To Our Fellow Non-Tourists,

This book has every detail you need about the little City on the Hill, from how to catch a game of one of our World Champion teams (Bruins! Sox! Pats!) to where you can get the best pizza on the entire east coast (Santarpio's!).

This book is not only a first-rate guidebook but also a love letter to this very unique and small city. The incredible people you see on the facing page have spent their time scouting out places in the nooks and crannies near and far—from breakfast joints hidden in the backroom of convenience stores to the incredibly new and ritzy restaurants that now circle the Fort Point Channel; from hobnobbing and enjoying a libation at Top of the Hub's no-cover bar seats in the highest-point-in-the-Prudential-Building's Jazz Lounge, to sidling up to talk philosophy at Harvard Square's basement bargain Grendel's Den, where food is half price much of the time with a three-buck beverage buy-in. We know, we know, it's a thankless job roaming around the city, making sure that every bar has fresh beer on tap, but somehow we'll survive.

If our fellow Non-Tourists will allow us, we want to send you to order a garlic and hot pepper pie in East Boston from Santarpio's and to sit at the bar at The Ashmont Grill to chat up the bartenders. We've got an extra ticket for the Sox game and we're going to have to hit up the Baseball Tavern to make sure to celebrate the right way, before catching a concert at Green Monster-abutting Lansdowne Street's House of Blues chapter. We're going to go see the craziness at Jacque's Cabaret and then pop into the Brattle Bookshop (downtown's Theatre District) to stock up for a quiet evening in, or take in a foreign flick at the landmark, art deco Coolidge Corner movie theatre and then browse in independent ink-on-paper icon Booksmith, across the street (Brookline). Put a whole group of crazy writers in your pocket, and you'll always find the best spot for everything.

While you're at it, make sure to visit the website, and its Boston page specifically, for up-to-the-minute hotspots at www.notfortourists.com/Boston.aspx and download our iPhone App to cram even more crazy locals into your already full pockets.

Here's hoping you find what you're looking for,

—Jane, Patrick, Scott, et al.

N F T™

Not For Tourists Guide to
BOSTON

Get more on
notfortourists.com

Keep connected with:

Twitter:
twitter/notfortourists

Facebook:
facebook/notfortourists

iPhone App:
nftiphone.com

Not For Tourists, Inc

Skyhorse Publishing

designed by:
Not For Tourists, Inc
NFT™—Not For Tourists™ Guide to Boston
www.notfortourists.com

Publisher Skyhorse Publishing	**City Editor** Patrick Hellen	**Graphic Design and** **Production** Aaron Schielke
Creative Direction & **Information Design** Jane Pirone	**Managing Editor** Scott Sendrow	**Information Systems** **Manager** Juan Molinari
Director Stuart Farr	**Production Manager** Aaron Schielke	

Printed in China
Print ISBN: 978-1-63450-139-2 $18.99
Ebook ISBN: 978-1-5107-0018-5
ISSN 2163-9043
Copyright © 2015 by Not For Tourists, Inc.
12th Edition

Every effort has been made to ensure that the information in this book is as up-to-date as possible a
press time. However, many details are liable to change — as we have learned.
Not For Tourists cannot accept responsibility for any consequences arising from the use of this book.

Not For Tourists does not solicit individuals, organizations, or businesses for listings inclusion in our
guides, nor do we accept payment for inclusion into the editorial portion of our book; the advertisin
sections, however, are exempt from this policy. We always welcome communications from
anyone regarding ANYTHING having to do with our books; please visit us on our website at www.
notfortourists.com for appropriate contact information.

Table of Contents

Boston Area Driving Map
and **Downtown Boston Map**
foldout, last page

Map 1 · **Beacon Hill / West End**

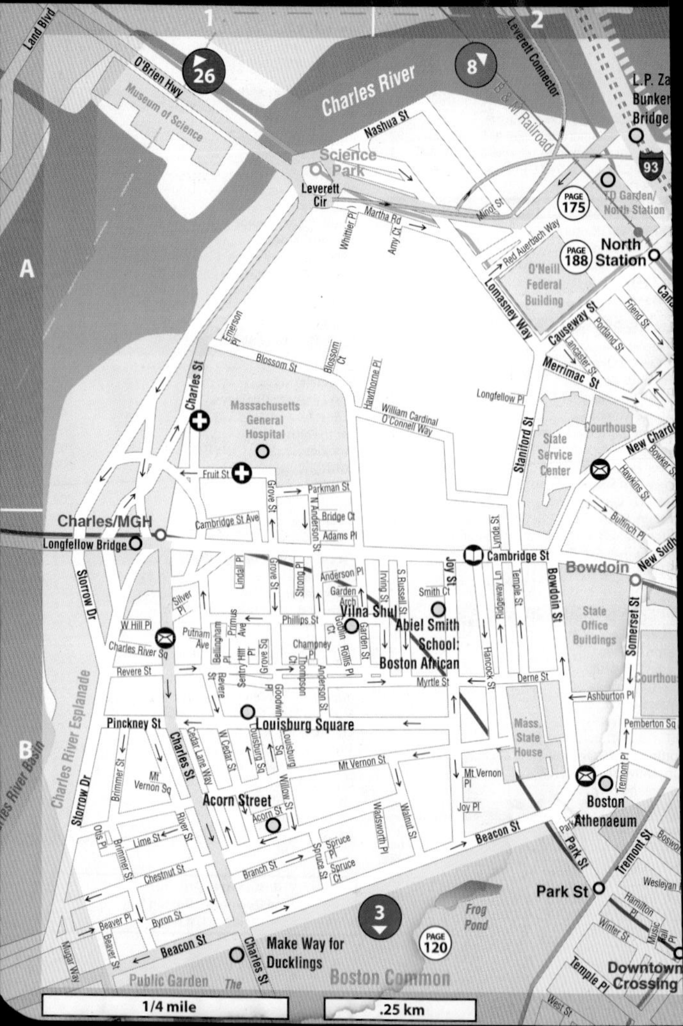

Land Blvd

1

2

O'Brien Hwy

26

Charles River

8

Leverett Connector

B&M Railroad

L.P. Za
Bunker
Bridge

Museum of Science

Nashua St

I-93

Science Park

PAGE 175

TD Garden/
North Station

Leverett Cir

Whittier Pl
Martha Rd
Amy Ct

Merill St

PAGE 188

North Station

O'Neill Federal Building

A

Lomasney Way

Causeway St
Portland St
Friend St
Canal St

Blossom St
Blossom Ct

Thorndike Pl

William Cardinal O'Connell Way

Longfellow Pl

Merrimac St

Massachusetts General Hospital

Stanford St

Courthouse

New Chard

Fruit St

Grove St
Parkman St
N Anderson St
Adams Pl

State Service Center

Hawkins St

Bulfinch Pl

Charles/MGH
Longfellow Bridge

Cambridge St Ave

Joy St

Cambridge St

Bowdoin

New Si

Somerset St

Silver Pl

Lindall Pl
Irving St
N Russell St
S Russell St

Smith Ct

Temple St

Bowdoin St

State Office Buildings

Courthou

W. Hill Pl
Charles River Sq

Putnam Ave
Primus Ave

Phillips St

Garden
Anderson St

Hancock St

Vilna Shul

**Abiel Smith School:
Boston African**

Ashburton Pl

Pemberton Sq

Revere St

Sentry Hill Pl

Chambney St

Grove Ct
Thompson St
Rollins Pl
Goodwin Pl
Anderson St

Myrtle St

Derne St

Mass.
State House

Pinckney St

Cedar Lane Way

Louisburg Square

Mt Vernon St

Mt. Vernon Pl

**Boston
Athenaeum**

Tremont St

Charles St

Acorn Street

Acorn St

Spruce St
Spruce Ct

Beacon St

Joy Pl

Park St

Courthou

B

Storrow Dr

Charles River Esplanade

Brimmer St

Mt Vernon Sq

W Cedar St
Willow St
Wadsworth St

Chestnut St

Branch St

Park St

Wesleyan

Charles River Basin

Otis Pl
Lime St

Byron St

3

Frog Pond

Hamilton Pl

Beaver Pl

Beaver St

Beacon St.

Charles St S

**Make Way for
Ducklings**

PAGE 120

Winter St

Magee Way

Mugar Way

Public Garden

The

Boston Common

Temple Pl

West St

**Downtown
Crossing**

1/4 mile	.25 km

acon Hill is still home to some of the most expensive real estate in
herica. Charming brick row houses reflect a long and storied history;
ere the State House stands, John Hancock once grazed cows. Full
ntrification has yet to reach the West End, where government buildings,
spitals, and tucked-away burrito joints mingle fairly harmoniously.

Landmarks

biel Smith School • 46 Joy St [Smith Ct]
enter of 19th-century African-American
oston.

corn Street • b/w West Cedar St & Willow St,
unning parallel to Chestnut St
he most photographed street in America.

oston Athenaeum •
0 Beacon St [Somerset St]
7-227-0270
ld books, including one true crime account
ound in the author's skin.

**Leonard P. Zakim
unker Hill Memorial Bridge** •
ambridge St [Causeway St]
World's widest cable-stayed bridge. Boston's
ewest landmark.

ongfellow Bridge •
ambridge St & Charles St
he "salt and pepper shaker bridge."

ouisburg Square •
t Vernon St & Pinckney St
harming square with elegant homes,
cluding John Kerry's.

Make Way for Ducklings •
eacon St & Charles St
spired by the Robert McCloskey children's
ook.

Massachusetts General Hospital •
5 Fruit St [N Grove St]
7-726-2000
he Ether dome, site of the first use of ether;
ontains an antique surgical museum.

D Garden • 150 Causeway St [Beverly St]
7-624-1050
ooking for the FleetCenter? This is it. Used to
e historic Boston Garden.

lna Shul • 18 Phillips St [Garden St]
7-523-2324
ecently revived Beacon Hill synagogue.

Nightlife

• **21st Amendment** •
150 Bowdoin St [Mt Vernon St]
617-227-7100
Favorite of the State House crowd.
• **6B Lounge** • 6 Beacon St [Tremont Pl]
617-742-0306
Martinis and snacks for the after-work crowd.
• **Alibi** • 215 Charles St [Fruit St]
857-241-1144
How many restaurants/bars are IN the Liberty
Hotel? Sweet lord.
• **Beacon Hill Pub** • 149 Charles St [Silver Pl]
Dive popular with young Hill residents.
• **Cheers** • 84 Beacon St [Brimmer St]
617-227-9605
If you must.
• **The Four's** • 166 Canal St [Causeway St]
617-720-4455
Sports tavern across from the Garden.
• **The Greatest Bar** •
262 Friend St [Causeway St]
617-367-0544
Big deal.
• **The Harp** • 85 Causeway St [Portland St]
617-742-1010
Pack in after an evening at the Garden.
• **The Hill Tavern** • 228 Cambridge St [Irving St]
617-742-6192
Middling Beacon Hill hangout.
• **The Sevens** • 77 Charles St [Mt Vernon St]
617-523-9074
Sturdy Beacon Hill local.
• **Sullivan's Tap** • 168 Canal St [Causeway St]
617-617-7617
Dive. Proper before Celtics and Bruins games.

Restaurants

- **75 Chestnut** • 75 Chestnut St [River St]
617-227-2175 • $$$$
Featuring a Sunday jazz brunch.
- **Artu** • 89 Charles St [Pinckney St]
617-227-9023 • $$$
Affordable Italian. Fresh ingredients. Take-out panini.
- **Beacon Hill Bistro** •
25 Charles St [Chestnut St]
617-723-7575 • $$$$
Elegant cooking in a cozy space.
- **Beacon Hill Chocolates** •
91 Charles St [Pinckney St]
617-725-1900 • $$$
Adorable chocolates and truffles in seasonal shapes.
- **Figs** • 42 Charles St [Chestnut St]
617-742-3447 • $$$
Beacon Hill branch of upscale pizza chain.
- **Grotto** • 37 Bowdoin St [Cambridge St]
617-227-3434 • $$$
Good value Italian in a Beacon Hill basement.
- **Harvard Gardens** •
316 Cambridge St [Grove St]
617-523-2727 • $$
More for meeting and drinking than eating.
- **The Hungry I** • 71 Charles St [Mt Vernon St]
617-227-3524 • $$$$
French. Cozy spot for intimate meals.

- **King & I** • 145 Charles St [Silver Pl]
617-227-3320 • $$
No-brainer for decent, inexpensive Thai.
- **Lala Rokh** • 97 Mt Vernon St [W Cedar St]
617-720-5511 • $$$
Alluring Persian in a pleasant Beacon Hill townhouse.
- **Panificio** • 144 Charles St [Silver Pl]
617-227-4340 • $
Paninis, pastries. Try the formaggio.
- **The Paramount** • 44 Charles St [Chestnut S
617-720-1152 • $$
Popular local spot for all three meals. Fantas brunch.
- **Pierrot Bistrot Francais** •
272 Cambridge St [Anderson St]
617-725-8855 • $$$$
Authentic French bistro.
- **Ristorante Toscano** •
47 Charles St [Chestnut St]
617-723-4090 • $$$
Northern Italian; change of pace from North End.
- **Scampo** • 215 Charles St [Fruit St]
617-536-2100 • $$$
Inventive Italian dished up for a toffee-nose crowd.
- **The Upper Crust** • 20 Charles St [Branch St
617-723-9600 • $$
Fancy schmancy, crisp-crust pizza.

...s praise the community feel of the square mile that constitutes ...on Hill. Pubs like **The Sevens** and **The Four's** cater to sports fans, ...the crispy pizza at **Upper Crust** causes mini sidewalk traffic jams. ...Public Garden and Boston Common function as the ...hborhood's backyard.

Shopping

...ack Ink • 101 Charles St [Pinckney St]
...7-723-3883
...musing tchotchkes, quirky gifts, purty paper.

...ugene Galleries •
...5 Charles St [Mt Vernon St]
...7-227-3062
...treasure chest of old maps, prints, books.

...he Flat of the Hill •
...0 Charles St [Mt Vernon St]
...7-619-9977
...uirky gifts. Lots of pink.

...ood • 133 Charles St [Silver Pl]
...7-722-9200
...vely gifts.

...ilton's Tent City •
...72 Friend St [Causeway St]
...7-227-9242
...ur floors of outdoors needs since 1947.

- **Moxie** • 51 Charles St [Mt Vernon St]
  617-557-9991
  Shoes, bags, accessories.
- **The Red Wagon** • 69 Charles St [Mt Vernon St]
  617-523-9402
  Pricey kids' clothes and toys.
- **Savenor's Market** •
  160 Charles St [Cambridge St]
  617-723-6328
  For a variety of gourmet goodies.
- **Second Time Around** •
  82 Charles St [Mt Vernon St]
  617-227-0049
  Upscale chic thrift.
- **Wish** • 49 Charles St [Mt Vernon St]
  617-227-4441
  Trendy, upscale women's clothing and accessories.

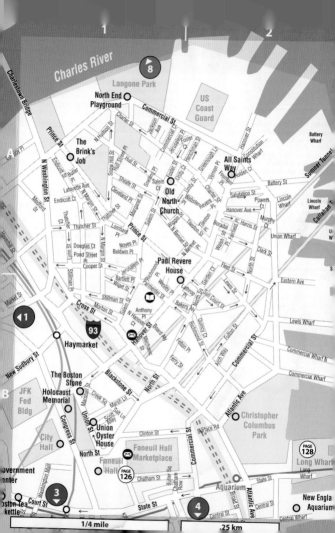

ton's version of Little Italy, the North End is a maze of narrow streets and
k buildings with a decidedly European air. With the Rose Kennedy
enway fully finished, the connection from the North End is once again
en, only this time it's grass instead of steel.

Landmarks

ll Saints Way • Hanover St & Battery St
eter Baldassari's folksy, handcrafted
evotional alley.

he Boston Stone • Marshall St [Hanover St]
entre of ye olde city.

oston Tea Kettle •
8 Court St [Cambridge St]
ong before Starbucks, this gigantic 1873
opper kettle was steaming.

he Brink's Job • 165 Prince St [Causeway St]
here Brink's Gang robbery occurred in 1950;
ow used for TD Banknorth Center parking.

hristopher Columbus Park •
tlantic Ave & Richmond St
estruction of the Artery gives this park new
reath.

ity Hall • 1 City Hall Plaza [Cambridge St]
7-635-4000
he box Faneuil Hall came in.

aneuil Hall • Congress St & North St
7-523-1779
aneuil Hall (that is, the building) dates from
742.

olocaust Memorial • Congress St & Union St
17-457-8755
x glass towers, with victims' numbers
presenting six camps.

eonard P. Zakim
unker Hill Memorial Bridge •
00 Beverly St [Causeway St]
Vorld's widest cable-stayed bridge. Boston's
ewest landmark.

ew England Aquarium •
entral Wharf [Central St]
17-973-5200
heck out penguin snack-time.

orth End Playground •
ommercial St & Foster St
te of the famous Great Molasses Flood.

ld North Church • 193 Salem St [Hull St]
17-523-6676
ne if by land, two if by sea.

aul Revere House • 19 N Sq [Garden Ct St]
17-523-2338
Vhere Paul was born and raised.

nion Oyster House •
1 Union St [Marshall St]
17-227-2750
ldest restaurant in America, saddle up to
yster bar.

Nightlife

• **Bell in Hand Tavern** •
45 Union St [Marshall St]
617-227-2098
Welcoming thirsty travelers since the 18th
century.

• **The Black Rose** • 160 State St [India St]
617-742-2286
Tourist-crowded, unremarkable. Try
somewhere else first.

• **Boston Beer Works** •
112 Canal St [Valenti Way]
617-896-2300
Cavernous suds shop near the Garden.

• **Boston Sail Loft** •
80 Atlantic Ave [Commercial Wharf]
617-227-7280
Big outside deck on the water, good crowds.

• **Green Dragon** • 11 Marshall St [Hanover St]
617-367-0055
Pretend you're Sam Adams while having the
same.

• **The Hong Kong** •
65 Chatham St [Chatham Row]
617-227-2226
Scorpion bowl anyone?

• **Paddy O's** • 33 Union St [Marshall St]
617-263-7771
The name tells you it's Oirish, you know.

• **The Place** • 2 Broad St [State St]
617-523-2081
A little bit of Jersey in Boston.

• **Tia's** • 200 Atlantic Ave [State St]
617-227-0828
Warm-weather party house.

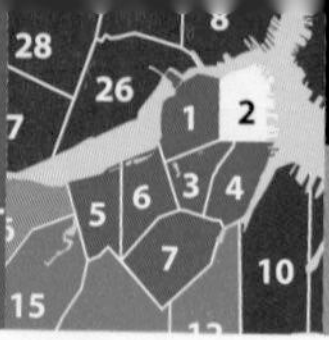

Map 2

North End / Faneuil Hall

🍴Restaurants

- **Al's State Street Café** • 112 State St [Broad St]
617-720-5555 • $
Good sandwiches on the cheap, but order fast.
You have been warned!
- **Antico Forno** • 93 Salem St [Wiget St]
617-723-6733 • $$$
A home-style North End stand-out. Great
pizza.
- **Artu** • 6 Prince St [Hanover St]
617-742-4336 • $$
Excellent Italian with a modern twist.
- **Billy Tse** • 240 Commercial St [Atlantic Ave]
617-227-9990 • $$$
Pan-Asian near the waterfront.
- **Boston Sail Loft** •
80 Atlantic Ave [Commercial Wharf]
617-227-7280 • $$
Good seafood with a great view.
- **Bova's Bakery** • 134 Salem St [Prince St]
617-523-5601 • $
Baked goods available 24/7!
- **Bricco** • 241 Hanover St [Cross St]
617-248-6800 • $$$$
Boutique Italian cuisine. Rather popular.
- **Caffe Paradiso** •
255 Hanover St [Richmond St]
617-742-1768 • $$
Coffee and cannoli. Local landmark.
- **The Daily Catch** • 323 Hanover St [Prince St]
617-523-8567 • $$$
For those who can stand the heat in the
kitchen.
- **Ducali Pizzeria & Bar** •
289 Causeway St [Prince St]
617-742-4144 • $$
Combines North End cuisine with the
rowdiness of Faneuil nightlife.

- **Durgin-Park** •
340 Faneuil Hall Marketplace [Congress St]
617-227-2038 • $$$$
Steak & New England comfort food since 18
- **Ernesto's** • 69 Salem St [Morton St]
617-523-1373 • $
One of the best slices in town.
- **Galleria Umberto** •
289 Hanover St [Richmond St]
617-227-5709 • $
Tasty, dirt cheap, greasy Italian lunch.
- **Green Dragon** • 11 Marshall St [Hanover St
617-367-0055 • $$
Pretend you're Sam Adams while having the
same.
- **Haymarket Pizza** •
106 Blackstone St [Hanover St]
617-723-8585 • $
Enjoy a great slice in the company of pigeo
- **L'Osteria** • 104 Salem St [Bartlett Pl]
617-723-7847 • $$$
Family-style red sauce joint.
- **La Famiglia Giorgio** •
112 Salem St [Cooper St]
617-367-6711 • $$
Cheap family style Italian without any fancy
pants.
- **La Summa** •
30 Fleet St [William F McClellan Hwy]
617-523-9503 • $$
More low-key than most North End places,
and it will leave your belly satisfied.
- **Lucca** • 226 Hanover St [Cross St]
617-742-9200 • $$$$
Stylish Northern Italian.
- **Mamma Maria** • 3 N Sq [Garden Ct St]
617-523-0077 • $$$$
High-end Italian in a charming townhouse.
- **Massimino's Cucina Italiana** •
207 Endicott St [Lafayette Ave]
617-523-5959 • $$
Out-of-the-way Italian, largely tourist-free.

le Boston is slowly becoming much more respected in culinary circles,
North End has been always been legit. Good luck finding a bad meal. By
it, young professionals reemerge from Faneuil Hall and hit the clubs—
d. Night owls stop by **Modern Pastry** for the best cannoli in the city.

Maurizio's • 364 Hanover St [N Bennet St]
517-367-1123 • $$$$
Tiny, yet amazing, Italian restaurant on the
main drag
McCormick & Schmick's •
1 Faneuil Hall Marketplace [S Market St]
617-720-5522 • $$$
Enormous fresh seafood selection in
steakhouse atmosphere.
Nebo • 90 N Washington St [Medford St]
617-723-6326 • $$
Decent North Endish spot. Perfect for a pizza
and a carafe of vino.
Neptune Oyster • 63 Salem St [Morton St]
617-742-3474 • $$$$
Great oysters, of course, and the most amazing
lobster roll —worth every penny.
Prezza • 24 Fleet St [Garden Ct St]
617-227-1577 • $$$$$
High-end Italian. Don't forget to try the Key
Lime Martini.
Regina Pizzeria • 11 Thacher St [N Margin St]
617-227-0765 • $$
If God made pizza, it would almost taste as
good as this.
Taranta • 210 Hanover St [Cross St]
617-720-0052 • $$$$
Delicious Italian food with a Peruvian twist.
Theo's Cozy Corner •
162 Salem St [Tileston St]
617-241-0202 • $
Cozy diner. Killer hash browns.
Trattoria Il Panino •
11 Parmenter St [Hanover St]
617-720-1336 • $$
In a sea of Italian restaurants Il Panino is a
pearl!
Union Oyster House •
41 Union St [Marshall St]
617-227-2750 • $$$
Authentic New England experience since
1826.
Wagamama Faneuil Hall •
Merchants Row [N Market St]
617-742-9242 • $
London noodle pros retrace journey of
Plymouth forebears.

🛍 Shopping

• **Bova's Bakery** • 134 Salem St [Prince St]
617-523-5601
Pastries, also deli and pizza. Open 24 hours.
• **Brooks Brothers** • 75 State St [Kilby St]
617-261-9990
Branch of venerable Back Bay clothier.
• **Green Cross Pharmacy** •
393 Hanover St [Clark St]
617-523-3728
Old-world pharmacy. Also sells Italian
sundries.
• **Maria's Pastry Shop** • 46 Cross St [Morton St]
617-523-1196
Sweet tooth heaven.
• **Mike's Pastry** • 300 Hanover St [Prince St]
617-742-3050
The most famous of the North End Italian
bakeries.
• **Modern Pastry** •
257 Hanover St [Richmond St]
617-523-3783
Boston's best cannoli? You decide.
• **Monica's Salumeria** • 130 Salem St [Prince St]
617-742-4101
Homemade takeout and Italian groceries.
• **Newbury Comics** • 1 Faneuil Hall Sq [Court St]
617-248-9992
Downtown location of successful music/
novelties chain.
• **Salumeria Italiana** •
151 Richmond St [North St]
617-523-8743
Well-regarded Italian specialties store.
• **Stanza dei Sigari** • 292 Hanover St [Prince St]
617-227-0295
17-year-olds take note: hookahs available.
• **Staples** • 25 Court St [Tremont St]
617-367-1747
Printer ink and other more reasonably priced
supplies.

Map 3 Downtown Crossing / Park Square / Bay Village

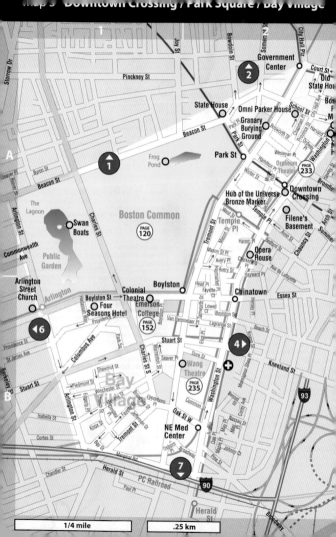

Slorrow Dr

Pinckney St

Joy St

Bowdoin St

Somerset St

City Hall Plz

2 Government Center

Court St

Old State St

Bds F M

State House

Omni Parker House

School St

Beacon St

Park Pl

Park St

Granary Burying Ground

Bosworth St

Washington

Harvard

A

Byron St

Beaver

Beacon St

Frog Pond

Park St

Wesleyan Pl

PAGE 233

Winter St

Hamilton Pl

Orpheum Theatre

Bromfield

1

Hub of the Universe Bronze Marker

Downtown Crossing

The Lagoon

Swan Boats

Charles St

Boston Common

PAGE 120

Temple Pl

Temple Pl

Filene's Basement

Summer

Chauncy St

Arlington St

Public Garden

Tremont St

Harem St

Mason Pl

Bedford St

Avery Pl

Opera House

Avery Pl

Hayward Pl

Lafayette

Commonwealth Ave

Avon St

Clickering

Boylston

Chinatown

Essex St

Arlington Street Church

Arlington

Boylston St

Colonial Theatre

Emerson College

PAGE 152

Head Pl

Fayette St

Lowell Ct

Boylston Pl

Van Rensselaer Pl

Lagrange St

Beach St

Four Seasons Hotel

Providence St

St James Ave

Providence St

Columbus Ave

Park Sq

Charles St S

Stuart St

Warrenton St

Dore St

Seaver Pl

4

Kneeland St

Stuart St

Berkeley St

Shawmut St

Piedmont St

Winchester St

Bay Village

Lyndeboro Pl

Wang Theatre

PAGE 235

Washington St

93

Isabella St

Knox St

Jefferson St

Church St

Tremont St

Common St

Oak St W

NE Med Center

Oak St

Ophan Pl

Broadway

Cortes St

Marginal Rd

Chandler St

7

Herald St

PC Railroad

90

Paul Pl

Herald

Broadway

1/4 mile

.25 km

owntown Crossing is abuzz with pedestrians from all walks of life. You'll
nd a lively mixture of financial types, shoppers, New England Medical
enter doctors, and the down-and-out. The giant hole in the ground from
alled development projects is still here, but maybe someday we'll have
at high rise we were promised.

Landmarks

Arlington Street Church •
351 Boylston St [Arlington St]
617-536-7050
Congregation dates from 1729, building from
1861.

Boston Common Frog Pond •
Boston Common
617-635-2120
Cool statues. Ribbit.

Boston Irish Famine Memorial •
Washington St & School St
Statue commemorating the Great Hunger of
the 1840s.

Boston Opera House •
539 Washington St [Ave de Lafayette]
617-259-3400
Beaux-Arts landmark open again after many
years.

Citi Emerson Colonial Theatre •
106 Boylston St [Tremont St]
617-482-9393
Boston's oldest continuously operating
theater, since 1900.

Four Seasons Hotel •
200 Boylston St [Charles St]
617-338-4400
The preferred local home of the Rolling
Stones.

Granary Burying Ground •
Tremont St & Park St
617-635-4505
Featuring John Hancock, Mother Goose, many
others.

Hub of the Universe Bronze Marker •
Washington St & Summer St
Um, located in the floor of a fruit and
vegetable stand.

John Hancock's Phallic Gravestone •
Tremont & Park St
Size matters.

Old South Meeting House •
310 Washington St [Milk St]
617-482-6439
Where Sam Adams gave the order for the
Boston Tea Party.

Old State House •
206 Washington St [Court St]
617-720-1713
Oldest surviving public building in Boston.

Omni Parker House •
60 School St [Chapman Pl]
617-227-8600
One-time employees include Ho Chi Minh and
Malcolm X.

Ritz-Carlton Boston Common •
10 Avery St [Washington St]
617-574-7100
Still classy.

State House • Beacon St & Park St
617-727-3679
Finished in 1797. Gold dome added later.

Swan Boats • Boylston St & Arlington St
617-522-1966
Since 1877. Ideal for wee ones.

Wang Theatre • 270 Tremont St [Hollis St]
617-482-9393
Eye-popping, opulent interior. A must see.

Nightlife

Jacque's Cabaret •
79 Broadway [Winchester St]
617-426-8902
Drag, but all welcome. Nightly cabaret.

Limelight Stage + Studios •
204 Tremont St [Lagrange St]
617-423-0785
Karaoke on a grand scale; private studios
available.

MJ O'Connor's • 27 Columbus Ave [Park Sq]
617-482-2255
Large Irish pub. Outdoor seating when warm.

Mojitos • 48 Winter St [Tremont St]
617-834-0552
For those who like their salsa hot.

Parker's Bar • 60 School St [Chapman Pl]
617-227-8600
Elegant. Try the Boston Creme martini.

Scholars • 25 School St [Province St]
617-248-0025
Popular for the after-work crowd. Giant
boozey punch bowls.

Sidebar • 14 Bromfield St [Washington St]
617-357-1899
Don a jersey and knock back some shots.

The Tam • 222 Tremont St [Stuart St]
Local dive.

Venu • 100 Warrenton St [Stuart St]
617-338-8061
Always changing; check before you go.

Map 3

Downtown Crossing / Park Square / Bay Vil

🍴 Restaurants

- **49 Social** • 49 Temple Pl [Washington St]
617-338-9600 • $$$$
Seasonal plus fresh seafood.
- **Dumpling Cafe** •
695 Washington St [Kneeland St]
617-338-8858 • $
Learn how to eat the soup dumplings. You're welcome.
- **Empire Garden** •
690 Washington St [Lagrange St]
617-482-8898 • $$$
Dim sum for the masses.
- **Erbaluce** • 69 Church St [Shawmut St]
617-426-6969 • $$$$
Italian food, Italian wine, Italian camaraderie.
Worth the price.
- **Herrera's Mexican Grille** •
11 Temple Pl [Tremont St]
617-426-2350 • $
Good and cheap Cali-Mex.
- **Intermission Tavern** •
228 Tremont St [Stuart St]
617-451-5997 • $$
Drinks and burgers until 1 am.
- **Jacob Wirth** • 31 Stuart St [Dartmouth St]
617-338-8586 • $$
German-y. Local institution since 1868 with barroom sing-a-long on Friday nights.
- **Legal Sea Foods** • 26 Park Plaza [Arlington St]
617-426-4444 • $$$
Fresh fish, famous chowder. Legal's sleekest space.
- **Marliave** • 10 Bosworth St [Chapman Pl]
617-422-0004 • $$
Cozy, old-time dead end street eats.
- **McCormick & Schmick's** •
34 Columbus Ave [Park Sq]
617-482-3999 • $$$$
$2 "social hour" bar menu is a great deal.
- **Mike and Patty's** • 12 Church St [Fayette St]
617-423-3447 • $
Eponymous owners whip up the sammies.

- **New Saigon Sandwich** •
696 Washington St [Kneeland St]
617-542-6296 • $
Cheap sandwiches, boxed lunches. Delicious
- **New York Pizza** •
224 Tremont St [Lagrange St]
617-482-3459 • $$
Perfect for late night noshing.
- **No. 9 Park** • 9 Park St [Beacon St]
617-742-9991 • $$$$
Consistently rated among Boston's best.
- **Penang** • 685 Washington St [Lagrange St]
617-451-6373 • $$$
Well-established Malaysian out of NYC.
- **Ruth's Chris Steak House** •
45 School St [City Hall Ave]
617-742-8401 • $$$$$
Ubiquitous chain serving gargantuan portion in Old City Hall.
- **Sam La Grassa's** •
44 Province St [Bosworth St]
617-357-6861 • $$
Monster sandwiches. Try the pastrami.
- **Silvertone Bar & Grill** •
69 Bromfield St [Tremont St]
617-338-7887 • $$
Great after-work lounge with tasty home cooking.
- **Smith & Wollensky** •
101 Arlington St [Stuart St]
617-423-1112 • $$$$$
The castle has been taken.
- **Sweet Cupcakes** •
11 School St [Washington St]
617-227-2253 • $
Give in to your Sweet tooth.
- **Teatro** • 177 Tremont St [Head Pl]
617-778-6841 • $$$
Sleek Italian next to Loews Cinema.
- **Via Matta** • 79 Park Plaza [Hadassah Wy]
617-422-0008 • $$$$
Stylish Italian, stylish crowd.
- **Viga** • 304 Stuart St [Arlington St]
617-542-7200 • $
Cheap and tasty take out.

Is still mourn the loss of Jordan Marsh. It's hard to get excited about **TJ x** and **Marshall's**. The best way to finish a weekday shopping excursion is with a scrumptious sandwich from the amazing **Mike & Patty's**. For a-end meal, try **No. 9 Park** across the Common.

Shopping

Beacon Hill Skate Shop •
35 Charles St S [Fayette St]
617-482-7400
Rentals available. Also has hockey gear.
Bromfield Camera Co. •
10 Bromfield St [Washington St]
617-426-5230
Decent selection of new and used cameras.
CD Spins • 58 Winter St [Tremont St]
617-357-0525
A great place to sell back your old CDs.
City Sports • 11 Bromfield St [Washington St]
617-423-2015
Covers all the basics in apparel and equipment.
DSW • 385 Washington St [Bromfield St]
617-556-0052
Oodles and oodles of sho[odl]es.
Eddie Bauer Outlet •
500 Washington St [West St]
617-423-4722
Good deals on quality clothes.
H&M • 350 Washington St [Franklin St]
855-466-7467
Disposable chic from Swedish mega-merchant.

L.J. Peretti • 2 Park Plaza [Charles St S]
617-482-0218
Oldest family-run tobacconist in the country.
Lambert's Marketplace •
140 Tremont St [Temple Pl]
617-338-6500
Fruit and veggie stand in the heart of Downtown Crossing.
Macy's • 450 Washington St [Temple Pl]
617-357-3000
Once Jordan Marsh. Big outdoor "holiday" tree in December.
Marshalls • 350 Washington St [Franklin St]
617-338-6205
Discount clothing and other stuff.
Roche Bobois • 2 Avery St [Washington St]
617-742-9611
Très trendy interior design and furnishings.
Sweet Cupcakes •
11 School St [Washington St]
617-227-2253
Give in to your Sweet tooth.
TJ Maxx • 350 Washington St [Franklin St]
617-695-2424
Put on your bargain-hunting hat. Off-price apparel and housewares.
Walgreens • 24 School St [Washington St]
617-372-8156
Huge, upscale, schmancy version of the chain drugstore.

Map 4 · **Financial District / Chinatown**

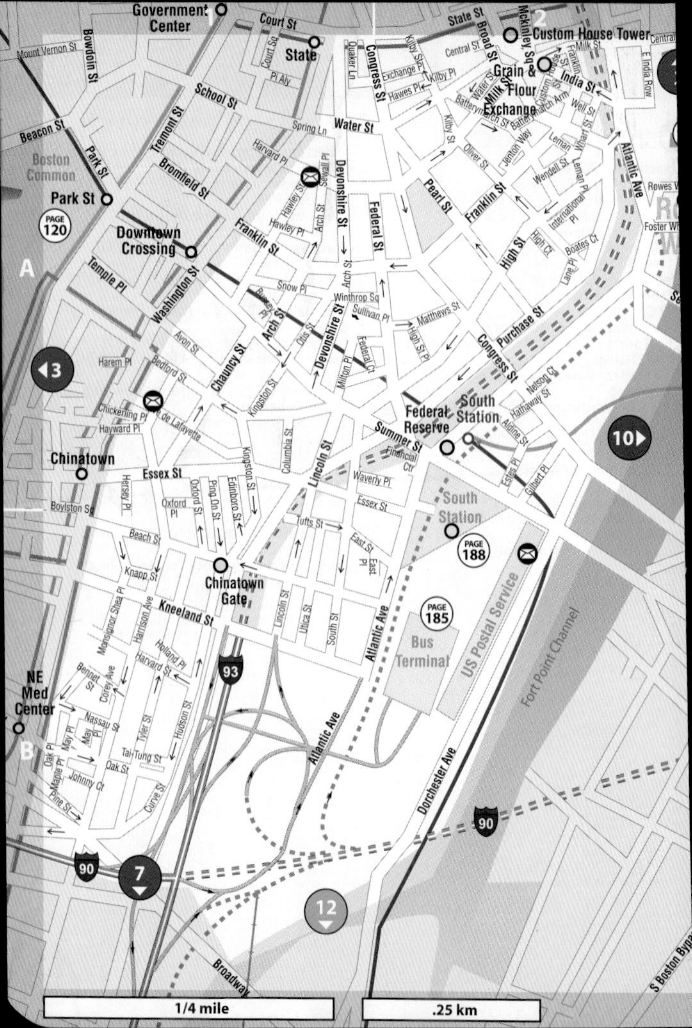

Ⓝ

Government Center

Court St
State
State St
Custom House Tower
McKinley Sq
Central St
Broad St
India St
Central
Milk St

Bowdoin St
Mount Vernon St
Quaker Ln
Quaker Ln Aly
Congress St
Exchange Pl
Kilby Pl
Hawes Pl
Grain & Flour Exchange
Milk St
E India Row
Atlantic Ave

Beacon St
School St
Spring Ln
Water St
Batterymarch St
Oliver St
Lemon Way
Wendell St
Rowes W

Boston Common
Tremont St
Bromfield St
Harvard Pl
Devonshire St
Pearl St
Franklin St
High St
Well St
Liberty Sq
International
Foster W

Park St
PAGE 120
Franklin St
Hawley St
Arch St
Federal St
Franklin St
High St
Broad St
Boates Ct
Lane Pl

Downtown Crossing
Washington St
Snow Pl
Winthrop Sq
Matthews St
High St Pl
Congress St
Purchase St

A

Temple Pl
Avery St
Chauncey St
Devonshire St
Sullivan Pl
Milton Pl

13

Harem Pl
Bedford St
Pl de Lafayette
Kingston St
Columbia St
Lincoln St
Summer St
Federal Reserve
South Station
Financial Ctr
Atlantic Ave

Chinatown
Chickering Pl
Hayward Pl
Essex St
Oxford St
Edinboro St
Tufts St
Waverly Pl
Essex St
South Station
PAGE 188

Boylston St
Harrison Ave
Beach St
Ping On St
East St
East St Pl
PAGE 185

Knapp St
Chinatown Gate
Kneeland St
Lincoln St
Utica St
South St
Bus Terminal
US Postal Service
Fort Point Channel

93

NE Med Center
Oak St
Nassau St
Tai-Tung St
Oak St
Curve St
Johnny Ct
Atlantic Ave
Dorchester Ave

90

7

12

90

Broadway

S Boston By

1/4 mile	.25 km

10

center of the Financial District has changed from The Big Dig to the Rose ...nedy Greenway, and as it's getting very little use, it's just as controversial as its ...decessor. Sit on the very pristine grass and then hit up the always bustling ...natown. For an introduction, stroll and windowshop along Beach Street and its ...ss-streets.

Map
16 5 6 3 4
15   7   1...
        13

Landmarks

...oston Harbor Hotel •
...0 Rowes Wharf [High St]
...7-439-7000
...he "building with a hole in the middle."
...hinatown Gate • Beach St & Hudson St
...verything under the sky is for the people.
...ustom House Tower •
...McKinley Sq [Central St]
...oston's first "skyscraper," completed in 1915.
...ederal Reserve Bank of Boston •
...00 Atlantic Ave [Summer St]
...617-973-3463
...asy-to-spot concrete monolith, built in 1983.
...rain & Flour Exchange •
...77 Milk St [India St]
...orgeous 1893 building from Shepley, Rutan,
...nd Goolidge.
...outh Station • Summer St & Atlantic Ave
...usier train station, with the new Silver Line
...nd bus terminal.

Nightlife

- **An Tain •** 31 India St [Milk St]
  617-426-1870
  For after work; DJs on Thursday, Friday.
- **Biddy Early's •** 141 Pearl St [Purchase St]
  617-654-9944
  Dive bar that tries a little too hard.
- **Bond •** 250 Franklin St [Oliver St]
  617-956-8765
  Prepare yourself for the line.
- **Elephant & Castle •**
  161 Devonshire St [Milk St]
  617-350-9977
  Large pub handy for groups. Skip the food.
- **Good Life •** 28 Kingston St [Bedford St]
  617-451-2622
  Martinis and jazz.
- **Howl at the Moon •**
  184 High St [Batterymarch St]
  617-292-4695
  Bros, bachelorettes, buckets of booze. Oh, and
  dueling pianos.
- **J.J. Foley's •** 21 Kingston St [Summer St]
  617-695-2529
  Attracts a big after-work crowd.
- **Les Zygomates •** 129 South St [Tufts St]
  617-542-5108
  Comprehensive wine list, pleasant bar.
- **Mr. Dooley's •** 77 Broad St [Custom House St]
  617-338-5656
  Irish. Popular after-work drinking spot.
- **Rowes Wharf Bar •** 70 Rowes Wharf [High St]
  617-439-7000
  Relax with scotch and an armchair.
- **The Times •** 112 Broad St [Wendell St]
  617-357-8463
  Irish. Live music and DJs.

Map 4

Financial District / Chinatown

Restaurants

- **Chacarero** • 101 Arch St [Winter St]
  617-542-0392 • $
  Unique Chilean sandwiches.
- **Chau Chow City** • 83 Essex St [Ping on St]
  617-338-8158 • $$
  Best known for their Dim Sum. Open late.
- **China Pearl** • 9 Tyler St [Beach St]
  617-426-4338 • $$
  Dim sum for beginners and experts.
- **Gourmet Dumpling House** •
  52 Beach St [Oxford St]
  617-338-6223 • $
  Destination dumplings with a wait to match.
- **Hei La Moon** • 88 Beach St [Lincoln St]
  617-338-8813 • $
  Best Dim Sum in Boston!
- **Hing Shing Pastry** • 67 Beach St [Hudson St]
  617-451-1162 • $
  Best buns in Chinatown.
- **The Hong Kong Eatery** •
  79 Harrison Ave [Knapp St]
  617-423-0838 • $
  Mountains of pork and rice for just a few
  bucks.
- **Les Zygomates** • 129 South St [Tufts St]
  617-542-5108 • $$$
  French bistro. Comprehensive wine list,
  pleasant bar.
- **Mei Sum** • 40 Beach St [Harrison Ave]
  617-357-4050 • $
  Another tasty option for bánh mi and baked
  goods in the heart of Chinatown.
- **Meritage** • 70 Rowes Wharf [High St]
  617-439-3995 • $$$$$
  Serious about pairing food with wine.

- **Milk Street Cafe** • 50 Milk St [Devonshire St]
  617-542-3663 • $
  Dependable lunch option.
- **New Shanghai** • 21 Hudson St [Kneeland St]
  617-338-6688 • $
  Critically acclaimed Shanghainese.
- **Peach Farm** • 4 Tyler St [Beach St]
  617-482-1116 • $$
  Family-style Cantonese. Cool seafood tanks.
- **Pho Hoa** • 17 Beach St [Monsignor Shea Rd]
  617-423-3934 • $
  Phat pho.
- **Sakurabana** • 57 Broad St [Broad St]
  617-542-4311 • $$$
  Good bet for low-key sushi.
- **Shabu-Zen** • 16 Tyler St [Beach St]
  617-292-8828 • $$
  Pay to cook your own food in a delicious
  broth? Yeah, it is worth it!
- **South Street Diner** •
  178 Kneeland St [South St]
  617-350-0028 • $
  Night shift dining excellence with a liquor
  license.
- **Sultan's Kitchen** • 116 State St [Broad St]
  617-570-9009 • $
  Terrific Turkish. A great lunch choice.
- **Taiwan Café** • 34 Oxford St [Oxford Pl]
  617-426-8181 • $$
  For opponents of the PRC's "one China" policy.
- **Umbria Prime** •
  295 Franklin St [Batterymarch St]
  617-338-1000 • $$$
  An Italian steakhouse during the week, and
  nightclub on the weekends.
- **Xinh Xinh** • 7 Beach St [Washington St]
  617-422-0501 • $$
  Exceptional Vietnamese. Not much ambiance.

...natown = **Hei La Moon** for dim sum, **Taiwan Café** for the real deal or
...rmet Dumpling House for real soup dumplings. For late-night bites,
...ember that the **South Street Diner** serves well into the night. Some of
...ton's top restaurants, including **Radius** and **Meritage**, call the Financial
...rict home.

Shopping

BRIX Wine Shop • 105 Broad St [Well St]
617-542-2749
Upscale wine shop.
Serenade Chocolatier •
2 South St [Summer St]
617-261-9941
Tastes of Vienna.

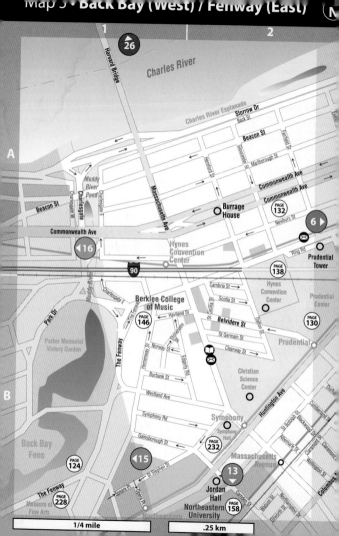

affic on Mass Ave! MassPIRG on Newbury Street! Berklee students
tween classes! This area is always insane, and always active. The striking
oup of buildings that comprises the **Christian Science Center**, together
th **the Pru** and 111 Huntington (the "Daily Planet"), looks great at night.

Landmarks

Burrage House •
14 Commonwealth Ave [Hereford St]
Nineteenth-century French-Renaissance
mansion. Private.

Christian Science Center •
275 Massachusetts Ave [Westland Ave]
617-450-3790
Mother Church, Mapparium, reflecting pool.
Quite nice.

Hynes Convention Center •
900 Boylston St [Gloucester St]
617-954-2000
Still a convention center, for now.

Jordan Hall •
30 Gainsborough St [Huntington Ave]
617-585-1260
Hundred-year-old theater seats over 1,000 and
has remarkable acoustics.

Prudential Tower •
800 Boylston St [Fairfield St]
617-236-3100
The other tall building. Equally loved and
reviled.

Symphony Hall •
301 Massachusetts Ave [Huntington Ave]
617-266-1492
Home of the Boston Symphony Orchestra.

Nightlife

• **Bukowski Tavern** • 50 Dalton St [Scotia St]
617-437-9999
100+ beers served with loud, eclectic music.
• **The Corner Tavern** •
421 Marlborough St [Massachusetts Ave]
617-262-5555
Locals only.
• **Dillon's** • 955 Boylston St [Hereford St]
617-421-1818
Revisiting the Roaring '20s.
• **King's Boston** • 50 Dalton St [Scotia St]
617-266-2695
Bowling, pool, TV sports. Goofy but fun.
• **Lir** • 903 Boylston St [Fenway]
617-778-0089
Upscale Irish. Large, handy for sports watchers.
• **McGreevey's** • 911 Boylston St [Hereford St]
617-262-0911
They remade the Foggy Goggle? Oh it's still an
overpriced meat market. Eh.
• **Our House East** •
52 Gainsborough St [St Stephen St]
617-236-1890
Branch of Allston college-kid hangout.
• **Pour House** • 907 Boylston St [Gloucester St]
617-236-1767
Wide beer selection, cool bartenders.
• **Sonsie** • 327 Newbury St [Hereford St]
617-351-2500
People-watching mainstay. Nice French-doors
street exposure.
• **Top of the Hub** • 800 Boylston St [Fairfield St]
617-536-1775
Great view from the top of the Pru.
• **Towne** • 900 Boylston St [Gloucester St]
617-247-0400
Stylish crowd can be a bit snobby.
• **Wally's Café** •
427 Massachusetts Ave [Columbus Ave]
617-424-1408
Cramped jazz landmark. For everyone at least
once.

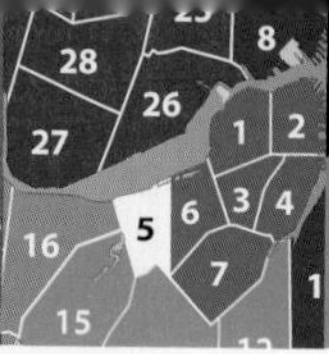

Map 5

🍴 Restaurants

- **5 Napkin Burger •**
  105 Huntington Ave [Belvidere St]
  617-375-2277 • $$
  Burgers so good you'll slap your momma.
- **Back Bay Social Club •**
  867 Boylston St [Gloucester St]
  617-247-3200 • $$
  One of the few brunch options in Back Bay.
- **Bangkok City •**
  167 Massachusetts Ave [Belvidere St]
  617-266-8884 • $$$
  Solid Thai served in a large, blue room.
- **Bukowski Tavern •** 50 Dalton St [Scotia St]
  617-437-9999 • $$
  Watering hole also has great chili, p.b.j.
  sandwiches, late hours.
- **Café Jaffa •** 48 Gloucester St [Boylston St]
  617-536-0230 • $
  Affordable, delicious Middle Eastern.
- **The Capital Grille •**
  900 Boylston St [Gloucester St]
  617-262-8900 • $$$$$
  Arise, Sir Loin!
- **Casa Romero •** 30 Gloucester St [Newbury St]
  617-536-4341 • $$$
  Mexican. Decent food, good atmosphere.
- **Chilli Duck •** 829 Boylston St [Fairfield St]
  617-236-5208 • $$
  Thai eatery with modern decor, slightly-
  elevated prices, and expectedly-tangy sauces.

- **Clio •**
  370 Commonwealth Ave [Massachusetts Ave]
  617-536-7200 • $$$$
  Sublime spot in the Eliot Hotel.
- **Jasper White's Summer Shack •**
  50 Dalton St [Scotia St]
  617-867-9955 • $$
  Chummy spot to share oysters with pals.
  Slightly overpriced.
- **Kashmir •** 279 Newbury St [Gloucester St]
  617-536-1695 • $$
  Excellent *murg saagwala*.
- **Pour House •** 907 Boylston St [Gloucester St]
  617-236-1767 • $
  Wonderful, cheap bar food. Opens at 8 am.
- **Sonsie •** 327 Newbury St [Hereford St]
  617-351-2500 • $$$$
  People-watching mainstay. Nice French-door
  street exposure.
- **Sweet Cupcakes •**
  49 Massachusetts Ave [Marlborough St]
  617-247-2253 • $
  Give in to your Sweet tooth.
- **Tapeo •** 266 Newbury St [Gloucester St]
  617-267-4799 • $$$
  Tasty tapas. Sip sangria outside on warm days.
- **Top of the Hub •** 800 Boylston St [Fairfield St]
  617-536-1775 • $$$$
  Almost worth the price for the amazing view
  atop the Pru.
- **Trident Booksellers & Café •**
  338 Newbury St [Hereford St]
  617-267-8688 • $
  All-day breakfast in a cool bookstore.

Back Bay (West) / Fenway (East)

...ent Booksellers and Café is a terrific spot for brunching and browsing. ... drinkers who can handle Tunnel-level stereo volume and a touch of ...ude should try Bukowski's. Berklee students often sit in at Wally's, ...ng more established musicians to play live jazz most nights of the ...k.

Shopping

DeLuca's Market •
239 Newbury St [Fairfield St]
617-262-5990
Good deli, pricey fruit, wine, and beer
downstairs.

Economy True Value Hardware •
219 Massachusetts Ave [Clearway St]
617-536-4280
Hardware, household needs, cheap furniture.
Very popular.

Emack & Bolio's •
290 Newbury St [Gloucester St]
617-536-7127
Innovative ice cream flavors.

Forever 21 •
343 Newbury St [Massachusetts Ave]
617-262-0212
Enormous—getting lost is a real concern.

John Fluevog • 302 Newbury St [Hereford St]
617-266-1079
Indulge the hipster in you with these funky
shoes.

Johnny Cupcakes •
279 Newbury St [Gloucester St]
617-375-0100
Trendy T-shirts. Not cupcakes.

Johnson Paint Co. •
355 Newbury St [Massachusetts Ave]
617-536-4244
Tony. Also a selection of stationery.

Newbury Comics •
332 Newbury St [Hereford St]
617-236-4930
Now featuring a large DVD section.

Orpheus Performing Arts • 362
Commonwealth Ave [Massachusetts Ave]
617-247-7200
Focusing on classical music.

Sephora • 800 Boylston St [Fairfield St]
617-262-4200
A makeup wonderland—play before you buy.

Sweet Cupcakes •
49 Massachusetts Ave [Marlborough St]
617-247-2253
Give in to your Sweet tooth.

Sweet-N-Nasty •
90 Massachusetts Ave [Commonwealth Ave]
617-266-7171
Saucy cakes for all [adult] occasions.

Trident Booksellers & Café •
338 Newbury St [Hereford St]
617-267-8688
Busy, independent bookstore/cafe with tons
of magazines.

Urban Outfitters •
361 Newbury St [Massachusetts Ave]
617-236-0088
Funky clothes, apartment stuff and novelties.

Utrecht Art Supply Center •
333 Massachusetts Ave [St Botolph St]
617-262-4948
Serious art store near Symphony Hall.

Map 6 • **Back Bay (East) / South End (Upper)**

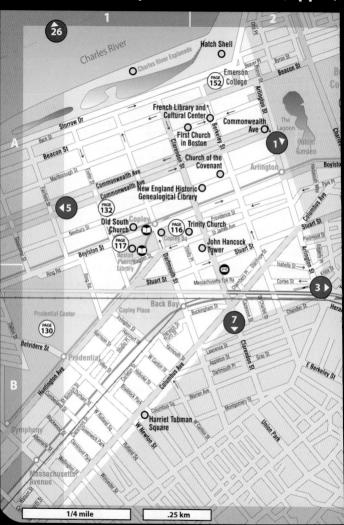

1

2

26

Charles River

Hatch Shell

Charles River Esplanade

Emerson College
PAGE 152

Beacon St

Byron St

Beaver Pl

Otis Pl

Co

Storrow Dr

French Library and Cultural Center

Commonwealth Ave

Berkeley St

Arlington St

The Lagoon

Back St

First Church in Boston

A

Beacon St

Clarendon St

Church of the Covenant

Arlington

Public Garden

Boylsto

Marlborough St

Commonwealth Ave

Commonwealth Ave

Columbus Ave

5

Fairfield St

Exeter St

New England Historic Genealogical Library

PAGE 132

Old South Church

Copley

Providence St

Stuart St

Piedmont St

Gloucester St

Newbury St

Copley Sq

PAGE 116

Trinity Church

St James Ave

Isabella St

Knox St

Boylston St

PAGE 117

Boston Public Library

Blagden St

Dartmouth St

Trinity St

John Hancock Tower

Stuart St

Cortes St

3

Ring Rd

Stuart St

Massachusetts Tpk Ra

Clearway Pl

Stanhope St

Back Bay

Copley Place

Buckingham St

7

St Charles St

Chandler St

Hera

Prudential Center
PAGE 130

Dalton St

Belvidere St

Prudential

Huntington Ave

Garrison St

Harcourt St

Studio

Yarmouth St

Lawrence St

Appleton St

Dartmouth Pl

Gray St

Columbus Ave

Warren Ave

E Berkeley St

B

Symphony

St Botolph St

Cumberland St

W Canton St

Holyoke St

Braddock Park

Columbus Sq

W Rutland Sq

Montgomery St

Union Park

Blackwood St

Harriet Tubman Square

W Newton St

Massachusetts Avenue

Albemarle St

Greenwich Park

Claremont Park

Wellington St

Pembroke St

W Rutland Sq

Rutland St

Worcester St

1/4 mile

.25 km

e eastern end of Back Bay features the "top" of Newbury Street, with its
ix of locals, tourists, and international students keeping its mainly
ghbrow merchants busy. The upper regions of the South End—especially
lumbus Avenue—are now home to excellent restaurant upon excellent
staurant, with a culturally correct number of galleries thrown in as well.

Landmarks

Boston Public Library—Central •
700 Boylston St [Exeter St]
617-536-5400

Charles River Esplanade • Storrow Drive
Great place to run or read a book.

Church of the Covenant •
67 Newbury St [Berkeley St]
617-266-7480
Gothic revival church called "absolutely
perfect" by Oliver Wendell Holmes.

Commonwealth Ave •
Commonwealth Ave & Mass Ave
Boston's most distinguished promenade with
oddest collection of statues.

Copley Square • Boylston St & Dartmouth St
Back Bay's living room.

First Church in Boston •
66 Marlborough St [Clarendon St]
617-267-6730
Founded 375 years ago.

French Library and Cultural Center •
53 Marlborough St [Berkeley St]
617-912-0417
Classes, food, and movies, tous en francais.

Hatch Shell • Esplanade [Congress St]
Where the Pops play each July 4th.

John Hancock Tower •
200 Clarendon St [St James Ave]
New England's tallest building, designed by
I.M. Pei.

New England Historic Genealogical Library •
101 Newbury St [Clarendon St]
617-536-5740
Trace your roots back to the Mayflower.

Old South Church •
645 Boylston St [Dartmouth St]
617-536-1970
Northern Italian Gothic, finished in 1875.

Trinity Church •
206 Clarendon St [St James Ave]
617-536-0944
Romanesque, with massive open interior.
Completed in 1877.

Nightlife

• **Anchovies** •
433 Columbus Ave [Braddock Park]
617-266-5088
Easy-going neighborhood joint.

• **Champions** •
110 Huntington Ave [Harcourt St]
617-927-5304
Sports. Food wins no trophies.

• **City Bar** • 65 Exeter St [Boylston St]
617-933-4800
At the Lenox Hotel.

• **Clery's** • 113 Dartmouth St [Columbus Ave]
617-262-9874
Bar with food. Location is its best attribute.

• **Club Café** • 209 Columbus Ave [Berkeley St]
617-536-0966
Gay: restaurant in front, scoping in back.

• **Lolita Cocina & Tequila Bar** •
271 Dartmouth St [Newbury St]
617-369-5609
Tacos and margaritas. Vampy with a tinge of
goth.

• **Poe's Kitchen at the Rattlesnake** •
384 Boylston St [Berkeley St]
617-859-7772
Hit the roof deck in the summer.

• **Rise** • 306 Stuart St [Columbus Ave]
617-423-7473
For clubbing after 2 a.m. Arrive with a
member.

• **Storyville** • 90 Exeter St [Huntington Ave]
617-236-1134
A pinch of New Orleans nightlife in Beantown.

Map 6

Back Bay (East) / South End (Uppe

🍴Restaurants

- **Abe & Louie's** • 793 Boylston St [Fairfield St]
617-536-6300 • $$$$
Popular local steakhouse.
- **b.good** • 131 Dartmouth St [Columbus Ave]
617-424-5252 • $
Healthy, quick lunches.
- **Brasserie Jo** •
120 Huntington Ave [W Newton St]
617-425-3240 • $$$$
French brasserie near Symphony Hall. Usually
very busy.
- **Davio's** • 75 Arlington St [Stuart St]
617-357-4810 • $$$$
Good food, but it's about the river view.
- **Flour Bakery + Café** •
131 Clarendon St [Stanhope St]
617-437-7700 • $
Beyond everyday bakery. Also serves
dinners for take-away.
- **Georgetown Cupcake** •
83 Newbury St [Clarendon St]
617-927-2250 • $
Best cupcakes hands down, flat out.
- **Grill 23 & Bar** • 161 Berkeley St [Stuart St]
617-542-2255 • $$$$$
Classic steakhouse. Ideal for business dinners.
- **House of Siam** •
542 Columbus Ave [Worcester St]
617-267-1755 • $$
If you are off to the symphony, this is a good
bet.
- **Lolita Cocina & Tequila Bar** •
271 Dartmouth St [Newbury St]
617-369-5609 • $$
Tacos and margaritas. Vampy with a tinge of
goth.

- **Mistral** • 223 Columbus Ave [Cahners Pl]
617-867-9300 • $$$$
Superb. Great bar, too. Look sharp.
- **Oak Long Bar + Kitchen** •
138 St James Ave [Trinity Pl]
617-585-7222 • $$$
Go for the old school Boston vibe, not the
overpriced menu and mediocre martinis.
- **Osushi** • 10 Huntington Ave [Dartmouth St]
617-266-2788 • $$$
Good sushi in the Westin? You better believe
- **Parish Café** • 361 Boylston St [Arlington St]
617-247-7777 • $$
Inventive sandwiches. Full bar too.
- **Red Lantern** • 39 Stanhope St [Clarendon St]
617-262-3900 • $$$$
Asian fusion in old Hard Rock Building;
industry hot spot.
- **The Salty Pig** •
130 Darthmouth St [Columbus Ave]
617-536-6200 • $$
Meat is king: Fantastic charcuterie plates and
excellent smoked meats.
- **Sweet Cupcakes** •
225 Newbury St [Fairfield St]
617-267-2253 • $
Give in to your Sweet tooth.
- **Tico** • 222 Berkeley St [St. James Ave]
617-351-0400 • $$$
Legit tapas joint that is always full and rockin
- **Zocalo** • 35 Stanhope St [Clarendon St]
617-456-7849 • $$
Vibrant and fun for a Friday night.

Map 6

a great sandwich at **Parish Café**, some tapas at **Tico**, or, if
e operating on an expense account, a steak at **Grill 23**. If
e just thirsty, you can always hit the roof-deck at
esnake.

Shopping

gent Provocateur •
3 Newbury St [Clarendon St]
7-267-0229
xe lingerie boutique.

nthropologie • 203 Newbury St [Fairfield St]
7-262-0545
othes, accessories and colorful *objets*
home.

pple Store • 815 Boylston St [Fairfield St]
7-385-9400
ac Mecca.

arneys New York •
0 Huntington Ave [Harcourt St]
7-385-3300
r those of you with lots of disposable
come.

est of Scotland Cashmere Outlet •
5 Newbury St [Clarendon St]
7-536-3048
ashmire outlet from the olde country.

rooks Brothers •
Newbury St [Berkeley St]
7-267-2600
agship store of company operating since
818.

ty Sports • 480 Boylston St [Clarendon St]
7-267-3900
overs all the basics in apparel and
quipment.

rate & Barrel • 777 Boylston St [Fairfield St]
7-262-8700
ck Bay location of Chicago behemoth.

&M • 100 Newbury St [Clarendon St]
5-466-7467
sposable chic from Swedish mega-
erchant.

he Hempest • 207 Newbury St [Exeter St]
7-421-9944
on't ask if they sell screens.

nternational Poster Gallery •
5 Newbury St [Exeter St]
7-375-0076
rints and posters from around the world.

ndt Master Chocolatier •
4 Boylston St [Exeter St]
17-236-0571
fty gifts for your Swiss miss.

ord & Taylor • 760 Boylston St [Fairfield St]
7-262-6000
eaturing new façade.

• Louis • 776 Boylston St [Fairfield St]
617-603-2944
High-end men's and women's designer
clothing.

• Lush • 166 Newbury St [Dartmouth St]
617-375-5874
British cosmetics merchant.

• Marathon Sports • 671 Boylston St [Exeter St]
617-267-4774
Run! Run! Run!

• Marc Jacobs • 81 Newbury St [Clarendon St]
617-425-0404
Will he make it in fashion-challenged Boston?

• Marshalls • 500 Boylston St [Clarendon St]
617-262-6066
Discount clothing and other stuff.

• Neiman Marcus • 5 Copley Pl [Dartmouth St]
617-536-3660
Needless Markup?

• Paper Source • 338 Boylston St [Arlington St]
617-536-3444
DIY paper crafts and quirky gifts.

• Saks Fifth Avenue •
800 Boylston St [Gloucester St]
617-262-8500
A posh shopping experience.

• Second Time Around •
176 Newbury St [Exeter St]
617-247-3504
Pre-owned chic.

• Second Time Around •
219 Newbury St [Fairfield St]
617-266-1113
Upscale chic thrift.

• Shreve, Crump & Low •
39 Newbury St [Berkeley St]
617-267-9100
Boston jewelers since 1796.

• Sweet Cupcakes •
225 Newbury St [Fairfield St]
617-267-2253
Give in to your Sweet tooth.

• The Tannery • 711 Boylston St [Berkeley St]
617-267-5500
Known for huge selection. Hit-or-miss service.

• Teuscher Chocolates •
230 Newbury St [Fairfield St]
617-536-1922
For the Swiss chocoholic in you.

• Urban Grape •
303 Columbus Ave [Dartmouth St]
857-250-2509
Wine rookies are welcomed in this friendly,
well-stocked shop.

Map 7 • South End (Lower)

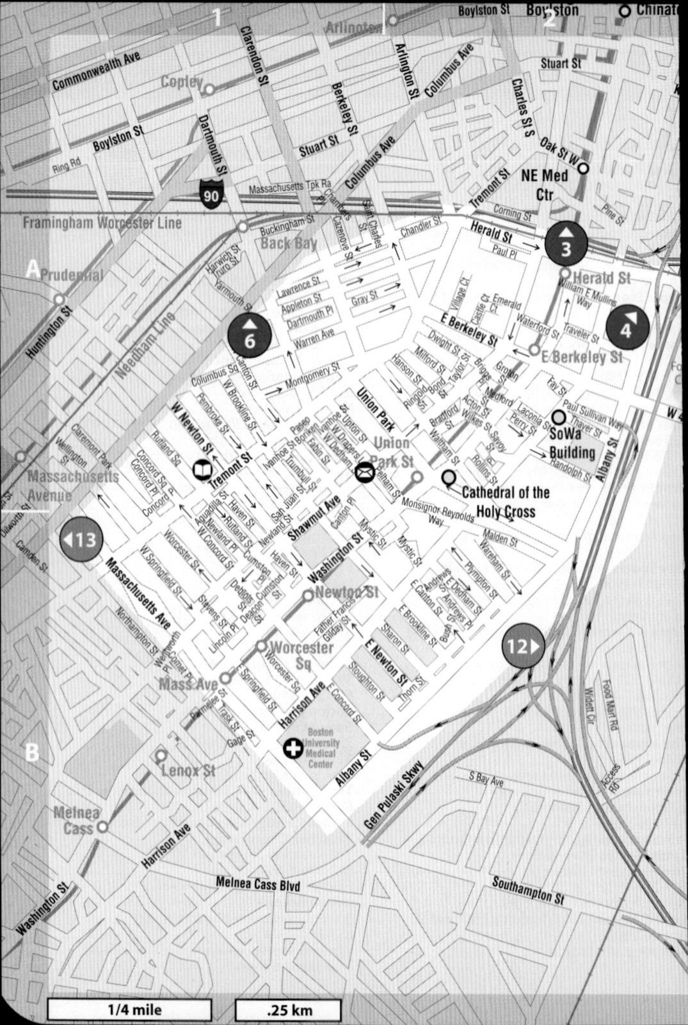
Boylston St
Boylston
Chinat
Arlington
Clarendon St
Arlington St
Columbus Ave
Stuart St
Charles St S
Commonwealth Ave
Copley
Berkeley St
Dartmouth St
Boylston St
Stuart St
Oak St W
Ring Rd
NE Med Ctr
Tremont St
Massachusetts Tpk Ra
90
Corning St
Pine St
Framingham Worcester Line
Buckingham St
Back Bay
Cazenove St
Saint Charles St
Chandler St
Herald St
Paul Pl
3
Herald St
William E Mullins Way
Prudential
Harwich St
Truro St
Yarmouth St
Lawrence St
Appleton St
Dartmouth Pl
Gray St
Village Ct
Castle Ct
Emerald Ct
Waterford St
Traveler St
4
Huntington St
Needham Line
6
Warren Ave
E Berkeley St
E Berkeley St
Dwight St
Milford St
Hanson St
Columbus Sq
Montgomery St
Canton St
Union Park
Ringgold St
Bond St
Taylor St
Briggs Pl
Groton St
Medford St
Fay St
Paul Sullivan Way
Thayer St
W Newton St
Pembroke St
W Brookline St
Paseo Borinquen
Ivanhoe St
Upton St
W Dedham St
Bradford St
Acton St
Wilkes St
Savoy St
Laconia St
Perry St
SoWa Building
Albany St
Randolph St
Claremont Park
Wellington St
Rutland Sq
Tremont St
Union Park St
Waltham St
Rollins St
Massachusetts Avenue
Concord Sq
Concord Pl
Fabin St
Trumbull St
San Juan St
Pelham St
Cathedral of the Holy Cross
Monsignor Reynolds Way
Dilworth St
13
Aquadilla St
Newland Pl
W Concord St
Haven St
Rutland St
Newland St
Shawmut Ave
Canton Pl
Mystic St
Mystic St
Malden St
Wareham St
Camden St
Worcester St
W Springfield St
Massachusetts Ave
Cumston Pl
Haven St
Washington St
Newton St
Andrews St
E Dedham St
Plympton St
Stevens St
Dedham St
Deacon St
Cunston St
Father Francis Gilday St
E Canton St
Andrews Pl
Northampton St
Wentworth Pl
Comet Pl
Lincoln Pl
Worcester Sq
E Brookline St
Sharon St
Bush St
12
Mass Ave
Springfield St
Worcester Sq
E Newton St
Stoughton St
Thorn St
Harrison Ave
E Concord St
Widett Cir
Food Mart Rd
Parmelee St
Trask St
Gage St
Boston University Medical Center
Albany St
B
Lenox St
S Bay Ave
Access Rd
Gen Pulaski Skwy
Melnea Cass
Harrison Ave
Melnea Cass Blvd
Southampton St
Washington St
1
2
A
1/4 mile
.25 km

South End is America's largest Victorian neighborhood, has the city's
est gay population, and, after years of gentrification, is now a
stination" spot. All this hipness, of course, makes the South End more
ensive than it was a decade ago. Ultra-trendy boutiques rub shoulders
h family-friendly brasseries (especially on happening Tremont Street).

Landmarks

athedral of the Holy Cross •
100 Washington St [Union Park St]
7-542-5682
other church of the Archdiocese of Boston.

oWa Artists Guild •
50 Harrison Ave [Thayer St]
converted warehouse, now home to several
alleries.

Nightlife

• **The Beehive** • 541 Tremont St [Milford St]
617-423-0069
There's an old-timey, speakeasy feel to the
place.
• **The Boston Eagle** •
520 Tremont St [Dwight St]
617-542-4494
Casual gay local, mostly denim and leather.
• **Delux Café** • 100 Chandler St [Clarendon St]
617-338-5258
Small, hip spot with good eats, music.
• **Franklin Café** • 278 Shawmut Ave [Hanson St]
617-350-0010
Mainly a restaurant, but a good bar choice too.
• **Fritz Lounge** • 26 Chandler St [Berkeley St]
617-482-4428
Best gay brunch spot.
• **J.J. Foley's** • 117 E Berkeley St [Fay St]
617-728-9101
One of the oldest family-run bars in the city.

31

Map
16 5 6 3 4
   7
15   1

🍴 Restaurants

- **Addis Red Sea** • 544 Tremont St [Waltham St]
617-426-8727 • $$
Ethiopian. Get jiggy with some injera.
- **Appleton Café** •
123 Appleton St [Appleton St]
617-859-8222 • $
Melt-in-your-mouth muffins meet sandwiches
with a twist.
- **Aquitaine** • 569 Tremont St [Union Park St]
617-424-8577 • $$$$
A solid French bistro.
- **B&G Oysters** • 550 Tremont St [Waltham St]
617-423-0550 • $$$$
Stylish oyster shop. Good wine list. Best lobster
rolls in town!
- **Da Vinci Ristorante** •
162 Columbus Ave [Isabella St]
617-350-0007 • $$$
South End's answer to the North End
hegemony on Italian food.
- **Delux Café** • 100 Chandler St [Clarendon St]
617-338-5258 • $$
Small, hip spot with good eats, music.
- **El Triunfo** • 147 E Berkeley St [Harrison Ave]
617-542-8499 • $
Cheap tacos. Good tongue!
- **Flour Bakery + Café** •
1595 Washington St [Rutland St]
617-267-4300 • $
Beyond exceptional bakery. Also serves
dinners for take-away.
- **Franklin Café** • 278 Shawmut Ave [Hanson St]
617-350-0010 • $$$
Delicious late-night option.
- **Gaslight Brasserie** •
560 Harrison Ave [Waltham St]
617-422-0224 • $$
Good French food. Stainless steel bar is a nice
touch.
- **Kitchen** • 560 Tremont St [Waltham St]
617-695-1250 • $$$
New spot with a classic American flair; get the
Toffee Pudding.
- **L'Espalier** • 774 Boylston St [Newbury St]
617-262-3023 • $$$$$
One of Boston's best. If you want the
experience and have the cash , spend it here.
- **Masa** • 439 Tremont St [Appleton St]
617-338-8884 • $$$$
Tiniest $1 tapas specials we've ever seen.
- **Mela** • 578 Tremont St [Upton St]
617-859-4805 • $$
Two words: lunch buffet.
- **Metropolis Café** • 584 Tremont St [Upton S
617-247-2931 • $$
Try the cranberry pancakes for brunch.
- **Mike's City Diner** •
1714 Washington St [W Springfield St]
617-267-9393 • $
A trusty not-too-greasy spoon.
- **Morse Fish** •
1401 Washington St [Union Park St]
617-262-9375 • $$
The neighborhood's only fish shack.
- **Myers + Chang** •
1145 Washington St [E Berkeley St]
617-542-5200 • $$
Fun Asian fusion.
- **Oishii Boston** •
1166 Washington St [E Berkeley St]
617-482-8868 • $$$$$
The only place with better sushi is their oth
location.
- **Orinoco** • 477 Shawmut Ave [W Concord St
617-369-7075 • $$$
The South End puts a twist on Venezuelan
food and it's delicious!
- **Picco** • 513 Tremont St [E Berkeley St]
617-927-0066 • $$
The gated community of ice cream. Serves
pizza, too.
- **South End Pita** • 473 Albany St [Union Park
617-556-2600 • $
South End shawarma that will hook you for
life.
- **Stella** • 1525 Washington St [E Brookline St,
617-247-7747 • $$$
Too Stylish, whitish spot. Mostly Italian men
- **Teranga** •
1746 Washington St [Massachusetts Ave]
617-266-0003 • $$
Senegalese—a welcome addition to the
worldly South End.
- **Tremont 647** •
647 Tremont St [W Brookline St]
617-266-4600 • $$$
One of the South End's best.
- **Union Bar and Grille** •
1357 Washington St [Waltham St]
617-423-0555 • $$$$
Expensive and tasty!
- **The Upper Crust** •
683 Tremont St [W Newton St]
617-927-0090 • $$
Fancy schmancy, crisp-crust pizza.

t your night at **Delux**, a beloved neighborhood bar complete with Elvis shrine. up some steaks for dinner at **The Butcher Shop**. When darkness falls, hit up **Beehive** for a great nightlife scene. The morning after, treat your stomach to e's **City Diner** or the pajama brunch at **Tremont 647**. If you're still alive after hat, call us. Bring pictures...and mimosas.

Shopping

Bobby from Boston •
19 Thayer St [Harrison Ave]
617-423-9299
Vintage clothing with a particularly awesome men's section.
BRIX Wine Shop •
1284 Washington St [Savoy St]
617-542-2749
Upscale wine shop.
The Butcher Shop •
552 Tremont St [Waltham St]
617-423-4800
Neighborhood meat shop. Also a wine bar serving specialties.
Holbrow Flowers •
540 Albany St [E Dedham St]
617-227-8669
Flowers!

• **Ilex** • 73 Berkeley St [Chandler St]
617-422-0300
Florist.
• **Lekker** • 1317 Washington St [Rollins St]
617-542-6464
Unique, modern home furnishings.
• **Picco** • 513 Tremont St [E Berkeley St]
617-927-0066
Ice cream handy to the BCA.
• **South End Buttery** •
314 Shawmut Ave [Union Park St]
617-482-4015
Churning out the treats.
• **South End Formaggio** •
268 Shawmut Ave [Milford St]
617-350-6996
Cheese, cured meats, dry goods, and wine.
• **Uniform** • 511 Tremont St [E Berkeley St]
617-247-2360
Top clothes for lads.

Map 8

s, Charlestown really is the same neighborhood depicted in Ben Affleck's
e Town—from Irish gangsters to the most bank robbers and car thieves
r capita. But despite the public housing blocks that still sit along the
dge of town, Charlestown is now an upscale, quaint community. Still, if
u see someone in a nun mask? Look away.

Landmarks

Bunker Hill Monument •
Monument Ave [High St]
617-242-5641
Battle actually took place on nearby Breed's
Hill.
Charlestown Navy Yard •
Warren St & Constitution Rd
617-242-5601
Home of the *USS Constitution* ("Old Ironsides").
Tobin Memorial Bridge • US-1
Lovingly photographed in *Mystic River*.
The Warren Tavern • 2 Pleasant St [Main St]
617-241-8142
One of Paul Revere's favorite watering holes.

Nightlife

Sullivan's Pub • 85 Main St [Harvard St]
617-242-9515
Relaxed pub off of Thompson Square.
The Warren Tavern • 2 Pleasant St [Main St]
617-241-8142
One of Paul Revere's favorite watering holes.

Restaurants

• **Figs** • 67 Main St [Monument Ave]
617-242-2229 • $$$
Charlestown branch of upscale pizza chain.
• **Ironside Grill** • 25 Park St [Warren St]
617-242-1384 • $$
Formerly managed by Raymond Burr.
• **Jenny's Pizza** • 320 Medford St [Allston St]
617-242-9474 • $$
Subs too. Nice view of the, erm, Autoport.
• **Navy Yard Bistro & Wine Bar** •
24 6th St [1st Ave]
617-242-0036 • $$
Mid-priced bistro fare near the ships.
• **Ninety Nine** • 29 Austin St [Lawrence St]
617-242-8999 • $$
Take your step-kids.
• **Paolo's Trattoria** • 251 Main St [Lawnwood Pl]
617-242-7229 • $$
Italian, including wood-oven-cooked pizzas.
• **Sorelle** • 100 City Sq [Park St]
617-242-5980 • $
Tasty sandwiches, baked goods, alcohol too.
• **Sorelle** • 1 Monument Ave [Main St]
617-242-2125 • $
Tasty sandwiches, baked goods, alcohol too.
• **Tangierino** • 83 Main St [Monument Ave]
617-242-6009 • $$$
Rockin' Moroccan.
• **The Warren Tavern** • 2 Pleasant St [Main St]
617-241-8142 • $$
One of Paul Revere's favorite watering holes.

Shopping

• **A Wild Flower** • 73 Main St [Monument Ave]
617-242-4214
Florist.
• **Bunker Hill Florist** •
1 Thompson Sq [Austin St]
617-242-2124
Florist.
• **The Joy of Old** • 85 Warren St [Pleasant St]
617-242-6066
Coming soon: "The Joy of Gay Old."

Map 9 · **East Boston**

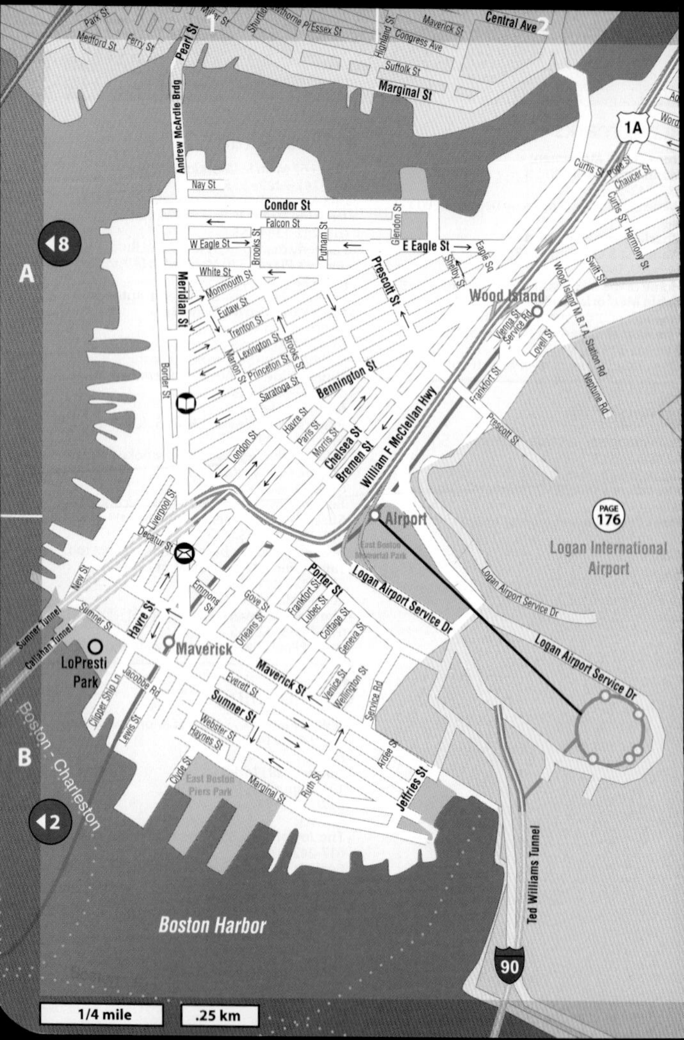

N

Park St
Medford St
Ferry St
Pearl St
Shelby St
Hawthorne St
Essex St
Central Ave
Highland St
Congress Ave
Maverick St
Suffolk St
Marginal St

Andrew McArdle Bridg

1A

Curtis St

Curtis St
Chauncy St
Harmony St

Nay St

Condor St
Falcon St
W Eagle St
Brooks St
Putnam St
E Eagle St
Glendon St
Eagle St

White St
Monmouth St
Eutaw St
Trenton St
W Eagle St
Meridian St

Lexington St
Princeton St
Saratoga St
Bennington St

Harris St
Morris St
Paris St
London St
Chelsea St
Bremen St

Border St

Liverpool St
Decatur St
Emmons St
Havre St
Sumner St
Maverick
Maverick St

LoPresti
Park
Chelsea St LA
Jacobus St
Everett St
Lewis St
Webster St
Sumner St
Haynes St

Boston - Charlestown

Sumner Tunnel
Callahan Tunnel

Cottage St

Orleans St

Porter St

Frankfort St
Lamson St
Paris St
Maverick St
Vienna St
Bennington St
Service Rd

Marion St
Brooks St
Marginal St
Cove St
Jenkins St
Ander St

East Boston
Piers Park

William F McClellan Hwy

Prescott St

Wood Island

Vienna St
Bennington St
Lovell St
Lovell St

Frankfort St

Prescott St

Airport
East Boston
Memorial Park

Logan Airport Service Dr

Logan Airport Service Dr

PAGE
176

Logan International
Airport

Logan Airport Service Dr

Ted Williams Tunnel

Boston Harbor

90

◄8

A

◄2

B

| 1/4 mile | .25 km |

of the last predominantly ethnic neighborhoods in Boston, and
...ated from the city by water, Eastie's tree-lined streets and classic triple-
...kers are home to a Latin American community that's just starting to see
... gentrification from Southie move in. Maverick Square is busy, but you'll
...nt to make the walk up to Day Square to get a better sense of the turf.

Landmarks

...Presti Park • Summer St
...est view of the Boston skyline and harbor for
...ndlubbers.

Nightlife

...elley's Square Pub •
...4 Bennington St [Marion St]
...7-567-4627
...eighborhood local, try the ribs.

Restaurants

...ngela's Cafe • 131 Lexington St [Brooks St]
...7-567-4972 • $$
... far the best Mexican food in town prepared
... someone else's Grandma…
...cco • 107 Porter St [Paris St]
...7-561-1112 • $$
...uperb craft cocktails and apps. An anomaly in
...astie.
...eveli's • 387 Chelsea St [Bennington St]
...7-567-9539 • $
...alian. Has a bar.
...a Frontera • 290 Bennington St [Chelsea St]
...17-569-8600 • $
...exican/Salvadoran hole in the wall.
...a Terraza • 19 Bennington St [Porter St]
...7-561-5200 • $$
...traight-forward Colombian cooking. Try the
...an.
...ollos A La Brasa El Chalan •
...05 Chelsea St [Saratoga St]
...7-567-9452 • $
...nest pollo in Eastie.

Rincon Limeno • 409 Chelsea St [Shelby St]
617-569-4942 • $
Specializing in Peruvian rotisserie chicken.
Santarpio's Pizza • 111 Chelsea St [Porter St]
617-567-9871 • $
Thin and crispy. Get a side of lamb and
homemade sausage from the grill.
Taco Mex • 65 Maverick Sq [Sumner St]
617-569-2838 • $
Tongue taco, a sign of real Mexican.
Taqueria Cancun •
192 Sumner St [Maverick Sq]
617-567-4449 • $
Don't count on tequila slammers.
Topacio • 120 Meridian St [London St]
617-567-9523 • $$
Pupusas! Specifically, the best ones of all time.

Shopping

Betty Ann Food Shop •
565 Bennington St [Moore St]
617-567-1479
Amazing donuts.
Brazilian Soccer House •
108 Meridian St [London St]
617-569-1164
The place to get your soccer kit.
Emack & Bolio's • 23 White St [Marion St]
617-492-1907
Innovative ice cream flavors.
Globos y Fiesta •
268 Bennington St [Chelsea St]
617-569-4908
Order your piñatas here.
Lolly's Bakery • 158 Bennington St [Brooks St]
617-567-9461
Quality panadería.

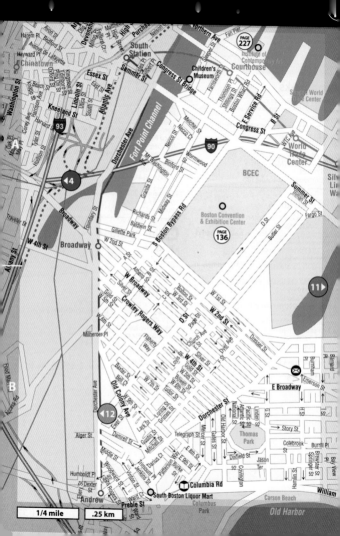

uthie seems to be in its renaissance. The formerly locals-only nghborhood has attracted yuppies, artists, and college students with a ry of new condos, restaurants, and a short commute downtown. For oof of this, take a look at the Fan Pier by the ICA, which is Boston's hippest dress, currently exploding with restaurants and new buildings.

Landmarks

oston Children's Museum •
08 Congress St [Sleeper St]
17-426-6500
eaturing the giant Hood milk bottle.

oston Convention & Exhibition Center •
15 Summer St [D St]
7-954-2100
ne Southie Starship.

oston Sailing Center •
ewis Wharf [Atlantic Ave]
17-227-4198
hoy, matey! Learn to sail the high seas.

oston Tea Party Ship & Museum •
06 Congress St [Sleeper St]
17-338-1773
te of not-so-civil disobedience.

nstitute of Contemporary Art •
00 Northern Ave [Boston Wharf Rd]
17-478-3100
Running new building. Oh, and the art's
retty good too.

outh Boston Liquor Mart •
95 Old Colony Ave [Jenkins St]
17-269-3600
Vhitey Bulger's HQ.

Nightlife

- **Atlantic Beer Garden •**
  146 Seaport Blvd [E Service Rd]
  617-357-8000
  Financial District Happy Hour spot and
  weekend sports bar
- **Blackthorn Bar •**
  471 W Broadway [Dorchester St]
  617-269-5510
  Real Irish. Pours a mean Guinness.
- **The Cornerstone •**
  16 W Broadway [Dorchester Ave]
  617-269-9553
  Broadway Square, erm, cornerstone. Parking in
  rear.
- **Drink •** 348 Congress St [Farnsworth St]
  617-695-1806
  Craft cocktail specialists; sit by the ice block.
- **The Junction •** 110 Dorchester St [Silver St]
  617-268-6429
  Low-key neighborhood spot.
- **Lincoln Tavern & Restaurant •**
  425 W Broadway St [F St]
  617-765-8636
  Fancy for Southie. Crazy crowded.
- **Lucky's Lounge •** 355 Congress St [A St]
  617-357-5825
  Well-liked retro cocktail lounge. Music most
  nights.
- **Shenannigans •** 332 W Broadway [D St]
  617-269-9509
  Popular watering hole.
- **Stadium •** 232 Old Colony Ave [Mitchell St]
  617-269-5100
  Two parts sports bar, one part dance club.
- **Stats •** 77 Dorchester St [W Broadway St]
  617-268-9300
  Sports bar by day, meat market by night.
- **The Whiskey Priest •** 150 Northern Ave [B St]
  617-426-8111
  Bro, I am like so seriously wasted, you know
  dude?
- **Whitey's •** 268 W Broadway St [D St]
  617-464-4869
  Bare bones bar with a patronage of tough
  guys.

🍴 Restaurants

- **Amrheins** • 80 W Broadway [A St]
617-268-6189 • $$
Has been here since Southie was mostly German.
- **Barking Crab** • 88 Sleeper St [Northern Ave]
617-426-2722 • $$
Make a mess while viewing the harbor skyline.
- **The Daily Catch** • 2 Northern Ave [Sleeper St]
617-772-4400 • $$$
Italian seafood specialists' Moakley Courthouse spot.
- **Flour Bakery + Café** •
12 Farnsworth St [Congress St]
617-338-4333 • $
Beyond exceptional bakery. Also serves dinners for take-away.
- **Kingston Station** • 25 Kingston St [Bedford St]
617-482-6282 • $$
Unusually tasty and reasonable grub downtown.

- **Legal Harborside** • 270 Northern Ave [D St]
617-477-2900 • $$$$
Three floors of ever-increasing cost; Seaport crown jewel doing gangbuster business.
- **Lucky's Lounge** • 355 Congress St [A St]
617-357-5825 • $$
Well-liked retro cocktail lounge. Music most nights.
- **Mul's Diner** • 80 W Broadway [A St]
617-268-5748 • $
Three words. Grilled blueberry muffins.
- **Salsa's Mexican Grill** •
118 Dorchester St [W Broadway]
617-269-7878 • $$
Legit Mexican.
- **Sportello** • 348 Congress St [A St]
617-737-1234 • $$$
Excellent modern Italian. Nice alternative to the North End.
- **Stadium** • 232 Old Colony Ave [Mitchell St]
617-269-5100 • $$
Not into sports? Don't eat here.
- **Teriyaki House** • 32 W Broadway [Dorcheste Ave]
617-269-2000 • $
The best Japanese delivery in an Irish 'hood.

fter-work drinks in the summer, nothing beats **Barking Crab**. Drinkin'
blishments are great here—especially **Lucky's** and **Shenannigans**.
n your new pad with retro pieces from **Front**. Foodies go crazy for
tello—their inventive cuisine is fantastic. Try the Bolognese.

Shopping

ront •
5 Channel Center St [Mt. Washington Ave]
57-362-7289
 hipster's wet dream for stationery and
 partment decoration.
ouis • 60 Northern Ave [S Bay Harbor Trail]
17-262-6100
 igh-end men's and women's designer
 othing.

- **Machine Age •** 645 Summer St [Fargo St]
  617-464-0099
  Modern furniture in a huge space.
- **Scooters Go Green •**
  220 Old Colony Ave [Gustin St]
  617-269-0050
  Want to save the earth and don't mind looking
  like a dork? Buy a scooter!

own as a working class Irish 'hood in a very Irish city, Southie's
nic and socioeconomic makeup is slowly changing. Many young
ofessionals, swayed by Southie's charm and priced out of other
ghborhoods, are renovating triple-deckers.

Landmarks

ank of America Pavilion •
90 Northern Ave [Massachusetts Tpke]
17-728-1690
Music venue.

lack Falcon Terminal •
Black Falcon Ave [Design Center Pl]
17-330-1500
eavily trafficked cruise boat terminal.

Boston Design Center •
Design Center Pl [Black Falcon Ave]
17-338-6610
or interior design junkies; several dozen
howrooms.

Boston Fish Pier • 212 Northern Ave [D St]
Opened in 1914, the oldest working fish port.

Giant Unholy Rat of Disease • P St
OMG! Kill it. It's dead? KILL IT AGAIN!

Harpoon Brewery •
306 Northern Ave [Harbor St]
17-574-9551
Brewery tours, seasonal special events.

Street Bathhouse • William J Day Blvd & L St
Old-timey bathhouse, home of the L Street
Brownies.

L Street Tavern • 658 E 8th St [L St]
617-268-4335
Infinitely better than "Cheers," Damon's pub in
that movie.

World Trade Center Boston •
200 Seaport Blvd [World Trade Center Ave]
617-385-5000
Event space that's part of "The Seaport
Experience."

Nightlife

- **Boston Beer Garden** • 732 E Broadway [L St]
  617-269-0990
  Had a makeover recently. Long wine list too.
- **L Street Tavern** • 658 E 8th St [L St]
  617-268-4335
  No nonsense local. Appeared in *Good Will
  Hunting*.
- **Murphy's Law** • 837 Summer St [E 1st St]
  617-269-6667
  Occasional live acoustic acts.
- **The Playwright** • 658 E Broadway [K St]
  617-269-2537
  For socializing and television watching.

Map 5 3 4 6 7 10 11 12

🍴Restaurants

- **Aura** • 1 Seaport Ln [Northern Ave]
  617-385-4300 • $$$$
  Seafood for doing deals over.
- **Boston Beer Garden** • 732 E Broadway [L St]
  617-269-0990 • $$
  If you are looking for a place right by the
  game, this is it.
- **Cafe Mamtaz** • 87 L St [Emerson St]
  617-464-4800 • $$
  Finally, ethnic food comes to Southie. For real
  this time.
- **Café Porto Bello** • 672 E Broadway [K St]
  617-269-7680 • $$
  Straight-forward, honest Italian.
- **Galley Diner** • 11 P St [E 2nd St]
  617-464-1024 • $
  Of *No Reservations* fame.

- **L Street Diner & Pizzeria** • 108 L St [E 5th S
  617-268-1155 • $
  Southie standby.
- **Local 149** • 149 P St [E 6th St]
  617-269-0900 • $$
  Replacing a beloved local isn't easy, but the
  best beer selection in Boston helps.
- **LTK** • 225 Northern Ave [D St]
  617-330-7430 • $$$
  Hip cousin to Legal chain has attentive servi
  iPod docks.
- **No Name Restaurant** •
  15 Fish Pier St E [Northern Ave]
  617-338-7539 • $$
  Attracts tourists and waterfront workers alik
- **The Playwright** • 658 E Broadway [K St]
  617-269-2537 • $$
  For socializing and television watching.

Map 11

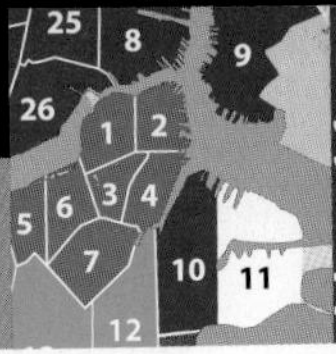

ring the summer, sea-bathers gather at the beaches along
chester Bay, or "The Irish Riviera." Good beer spots abound—take
ur of **Harpoon Brewery** for the samples of the freshest possible
Take your pick from several great restaurants along the waterfront
it up **No Name Restaurant** for reliable seafood.

🛍 Shopping

K and 8th Street Market • 362 K St [8th St]
617-269-9810
Old school neighborhood market, fantastic
meats.
Ku De Ta • 663 E Broadway [K St]
617-269-0008
A slice of Newbury St prices, in Southie.

• **Miller's Market** • 336 K St [E 7th St]
617-268-2526
Apparently, the coldest beer in town.
• **Stapleton Floral** •
635 E Broadway [Emerson St]
617-269-7271
Florist.
• **Stapleton Floral** • 200 Seaport Blvd [D St]
617-399-9960
Strategically designed horticultural fauna to
please the eye…? Florist.

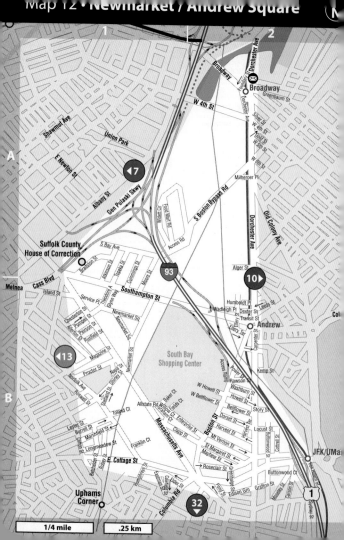

Map 12 • Newmarket / Andrew Square

N

1
2

Dorchester Ave
Broadway
Broadway
Greenbaum St
W 4th St
Snow St
W 5th St
Dexter St
W 5th St
W 6th St
W 7th St
W 8th St

Shawmut Ave
Union Park
E Newton St

A

◄7

Milheroer Pl
S Boston Bypass Rd
Dorchester Ave
Old Colony Ave

Albany St
Gen Pulaski Skwy

Suffolk County
House of Correction

S Bay Ave
Alger St
10►

Cass Blvd
Island St
Broxton St
Atkinson St
Topeka St
Quimanga St
Maine St
93

Melnea
Service Pl
Clipp Way
Southampton St
Humboldt Pl
Wadleigh Pl
Dexter St
Leeds St
Transit St

Chesterton St
Pomau St
Alberto St
Pierson St
Burfield St
Newmarket Sq
Newmarket St
Ferry Ter
Andrew

◄13

Magazine St
Capen St

Proctor St
Rand St
South Bay
Shopping Center
Kemp St

Norfolk Ave
Boston St
Access Rd
Rawson St

B

Lester St
Burrill St
Marshfield St
Longmeadow St
Speedwell St
Spring St
Tolland Ct
Franklin Ct
Baker Ct
Allstate Rd
Miller Fields Ct
Enterprise St
Clapp St
W Howell St
W Bellflower St
Washburn St
Howell St
Bellflower St
Story St
Dorset St
Harvest St
Locust St

E Cottage St
Humphreys St
St Margaret St
Mt Vernon St
Mayhew St
Roselclair St
JFK/UMass
Buttonwood Ct

Uphams
Corner
Columbia Rd
Edson Grn
Grafton St
Edson St
32▼
1

1/4 mile   .25 km

...d distributors, u-store warehouses, and the big box chains at South Bay ...opping Center are the heart of this commercial and industrial area. ...less you've got a trip to Target, Home Depot, or are visiting family at the ...ffolk County House of Correction, you'll find only the fraying edges of ...uthie, Dorchester, and Roxbury worth a deeper look.

Landmarks

...uffolk County House of Correction •
...0 Bradston St [Southampton St]
...17-635-1000
...ust so you know.

Nightlife

Dot Tavern • 840 Dorchester Ave [Harvest St]
...17-288-6288
Neighborhood local.
Sports Connection Bar & Grill •
...60 Dorchester Ave [Leeds St]
...17-268-4119
Featuring "a big screen TV."

Restaurants

224 Boston Street •
224 Boston St [St Margaret St]
...17-265-1217 • $$$
Big Portions, Good Prices! Oh crap!
Andrew Square House of Pizza •
395 Dorchester St [Dorchester Ave]
...17-268-1940 • $
No frills Greek-style pizza.
The Avenue Grille •
...56 Dorchester Ave [Mt Vernon St]
...17-288-8000 • $$
Always something tasty here. A good choice.
Baltic Deli & Café •
...32 Dorchester Ave [Father Songin Way]
...17-268-2435 • $
Foods from the old country.
Café Polonia • 611 Dorchester St [Boston St]
...17-269-0110 • $
Polish. Small, inviting, authentic. Have a
Zywiec.
Franklin Southie •
152 Dorchester Ave [W 4th St]
...17-269-1003 • $$$
Cocktails proving Southie isn't all rough edges.

• The Hen House Wings 'n Waffles •
1033 Massachusetts Ave [Proctor St]
617-442-9464 • $
Chicken, waffles, cholesterol.
• Liberty Diner •
1003 Massachusetts Ave [Magazine St]
617-442-9262 • $
Who doesn't love a good egg sandwich?
• Restaurant Laura •
688 Columbia Rd [Elder St]
617-825-9004 • $$
Scary outside, lovely Cabo Verde inside. Live
music.
• Singh's Roti Shop •
692 Columbia Rd [Elder St]
617-282-7977 • $
Huge roti. Also try the channa doubles.
• Taqueria Casa Real •
860 Dorchester Ave [Mt Vernon St]
617-282-3135 • $
Mexican; good hot sauce options.
• Venetian Garden •
1269 Massachusetts Ave [Columbia Rd]
617-288-9262 • $$
A '60s time warp for Rat Pack Mexican food.
• Victoria's Diner •
1024 Massachusetts Ave [Proctor St]
617-442-5965 • $
Great diner chow, loads of sausage, and open
24 hours on weekends!

Shopping

• Home Depot •
5 Allstate Rd [Massachusetts Ave]
617-442-6110
Got wood?
• Marshalls • 8 Allstate Rd [Massachusetts Ave]
617-442-5050
Discount clothing and other stuff.

re's a beauty to Roxbury, despite its roughness. Dudley Square is
bury's commercial center, but businesses are also finding opportunity
ser to the busy Orange Line and along Blue Hill Avenue. Highlights
ude **The National Center of Afro-American Artists**, the largest
sque in New England, and the view from Fort Hill.

Landmarks

ighland Park • Fort Ave & Beech Glen St
tle visited Fort Hill monument with great
ews

lamic Cultural Center •
00 Malcolm X Blvd [Elmwood St]
17-427-2636
argest mosque in the Northeast.

alcolm X Ella Little Collins House •
2 Dale St [Wakullah St]
alcolm X lived here with his sister during
rmative years.

ational Center for Afro-American Artists •
00 Walnut Ave [Cobden St]
17-442-8614
uddingstone mansion holds Nubian tomb
odel, afternoon hours.

hirley-Eustis House •
3 Shirley St [Clifton St]
17-442-2275
our this 18th-century royal governor's
ountry estate.

Nightlife

&S Tavern • 380 Warren St [Maywood St]
17-442-7023
eighborhood local.

ade's • 958 Tremont St [Davenport St]
17-442-4600
ancing, mostly R&B and hip-hop.

Restaurants

- **Ali's Roti Restaurant** •
  1035 Tremont St [Coventry St]
  617-427-1079 • $
  Indian food lovers will take naturally to this
  Trinidadian gem.
- **Dayib Cafe** • 722 Shawmut Ave [Williams St]
  617-427-0599 • $
  Authentic Middle Eastern. The tea is an
  absolute must.
- **Eddie's Restaurant** •
  2253 Washington St [Warren St]
  617-427-1076 • $$
  Satisfy your Spanish craving for minimal
  moolah.
- **Haley House Bakery Café** •
  12 Dade St [Washington St]
  617-445-0900 • $
  The best jerk chicken. Ever.
- **Ideal Sub Shop** • 522 Dudley St [Burrell St]
  617-442-1560 • $
  The freshest, largest, best-deal-ever subs.
- **M & M Ribs** •
  155 Southampton St [Theodore Glynn Way]
  617-306-0788 • $
  Saucy ribs, tangy baked beans, gooey mac 'n'
  cheese.
- **Merengue** • 156 Blue Hill Ave [Julian St]
  617-445-5403 • $$
  Dominican. Tropical vibe. Gets props from the
  Sox.
- **Peking House** • 160 Dudley St [Warren St]
  617-442-9215 • $$
  Solid chicken dishes and fried rice.
- **Silver Slipper Restaurant** •
  2387 Washington St [Dudley St]
  617-442-4853 • $
  Breakfast in all its greasy glory; great grits.
- **Ugi's Subs** • 68 Warren St [Dudley St]
  617-427-7032 • $
  Old school sandwich shop with a mean steak
  and cheese.

avy gentrification in Jamaica Plain means that the population of new parents pushing llers is at an all-time high. Other residents include artists, hipsters, young professionals, -friendly folk, and lesbians. Perhaps the neighborhood with the most access to green as, Jamaica Pond and the Arnold Arboretum provide ample space for joggers to sprint d bikers to ride. The addition of a **Whole Foods**, joining the **Harvest Co-op Market**, has dified the community's reputation as being pro-organic and locally farmed foods.

Landmarks

rnold Arboretum • 125 Arborway [Centre St]
17-524-1718
he most famous collection of trees in
merica, an oasis.

oyle's Café •
484 Washington St [Williams St]
17-524-2345
century's worth of pols have slapped backs
ere.

irst Church in Jamaica Plain •
Eliot St [Centre St]
17-524-1634
he first church in Jamaica Plain, ca. 1853.
mpressive stone facade, creepy graveyard.

he Footlight Club • 7 Eliot St [Centre St]
17-524-3200
ldest running theatre in the US.

he Loring-Greenough House •
2 South St [Centre St]
17-524-3158
uilt as a country estate in 1760. Open for
ours.

amuel Adams Brewery •
0 Germania St [Brookside Ave]
17-368-5080
ove the product, but not much of an
experience.

pontaneous Celebrations •
5 Danforth St [Boylston St]
17-524-6373
P community arts organization.

Nightlife

- **Bella Luna Restaurant and Milky Way Lounge** •
284 Amory St [Minton St]
617-524-6060
Dance club-Chuck E. Cheese's hybrid.
- **Brendan Behan Pub** •
378 Centre St [Sheridan St]
617-522-5386
Well-liked Irish local. Relaxed atmosphere.
- **Canary Square** •
435 S Huntington Ave [Moraine St]
617-524-2500
Swanky haven for craft beer fanatics.
- **Costello's Tavern** • 723 Centre St [Harris Ave]
617-522-9263
Friendly JP tavern; decent food and darts.
- **Doyle's Café** •
3484 Washington St [Williams St]
617-524-2345
Trusty Irish landmark. Good grub and a mean Bloody Mary.
- **James's Gate** • 5 McBride St [South St]
617-983-2000
Enjoy the fireplace while getting busy on your shepherd's & your Guinness.
- **Jeanie Johnston Pub** • 144 South St [Hall St]
617-983-9432
Darts, karaoke, live music, local flavor.
- **Midway Cafe** •
3496 Washington St [Williams St]
617-524-9038
Local watering hole featuring a variety of live bands.
- **Samuel Adams Brewery** •
30 Germania St [Brookside Ave]
617-368-5080
Tours and samples.

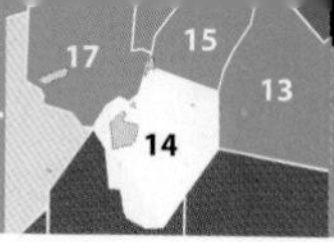

Map 14

17 15
13
14

Restaurants

- **Alex's Chimis** • 358 Centre St [Forbes St]
  617-522-5201 • $
  How can you complain about a giant plate full of chicken and chicharrones?
- **The Blue Nile** • 389 Centre St [Day St]
  617-522-6453 • $$
  Ethiopian. Heaping servings for small prices.
- **Bukhara** • 701 Centre St [Burroughs St]
  617-522-2195 • $$
  Well-liked Indian bistro. Level of tastiness is like a mystery wheel.
- **Cafe Beirut** • 654 Centre St [Green St]
  617-522-7264 • $
  Scrumptious Middle Eastern street food on the cheap.
- **Captain Nemo's** • 367 Centre St [Creighton St]
  617-971-0100 • $
  Run by sweet as pie siblings.
- **Centre Street Sanctuary** •
  365 Centre St [Creighton St]
  617-942-8951 • $$
  Very sweet drinks due to a "liqueurs only" bar license.
- **The Dogwood Café** •
  3712 Washington St [Arborway]
  617-522-7997 • $$
  Enjoy your wood-fired pizzas while listening to an actual human playing an actual piano.
- **Doyle's Café** •
  3484 Washington St [Williams St]
  617-524-2345 • $$
  The history and great atmosphere make up for the mediocre food.
- **El Oriental de Cuba** •
  416 Centre St [Paul Gore St]
  617-524-6464 • $$
  Always packed. So, be ready to wait for your cubano.
- **FoMu** • 617 Centre St [St John St]
  617-553-2299 • $
  Damn good vegan ice cream. (It's vegan?!)
- **Galway House** • 710 Centre St [Burroughs St]
  617-524-9677 • $
  Resisting the onion rings is futile.
- **Grass Fed** • 605 Centre St [Pond St]
  617-553-2278 • $
  Gourmet burgers and alcoholic milkshakes. Counter seating only.
- **The Haven** • 2 Perkins St [Centre St]
  617-524-2836 • $$
  Fortifying Scottish fare. Heart attack alert: deep fried Mars bars.

- **James's Gate** • 5 McBride St [South St]
  617-983-2000 • $$
  Enjoy the fireplace while getting busy on yo shepherd's & your Guinness.
- **JP Seafood Café** • 730 Centre St [Harris Ave]
  617-983-5177 • $$
  Some like it. Some don't. I don't.
- **Miami Restaurant** •
  381 Centre St [Sheridan St]
  617-522-4644 • $
  Go for the cubano…don't leave without a b patty.
- **Monumental Cupcakes** •
  36 South St [Sedgwick St]
  617-522-1729 • $
  Epic desserts (obviously) and rotating vegetarian/vegan lunch specials.
- **The Real Deal** • 736 Centre St [Harris Ave]
  617-522-1181 • $
  Sandwiches and wraps named after gangst
- **Ruggerio's** • 3345 Washington St [Green St
  617-522-7184 • $
  Everything sold can be delivered. Yes, even cigarettes and booze.
- **Sorella's** • 388 Centre St [Sheridan St]
  617-524-2016 • $
  Worth waiting for famous, diner-style breakfasts.
- **Ten Tables** • 597 Centre St [Pond St]
  617-524-8810 • $$$
  Short, precise, inspired menu. Delicious.
- **Tostado Sandwich Bar** •
  300 Centre St [Estrella St]
  617-477-8691 • $
  New spins on standard Cubans. Freshest frui smoothies around.
- **Tres Gatos** • 470 Centre St [Boylston St]
  617-477-4851 • $$
  Record store, tapas bar and bookstore ingeniously fused.
- **Vee Vee** • 763 Centre St [Elliot St]
  617-522-0145 • $$
  Not only cares about your eating experience but also where the food comes from.
- **Wonder Spice Café** •
  697 Centre St [Burroughs St]
  617-522-0200 • $$
  Tasty Cambodian/Thai. Well named. Get the Crispy Fish!
- **Yely's Coffee Shop** •
  284 Centre St [Chestnut Ave]
  617-524-2204 • $
  Coffee? The counter is stacked full of pork, chicken, sausages, and plantains.

re Street functions as the main artery in JP, lined with restaurants, boutiques, and ge/consignment shops. **The Blue Nile** dishes out heaping sharing-sized platters of pian delicacies on the cheap. If Middle Eastern's your bag, it doesn't get much better the shawarma at **Café Beirut**. Grab a Guinness and a shot of Fernet at the **Brendan n Pub**. Jackson Square and Washington Street offer the flavors of its Puerto Rican, ican, and Cape Verdean communities.

Shopping

40 South Street • 40 South St [Sedgwick St]
17-522-5066
etro duds, mostly from the '80s.

Blue Frog Bakery • 3 Green St [Centre St]
17-983-3765
read pudding muffins, whoopie pies, coffee nd espresso.

Boing! JP's Toy Shop •
67 Centre St [Harris Ave]
17-522-7800
riendly toy shop.

Boomerangs • 716 Centre St [Burroughs St]
17-524-5120
sed clothing and housewares.

Canto 6 • 3346 Washington St [Green St]
17-983-8688
aked goodies and a good cup of joe.

City Feed and Supply •
6 Boylston St [Chestnut Ave]
17-524-1657
opular neighborhood grocery, meeting spot.

City Feed and Supply •
72 Centre St [Seaverns Ave]
17-524-1700
opular neighborhood grocery, meeting spot.

ye Q Optical • 615 Centre St [Pond St]
17-983-3937
Designer eyeglasses.

• **Fat Ram's Pumpkin Tattoo** •
374 Centre St [Sheridan St]
617-522-6444
Skilled ink artists with degrees in fine art.

• **Fire Opal** • 683 Centre St [Seaverns Ave]
617-524-0262
Upscale craft gallery.

• **Hatched** • 668 Centre St [Seaverns Ave]
617-524-5402
Small boutique specializing in organic clothing for little ones.

• **J.P. Licks** • 659 Centre St [Starr Ln]
617-524-6740
Popular ice cream shop.

• **JP Knit and Stitch** • 461 Centre St [Moraine St]
617-942-2118
Yarn store + knitting classes.

• **Kitchenwitch** • 671 Centre St [Seaverns Ave]
617-524-6800
Adorable cooking gadgets galore.

• **Salmagundi** • 765 Centre St [Eliot St]
617-522-5047
Check out the coolest selection in the city.

• **Tres Gatos** • 470 Centre St [Boylston St]
617-477-4851
Record store, tapas bar and bookstore ingeniously fused.

• **When Pigs Fly** • 613 Centre St [Pond St]
617-522-4948
Old-world style, handcrafted, artisanal breads.

, Mission Thrill. The place where culture, education, and sports meet, you n wander among fine art museums, green parks, eclectic colleges, top edical centers, and historic Fenway Park. While high-rise condos are anging the face of Fenway, Mission Hill remains a funky mix of students, milies, and young professionals.

Landmarks

sabella Stewart Gardner Museum •
5 Evans Way [Palace Rd]
17-566-1401
ccentric collection highlighting the enaissance and the pleasures of having noney. A gem.

Mission Church of Boston •
545 Tremont St [Pontiac St]
17-445-2600
Mission Hill landmark. Recently renovated.

Museum of Fine Arts •
65 Huntington Ave [Museum Rd]
17-267-9300
rguably one of the top museums in the ountry. Go for the Copleys.

Warren Anatomical Museum •
0 Shattuck St [Binney St]
17-432-6196
Phineas Gage's skull and other medical oddities.

Nightlife

- **The Baseball Tavern •**
  1270 Boylston St [Yawkey Way]
  617-867-6526
  Sports tavern with a focus on Fenway.
- **Church •** 69 Kilmarnock St [Queensberry St]
  617-236-7600
  Music, beer, and food—all in the shadow of Fenway.
- **The Crossing •**
  1592 Tremont St [Wigglesworth St]
  617-487-4851
  Karaoke and cornhole; cheap drinks and friendly faces.
- **Flann O'Brien's •**
  1619 Tremont St [Wigglesworth St]
  617-566-7744
  Spirited Brigham Circle local.
- **Jerry Remy's •** 1265 Boylston St [Yawkey Way]
  617-236-7369
  Staggering amount of TVs and boisterous Sox fans.
- **Machine •** 1254 Boylston St [Ipswich St]
  617-536-1950
  Large gay club.
- **Punter's Pub •** 450 Huntington Ave [Parker St]
  Student dive.
- **Ramrod •** 1254 Boylston St [Yawkey Wy]
  617-266-2986
  Gay denim-and-leather crowd; various theme nights.
- **Sweet Caroline's •**
  1260 Boylston St [Ipswich St]
  617-424-1260
  Bar food has never been so good (so good! so good!).

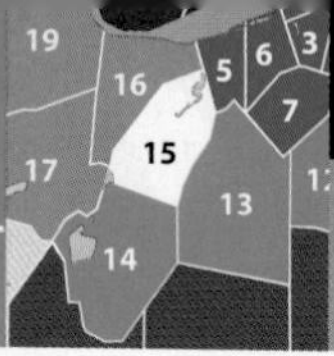

Map 15

Fenway (West) / Mission Hill

🍴Restaurants

- **Bravo** • 465 Huntington Ave [Museum Rd]
  617-369-3474 • $$$$
  At the MFA. Stick with the art.
- **Brigham Circle Chinese Food** •
  728 Huntington Ave [Fenwood Rd]
  617-278-2000 • $
  Two words: Wonton soup. Or is that three?
  Won ton soup? Eh. Get it.
- **Chacho's** • 1502 Tremont St [Burney St]
  617-445-6738 • $
  Pizza and subs.
- **Chicken Lou's** • 50 Forsyth St [Greenleaf St]
  617-859-7017 • $
  "Sex on a bagel" and spicy fries. Slobber.
- **Citizen Public House and Oyster Bar** •
  1310 Boylston St [Kilmarnock St]
  617-450-9000 • $$
  Whole suckling pig roasts. You read that right.

- **Crispy Dough Pizzeria** •
  1514 Tremont St [Burney St]
  617-445-7799 • $
  Specialty thin crust pies and slices.
- **Halal Indian Cuisine** •
  736 Huntington Ave [Fenwood Rd]
  617-232-5000 • $
  Decent and different for this part of town.
- **J.P. Licks** • 1618 Tremont St [Huntington Ave]
  617-566-6676 • $
  Homemade ice cream plus cafe.
- **Jerry Remy's** • 1265 Boylston St [Yawkey Wa]
  617-236-7369 • $$
  Staggering amount of TVs and boisterous Sc
  fans.
- **Longwood Grille & Bar** •
  342 Longwood Ave [Brookline Ave]
  617-232-9770 • $$$
  Hotel restaurant serving medical communit
  designed like a chain restaurant.
- **Mama's Place** • 764 Huntington Ave [Wait S
  617-566-1300 • $
  Greek goodness. Gyros and baklava.

dies began flocking to the booming Fenway side of Boylston Street places like **Tasty Burger** and **Citizen's Public House** set up shop. In ion Hill, **Penguin Cafe** makes delicious pizzas with creative toppings, the best pints flow at **Flann O'Brien's**. **Chicken Lou's** has been a heastern breakfast institution for years.

The Mission •
*24 Huntington Ave [Tremont St]
617-566-1244 • $$
Convenient, full-service bar & grill.

Montecristo Mexican Grill •
*48 Huntington Ave [Fenwood Rd]
617-232-2228 • $$
Nachos piled high with everything except the kitchen sink.

Penguin Pizza •
*35 Huntington Ave [Francis St]
617-277-9200 • $
Recommended, and not just for the name.

The Squealing Pig •
*34 Smith [Washington St]
617-566-6651 • $
Toasties served by indifferent staff.

Sushi Station •
*562 Tremont St [St Alphonsus St]
617-738-0888 • $
Quality maki; wallet-friendly.

• **Sweet Caroline's •**
1260 Boylston St [Ipswich St]
617-424-1260 • $$
Bar food has never been so good (so good! so good!).

• **Sweet Cheeks •**
1381 Boylston St [Kilmarnock St]
617-266-1300 • $$
Sloppy and smoky BBQ. Can be ordered by the pound.

• **Swish Shabu •**
86 Peterborough St [Kilmarknock St]
617-236-0255 • $$
Very popular hot pot spot. The wait is worth it.

• **Tasty Burger •** 1301 Boylston St [Yawkey Way]
617-425-4444 • $
Huge selection of canned beers—all served in koozies.

• **Thaitation •** 129 Jersey St [Park Dr]
617-585-9909 • $$
Head and shoulders above Brown Sugar. Go for lunch.

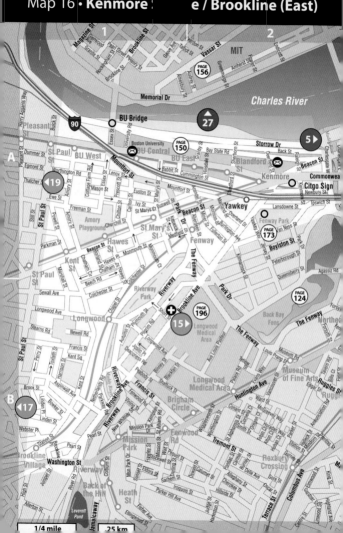

Map 16 • **Kenmore** S----e / **Brookline (East)**

der the watchful triangular eye of the **Citgo Sign**, the Kenmore Square ea is notable for sprawling Boston University, the nightclub scene on nsdowne Street, and, of course, **Fenway Park**. Beyond Fenway and the re of Kenmore Square, urban bustle gives way to the more serene idential neighborhoods of affluent Brookline.

Landmarks

U Bridge • Essex St & Mountfort St
rguably Boston's best river/skyline view.
itgo Sign • Commonwealth Ave & Beacon St
eloved Kenmore Square landmark.
enway Park • 4 Yawkey Way [Brookline Ave]
17-267-9440
ome to the Sox since 1912.

Nightlife

• **Bleacher Bar** •
82 Lansdowne St [Brookline Ave]
617-262-2424
Just your average looks-into-Fenway-Park sports bar.
• **Cask 'N Flagon** •
62 Brookline Ave [Lansdowne St]
617-536-4840
Just behind the Green Monster. Nothing special.
• **The Dugout** •
722 Commonwealth Ave [St Marys St]
617-247-8656
Babe Ruth's basement dive bar of choice.
• **Game On!** • 82 Lansdowne St [Brookline Ave]
617-351-7001
Yet another sports bar near Fenway.
• **House of Blues** • 15 Lansdowne St [Ipswich St]
888-693-2583
Huge new Landsdowne Street spot for all things musical.
• **Lansdowne Pub** • 9 Lansdowne St [Ipswich St]
617-247-1222
Bawdy, brawly and lowbrow.
• **The Lower Depths** •
476 Commonwealth Ave [Kenmore St]
617-266-6662
Gourmet tater tot platters and craft beer.
• **Lucky Strike Lanes** •
145 Ipswich St [Lansdowne St]
617-437-0300
Uber gaming and lounge establishment.
• **Tequila Rain** • 3 Lansdowne St [Ipswich St]
617-437-0300
Woooo! Woooo!
• **Who's on First?** •
19 Yawkey Way [Brookline Ave]
617-247-3353
Fun Fenway dive.
• **Yard House** •
126 Brookline Ave [Burlington Ave]
617-236-4083
Drinking a yard of beer is actually kinda awkward.

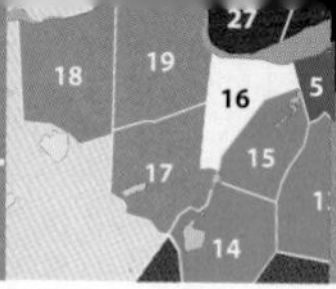

Map 16

Kenmore Square / Brookline (East)

Restaurants

- **Bon Me** •
602 Commonwealth Ave [Blandford St]
617-945-2615 • $
No, it does NOT say "bone me".
- **Boston Beer Works** •
61 Brookline Ave [Lansdowne St]
617-536-2337 • $$
Cavernous suds shop across from Fenway Park.
- **Clover Boston University** •
594 Commonwealth Ave [Blandford Mall]
$
You won't even notice it's vegetarian.
- **Cornwall's** •
654 Beacon St [Commonwealth Ave]
617-262-3749 • $$
Eat only to soak up pints.
- **Eastern Standard** •
528 Commonwealth Ave [Kenmore St]
617-532-9100 • $$$
At the Hotel Commonwealth with lip-smackingly good drinks.
- **The Elephant Walk** • 900 Beacon St [Park Dr]
617-247-1500 • $$$
French-Cambodian local legend.

- **Emack and Bolio's** •
160 Brookline Ave [Fullerton St]
617-262-1569 • $
Fruity Pebbles-encrusted cones. Need I say more?
- **India Quality** •
484 Commonwealth Ave [Kenmore St]
617-267-4499 • $$
Quality Indian. The name says it all.
- **New England Soup Factory** •
2 Brookline Pl [Brookline Ave]
617-739-1899 • $
Creative, home-style soups. Recommended.
- **Noodle Street** •
627 Commonwealth Ave [Sherborn St]
617-536-3100 • $
Unexpected spices transcend everyday Asian fare.
- **Nud Pob** •
738 Commonwealth Ave [St Marys St]
617-232-9992 • $
Yes, you can call it "nude pub." We do.
- **O'Leary's Pub** • 1010 Beacon St [St Marys St]
617-734-0049 • $$
Try the Guinness stew.
- **Taberna de Haro** • 999 Beacon St [St Marys]
617-277-8272 • $$$
Solid tapas spot with a great sherry menu.
- **Uburger** • 636 Beacon St [Raleigh St]
617-536-0448 • $
Burgers and frappes right by BU.

the addition of the gigantic **House of Blues**, some of the former club ions have lessened in quantity, but not in quality. For non-clubbers, **hant Walk** or **Taberna de Haro** are both excellent dining options. For e lucky enough to score tickets, the best entertainment in the world is :nway Park.

Shopping

ed Bath & Beyond •
01 Park Dr [Brookline Ave]
17-536-1090
or when holes are growing in your towels.

lick Art Materials •
01 Park Dr [Brookline Ave]
17-247-3322
rt-supply megashop plus custom framing.

Economy True Value Hardware •
012 Beacon St [St Marys St]
17-277-8811
lardware, household needs, cheap furniture.
/ery popular.

Guitar Center • 1255 Boylston St [Ipswich St]
17-247-1389
\lso has drums, keys, etc.

• **Hunt's Photo and Video •**
520 Commonwealth Ave [Kenmore St]
617-778-2222
Good selection of used cameras.

• **Japonaise Bakery •**
1020 Beacon St [Carlton St]
617-566-7730
Mmmm…curry donut.

• **Nuggets •**
486 Commonwealth Ave [Kenmore St]
617-536-0679
Sells only used recordings. Quite fun to
browse.

• **REI •** 401 Park Dr [Brookline Ave]
617-236-0746
Seattle co-op for the gearhead.

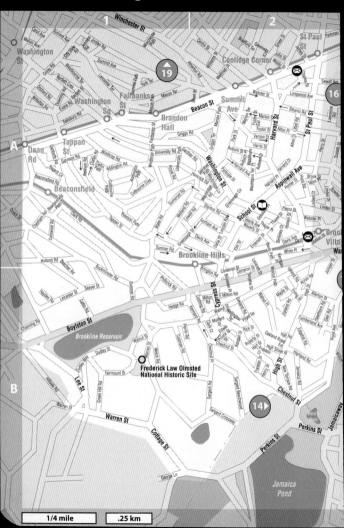

Map 17 · Coolidge Corner / Brookline Hills

1/4 mile   .25 km

s neighborhood is a vibrant mix of old and new, urban and suburban,
-fashioned and eclectic. Long-time residents in stately Victorian homes
re quiet neighborhood parks, diverse restaurants and shops, and a
zing nightlife with transient college students and well-paid young
fessionals.

Landmarks

**ederick Law Olmsted
ational Historic Site** • 99 Warren St [Welch
]
7-566-1689
enius of American landscapes, the ultimate
ome office.

Nightlife

- **Matt Murphy's Pub** •
  14 Harvard St [Webster Pl]
  617-232-0188
  Popular Irish pub. Good food and music.
- **The Publick House** •
  1648 Beacon St [Washington St]
  617-277-2880
  Focus here is on the beers.
- **The Washington Square Tavern** •
  714 Washington St [Beacon St]
  617-232-8989
  Pub/restaurant with slightly overpriced food.

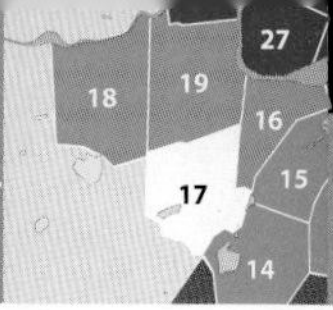

Map 17

Coolidge Corner / Brookline Hil

🍴 Restaurants

- **The Abbey** • 1657 Beacon St [Winthrop Rd]
617-730-8040 • $$
Homey neighborhood joint with an impressive beer list.
- **Boca Grande** • 1294 Beacon St [Pleasant St]
617-739-3900 • $
Lots of good taqueria fare. Consider ordering carnitas.
- **Brookline Family Restaurant** •
305 Washington St [Holden St]
617-277-4466 • $$
Top notch Turkish food.
- **Chef Chow's House** •
230 Harvard St [Webster St]
617-739-2469 • $$
Decent Chinese food outside of Chinatown.
- **Curry House** • 1335 Beacon St [Harvard St]
617-734-3971 • $
Fast food Indian.
- **Dok Bua** • 411 Harvard St [Fuller St]
617-232-2955 • $
Tastiest Thai around! Their best dishes are not the noodle dishes.
- **The Fireplace** •
1634 Beacon St [Washington St]
617-975-1900 • $$$
Warning: food also capable of inducing nap.
- **Fugakyu** • 1280 Beacon St [Pleasant St]
617-738-1268 • $$$
Sushi, very popular. Be prepared to wait.
- **Hops N Scotch** • 1306 Beacon St [Pleasant St]
857-242-4980 • $$
Order scotch or beer, but avoid the signature drink.
- **Khao Sarn** • 250 Harvard St [Longwood Ave]
617-566-7200 • $$
Relax and enjoy excellent Thai.
- **La Morra** • 48 Boylston St [High St]
617-739-0007 • $$$$
Popular Northern Italian.
- **Lineage** • 242 Harvard Ave [Longwood Ave]
617-232-0065 • $$$
Fine dining in a bright, airy setting.
- **Martin's Coffee Shop** •
35 Harvard St [Pierce St]
617-566-0005 • $
Brookline Village's own greasy spoon features breakfast, heavenly home fries.

- **Matt Murphy's Pub** •
14 Harvard St [Webster Pl]
617-232-0188 • $$
Stylish Irish pub with good food and occasional live music.
- **Michael's Deli** •
256 Harvard St [Longwood Ave]
617-738-3354 • $
Deli authenticity in Coolidge Corner.
- **Orinoco** • 22 Harvard St [Pierce St]
617-232-9505 • $$$
Make sure to make a reservation for their Saturday tasting table.
- **Pho Lemongrass** •
239 Harvard St [Webster St]
617-731-8600 • $$
Pho, Brookline-style.
- **Pomodoro** • 24 Harvard St [Webster Pl]
617-566-4455 • $$
That means tomato in Italian.
- **Rani Indian Bistro** •
1353 Beacon St [Webster St]
617-734-0400 • $$
Serving all your Indian favorites alongside some Hyderabadi specialties.
- **The Regal Beagle** •
308 Harvard Ave [Babcock St]
617-739-5151 • $$
The moonshine cocktail is one of the best Boston.
- **Rod Dee** • 1424 Beacon St [Summit Ave]
617-738-4977 • $
So tasty that we wish it was more than just small take-out joint.
- **Shawarma King** • 1383 Beacon St [Park St
617-731-6035 • $
Excellent Middle Eastern; informative servi fresh fruit beverages, traditional desserts.
- **Super Fusion Cuisine** •
690 Washington St [Beacon St]
617-277-8221 • $$
Sushi purists will appreciate the lack of sau and toppings.
- **Virginia's Fine Foods** •
8 Cypress St [Washington St]
617-566-7775 • $
Slightly pricey shop with multiple breads fo sandwiches, including veggie-friendly fare
- **The Washington Square Tavern** •
714 Washington St [Beacon St]
617-232-8989 • $$$
Good American food, but not as cheap as name might suggest.

Coolidge Corner / Brookline Hills

...kline is a place where specialty shops mingle with chain stores, and an ...ic array of food spans from the inexpensive **Rani Indian Bistro** and ... **Grande** to the upscale **Fireplace** and **Fugakyu**. The popular Art Deco ...idge Corner Theater** shows first-run, repertory, midnight movies, and ...sional burlesque.

⊃Shopping

...than's European Bakery •
...621 Beacon St [Washington St]
...17-734-7028
...o Exquisite baked goods, chocolates, gelato,
...nd espresso.

...C Florist • 224 Washington St [Davis Ct]
...17-232-3693
...orist.

...mack & Bolio's •
...563 Beacon St [Winthrop Rd]
...17-731-6256
...nnovative ice cream flavors.

...ureka Puzzles • 1349 Beacon St [Centre St]
...17-738-7352
...ld-timey gamers' heaven.

...adras Masala • 191 Harvard St [Marion St]
...17-566-9943
...dian Grocery store with a good selection of
...hutneys and prepared food

...arathon Sports •
...538 Beacon St [University Rd]
...17-735-9373
...un! Run! Run!

Mint Julep • 1302 Beacon St [Harvard St]
617-232-3600
Boutique for the ladies or for the men looking
for a gift for the ladies.

New England Comics •
316 Harvard St [Babcock St]
617-566-0115
Study break reading material, some
independent comics.

Paper Source • 1361 Beacon St [Webster St]
617-264-2800
DIY paper crafts and quirky gifts.

Party Favors • 1356 Beacon St [Webster St]
617-566-3330
Satisfies your sweet tooth and your inner
party animal.

Pier 1 Imports • 1351 Beacon St [Webster St]
617-232-9627
Brought to you by Fat Actress Kirstie Alley.

Ten Thousand Villages •
226 Harvard St [Sewall Ave]
617-277-7700
Free-trade, handmade crafts from around
the world.

Wild Goose Chase •
1355 Beacon St [Webster St]
617-738-8020
Crafts, gifts. A flea market, Brookline-style.

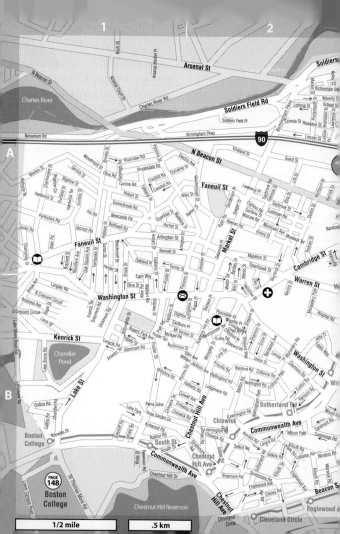

Map 18

ighton is the more sedate half of the Allston-Brighton duo but, like its
wdier neighbor, it attracts plenty of college students and young folk.
rrow, tangled, residential streets surround the cluster of shops and
staurants on Washington Street in Brighton Center.

Nightlife

Cityside • 1960 Beacon St [Sutherland Rd]
617-566-1002
Hit the patio if it's nice outside.
The Green Briar • 304 Washington St [Wirt St]
617-789-4100
Pub with frequent live rock.
Irish Village • 224 Market St [Saybrook St]
617-787-5427
Popular, relaxed local.
Mary Ann's • 1937 Beacon St [Ayr Rd]
BC student dump.
Roggie's •
356 Chestnut Hill Ave [Englewood Ave]
617-566-1880
52 beers, televised soccer.

Restaurants

Bamboo •
1616 Commonwealth Ave [Washington St]
617-734-8192 • $$
Very good Thai at Washington Street.
Cityside • 1960 Beacon St [Sutherland Rd]
617-566-1002 • $$
More for watching television than dining.
Corrib Pub • 396 Market St [Surrey St]
617-787-0882 • $$
Irish breakfast of champions.
Devlin's • 332 Washington St [Waldo Terrace]
617-779-9822 • $$$
A little bit of downtown in Brighton.
Eagle's Deli • 1918 Beacon St [Ayr Rd]
617-731-3232 • $
BC meatheads eating meat.
The Green Briar • 304 Washington St [Wirt St]
617-789-4100 • $$
Generic pub food. Stick with beer.
IHOP • 1850 Soldiers Field Rd [N Beacon St]
617-787-0533 • $
Pancakes anytime.

• **Moogy's** • 154 Chestnut Hill Ave [Colwell Ave]
617-254-8114 • $
Enjoy a cheese omelette while playing
Connect Four.
• **Roggie's** •
356 Chestnut Hill Ave [Englewood Ave]
617-566-1880 • $$
Hang out with BC kids, drink beer, and eat
greasy food.
• **Tasca** •
1612 Commonwealth Ave [Washington St]
617-730-8002 • $$
Good (but not great) tapas for all budgets!
• **TREATS on Washington** •
379 Washington St [Leicester St]
617-202-5837 • $
Hibiscus ginger soda and ham and cheese
scones? Yes, please.

Shopping

• **Amanda's Flowers** •
347 Washington St [Academy Hill Rd]
617-782-0686
Ever watch *Bed of Roses*? Hand delivered with
a smile.
• **New Balance Factory Store** •
40 Life St [Guest St]
617-779-7429
Running gear for cheap runners.
• **Petropol** •
1845 Commonwealth Ave [Sidlaw Rd]
617-232-8820
Russian-language books and media.
• **Staples** •
1660 Soldiers Field Rd [Soldiers Field Pl]
617-254-4822
Printer ink and other more reasonably priced
supplies.

Map 19 • **Allston (South) / Brookline (North)**

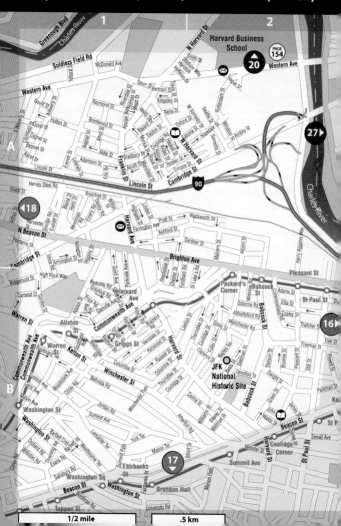

most Bostonians, crowded living and rowdy students define Allston.
re's no place in the city where so many cheap eats, dive bars, and used
ods are crammed into so few blocks. It's a dirty mashup and the city is
ter for it.

Landmarks

FK National Historic Site •
3 Beals St [Harvard St]
7-566-7937
nderstated residential home, open only in
ummer.

Nightlife

he Avenue •
249 Commonwealth Ave [Royce Rd]
17-903-3110
heap drafts and college kids.

ig City • 138 Brighton Ave [Harvard Ave]
17-782-2020
or beer and pool, not food and service.

righton Music Hall •
58 Brighton Ave [Harvard Ave]
7-562-8800
ee some great bands up close. Real close.

us Stop Pub •
52 Western Ave [N Harvard St]
17-254-4086
ownie bar with sports.

ommon Ground •
5 Harvard Ave [Gardner St]
17-783-2071
efending Allston.

eep Ellum •
77 Cambridge St [Brighton Ave]
17-787-2337
hic enough to make you forget you're in
llston.

oremi Music Studio •
42 Cambridge St [Craftsman St]
17-783-8900
araoke with private rooms.

he Draft • 34 Harvard Ave [Cambridge St]
17-783-9400
ipsters and jocks make nice.

reat Scott •
222 Commonwealth Ave [Harvard Ave]
17-566-9014
oud, live music in a small, dark place.

arry's Bar & Grill •
430 Commonwealth Ave [Kelton St]
17-738-9990
asual and roomy, with a mostly
eighborhood crowd.

• Model Café • 7 N Beacon St [Cambridge St]
617-254-9365
Allston staple, with all the usual suspects.

• Myung Dong 1st Ave •
90 Harvard Ave [Brighton Ave]
617-206-3229
Korean equivalent of *Saved by the Bell*'s The
Max. Win.

• O'Brien's • 3 Harvard Ave [Cambridge St]
617-782-6245
Live rock, mostly local acts.

• Paradise Rock Club •
967 Commonwealth Ave [Harry Agganis Wy]
617-562-8800
Major rock acts. Tasty food and smaller bands
in lounge.

• Patron's Mexican Kitchen & Watering Hole •
138 Brighton Ave [Harvard Ave]
617-782-2020
Come only after having a few drinks
downstairs first.

• Scullers Jazz Club •
400 Soldiers Field Rd [Cambridge St]
617-562-4111
Live jazz most nights. In the Doubletree.

• Silhouette Lounge •
200 Brighton Ave [Allston St]
617-254-9306
A room full of darts and drunks.

• Sunset Grill & Tap •
130 Brighton Ave [Linden St]
617-254-1331
Hundreds of beers to choose from, food until
1 am.

• Tavern in the Square •
161 Brighton Ave [Harvard Ave]
617-782-8100
All you can eat brunch buffet. All you can
watch sports.

• White Horse Tavern •
116 Brighton Ave [Linden St]
617-254-6633
Always hopping, great for sports.

• Wonder Bar • 186 Harvard Ave [Glenville Ter]
617-351-2665
Wannabe Soho, patronized by wannabe yups.

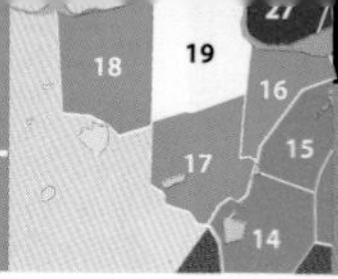

Map 19

Allston (South) / Brookline (North)

🍴 Restaurants

- **@Union** • 174 Harvard Ave [Glenville Terrace]
617-779-0077 • $$
The perfect place to nurse a hangover.
- **Allston Diner** • 431 Cambridge St [Denby Rd]
617-208-8741 • $$
Soul food, Allston-style.
- **Angora Café** •
1024 Commonwealth Ave [Babcock St]
617-232-1757 • $
Great wraps and not-to-miss fro-yo with
exhaustive and surprising toppings.
- **Anna's Taqueria** •
446 Harvard St [Thorndike St]
617-277-7111 • $
It doesn't mean much, but they roll up one of
the best burritos in town.
- **Big City** • 138 Brighton Ave [Harvard Ave]
617-782-2020 • $$
For the beer and pool, not food and service.
- **BonChon** • 123 Brighton Ave [Linden St]
617-254-8888 • $$
The other KFC: Korean fried chicken. Better
than the Colonel's.
- **Bottega Fiorentina** •
313 Harvard St [Babcock St]
617-232-2661 • $
Tuscan sandwiches to go.
- **The Breakfast Club** •
270 Western Ave [McDonald Ave]
617-783-1212 • $$
The shiniest diner found outside New Jersey.
- **Buk Kyung II** • 151 Brighton Ave [Harvard Ave]
617-254-2775 • $
Top-notch Korean food. Good luck finding a
parking space on weekends.

- **Camino Real** •
48 Harvard Ave [Farrington Ave]
617-254-5088 • $$
Good-value Colombian.
- **Charlie's Pizza & Café** •
177 Allston St [Kelton St]
617-277-3737 • $
You would never guess by the name, but th
also have Middle Eastern food.
- **Coolidge Corner Clubhouse** •
307 Harvard St [Babcock St]
617-566-4948 • $$
Home of the Big Papi Burger.
- **Dante's Frozen Yogurt** •
1236 Commonwealth Ave [Harvard Ave]
617-739-0215 • $
Self-serve froyo you can grab while waiting
for the T.
- **Dorado** • 401 Harvard St [Naples Street]
617-566-2100 • $
Never had a cemita? Best sandwich ever.
- **Garlic 'n Lemons** •
133 Harvard Ave [Brighton Ave]
617-783-8100 • $
Get your shawarma fix.
- **Grasshopper** • 1 N Beacon St [Cambridge S
617-254-8883 • $$
Hip Asian vegan.
- **Habanero Mexican Grill** •
166 Brighton Ave [Park Vale Ave]
617-254-0299 • $
El Salvadoran chow. Hell yes to the fried
plantains.
- **La Mamma** • 190 Brighton Ave [Quint Ave]
617-783-1661 • $
Stick with the empanadas and Chilean
specialties.
- **Lone Star Taco Bar** •
477 Cambridge St [Brighton Ave]
617-782-8226 • $$
Tacos and tequila—what could go wrong?

Allston (South) / Brookline (North)

Map 19

...n Rock City! Clubs drive the scene here, with live music and DJs every ...of the week. Check **Paradise**, **Great Scott**, and even the velvet rope ...nder Bar. Taps dominate **Sunset Grill** and **Big City**. As for food, we've ...known to fantasize about kebabs at **Saray** and bánh mì at **Super 88**.

...ixx Frozen Yogurt •
5 Brighton Ave [Chester St]
17-782-6499 • $
...e search ends here! Boston's best froyo.

...r. Sushi • 329 Harvard St [Babcock St]
17-731-1122 • $$
...ood basic sushi with no frills.

...adaria Brasil •
25 Harvard Ave [Brighton Ave]
17-202-6783 • $
...e pão de queijo, please.

...aradise Rock Club •
57 Commonwealth Ave [Harry Agganis Wy]
17-562-8800 • $
...ajor rock acts. Tasty food and smaller bands
Lounge.

...ho Viet •
095 Commonwealth Ave [Brighton Ave]
17-562-8828 • $
...est Vietnamese subs (bánh mì) in town for
...st a few bucks.

...uan's Kitchen •
026 Commonwealth Ave [Winslow Rd]
17-232-7617 • $
...ast, cheap Chinese; open late, good lemon
...hicken, flat-screen TV.

...efuge Café • 155 Brighton Ave [Harvard Ave]
17-562-8888 • $
...écor says "hipster hunting lodge." Go for
...runch.

...oast Beast •
080 Commonwealth Ave [Naples Rd]
17-505-9999 • $
...tuffed deli sandwiches with your choice of a
...azillion sauces.

...aray •
098 Commonwealth Ave [Brighton Ave]
17-383-6651 • $$
...ust the thought of their kabobs and eggplant
...ishes is making me drool.

• **Spike's Junkyard Dogs** •
108 Brighton Ave [Linden St]
617-254-7700 • $
Quick sausage fix.

• **Steve's Kitchen** •
120 Harvard Ave [Brighton Ave]
617-254-9457 • $
The best diner in Allston even though Lisa no
longer works there.

• **Sunset Grill & Tap** •
130 Brighton Ave [Linden St]
617-254-1331 • $$
Huge Mexican platters and tons of great beer.

• **Super 88 Food Court** •
1 Brighton Ave [Malvern St]
617-787-2288 • $
Boston's largest Asian food court.

• **Tavern in the Square** •
161 Brighton Ave [Harvard Ave]
617-782-8100 • $
All-you-can-eat brunch buffet. All-you-can-
watch sports.

• **The Upper Crust** • 286 Harvard St [Green St]
617-734-4900 • $
Fancy schmancy pizza with Wi-Fi.

• **Victoria Seafood** •
1029 Commonwealth Ave [Winslow Rd]
617-783-5111 • $
Good food and dirt cheap prices! Great
Chinese seafood options.

• **YoMa** • 5 N Beacon St [Cambridge St]
617-783-1372 • $
Fantastic Burmese food finally arrives to
Boston!

• **Zaftigs Delicatessen** •
335 Harvard St [Shailer St]
617-975-0075 • $$
Comfort food for breeders who brunch.

71

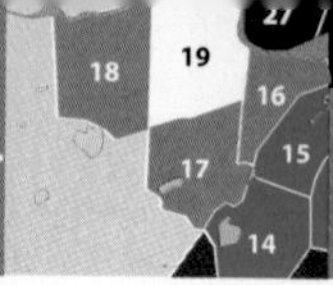

Map 19

18 19
16
17 15
14

🛍 Shopping

• **Berezka International Food Store** •
1215 Commonwealth Ave [Linden St]
617-787-2837
Russian goods for the slavophile.
• **Brookline Booksmith** •
279 Harvard St [Green St]
617-566-6660
Indie + used, with book clubs and readings monthly.
• **Brookline News and Gifts** •
313 Harvard St [Babcock St]
617-566-9634
Since 1963, chances are they have what you're looking for.
• **Catering by Andrew** •
402 Harvard St [Naples Rd]
617-731-6585
Shabbot bakery, Thursdays and Fridays only.
• **City Sports** •
1035 Commonwealth Ave [Winslow St]
617-782-5121
Covers all the basics in apparel and equipment.

• **Clear Flour Bread** •
178 Thorndike St [Lawton St]
617-739-0060
Lines out the door for Boston's honest bread
• **The Compleat Strategist** •
957 Commonwealth Ave [Pleasant St]
617-254-1166
Gaming paraphernalia.
• **Eastern Mountain Sports** •
1041 Commonwealth Ave [Winslow Rd]
617-254-4250
Gear for the New England outdoor enthusia
• **Fire Opal** • 320 Harvard St [Babcock St]
617-739-9066
Upscale craft gallery.
• **Herb Chambers Vespa Boston** •
22 Brighton Ave [St Lukes Rd]
617-254-4000
Imagine you are in Italy with its better driver
• **In Your Ear** •
957 Commonwealth Ave [Harry Agganis Wy
617-787-9755
Good selection of independent, experiment music.
• **Israel Book Shop** • 410 Harvard St [Fuller St
800-323-7723
Books in Hebrew.

porty and outdoorsy converge on **City Sports** and **Eastern Mountain**
ts. Boston's also a biking town, and riders can get tune-ups, gear, and
st advice at **International Bicycle Center**. You can always find some
d stuff at spots like **TJ Maxx** and **Urban Outfitters**, both of which come
ndy more often than not. Oh, and we love the ice cream at **J.P. Licks**.

P. Licks • 311 Harvard St [Babcock St]
17-738-8252
opular Boston ice cream institution.

olbo Fine Judaica Gallery •
37 Harvard St [Coolidge St]
17-731-8743
ood place for Jewish gifts.

upel's Bakery • 421 Harvard St [Fuller St]
17-566-9528
ld school bagel joint.

rchard Skate Shop •
56 Harvard Ave [Brighton Ave]
17-782-7777
or hipsters who travel by skateboard instead
f bicycle.

egeneration Tattoo •
55 Harvard Ave [Glenville Ave]
17-782-1313
ood addition to the Allston punk scene.

taples •
14 Harvard Ave [Commonwealth Ave]
17-566-8605
rinter ink and other more reasonably priced
upplies.

• **Stingray Body Art** •
1 Harvard Ave [Cambridge St]
617-254-0666
Huge tattoo parlor with sassy boutique.

• **TJ Maxx** • 525 Harvard St [Verndale St]
617-232-5420
Off-price apparel and housewares.

• **Unique Furnishings** •
144 Harvard Ave [Brighton Ave]
617-208-8505
Real hipsters get their furniture here. Forget
Ikea.

• **Urban Outfitters** •
226 Harvard Ave [Brainerd Rd]
617-232-0321
Hipster funky outfits for the urbanites.

• **Urban Renewals** •
122 Brighton Ave [Linden St]
617-783-8387
Top thrift shop with clothes, gifts, and kitsch.

• **Wulf's Fish Market** • 407 Harvard St [Fuller St]
617-277-2506
Respected fishmonger.

• **Zipper Hospital** • 318 Harvard St [Babcock St]
617-277-0039
The place to go for fixing zippers and tailoring.

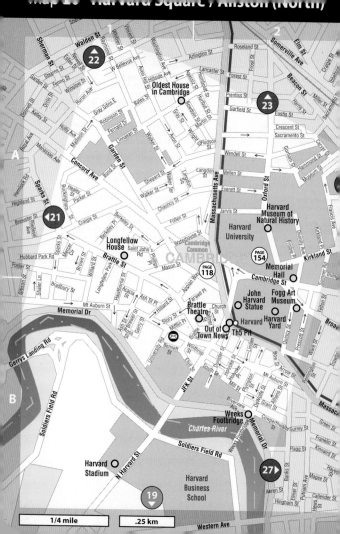

Map 20 Harvard Square / Allston (North)

1   2

Sherman St   Walden St   Roseland St   Somerville Ave

22

W Bellevue Ave   Arlington St   Elm St   Beacon St

Stearns St   Whittier St   Lancaster St   Forest St   Harris St

Fenno St   Winslow St   Washington Ave   Prentiss St   Miller St

Huron Ave   Hillside Ave   **Oldest House in Cambridge**   Garfield St   Eustis St

Gray Gdns E   Bates St   **23**

Crescent St   Sacramento St

Robinson St   Fernald Dr   Linnaean St   Avon St

Holly Ave   Madison St

A

Concord Ave   **Garden St**   Shepard St   Wendell St   Gorham St

Highland St   Healey St   Parker St   Walker St   Walker Ter   Mellen St   Hammond St

Brewster St   **21**   Berkeley St   Chauncy St   Everett St   Oxford St   Museum St

Sparks St   Craigie St   Follen St   Jarvis St   **Harvard Museum of Natural History**   Francis Ave

Hubbard Park Rd   Mercer Cir   Brown St   Saint John's Rd   **Longfellow House**   Langdon St   **Harvard University**   Kirkland St

Foster St   Willard St   **Brattle St**   Phillips Pl   Mason St   **Cambridge Common**   **PAGE 154**   Irving St

Shaler Ln   Bradbury St   Longfellow Park   Hawthorne St   Warehouse St   **Memorial Hall**   Kirkland St

Memorial Dr   Mt Auburn St   Acacia St   Story St   Farwell Pl   **PAGE 118**   **Cambridge St**   Irving St

B

Gerrys Landing Rd   Ash St Pl   **Brattle Theatre**   Church St   **John Harvard Statue**   **Fogg Art Museum**   Broadway

Ash St   Brewster St   **Out of Town News**   **Harvard**   **Harvard Yard**   Prescott St   Quincy St

Mifflin Pl   Bennett St   Winthrop St   **T5 Pl**   Bow St   Ware St

Soldiers Field Rd   **JFK St**   S Flagg St   Eliot St   Mt Auburn St   Arrow St   Massachusetts Ave

Riverview Ave   Plympton St   Grant St

Weeks Footbridge   DeWolfe St   Cowperthwaite St   Surrey St   Green St

Charles River   Memorial Dr   Franklin St

Soldiers Field Rd   Weeks Footpath   Kinnaird St

Harvard Stadium   N Harvard St   **27**   Banks St   Hayes St   Magee St

19   **Harvard Business School**   Akron St   Elmer St   Putnam Ave   Callender St   Hano St

1/4 mile   .25 km   Western Ave

r nearly 400 years of existence, Harvard Square remains more than just a ination for students. It is, in fact, a beautiful intersection between old and , where historic buildings and austere colonial brick mingle with trendy ans and hip indie boutiques. The neighborhood shines in spring and fall, but is a surprisingly charming spot during the holiday season—especially if you d to get some shopping done.

Landmarks

rattle Theatre • 40 Brattle St [Church St]
7-876-6837
dest repertory cinema in Boston, since 1953
d still projecting.

ogg Art Museum • 32 Quincy St [Broadway]
7-495-9400
ne collection, more humane scale than the
FA.

Harvard Museum of Natural History •
Oxford St [Kirkland St]
17-495-3045
ne public face of the botanical, zoological,
d geological museums.

Harvard Stadium •
Harvard St & Soldiers Field Rd
ne nation's oldest stadium.

Harvard Yard • Kirkland Street, b/w Broadway,
uincy St, Peabody St, & Massachusetts Ave
ne core of the campus, full of historical
ndmarks.

ohn Harvard Statue •
assachusetts Ave [Quincy St]
ne "statue of the three lies."

• **Longfellow House** •
105 Brattle St [Longfellow Park]
617-876-4491
Home of Henry W. Longfellow, as well as
Washington's HQ.

• **Memorial Hall** • 45 Quincy St [Cambridge St]
617-496-4595
Gorgeous architecture and interior. Try to see a
show there.

• **Oldest House in Cambridge** •
21 Linnaean St [Bowdoin St]
Built in 1681. Tours available by appointment
in the summer.

• **Out of Town News** •
Harvard Sq [John F Kennedy St]
617-354-1441
The sensible Harvard Square rendezvous spot.

• **The Pit** • Harvard Sq [John F Kennedy St]
Favorite hang-out for the counter-culture kids.

• **Weeks Footbridge** •
Memorial Dr & DeWolfe St
Most beautiful bridge on the Charles, hosts full
moon tangos.

Map 20

Harvard Square / Allston (North

Nightlife

- **Cambridge Common** •
  1667 Massachusetts Ave [Hudson St]
  617-547-1228
  Dark, comfy, familiar, yummy food.
- **Charlie's Kitchen** • 10 Eliot St [Winthrop St]
  617-492-9646
  Old School by the old school. Great jukebox.
- **Club Passim** • 47 Palmer St [Church St]
  617-492-7679
  Folk singer-songwriter landmark and
  vegetarian restaurant.
- **The Comedy Studio** •
  1238 Massachusetts Ave [Plympton St]
  617-661-6507
  A few scorpion bowls and you'll laugh at
  anything.
- **Grendel's Den** • 89 Winthrop St [JFK St]
  617-491-1160
  Harvard Square mainstay.
- **Hong Kong** •
  1238 Massachusetts Ave [Plympton St]
  617-864-5311
  The scorpion bowls are a Harvard Square
  tradition.
- **John Harvard's Brewery** •
  33 Dunster St [Mt Auburn St]
  617-868-3585
  Large and loud, good for crowds.

- **Lizard Lounge** •
  1667 Massachusetts Ave [Hudson St]
  617-547-0759
  Great spot to kick back to live music.
- **Noir Bar** • 1 Bennett St [Eliot St]
  617-661-8010
  More pretentious than sophisticated.
- **Nubar** • 16 Garden St [Waterhouse St]
  617-234-1365
  Classy comfort in the Sheraton Commander.
- **Regattabar** • 1 Bennett St [Eliot St]
  617-661-5000
  Serious jazz club.
- **Russell House Tavern** • 14 JFK St [Brattle St]
  617-500-3055
  Soak up the history AND the booze!
- **Shay's Pub & Wine Bar** • 58 JFK St [South St]
  617-864-9161
  Lo-fi wine bar and pub with outdoor seating
- **Temple Bar** •
  1688 Massachusetts Ave [Sacramento St]
  617-547-5055
  Popular and impressed with itself.
- **West Side Lounge** •
  1680 Massachusetts Ave [Sacramento St]
  617-441-5566
  For those who find Temple Bar too pretentio
- **Whitney's Cafe** • 37 JFK St [Mt Auburn St]
  617-354-8172
  One of the last dives in Harvard Square.

Harvard Square / Allston (North)

...out skipping a beat, a new crop of cocktail lounges, rustic taverns, and ...national eateries has found its way into Harvard Square's heart. Visit **Russell ...e Tavern** and **First Printer** for rustic fare with a dash of history. For street grub, **Zinneken's** or **Otto**. Old standbys remain, showing no signs of stopping: ...lie's Kitchen for juicy burgers, **Shay's** for people watching, and **Cardullo's** for ...of drool-inducing goodies.

Restaurants

Algiers • 40 Brattle St [Story St]
617-492-1557 • $
An excellent, and oddly tourist-free, lunch and coffee spot.

b. good • 24 Dunster St [Massachusetts Ave]
617-354-6500 • $
Healthier fast food.

BerryLine •
1668 Massachusetts Ave [Hudson St]
617-492-3555 • $
Fro-yo a go-go.

BonChon • 57 JFK St [Winthrop St]
617-868-0981 • $$
Korean fried chicken comes to Cambridge.

Border Café • 32 Church St [Palmer St]
617-864-6100 • $$
Feeding students sub-par Tex-Mex for years.

Café Pamplona • 12 Bow St [Arrow St]
617-492-0352 • $
Mellow Cuban hangout with outdoor patio.

Cambridge, 1 • 27 Church St [Palmer St]
617-576-1111 • $$
Tasty innovative pizzas and salads. Relaxed, stripped-down space.

Charlie's Kitchen • 10 Eliot St [Winthrop St]
617-492-9646 • $
Old School at the old school. Best jukebox around!

Clover Harvard Square •
7 Holyoke St [Massachusetts Ave]
$
Locavores 'n herbivores. Based on the popular foodtruck.

Crazy Dough's Pizza •
36 JFK St [Mt Auburn St]
617-492-4848 • $
Pizza in The Garage.

Darwin's Ltd. • 148 Mt Auburn St [Brewer St]
617-354-5233 • $
Hidden Harvard Square refuge.

Falafel Corner • 8 Eliot St [Mt Auburn St]
617-441-8888 • $
Late-night Greek on the quick and cheap.

Felipe's Taqueria •
83 Mt Auburn St [Dunster St]
617-354-9944 • $
Late night burritos in The Garage. Mind the drunks.

Flat Patties • 33 Brattle St [Brattle Sq]
617-871-6871 • $
Try their shredded pork sandwich and an order of fries.

Grafton Street •
1230 Massachusetts Ave [Bow St]
617-497-0400 • $$$
High-volume, high-end Irish restaurant offering an eclectic menu.

Grendel's Den • 89 Winthrop St [JFK St]
617-491-1160 • $
For the laid-back academic. Reasonable prices. Excellent after work specials.

Harvest • 44 Brattle St [Story St]
617-868-2255 • $$$$
Excellent. Nice garden terrace.

John Harvard's Brewery •
33 Dunster St [Mt Auburn St]
617-868-3585 • $$
Large and loud, good for crowds.

Le's • 35 Dunster St [Mt Auburn St]
617-864-4100 • $$
Reliable Vietnamese. You can't go wrong here.

Legal Sea Foods •
20 University Rd [Bennett St]
617-491-9400 • $$$
Charles Square outpost of the popular chain.

Maharaja • 57 JFK St [Winthrop St]
617-547-2757 • $$
Ornate Northern Indian.

Mr. Bartley's •
1246 Massachusetts Ave [Plympton St]
617-354-6559 • $
Classic burger joint across from the Yard.

Map 20

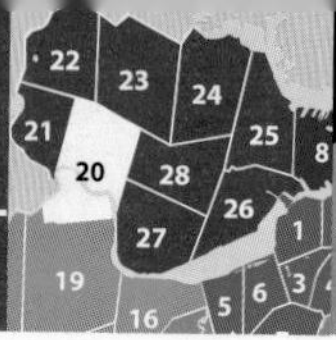

Harvard Square / Allston (North

Map 20

22 23 24
21 20 25 8
27 26 5
22 6 1
19 7
16

- **Nubar** • 16 Garden St [Waterhouse St]
617-234-1365 • $$$
Classy comfort in the Sheraton Commander.
- **Otto** • 1432 Massachusetts Ave [Church Ave]
617-499-3352 • $
Eclectic slices by way of Portland, Maine.
- **Park** • 59 JFK St [Eliot St]
617-491-9851 • $$
Choose-your-own-adventure gastropub.
- **The Red House** • 98 Winthrop St [JFK St]
617-576-0605 • $$
Seasonal menus served in an old red house.
- **Rialto** • 1 Bennett St [Eliot St]
617-661-5050 • $$$$$
Probably Cambridge's finest restaurant.
- **Russell House Tavern** • 14 JFK St [Brattle St]
617-500-3055 • $$
Modern tavern, heavy on the meat.
- **Sabra Grill** • 20 Eliot Sq [JFK St]
617-868-5777 • $
Tasty, cheap Greek food.
- **Sandrine's** • 8 Holyoke St [Massachusetts Ave]
617-497-5300 • $$$
Have a flammekueche; hard to say, easy to eat.
- **Sweet Cupcakes** • 0 Brattle St [Palmer St]
617-547-2253 • $
Give in to your Sweet tooth.
- **Takemura Japanese Restaurant** •
18 Eliot St [Brattle St]
617-492-6700 • $$
Creative sushi on a budget.
- **Tasty Burger** • 40 JFK St [Mt Auburn St]
617-425-4444 • $
Reads more like a fast food joint than the
Fenway outpost.
- **Tory Row** • 3 Brattle St [JFK St]
617-876-8769 • $$
Sister of Middlesex Lounge and Miracle of
Science. Same vibe.
- **Veggie Planet** • 47 Palmer St [Church St]
617-661-1513 • $$
At Club Passim. Mostly for pizzas, some vegan.
- **Wagamama** • 57 JFK St [Holyoke Pl]
617-499-0930 • $$
London noodle pros retrace journey of
Plymouth forebears.
- **Zinneken's** •
1154 Massachusetts Ave [Arrow St]
617-876-0836 • $
Belgian waffle emporium. 'Nuff said.

🛍 Shopping

- **Abodeon** •
1731 Massachusetts Ave [Prentiss St]
617-497-0137
Retro housewares.
- **American Apparel** • 47 Brattle St [Church S
617-661-2770
Basic threads for hipsters.
- **Anthropologie** • 48 Brattle St [Story St]
617-354-3031
For the wealthy hipster.
- **Berk's Shoes** • 50 JFK St [Winthrop St]
617-492-9511
Arm yourself with the right kicks for the
neighborhood.
- **Black Ink** • 5 Brattle St [Brattle Sq]
866-497-1221
A blend of quirky and handy gifts.
- **Bob Slate Stationer** • 30 Brattle St [Eliot St]
617-547-1230
Fancy paper and some art supplies.
- **Brattle Square Florist** • 31 Brattle St [Eliot S
617-876-9839
Delphinium paradise.
- **Cardullo's Gourmet Shoppe** •
6 Brattle St [Brattle Sq]
617-491-8888
Craving Swedish ginger cookies? Internation
gourmet goodies.
- **City Sports** • 44 Brattle St [Story St]
617-492-6000
Moved from Dunster Street.
- **Eastern Mountain Sports** •
1 Brattle Sq [Massachusetts Ave]
617-864-2061
Gear for the New England outdoor enthusias
- **Eye Q Optical** • 12 Eliot St [Bennett St]
617-354-3303
Designer eyeglasses.
- **The Games People Play** •
1100 Massachusetts Ave [Remington St]
617-492-0711
Games, puzzles, and other items humans are
wont to play.

Map 20

...can spend a solid afternoon shopping around Harvard Square. **...bury Comics**, **Black Ink**, and **Leavitt & Peirce** are great for gift ...ping (for yourself or anyone else). The **Urban Outfitters** bargain ...ment has savings that will melt your face off. Recharge at **Tealuxe**, and ...through a book at the **Co-op** or **Harvard Bookstore**.

Harvard Book Store •
256 Massachusetts Ave [Plympton St]
617-661-1515
An independent bookstore selling new, used,
and remainders.

Harvard Co-op •
400 Massachusetts Ave [Dunster St]
617-499-2000
Good for books, maps, and school stuff.

Hidden Sweets • 25 Brattle St [Church St]
617-497-2600
Bulk candy and other crap.

In Your Ear • 72 Mt Auburn St [Holyoke Pl]
617-491-5035
Good selection of independent, experimental
music.

J.P. Licks •
1312 Massachusetts Ave [Holyoke St]
617-492-1001
Bostonian ice cream institution. Try the Peanut
Butter Sauce.

L.A. Burdick Homemade Chocolates •
52 Brattle St [Story St]
617-491-4340
Sublime confections and some killer hot
chocolate.

Leavitt & Peirce •
1316 Massachusetts Ave [Holyoke St]
617-547-0576
Best bookstore in Cambridge. Chess sets too.

Lizzy's Ice Cream • 29 Church St [Palmer St]
617-354-2911
Homemade.

Lush • 30 JFK St [Winthrop St]
617-497-5874
British cosmetics merchant.

Marathon Sports •
1654 Massachusetts Ave [Shepard St]
617-354-4161
Run! Run! Run!

Mint Julep • 6 Church St [Palmer St]
617-576-6468
Boutique for the ladies or for the men looking
for a gift for the ladies.

Newbury Comics • 36 JFK St [Mt Auburn St]
617-491-0337
A zoo on weekends.

• **Nomad** • 1741 Massachusetts Ave [Prentiss St]
617-497-6677
An eclectic mix with a Mexican bent.

• **Oona's** • 1210 Massachusetts Ave [Bow St]
617-491-2654
Nifty little vintage shop.

• **Out of Town News** •
Harvard Sq [John F Kennedy St]
617-354-1441
The sensible Harvard Square rendezvous spot.

• **Planet Records** •
144 Mt Auburn St [Brewer St]
617-492-0693
CDs, some vinyl. Grab a $1 "mystery bag."

• **Raspberry Beret** •
1704 Massachusetts Ave [Martin St]
617-354-3700
Vintage and consignment threads and jewelry.

• **Staples** • 57 JFK St [Winthrop St]
617-491-1166
Printer ink and other more reasonably priced
supplies.

• **Stereo Jack's Records** •
1686 Massachusetts Ave [Sacramento St]
617-497-9447
Specializing in jazz, blues, and the like.

• **Sweet Cupcakes** • 0 Brattle St [Palmer St]
617-547-2253
Give in to your Sweet tooth.

• **The Tannery** • 39 Brattle St [Brattle Sq]
617-491-1811
Known for huge selection. Hit-or-miss service.

• **Tealuxe** • 0 Brattle St [Hague St]
617-441-0077
Good spot to hide from Harvard Square
crowds.

• **Tess and Carlos** • 20 Brattle St [Church St]
617-864-8377
Well-chosen selection of pricey designer
clothing and accessories.

• **Urban Outfitters** • 11 JFK St [Brattle Sq]
617-864-0070
Funky clothes and apartment stuff. Great
bargain basement.

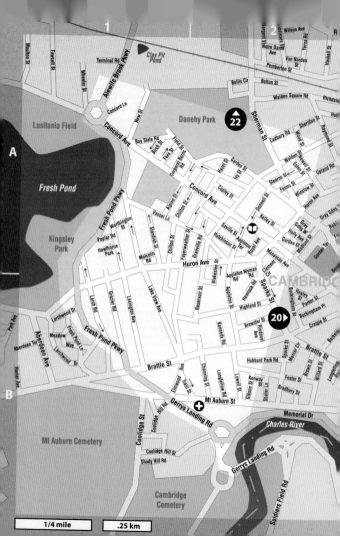

...ked behind bustling Harvard Square, this hushed suburban community ...nice for a pleasant, house-viewing stroll, but little else. Beautiful **Mt. ...burn Cemetery** is certainly a neighborhood highlight. Stop by and pay ...r respects to such long-ago dignitaries as Winslow Homer and Henry ...bot Lodge.

Restaurants

...rmando's • 163 Huron Ave [Concord Ave]
...17-354-8275 • $
...heap and delicious pizza.
...ull Moon • 344 Huron Ave [Chilton St]
...17-354-6699 • $$
...or a night out with the children.
...enki Ya •
...31 Alewife Brook Pkwy [Concord Ave]
...17-661-8200 • $$
...mpressive, organic strip-mall sushi.
...i-Rise Bread Company •
...08 Concord Ave [Huron Ave]
...17-876-8766 • $
...very neighborhood should have a place this
...ood.
...a Magoo's Pizza & Sub Shop •
... Concord Ln [Alewife Brook Pkwy]
...17-354-9139 • $
...he chicken finger sub is a local favorite.
...rattoria Pulcinella •
...47 Huron Ave [Concord Ave]
...17-491-6336 • $$$$
...or those not going to the North End.

Shopping

• **Circle Furniture** •
199 Alewife Brook Pkwy [Concord Ave]
617-876-3988
Tons of cool, unique home furnishings.
• **Formaggio Kitchen** •
244 Huron Ave [Appleton St]
617-354-4750
Cheese and other gourmet imports.
• **Henry Bear's Park** •
Porter Square Shopping Center
[Massachusetts Ave]
617-547-8424
Chi-chi toy store.

Map 22 • North Cambridge / West Somerville

PAG 16
Tufts Uni

SOMER

1

2

Professors Row
Conwell Ave
Raymond Ave
Sawyer Ave
Whitfield Rd
Teele Ave
Talbot

Broadway
Hamilton Rd
Curtis St
Powderhouse Blvd

Ware St

Watson St
Barton St
Bellevue Ave
Russell St
Fairmount Ave

Waterhouse St
Victoria St
Hooker St
Garrison St
Farragut Ave
Endicott Ave

Woodson St
Weston Ave
Dickson St
Clarendon Ave

Ossipee Rd
Westminster
Lovell
Electric Ave
Whitman St
Mason St

Broadway

Massachusetts Ave
Alewife Brook Pkwy

2A

Newbury St
Moore St
Clarence St
Mead St
Elmwood St
Gorham St

Holland St
Paulina St
Columbian St
Simpson Ave

Willa

Eberle Rd
Melrose St
Thorndike St
Fairmont St
Magnolia St

Cleveland St
Marathon St
Waldo Rd
Windsor St
Amsden St
Lee St
Teel St
Henderson Rd
Cottage Ave

Murray Hill Rd
Foch St
Irving St
Matignon Rd
Churchill Ave
Gold Star Rd
Camp St
Seven
Pines Ave

Clarendon
St
Jay St
Park Ave

Chandler St
Orchard St
College Ave

A

Boulevard Rd

3

Harrison Ave
Madison Ave
Brookford
Magoun St

Washburn Ave

Elmwood
Howard St
Thorndike St
Buena Vista
Kingston St
Winter St

Highland A
College Ave
More

Whittemore St
Kimball St
Seagrave Rd

Clay Pit
Pond
Alewife

Harvey St
Hamilton
Belmont St
Alberta St
Ter
Shea St
Lowden Ave
Woodbridge
Cambridge St

Davis
Somerville
Theatre

Highland A

Russell Field

Dudley St
Reed St
Norris St
Madham St
Dover St

Elm St

Jerry's
Pond
Rindge Ave

Jackson St
Clay St
Montgomery St
Cedar St
Rice St

Orchard St
Day St
Chester St
Milton St

Bowers
Cutter Ave
Tannery

CAMBRIDGE

Fitchburg Line

Catholic
Cemetery
Sherman St

Hollis St
Sargent St
Wilson Ave
Notre Dame
Ave
Haskell St

Middlesex St
Fairfield St
Pemberton St

Russell St
Hadley St
Blake St

Clay Pit
Pond

Bellis Cir.
Bolton St

21

Walden Mews
Walden Square Rd
Cameron Mead St
Bolton St
Richdale Ave
Creighton St
Regent St

Herbert St

Concord Ln
Tank Ct.
Hubbard Ave
Mt Pleasant
Cambridge Ter

B

Bay State Rd
Danehy Park
Cadbury Rd
Sheridan
Lincoln
Way
Wood St
Whittier St

Walden St

Upland

Mt Ve

Arlington

20

Concord Ave
Copley St
Stearns St
Ferno St
Winslow St
Huron Ave
Raymond Ave
Hillside Ave
Gray Gdns E

1/4 mile   .25 km

Once upon a time, this neighborhood was dominated by slaughterhouses and a slightly less refined clientele. Today it's a bit different, blending NPR culture with town-center appeal. (Peter Sagal used to hang out here!) Artisan vittles, farmers markets, hip taverns, and young families abound—quite an advance over the slaughterhouses.

Landmarks

- **Somerville Theatre** •
  55 Davis Sq [Highland Ave]
  617-625-5700
  Movies, concerts, and more.

Nightlife

- **The Burren** • 247 Elm St [Chester St]
  617-776-6896
  Well-known Irish; live music.
- **Five Horses Tavern** •
  400 Highland Ave [Grove St]
  617-764-1655
  All hail the Beer Star!
- **Foundry on Elm** • 255 Elm St [Chester St]
  617-628-9999
  Decent draft list, excellent cocktails.
- **Johnny D's Uptown** •
  17 Holland St [Winter St]
  617-776-2004
  Music nightly, wide variety.
- **The Painted Burro** • 219 Elm St [Summer St]
  617-776-0005
  Flights of tequila, trips to the floor.
- **PJ Ryan's** • 239 Holland St [Broadway]
  617-625-8200
  Brick and beer bar.
- **Redbones** • 55 Chester St [Herbert St]
  617-628-2200
  Don't dig on swine? Then come spin the beer wheel.
- **Saloon** • 255 Elm St [Chester St]
  617-628-4444
  Brown liquors and local brews a la speakeasy.
- **Sligo Pub** • 237 Elm St [Bowers Ave]
  617-623-9561
  A landmark of sorts.
- **Somerville Theatre** •
  55 Davis Sq [Highland Ave]
  617-625-5700
  Occasional live music.

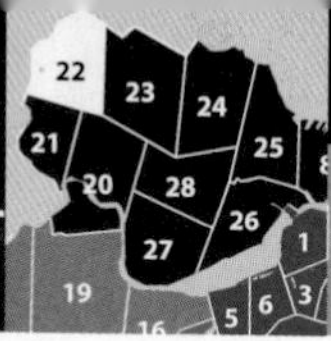

Map 22

North Cambridge / West Somervil

🍴 Restaurants

- **Amsterdam Falafel Shop** •
  248 Elm St [Chester St]
  617-764-3334 • $
  Pros: mouthwatering pita and huge toppings bar. Con: sparse seating.
- **Anna's Taqueria** • 236 Elm St [Chester St]
  617-666-3900 • $
  Fastest burritos in town.
- **Blue Shirt Cafe** • 424 Highland Ave [Elm St]
  617-629-7641 • $
  Feel the force of vitamin B12.
- **Café Barada** •
  2269 Massachusetts Ave [Dover St]
  617-354-2112 • $
  Relaxed Middle Eastern.
- **Dave's Fresh Pasta** • 81 Holland St [Irving St]
  617-623-0867 • $
  Homemade pasta and sauces.
- **Diesel Café** • 257 Elm St [Chester St]
  617-629-8717 • $
  Coffee and sandwich shop with an attitude.
- **Diva Indian Bistro** • 246 Elm St [Chester St]
  617-629-4963 • $$
  Flashy and tasty, but pricey.
- **The Elephant Walk** •
  2067 Massachusetts Ave [Walden St]
  617-492-6900 • $$$
  French-Cambodian local legend.
- **Five Horses Tavern** •
  400 Highland Ave [Grove St]
  617-764-1655 • $$
  Coat your stomach before the booze kicks in.
- **Foundry on Elm** • 255 Elm St [Chester St]
  617-628-9999 • $$
  Popular (read: crowded) brasserie-tavern hybrid.
- **Golden Light** • 24 College Ave [Winter St]
  617-666-9822 • $$
  Late night, dynamite spring rolls.
- **Greek Corner** •
  2366 Massachusetts Ave [Dudley St]
  617-661-5655 • $$
  Small corner, huge portions.

- **House of Tibet** • 235 Holland St [Broadway]
  617-629-7567 • $$
  Delicious. But where's the yak butter?
- **Istanbul'lu** • 237 Holland St [Broadway]
  617-440-7387 • $$
  Delightful Turkish.
- **iYo Cafe** • 234 Elm St [Grove St]
  617-764-5295 • $
  Make your own froyo…or waffle.
- **Jasper White's Summer Shack** •
  149 Alewife Brook Pkwy [Rindge Ave]
  617-520-9500 • $$$
  Seafood. More a hangar than a shack.
- **Jose's** • 131 Sherman St [Bellis Cir]
  617-354-0335 • $$
  It's all about the margaritas.
- **Joshua Tree** • 256 Elm St [Chester St]
  617-623-9910 • $$
  Achtung, baby.
- **L'Impasto** •
  2263 Massachusetts Ave [Dover St]
  617-491-1901 • $$
  Quite possibly the best Italian in Cambridge
- **Martsa on Elm** • 233 Elm St [Grove St]
  617-666-0660 • $$
  Your meal is best accompanied by a Tibetan tea.
- **Orleans** • 65 Holland St [Buena Vista Rd]
  617-591-2100 • $$$
  People-watching, food. Don't look so expectant.
- **Out of the Blue** • 215 Elm St [Grove St]
  617-776-5020 • $$
  Good value for seafood, Italian. Colorful roo
- **The Painted Burro** • 219 Elm St [Summer St]
  617-776-0005 • $$
  Hip, high-end hacienda.
- **Posto** • 187 Elm St [Windom St]
  617-625-0600 • $$
  Rustic, wood-fired pizza and the like.
- **Qingdao Garden** •
  2382 Massachusetts Ave [Alberta Ter]
  617-492-7540 • $
  Casual, delicious. Sells dumplings-to-go in bulk.

Map 22

's 'hood, there's no shortage of variety with food and entertainment. **Redbones** elivers with colossal 'cue and beer. **Dave's Fresh Pasta** keeps slingin' awesome nies and perfecto pasta. Newer editions like **Five Horses**, **Saloon**, and **True o** have found their niche as welcome neighborhood scenes. **Sacco's Bowl** n has joined forces with Flatbread Company to create fantastic 'za, cocktails, andlepin bowling—don't even think about skipping out.

edbones • 55 Chester St [Herbert St]
17-628-2200 • $$
on't dig on swine? Then come spin the beer
wheel.

enee's Cafe • 198 Holland St [Claremon St]
17-623-2727 • $
o-cash, early-closing pancake heaven. Try the
pecials.

udy's Café • 248 Holland St [Newbury St]
17-623-9201 • $$
erving up generous Tex-Mex portions with a
oco selection of tequila.

abur • 212 Holland St [Moore St]
17-776-7890 • $$$
ood from Greece, North Africa, and the
alkans in a casbah-like atmosphere.

nappy Sushi • 420 Highland Ave [Elm St]
17-625-0400 • $$
ummy brown rice sushi.

rue Bistro • 1153 Broadway [Holland St]
17-627-9000 • $$
egan date spot.

Shopping

uffalo Exchange • 238 Elm St [Grove St]
17-629-5383
rendy recycled duds.

aning Shoppe • 99 Albion St [Lowell St]
17-776-0100
and-crafted chairs, vintage pieces, and other
ome furnishings.

apone Foods •
285 Massachusetts Ave [Meacham Rd]
17-629-2296
asta, sauces, and other specialties from The
oot.

hina Fair Inc. •
100 Massachusetts Ave [Walden St]
17-864-3050
nexpensive kitchen gear and housewares.

• **Dave's Fresh Pasta** • 81 Holland St [Irving St]
617-623-0867
Homemade pasta, sammies, produce, beer, &
wine: heaven in Davis.

• **Davis Squared** •
409 Highland Ave [College Ave]
617-666-6700
Somerville-centric gift shop. Not that there's
anything wrong with that.

• **Found** • 255 Elm St [Chester St]
617-764-3131
Secondhand store for upscale clothes.

• **Magpie** • 416 Highland Ave [Grove St]
617-623-3330
Featuring over 350 indie crafters and artists.

• **McKinnon's Meat Market** •
239 Elm St [Grove St]
617-666-0888
Smart choice before a barbecue.

• **Modern Homebrew Emporium** •
2304 Massachusetts Ave [Rice St]
617-498-0400
Everything for your home-brewing needs.

• **Nellie's Wildflowers** •
72 Holland St [Buena Vista Rd]
617-625-9453
Ask for assistance from Joyce, the friendly
owner.

• **Pemberton Farms** •
2225 Massachusetts Ave [Rindge Ave]
617-491-2244
Local and organic groceries, sammies, and
plants.

• **Staples** •
186 Alewife Brook Pkwy [Terminal Rd]
617-547-3948
Printer ink and other more reasonably priced
supplies.

• **Sunshine Lucy's** •
93 Holland St [Simpson Ave]
617-776-2011
Awesome vintage pieces.

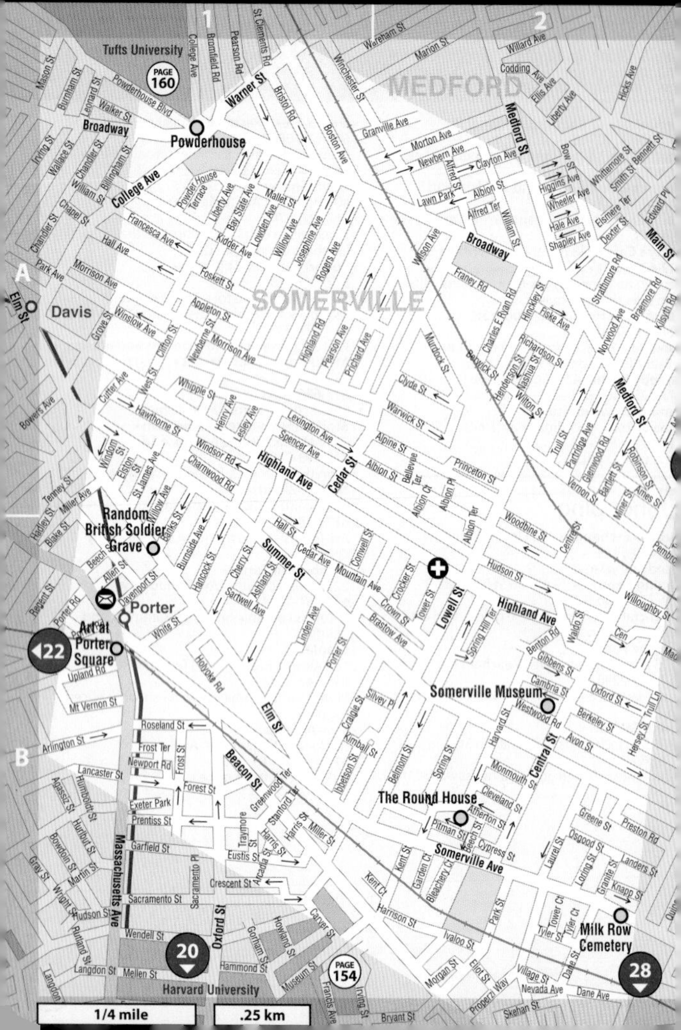

Map 23 • **Central Somerville / Porter Square**

Tufts University

PAGE 160

Broadway

Powderhouse

College Ave

MEDFORD

SOMERVILLE

Davis

Elm St

Random British Soldier Grave

Porter

Art at Porter Square

22

Somerville Museum

The Round House

Somerville Ave

Milk Row Cemetery

20

PAGE 154

Harvard University

28

Massachusetts Ave

Broadway

Highland Ave

Summer St

Cedar St

Lowell St

Central St

Medford St

Beacon St

1/4 mile   .25 km

rter Square feels less polished than Harvard and Davis, and living space
re and in neighboring Somerville is slightly more affordable. Shops and
staurants are concentrated on Mass Ave, and a mix of young people,
milies, and townies populates the residential neighborhoods.

Landmarks

Art at Porter Square •
Massachusetts Ave & Somerville Ave
The T's best public art display.

Milk Row Cemetery •
-39 Somerville Ave [School St]
Historic 1804 boneyard. Next to a
supermarket.

Powder House • Broadway & College Ave
Revolutionary War-era gunpowder store, park
centerpiece.

The Round House • 36 Atherton St [Beech St]
Around since 1856. Not open to the public.

Somerville Museum •
 Westwood Rd [Central St]
17-666-9810
Great exhibits of Somerville history.

Nightlife

• **Christopher's** •
1920 Massachusetts Ave [Porter Rd]
617-876-9180
Large selection of drafts, friendly staff, warm
food.

• **Newtowne Grille** •
1945 Massachusetts Ave [Davenport St]
617-661-0706
Divey, but lively.

• **Olde Magoun's Saloon** •
518 Medford St [Lowell St]
617-776-2600
Nicer than it looks. Neighborhood favorite
with good beer and Sox games.

• **On the Hill Tavern** •
499 Broadway [Medford St]
617-629-5302
DJs Thursday through Saturdays.

• **Samba Bar & Grill** •
608 Somerville Ave [Kent St]
617-718-9177
Brazilian vibe.

• **Toad** • 1912 Massachusetts Ave [Porter Rd]
617-497-4950
Cramped but fun. Live music nightly.

Map 23 · Central Somerville / Porter Squar

🍴Restaurants

- **Anna's Taqueria** ·
822 Somerville Ave [Acadia Park]
617-661-8500 · $
Fastest burritos in town.
- **Ball Square Cafe** ·
708 Broadway St [Willow Ave]
617-623-2233 · $
Belgian waffles loaded with whipped cream.
Drool.
- **Blue Fin** ·
1815 Massachusetts Ave [Roseland St]
617-497-8022 · $$
Not the best sushi, but close to the cheapest.
- **Café Mami** ·
1815 Massachusetts Ave [Roseland St]
617-547-9130 · $
It's amazing what they can do with a little
ground beef and an egg.
- **Café Rustica** · 356 Beacon St [Roseland St]
617-491-8300 · $
Friendly neighborhood café.
- **Christopher's** ·
1920 Massachusetts Ave [Porter Rd]
617-876-9180 · $$
Good for relaxing on a wet day.
- **Eat at Jumbo's** · 688 Broadway [Boston Ave]
617-666-5862 · $
Pizza, burgers, and above par vegan vittles.
- **Highland Kitchen** ·
150 Highland Ave [Central St]
617-625-1131 · $$
Lovely liquids and solids.
- **Kelly's Diner** · 674 Broadway [Boston Ave]
617-623-8102 · $
Old-school greasy spoon known for its "Kiss
My Grits!" service.
- **Lyndell's Bakery** · 720 Broadway [Willow Ave]
617-625-1793 · $
Old-fashioned bakery.

- **Passage to India** ·
1900 Massachusetts Ave [Porter Rd]
617-497-6113 · $$
Good Indian, served late. Try the curries.
- **Pescatore** · 158 Boston Ave [Broadway]
617-623-0003 · $$
Secret spot for amazing Italian seafood.
- **Petsi Pies** · 285 Beacon St [Sacramento St]
617-661-7437 · $
Name a dinner or dessert pie…any pie…and
they probably make it.
- **R.F. O'Sullivan & Son** ·
282 Beacon St [Sacramento St]
617-492-7773 · $
Quite possibly the best burgers in Boston.
- **Sound Bites** · 704 Broadway [Willow Ave]
617-623-8338 · $
For filling breakfasts.
- **Stone Hearth Pizza Co.** ·
1782 Massachusetts Ave [Stone Ct]
617-492-1111 · $$
Pizza chain using organic, sustainable
ingredients.
- **Sugar & Spice** ·
1933 Massachusetts Ave [Davenport St]
617-868-4200 · $$$
Thai food when you're not in the mood for th
Japanese.
- **Tavern in the Square** ·
1815 Massachusetts Ave [Mt Vernon St]
617-354-7766 · $$
TVs blaring sports as far as the eye can see.
- **Tu Y Yo** · 858 Broadway [Walker St]
617-623-5411 · $$
Authentic Mexican—no burritos here.
- **Wang's Fast Food** ·
509 Broadway [Hinckley St]
617-623-2982 · $
Best Mandarin hole-in-the-wall on this side
the river. Try the dumplings.
- **Yume Wo Katare** ·
1923 Massachusetts Ave [Davenport St]
617-714-4008 · $$
All the rage ramen joint. Be prepared to star
in line.

a less concentrated bar and restaurant scene than Davis or Harvard, Porter
gets overlooked—but that just means fewer crowds for those in the know.
k out **Highland Kitchen** for wicked cocktails and tip-top pub grub, or head
ad where there's live music every night. Get baked at some of the best
ries in the Boston area: **Petsi Pies**, **When Pigs Fly**, or **Lyndell's Bakery**.

◯Shopping

ig Fish, Little Fish • 55 Elm St [Cedar St]
17-666-2444
et store with more than just fish.

afe Japonaise •
315 Massachusetts Ave [Roseland St]
17-547-5531
Mmm…curry donut.

ambridge Clogs •
798 Massachusetts Ave [Stone Ct]
17-497-1516
reat for sock enthusiasts, too.

ity Sports •
315 Massachusetts Ave [Roseland St]
17-661-1666
overs all the basics in apparel and
quipment.

oie de Vivre •
792 Massachusetts Ave [Arlington St]
17-864-8188
illy gifts, nostalgic toys, good stocking
tuffers.

Lyndell's Bakery • 720 Broadway [Willow Ave]
617-625-1793
Tasty pastries.

Paper Source •
1810 Massachusetts Ave [Arlington St]
617-497-1077
DIY paper crafts and quirky gifts.

Porter Square Books •
25 White St [Somerville Ave]
617-491-2220
Fiercely independent!

WardMaps •
1735 Massachusetts Ave [Prentiss St]
617-497-0737
Antique maps and other local images for sale.
Worth visiting.

When Pigs Fly •
378 Highland Ave [Cutter Ave]
617-776-0021
All-natural sourdough breads.

Yesterday Service, Inc. •
191 Highland Ave [Benton Rd]
617-547-8263
Sells instruments and hard-to-find sheet
music.

re you'll find remnants of Somerville's working-class neighborhoods, **City** ll, the charming Italian Renaissance Revival central library donated by drew Carnegie, and **Prospect Hill**, where America's first flag was raised in 76. Still, lively and diverse Union Square continues to grow into an tension of Davis Square, with farm-to-table restaurants, hip boutiques, and tdoor film series.

Landmarks

- **Prospect Hill Monument** •
  Munroe St b/w Prospect Hill Ave & Walnut St
  xcellent view of Boston from Somerville.
- **Somerville City Hall** •
  93 Highland Ave [School St]
  17-625-6600
  A classic New England municipal building.

Nightlife

- **Backbar** • 9 Sandborn Ct [Union Sq]
  17-718-0249
  Jnique, locally sourced beers and old-timey
  cocktails.
- **The Independent** • 75 Union Sq [Stone Ave]
  517-440-6022
  rish pub on one side, upscale bar on the
  other.
- **P.A.'s Lounge** •
  345 Somerville Ave [Hawkins St]
  517-776-1557
  Cool spot for live, modern rock.
- **Sally O'Brien's** •
  335 Somerville Ave [Hawkins St]
  517-666-3589
  Local bands, local sports, decent pub food.

Restaurants

- **Cantina La Mexicana** •
  247 Washington St [Bonner Ave]
  517-776-5232 • $
  The real deal. Terrific flautas.
- **Casa B** • 253 Washington St [Bonner Ave]
  517-764-2180 • $$$
  Tasty tapas in a button-cute setting.
- **Ebi Sushi** • 290 Somerville Ave [Union Sq]
  517-764-5556 • $$
  Decent sushi finally comes to Union.
- **Fasika Ethiopian Restaurant** •
  145 Broadway [Rush St]
  617-628-9300 • $$
  Best Ethiopian in town in the oddest setting.
- **J & J Restaurant & Takeout** •
  157 Washington St [McGrath Hwy]
  617-625-3978 • $
  Cheap, generously-portioned Portuguese with
  attached grocery store!

- **Journeyman** • 9 Sandborn Ct [Union Sq]
  617-718-2333 • $$$$
  Farm-to-table fine dining in an unpretentious
  setting.
- **Leone's** • 292 Broadway [Marshall St]
  617-776-2511 • $
  Meatball subs that are To-Die-For.
- **Machu Picchu** • 25 Union Sq [Webster Ave]
  617-623-7972 • $
  Peruvian. Definitely worth trying.
- **Neighborhood Restaurant & Bakery** •
  25 Bow St [Walnut St]
  617-623-9710 • $
  Big, good breakfasts + patio = summer
  morning bliss.
- **Sweet Ginger** • 22 Bow St [Walnut St]
  617-625-5015 • $$
  Typical, tasty Thai.

Shopping

- **Bombay Market** •
  359 Somerville Ave [Kilby St]
  617-623-6614
  Good Indian grocery, Bollywood movies.
- **Bostonian Florist** •
  92 Highland Ave [School St]
  617-629-9300
  Florist.
- **Christmas Tree Shops** •
  177 Middlesex Ave [Cummings St]
  617-623-3428
  Everything including the kitchen sink.
- **Mudflat Studio** •
  81 Broadway [Wisconsin Ave]
  617-628-0589
  Pottery classes and studios.
- **Reliable Market** • 45 Union Sq [Warren Ave]
  617-623-9620
  Overflowing East Asian grocer.
- **Ricky's Flower Market** •
  238 Washington St [Union Sq]
  617-628-7569
  Great outdoor market. Mind the traffic,
  though.
- **Somerville Grooves** •
  26 Union Sq [Somerville Ave]
  617-666-1749
  Post-punk vinyl, t-shirts, books, and the like.

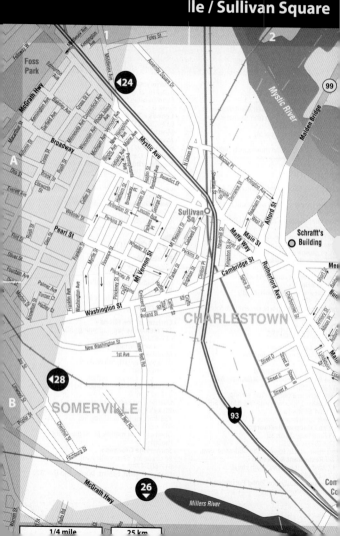

ple go to Sullivan Square for the Orange Line or if they have a package JPS. The historic **Schrafft's Building**, formerly the country's largest dy factory, looms over this throughway of a neighborhood from nbridge/Somerville to Charlestown, Everett, and Malden.

Landmarks

chrafft's Building •
29 Main St [Mishawum St]
nce the country's largest candy factory.

Nightlife

vern at the End of the World •
08 Cambridge St [Parker St]
7-241-4999
ot as far as it sounds, but worth the trip.

Restaurants

- **Beijing Taste** • 99 Cambridge St [Brighton St]
  617-241-5077 • $
  For emergencies only.
- **Mount Vernon** • 14 Broadway [Mt Pleasant St]
  617-666-3830 • $$
  Sleepy spot with occasional lobster specials.
- **Vinny's** • 76 Broadway [Hathorn St]
  617-628-1921 • $$$
  Quality home-style Italian tucked behind a
  deli.

Shopping

- **Home Depot** • 75 Mystic Ave [N Union St]
  617-623-0001
  Got wood?
- **Vinny's** • 76 Broadway [Hathorn St]
  617-628-1921
  Damn good Italian cold-cuts.

Map 20 • **East Cambridge / Kendall Square / MIT**

Map 26

ce dominated by countless factories producing candy and candles, East
mbridge is now dominated by MIT and countless labs and tech companies. The
tory buildings still stand, but have been repurposed as post-industrial offices,
dos, and trendy bars and restaurants. There are some newer, sleeker
hitectural specimens 'round these parts, the most striking example being the
ta Center.

Landmarks

Harvard Bridge •
Massachusetts Ave [Memorial Dr]
64 smoots and an ear, the Harvard Bridge
eads to MIT.
Kendall / MIT T Station • Main St [Broadway]
very T-Stop should have musical instruments
y MIT students.
MIT Stata Center • 32 Vassar St [Main St]
rank Gehry's curvy and colorful MIT building.

Nightlife

• **Cambridge Brewing Company** •
1 Kendall Sq [Hampshire St]
617-494-1994
Decent microbrews. Some outdoor seating.
• **Champions Sports Bar** •
2 Cambridge Ctr [3rd St]
617-252-4444
Ultra-modern setting, hotel bar clientele.
• **Flat Top Johnny's** •
1 Kendall Sq [Hampshire St]
617-494-9565
Cambridge's best large pool hall.
• **Meadhall** • 4 Cambridge Ctr [Ames St]
617-714-4372
Mead, of course, but over 100 draft beers, too.
• **West Bridge** • 1 Kendall Sq [Binney St]
617-945-0221
Vino collapso.

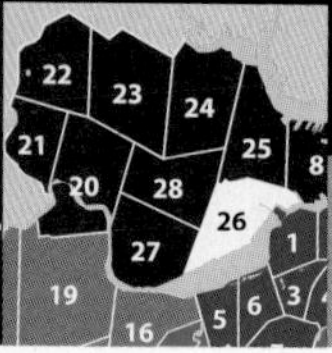

Map 26

East Cambridge / Kendall Square / MI

🍴 Restaurants

- **Abigail's** • 291 3rd St [Binney St]
  617-945-9086 • $$
  Satisfactory New American with lots of libations.
- **Aceituna Cafe** •
  605 W Kendall St [Athenaeum St]
  617-252-0707 • $$
  Mediterranean for lunch at the Genzyme building.
- **Bambara** • 25 Land Blvd [Cambridgeside Pl]
  617-868-4444 • $$$$
  Hit-or-miss at Hotel Marlowe.
- **Belly Wine Bar** • 1 Kendall Sq [Hampshire St]
  617-494-0968 • $$
  Charcuterie, wine pairings and…family-style fried chicken dinners?
- **Black Sheep** • 350 Main St [Dock St]
  617-577-1300 • $$
  In the Kendall Hotel. Go for breakfast.
- **The Blue Room** • 1 Kendall Sq [Hampshire St]
  617-494-9034 • $$$
  Terrific food, popular. Somehow elegant and casual.
- **Catalyst** • 300 Technology Sq [Albany St]
  617-576-3000 • $$$
  Mostly New England fare, with a farm-to-table twist.
- **Courthouse Seafood** •
  498 Cambridge St [6th St]
  617-491-1213 • $$
  One step removed from bobbing for fish.

- **Desfina** • 202 3rd St [Charles St]
  617-868-9098 • $$
  Old-school Greek for new school geeks.
- **Firebrand Saints** • 1 Broadway [3rd St]
  617-401-3399 • $$
  Pay attention to the artsy television wall.
- **Fuji at Kendall** • 300 3rd St [Binney St]
  617-252-0088 • $$
  Runs the Japanese gamut, with delicious smoothies to boot.
- **Helmand Restaurant** • 143 1st St [Bent St]
  617-492-4646 • $$$
  Delightful, authentic. Family ties with Afghanistan's president.
- **Legal Sea Foods** •
  5 Cambridge Center [Dock St]
  617-864-3400 • $$$
  Another Legal Seafoods for your fishy pleasure.
- **Momogoose** • 70 Carleton St [Ames St]
  617-807-0706 • $
  Food truck serving pho and ramen for cheap money.
- **Second Street Café** • 89 2nd St [Spring St]
  617-661-1311 • $$
  Plenty of fresh, inexpensive choices.
- **West Bridge** • 1 Kendall Sq [Binney St]
  617-945-0221 • $$$
  Modern industrial French-fusion fare.

a few years ago, this neck of the woods was Deadsville after 5 p.m.
y it's home to a growing contingent of taverns, lounges, and eateries,
g it a new life after the whistle blows. Grab some grub at **Fuji**, libations
ambridge Brewing Company or **Meadhall**, and a flick at **Kendall
re Cinema**.

Shopping

pple Store •
00 Cambridgeside Pl [Land Blvd]
17-528-7970
ac heaven in the Galleria.

est Buy • 100 Cambridgeside Pl [Land Blvd]
7-225-2420
wful, annoying electronics retailer.

ambridge Antique Market •
01 Monsignor O'Brien Hwy [Water St]
17-868-9655
ive floors to keep you busy.

avid's Famous Name Shoes •
5 First St [Spring St]
17-354-3730
ans mall shoe shop!

• **H&M** •
100 Cambridgeside Pl [Commercial Ave]
855-466-7467
Disposable chic from Swedish mega-
merchant.

• **Marshalls** • 22 McGrath Hwy [Gore St]
617-776-0674
Discount clothing and other stuff.

• **Mayflower Poultry Company** •
621 Cambridge St [8th St]
617-547-9191
Live poultry, fresh killed.

• **New Deal Fish Market** •
622 Cambridge St [Fulkerson St]
617-876-8227
Relief, reform, and recovery in fish form.

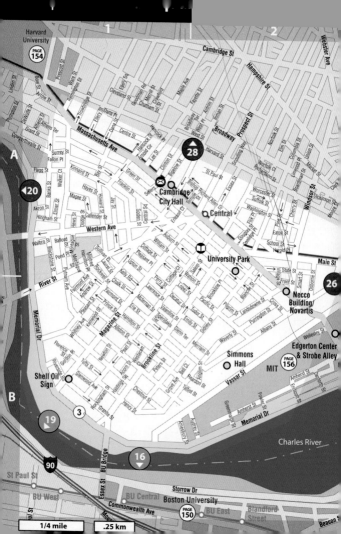

ral Square is a mix of MIT residences, biotech companies, and rock clubs—a
e where hipsters, scientists, and vagrants live in harmony. And somehow there
o surprisingly nice apartments in Cambridgeport. Sadly, the old Necco Candy
ory is now a research facility. However, the gorgeous **Cambridge City** Hall has
been converted to a biotech lab...yet. Satisfy your grocery needs (and tasty
nic food supplies) at **Harvest Co-op.**

Landmarks

ambridge City Hall •
5 Massachusetts Ave [Bigelow St]
7-349-4000
ecently got a needed facelift.

ormer Necco Building •
0 Massachusetts Ave [Landsdowne St]
t another candy company leaves
mbridge.

IT Edgerton Center •
Massachusetts Ave [Vassar St]
7-253-4629
h floor of Building 4 displays of slow-mo
structive photography and tech.

hell Oil Sign • 187 Magazine St [Granite St]
n't miss it. Logo designed by Raymond
ewy.

immons Hall • 229 Vassar St [Concord Ave]
7-253-5107
gressively modernist MIT dorm by Stephen
oll.

niversity Park •
assachusetts Ave & Sidney St
mplex of cool structural and landscape
chitecture.

🍸 Nightlife

- **Cantab Lounge •**
738 Massachusetts Ave [Pleasant St]
617-354-2685
Legendary quasi-dive. Little Joe Cook still
plays.
- **The Field •** 20 Prospect St [Massachusetts Ave]
617-354-7345
Dark and gritty Irish pub.
- **Garden at the Cellar •**
991 Massachusetts Ave [Dana St]
617-475-0045
Stuck between Central and Harvard? Here you
go.
- **The Middle East •**
472 Massachusetts Ave [Douglas St]
617-864-3278
Venerable venue that gets high-profile music
bookings.
- **Middlesex Lounge •**
315 Massachusetts Ave [State St]
617-868-6739
Rotating DJ line-up, fun modular seating.
- **Miracle of Science •**
321 Massachusetts Ave [State St]
617-868-2866
Energetic mainstay, always playing cool music.
- **The People's Republik •**
876 Massachusetts Ave [Lee St]
617-491-6969
Toast 'til 2:00.
- **Phoenix Landing •**
512 Massachusetts Ave [Brookline St]
617-576-6260
Irish pub with club music every night.
- **The Plough & Stars •**
912 Massachusetts Ave [Hancock St]
617-576-0032
Well-loved local. Frequent live music.
- **River Gods •** 125 River St [Kinnaird St]
617-576-1881
Hipster house. DJs spin frequently.
- **TT the Bear's Place •**
10 Brookline St [Green St]
617-492-2327
Live rock nightly. Showcases local bands.
- **The Western Front •**
343 Western Ave [Putnam Ave]
617-492-7772
Mostly reggae and world, occasional hip-hop.

Map 27

Central Square / Cambridgepo

Restaurants

- **Area Four** • 500 Technology Sq [Main St]
617-758-4444 • $$
Techster coffee in Cambridge's Area IV.
- **The Asgard** •
350 Massachusetts Ave [Blanche St]
617-577-9100 • $$
Enormous "Celtic" gastropub.
- **Asmara** • 739 Massachusetts Ave [Pleasant St]
617-864-7447 • $$
Once was the only Ethiopian restaurant in
Cambridge.
- **Baraka Café** • 80 Pearl St [William St]
617-868-3951 • $$
A tiny restaurant serving up some good
Moroccan cuisine.
- **Beantown Taqueria** •
245 Massachusetts Ave [Lansdowne St]
617-441-8689 • $
There's always room for late-night tacos.
- **Brookline Lunch** •
9 Brookline St [Massachusetts Ave]
617-354-2983 • $
Popular diner. For food, not service.
- **Central Kitchen** •
567 Massachusetts Ave [Pearl St]
617-491-5599 • $$$
Simple Mediterranean menu featuring
incredibly flavorful dishes with great wines to
match.
- **Coast Cafe** • 233 River St [Rockwell St]
617-354-7644 • $
Breadcumb-laden fried chicken, mac 'n cheese
'n collard greens.
- **Craigie on Main** •
853 Main St [Massachusetts Ave]
617-497-5511 • $$$$$
Expensive and slow but wonderful
French-American bistro on Main St.
- **Cuchi Cuchi** • 795 Main St [Cherry St]
617-864-2929 • $$$
You either love this place or hate it. Find out
for yourself!
- **Dolphin Seafood** •
1105 Massachusetts Ave [Remington St]
617-661-2937 • $$
Unpretentious fish house.
- **Falafel Palace** • 25 Central Sq [Pleasant St]
617-864-0827 • $
Located in what was once a White Castle.
- **Flour Bakery + Café** •
190 Massachusetts Ave [Albany St]
617-225-2525 • $
Beyond exceptional bakery. Also serves
dinners for take-away.
- **Four Burgers** •
704 Massachusetts Ave [Prospect St]
617-441-5444 • $
Truth in advertising. The menu? Four Burger
- **Green Street Grill** •
280 Green St [Magazine St]
617-876-1655 • $$$
New American, seasonal, local-based menu.
- **India Pavilion** • 17 Central Sq [Pleasant St]
617-547-7463 • $$
Reliable Indian that's been a part of Central
Square forever. A decent value.
- **Life Alive** • 765 Massachusetts Ave [Inman
617-354-5433 • $$
Colorful vegetarian cuisine served in a
cheerful locale.

y not being the prettiest girl at the ball, but Central sure knows how to have
eeing a rock show at **The Middle East** earns you instant cred. Sophisticated
ers frequent **Central Kitchen**, **Falafel Palace**, **Cantab**, and **Miracle of**
ce. The sweet-toothed love **Flour + Bakery**, but to forgo a scoop from
nini's is a downright sin.

lary Chung •
54 Massachusetts Ave [Douglas St]
17-864-1991 • $$
nis Central Square institution is still going
trong.

he Middle East •
72 Massachusetts Ave [Douglas St]
17-864-3278 • $$
heap and tasty food before going to see a
how.

liracle of Science •
21 Massachusetts Ave [State St]
17-868-2866 • $$
nergetic neighborhood mainstay. Great
urgers, quesadillas.

loksa • 450 Massachusetts Ave [Brookline St]
17-661-4900 • $$
sian tapas, some on a stick.

icante Mexican Grill •
35 Massachusetts Ave [Pleasant St]
17-576-6394 • $
ali-Mex. Pretty good salsas.

Rangzen Tibetan Restaurant •
4 Pearl St [Green St]
17-354-8881 • $$
or a feast fit for a monk try the Gyakor Tibetan
lot Pot.

ialts • 798 Main St [Windsor St]
617-876-8444 • $$$$
lew ownership, higher prices. Tasty.

helonious Monkfish •
24 Massachusetts Ave [Norfolk St]
617-441-2116 • $$
ushi and jazz, together at last!

Zoe's •
105 Massachusetts Ave [Remington St]
17-495-0055 • $
Retro-ish diner food, breakfast all day.

ZuZuBar •
474 Massachusetts Ave [Douglas St]
617-864-3278 • $$$
Funky, colorful. Make a meal of maza.

🛍 Shopping

• **Cheapo Records** •
538 Massachusetts Ave [Norfolk St]
617-354-4455
A treasure trove of older tunes.
• **Economy True Value Hardware** •
438 Massachusetts Ave [Main St]
617-500-1595
Hardware, household needs, cheap furniture.
Very popular.
• **Great Eastern Trading Company** •
49 River St [Auburn St]
617-354-5279
Like the Garment District's little sister on crack.
• **Hubba Hubba** •
534 Massachusetts Ave [Norfolk St]
617-492-9082
Focusing on the naughty bits.
• **Micro Center** • 730 Memorial Dr [Riverside Rd]
617-234-6400
Computer have-it-all. Avoid going on
Saturdays.
• **Pandemonium Books** •
4 Pleasant St [Massachusetts Ave]
617-547-3721
Books, Role-Playing Supplies, and tables for all
your D&D needs.
• **Shalimar India Food and Spices** •
571 Massachusetts Ave [Pearl St]
617-868-8311
Huge selection of spices.
• **Ten Thousand Villages** •
694 Massachusetts Ave [Western Ave]
617-876-2414
Free-trade, handmade crafts from around the
world.
• **Toscanini's** • 899 Main St [Columbia St]
617-491-5877
In our opinion, Boston's best ice cream.
• **University Stationery** •
311 Massachusetts Ave [State St]
617-547-6650
A friendly little shop near MIT.

Map 28 • Inman Square

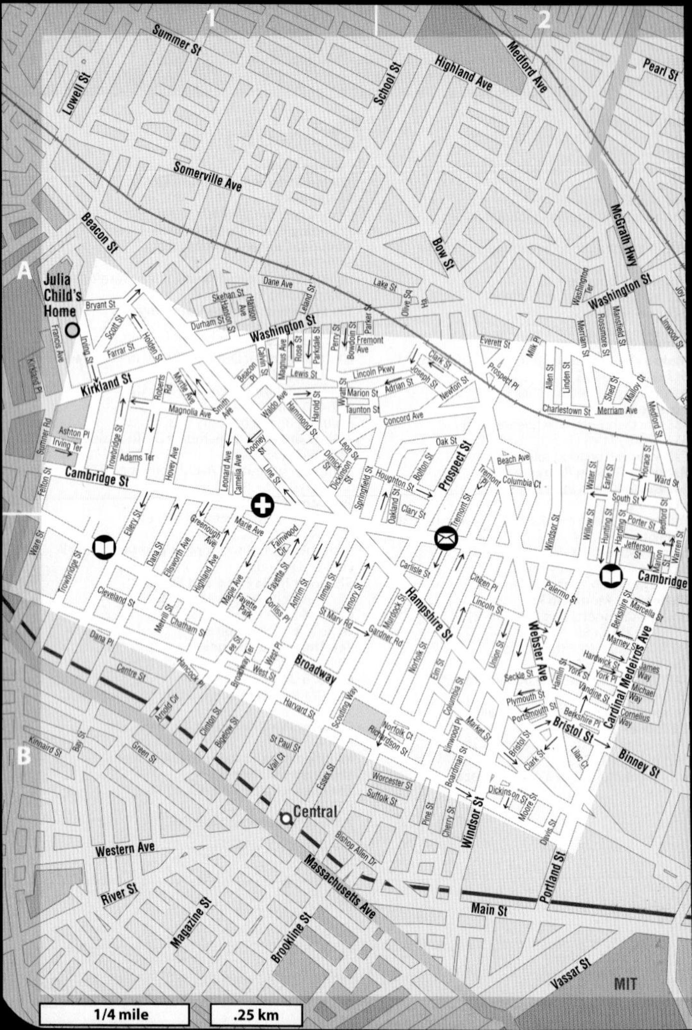

N
1
2
A
B
Summer St
Lowell St
School St
Highland Ave
Medford Ave
Pearl St
Somerville Ave
Beacon St
McGrath Hwy
Bow St
Julia Child's Home
Bryant St
Scott St
Farrar St
Holden St
Irving St
Francis Ave
Kirkland Pl
Kirkland St
Dane Ave
Lake St
Olive Sq
Skehan St
Hanson St
Hanson Ave
Leland St
Durham St
Washington St
Parker St
Fremont Ave
Washington Ter
Washington St
Joy St
Merriam St
Rossmore St
Mansfield St
Linwood St
Everett St
Milk Pl
Calvin St
Magnus Ave
Rose St
Parkdale St
Perry St
Bowdoin St
Beacon Pl
Lewis St
Lincoln Pkwy
Clark St
Joseph St
Prospect Pl
Allen St
Linden St
Shed St
Malloy Ct
Medford St
Roberts Rd
Myrtle Ave
Waldo Ave
Marion St
Adrian St
Newton St
Charlestown St
Merriam Ave
Magnolia Ave
Smith Ave
Hammond St
Harold St
Wyatt St
Taunton St
Concord Ave
Sumner Rd
Ashton Pl
Irving Ter
Trowbridge St
Adams Ter
Hovey Ave
Leonard Ave
Camelia Ave
Cooney St
Line St
Leon St
Dimick St
Dickinson St
Springfield St
Houghton St
Bolton St
Oak St
Prospect St
Beach Ave
Tremont Pl
Columbia Ct
Water St
Earle St
Horace St
Ward St
Felton St
Cambridge St
Ellery St
Greenough Ave
Marie Ave
Oakland St
Clary St
Tremont St
Windsor St
Willow St
Hunting St
Harding St
South St
Porter St
Bedford St
Jefferson St
Marion St
Warren St
Ware St
Trowbridge St
Dana St
Ellsworth Ave
Highland Ave
Fairwood Cir
Fayette St
Maple Ave
Inman St
Amory St
Carlisle St
Citizen Pl
Palermo St
Cambridge
Berkshire St
Marcella St
Cleveland St
Merrill St
Chatham St
Fayette Park
Corliss Pl
Antrim St
St Mary Rd
Gardner Rd
Murdock St
Hampshire St
Lincoln St
Union St
Webster Ave
Marney St
Cardinal Medeiros Ave
Hardwick St
James Way
Dana Pl
Lee St
Broadway Ter
West Pl
West St
Broadway
Norfolk St
Elm St
Seckle St
Hamlin St
York St
York Pl
Vandine St
Michael Way
Centre St
Hancock Pl
Columbia St
Plymouth St
Portsmouth St
Berkshire Pl
Cornelius Way
Arnold Cir
Clinton St
Bigelow St
Harvard St
Scouting Way
Norfolk Ct
Richardson St
Market St
Linwood Pl
Bristol St
Bristol St
Lilac Ct
Binney St
Clark St
Kinnaird St
Bay St
Green St
St Paul St
Vail Ct
Essex St
Worcester St
Suffolk St
Boardman St
Dickinson St
Moore St
Pine St
Cherry St
Windsor St
Davis St
Central
Bishop Allen Dr
Western Ave
Massachusetts Ave
Portland St
River St
Main St
Magazine St
Brookline St
Vassar St
MIT
1/4 mile
.25 km

nan Square is an almost-hidden treasure at the center of the Cambridge/ merville vortex. But its older, cozy Cantabrigian apartments are slowly ng converted to condos, which means the secret is getting out. Folks m the rest of Boston are increasingly finding their way to Inman, rticularly when they're hungry.

Landmarks

ulia Child's Home • 103 Irving St [Bryant St]
he kitchen was dismantled and moved to the mithsonian.

Nightlife

- **Atwood's Tavern** •
  877 Cambridge St [Hunting St]
  617-864-2792
  Food 'til late and live local music.
- **Bukowski Tavern** •
  1281 Cambridge St [Oakland St]
  617-497-7077
  100+ beers. More chill than its Boston brother.
- **The Druid** •
  1357 Cambridge St [Springfield St]
  617-497-0965
  Well-liked Irish pub.
- **Lord Hobo** • 92 Hampshire St [Windsor Street]
  617-250-8454
  Good food, good beer, good God, let's cheer!
- **Parlor Sports** • 1 Beacon St [Dickinson St]
  617-576-0231
  Best sports bar in Cambridge.
- **Ryles Jazz Club** • 212 Hampshire St [Inman St]
  617-876-9330
  Two-level club with jazz, world, Latin.
- **Thirsty Scholar Pub** •
  70 Beacon St [Cooney St]
  617-497-2294
  Laid-back neighborhood local. Good food, too.

Map 28

Restaurants

- **All Star Pizza Bar** •
  1238 Cambridge St [Prospect St]
  617-547-0836 • $$
  Foodie pies. Pricey but creative.
- **All-Star Sandwich Bar** •
  1245 Cambridge St [Prospect St]
  617-868-3065 • $
  Old-fashioned favorites like Mom used to
  make.
- **Amelia's Trattoria** • 111 Harvard St [Davis St]
  617-868-7600 • $$$
  The best Italian in this area.
- **Bergamot** • 118 Beacon St [Kirkland St]
  617-576-7700 • $$$
  Modern fine-dining with simple, local fare.
  Excellent.
- **Bondir** • 279 Broadway [Elm St]
  617-661-0009 • $$$
  Another farm-to-table joint—not that we're
  complaining.
- **City Girl Café** • 204 Hampshire St [Inman St]
  617-864-2809 • $$
  Comfy and cool. Try the lasagna.
- **Dali** • 415 Washington St [Beacon St]
  617-661-3254 • $$$
  Fun taparia. Worth the wait. Usually worth the
  price.
- **East by Northeast** •
  1128 Cambridge St [Norfolk St]
  617-876-0286 • $$
  Asian fusion sharing plates. Romantic and
  delicious.
- **East Coast Grill** •
  1271 Cambridge St [Oakland St]
  617-491-6568 • $$$$
  Awesome seafood, barbecue. Try the Hell
  Sausage.
- **Emma's** • 40 Hampshire St [Webster Ave]
  617-864-8534 • $$
  Design your own gourmet pie. Worth waiting.

- **The Friendly Toast** •
  1 Kendall Sq [Hampshire St]
  617-621-1200 • $$
  Late-night spot for the domestic American
  hipster.
- **Ginger Exchange** •
  1287 Cambridge St [Oakland St]
  617-250-8618 • $$
  Adequate sushi. Great happy hour roll speci‹
- **Koreana** • 154 Prospect St [Broadway]
  617-576-8661 • $$
  Cooking tasty bulgogi right at your table.
- **Midwest Grill** •
  1124 Cambridge St [Norfolk St]
  617-354-7536 • $$$
  Brazilian sword-play.
- **Muqueca** • 1008 Cambridge St [Columbia S‹
  617-354-3296 • $$
  Their specialty is a Brazilian-style seafood ste
- **Ole Mexican Grill** •
  11 Springfield St [Cambridge St]
  617-492-4495 • $$
  Delicious guacamole made right at your tab‹
- **Oleana** • 134 Hampshire St [Elm St]
  617-661-0505 • $$$$
  Top-notch Mediterranean. Patio seating in
  warm weather.
- **Punjabi Dhaba** •
  225 Hampshire St [Cambridge St]
  617-547-8272 • $
  Some of the best Indian food for dirt cheap.
- **Puritan & Company** •
  1166 Cambridge St [Tremont St]
  617-615-6195 • $$$
  Fresh New American with an emphasis on
  local flavors.
- **S&S Restaurant** • 1334 Cambridge St [Oak S
  617-354-0777 • $$
  Serving deli, comfort food for eighty years.
- **Trina's Starlight Lounge** •
  3 Beacon St [Dickinson St]
  617-576-0006 • $$$
  Old school Southern cocktails and vittles.
- **Tupelo** • 1193 Cambridge St [Tremont St]
  617-868-0004 • $$
  Food for the southerner in y'all.

and treats. Choose from over 100 beers at **Bukowski's**, relax with a classy
...tail at **Trina's Starlight Lounge**, or get the best of both worlds at Lord Hobo.
...ple farm-to-table Mediterranean fare at **Oleana** or homestyle Southern
...n' at **Tupelo**. Tour the famous **Taza Chocolate**, sift through threaded
...ures at **The Garment District**, then sit in a hot tub at **Inman Oasis** and call it

Shopping

Boston Costume Company •
...00 Broadway [Davis St]
...17-482-1632
...entals and sales.

Boutique Fabulous •
...309 Cambridge St [Oak St]
...17-864-0656
...nman Square maxi-boutique.

Christina's Homemade Ice Cream •
...255 Cambridge St [Prospect St]
...17-492-7021
...lever flavors; good spice shop next door.

The Garment District •
...200 Broadway [Davis St]
...17-876-5230
...intage threads, costumes, clothing
...y-the-pound.

• **Inman Oasis** •
243 Hampshire St [Cambridge St]
617-491-0176
Get hydrated in the community hot tubs.

• **Royal Pastry Shop** •
738 Cambridge St [Marion St]
617-547-2053
Caters to a devoted clientele.

• **Target** • 180 Somerville Ave [Mansfield St]
617-776-4036
Oh, you know.

• **Taza Chocolate** • 561 Windsor St [South St]
617-284-2232
Local, stone-ground chocolate.

• **Wine & Cheese Cask** •
407 Washington St [Beacon St]
617-623-8656
Wine, cheese, specialties.

st Roxbury is a suburb-within-the-city community, with selective shopping and ne good food. **Millennium Park** has fields, paths, and playgrounds, and a drive ng VFW can be nice when the construction isn't bad and the trees are in bloom. The a exists as a middle ground between suburban Newton and city communities like lindale. With supermarkets and places to park, West Roxbury is a good place to tle if you want to stay in the city and own an affordable house.

Landmarks

Millennium Park • VFW Pkwy & Gardner St
Clear your head by flying a kite.

Restaurants

Comella's • 1844 Centre St [Corey St]
617-327-8600 • $$
Get a mess of eggplant parm, lasagna, ziti, mozz…
Himalayan Bistro •
4735 Centre St [Manthorne Rd]
617-325-3500 • $$$
Nepali for your inner sherpa.
Mary Ann's Breakfast and Lunch •
223 Grove St [Washington St]
617-469-7426 • $
Solid breakfast shop.
Masona Grill • 4 Corey St [Park St]
617-323-3331 • $$$$
Euro-Peruvian eclectic grill, West Roxbury's best
Porter Cafe • 1723 Centre St [Esther Rd]
617-942-2579 • $$
Comfort food and heavy beer. You'll need a nap after.
The Real Deal • 1882 Centre St [Hastings St]
617-325-0754 • $
Imagine a typical sub shop with creative fixin's.
Rox Diner • 1881 Centre St [Corey St]
617-327-1909 • $$
Who says diner food can't be refined?
Viva Mi Arepa •
5197 Washington St [Grove St]
617-323-7844 • $
Empanadas and arepas to die for.
West on Centre •
1732 Centre St [Manthorne Rd]
617-323-4199 • $$$
Casual American; plenty of brick and mahogany.

Shopping

• **Bay Sweets Market** •
120 Spring St [Gardner St]
617-327-3737
Middle Eastern grocery.
• **Boomerangs** • 1870 Centre St [Hastings St]
617-323-0262
Resale store that supports the AIDS Action Committee. Good karma, great prices.
• **Jack Davis Florist** • 2097 Centre St [Temple St]
617-323-4237
Florist.
• **Roche Bros** • 1800 Centre St [Willow St]
617-469-5747
Pre-made meat kabobs.

er the last few decades, **Roslindale Square** (also known as Roslindale Village)
received awards for turning a virtual ghost town into a nice place to live
ome to such literary greats as e.e. cummings
ough local shops and some great restaurants. The city subsidies didn't hurt
her. Walking through the village area, one gets the sense of a community proud
tself. As a bonus, Roslindale Village is within walking distance of the **Arnold**
oretum, the best park in Boston and possibly the best urban park in America.

Landmarks

orest Hills Cemetery •
5 Forest Hills Ave [Morton St]
17-524-0128
his 250-acre beautiful cemetery is not only
ome to such literary greats as e.e. cummings
ut is also great spot to picnic and bike ride.

oslindale Square •
Vashington St [Belgrade Ave]
r, Roslindale Village.

Nightlife

ugene O'Neill's •
700 Washington St [Tower St]
17-553-2492
tart here, then stumble to J.J. Foley's when
ruly gone.

J Foley's Fireside Tavern •
0 Hyde Park Ave [Weld Hill St]
17-524-9849
 great old man bar that is slowly being taken
ver the young'uns.

Restaurants

Birch Street Bistro • 14 Birch St [Corinth St]
617-323-2184 • $$
nviting place to kick back for dinner.
Delfino • 754 South St [Taft Ct]
617-327-8359 • $$$
Tiny, popular spot serving good-quality Italian.
Diane's Bakery • 9 Poplar St [South St]
617-323-1877 • $
Croissant sandwiches, snack cakes.
Napper Tandy's •
4195 Washington St [Basile St]
617-323-8400 • $$
Townies abound.
Pleasant Cafe •
4515 Washington St [Cedrus Ave]
617-323-2111 • $$
Pizza and other basics. Don't be scared of the
sketchy exterior.
Redd's in Rozzie •
4257 Washington Ave [Corinth St]
617-325-1000 • $$
Southern American feel good, stick to your
ribs food. Get the hush puppies!
Romano's Pizzeria & Taqueria •
4249 Washington St [Poplar St]
617-325-2885 • $
Two great foods under one roof.

Roslindale House of Pizza •
4168 Washington St [Bexley Rd]
617-327-9170 • $
Pizza. Ya know, pizza.
Seven Star Street Bistro •
153 Belgrade Ave [Walworth St]
617-325-8686 • $$
Extraordinarily tender ribs.
Shanti Taste of India •
4197 Washington St [Basile St]
617-325-3900 • $$
Authentic Indian with a posh backdrop.
Sophia's Grotto • 22 Birch St [Corinth St]
617-323-4595 • $$
Cozy family trattoria. Enjoy the mussels in the
courtyard.
Village Sushi & Grill • 14 Corinth St [Birch St]
617-363-7874 • $$
Japanese and Korean.
Yucatan Tacos • 1417 Centre St [Knoll St]
617-323-7555 • $
Authentic Mexican food, apparently.

Shopping

Atlas Liquors •
591 Hyde Park Ave [Cummins Hwy]
617-323-8202
Sousing the locals since 1933.
Boston Cheese Cellar • 18 Birch St [Corinth St]
617-325-2500
NFT loves cheese. And free samples.
Droubi Bakery • 748 South St [Cohasset St]
617-325-1585
Cheap veggies and fruit along with delicious
Middle Eastern baked goods.
Exotic Flowers •
609 American Legion Hwy [Canterbury St]
617-247-2000
Florist.
Fornax Bread Company •
27 Corinth St [Washington St]
617-325-8852
Sandwiches, too.
Joanne Rossman • 6 Birch St [Belgrade Ave]
617-323-4301
Curios for the rich. Cool stuff, nice lady.
Roslindale Fish Market •
38 Poplar St [Washington St]
617-327-9487
Come early for fresh fish.
Solera • 16 Birch Street [Corinth St]
617-469-4005
A shrine to wine.

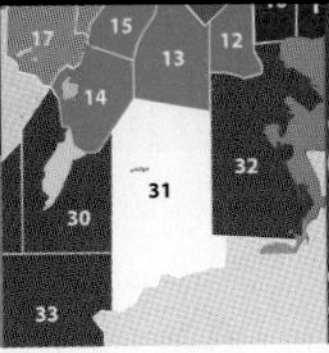

Map 31

attapan is mostly residential and home to about 40,000 people. It has a owing Haitian-American community (the largest in Massachusetts), and s smaller communities whose roots are in many of the nations of the aribbean. This is reflected in the wealth of Caribbean restaurants located Blue Hill Avenue.

Landmarks

Franklin Park Zoo Bear Cages •
Franklin Park Rd [Blue Hill Ave]
The abandoned bear cages outside the zoo's ences make for a creepy outing.
United House of Prayer •
206 Seaver St [Elm Hill Ave]
617-445-3246
mpressive Mishkan Tefila synagogue, now church and soul food kitchen.

Restaurants

Ali's Roti • 1188 Blue Hill Ave [Morton St]
617-298-9850 • $
You have not experienced life until you dive into a delicious roti.
Bon Appetit •
1138 Blue Hill Ave [Livingstone St]
617-825-5544 • $$
Haitian food supposedly makes you a better lover.
Brothers • 1638 Blue Hill Ave [Fairway St]
617-298-5224 • $
Southern. Huge side portions.
Flames • 469 Blue Hill Ave [Georgia St]
617-989-0000 • $$
Unusually stylish for this neighborhood.
Flames • 663 Morton St [Rhoades St]
617-296-4972 • $$
Jamaican. Serves ackee!
Genki Ya • 398 Harvard St [Naples Rd]
617-277-3100 • $$
Mr. T says that's how sushi is done foo!

• **Lenny's Tropical Bakery •**
1195 Blue Hill Ave [Deering Rd]
617-296-2587 • $
Double parking for the patties.
• **P&R Ice Cream •** 1284 Blue Hill Ave [Evelyn St]
617-296-0922 • $
Nothing beats a beef patty followed by a scoop of Grape Nut ice cream.
• **Pit Stop Bar-B-Q •**
888 Morton St [Cemetery Rd]
617-436-0485 • $
A rib shack, literally. Stick to the ribs.
• **Simco's •** 1509 Blue Hill Ave [Regis Rd]
617-296-3800 • $
Boston's best hotdogs since the 1930s.
• **United House of Prayer •**
206 Seaver St [Elm Hill Ave]
617-445-3246 • $
Friendly soul food in basement of Boston's old stadt shul.

Shopping

• **Dark Horse Antiques •**
2297 Dorchester Ave [Adams St]
617-298-1031
Antiques. Friendly.
• **Le Foyer Bakery •** 132 Babson St [Fremont St]
617-298-0535
Long lines for patties at this Haitian bakery.
• **Taurus Records •**
1282 Blue Hill Ave [Evelyn St]
617-298-2655
Small shop is best source for reggae, tons of singles.

Map 32 • **Dorchester (East)**

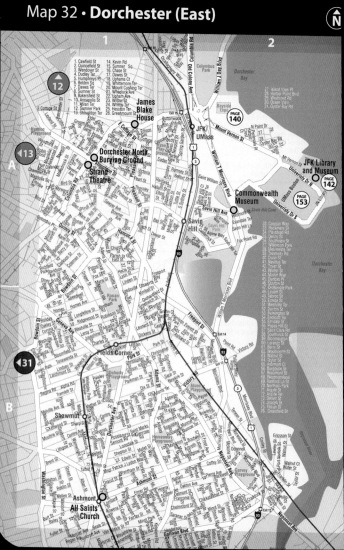

1. Cawfield St
2. Quincefield St
3. Wendover St
4. Dudley Ter
5. Humphreys Pl
6. Belden Sq
7. Dawes Ter
8. Sumner St
9. Bakersfield St
10. Annapolis St
11. Alvan Ter
12. Sumner Park
13. Stoughton Ter
14. Kevin Rd
15. Sumner Sq
16. Chase St
17. Dawes St
18. Uphams Ct
19. Whittemore Ter
20. Mount Cushing Ter
21. Wheelock Ave
22. Upham Ave
23. Wilbur St
24. Hessfuln Ter
25. Greenmount St
26.

27. Island View Pl
28. Harbor Point Blvd
29. Westwood Rd
30. Ocean Pkin
31. Oyster Bay Rd

32. Caspian Way
33. Rockmere St
34. Plumstead Rd
35. Denny St
36. Southview St
37. Waterson Ave
38. Meadowdale Ter
39. Treadway Rd
40. Duon St
41. Savihw Ter
42. Troon St
43. Winter St
44. Monte Way
45. Dorcas Pl
46. Clayton St
47. Centerville Park
48. Levant St
49. Tabnic St
50. Ennox St
51. Westville Ter
52. Davros St
53. Remington St
54. Endicott Ter
55. Ramsey St
56. Poppa Hill St
57. Saint Clara Rd
58. Southview St
59. Bloomingdale St
60. Lorenzo St
61. Bruzy St
62. Woodworth St
63. Walnut St
64. Taylor St
65. Ashmont Ct
66. Burgoyne St
67. Beaumont St
68. Westmoreland
69. Radford La St
70. Newmarch Park
71. Argyle St
72. Argyle Ter
73. Denver St
74. Shwegh St
75. Retun St
76. Greenhmd St

PAGE 140
PAGE 142
PAGE 153

James Blake House

Dorchester North Burying Ground

Strand Theatre

JFK/ UMass

Commonwealth Museum

JFK Library and Museum

Savin Hill

Fields Corner

Shawmut

Ashmont
All Saints' Church

famous for protecting turf, Dorchester is a collection of distinct neighborhoods and ethnicities. Uphams Corner, Savin Hill, Fields Corner, [...]mont, Codman Square, and Grove Hall are but a few of the areas that comprise Boston's largest district. If all you think about when you hear [...]chester is crime, you're missing out on an amazing section of the city—for [...]ing, and for cheaper rents than some of the more upscale 'hoods.

Landmarks

[A]ll Saints' Church •
[...]9 Ashmont St [Bushnell St]
[6]17-436-6370
[F]ounded in 1867. Beautiful stained glass.
[T]he Blake House • 735 Columbia Rd [Pond St]
[B]uilt in 1648, Boston's oldest house.
[C]ommonwealth Museum •
[2]20 Morrissey Blvd [Dominic J Bianculli Blvd]
[6]17-727-9268
[O]perated by the Massachusetts Historical
[S]ociety.
[D]orchester North Burying Ground •
[C]olumbia Rd & Stoughton St
[I]nteresting and eerie gravestones spanning 4
[c]enturies.
**[J]ohn F. Kennedy Presidential Library
[a]nd Museum •** Morrissey Blvd & Columbia Pt
[6]17-514-1600
[H]ouses 21 permanent exhibits examining JFK's
[li]fe and work.
[S]trand Theatre • 543 Columbia Rd [Dudley St]
[6]17-635-1403
[V]audeville, movie house time capsule. Under
[r]enovation.

Nightlife

[B]oston Bowl •
[8]20 Morrissey Blvd [Freeport St]
[6]17-825-3800
[O]pen 24 hours. Family fun all night long.
[d]bar • 1236 Dorchester Ave [Hoyt St]
[6]17-265-4490
[H]ip, gay bar. Food till 10 pm, then the dancing
[s]tarts.
[E]ire Pub • 795 Adams St [Gallivan Blvd]
[6]17-436-0088
[P]oliticians and sports fans welcome.
[H]arp & Bard •
[1]099 Dorchester Ave [Savin Hill Ave]
[6]17-265-2893
[P]atio makes this a summertime Irish standout.
[T]om English Bar •
[9]57 Dorchester Ave [Howes St]
[6]17-288-7748
[A] dive, no doubt, but a friendly one.

Restaurants

[A]shmont Grill • 555 Talbot Ave [Ashmont St]
[6]17-825-4300 • $$$
[B]ringing flair to Peabody Square.

• Banh Mi Ba Le •
1052 Dorchester Ave [William St]
617-265-7171 • $
Wonderful crisp Vietnamese sandwiches.
• The Blarney Stone •
1505 Dorchester Ave [Park St]
617-436-8223 • $$
Hodgepodge of good pub-type food.
• Gerard's • 772 Adams St [Minot St]
617-282-6371 • $
Traditional Irish breakfast with conveniently
contiguous convenience store.
• McKenna's Cafe •
109 Savin Hill Ave [S Sydney St]
617-825-8218 • $
Four words: sweet potato home fries.
• O Ya • 9 East St [South St]
617-654-9900 • $$$$$
Amazing sushi that is not easy on the wallet.
• Pho 2000 • 198 Adams St [Arcadia St]
617-436-1908 • $$
Serving a delicious 7 course beef dinner.
• Pho So 1 Boston •
223 Adams St [Dorchester Ave]
617-474-1999 • $
Fantabulous bowls of wontons.
• Restaurante Cesaria •
266 Bowdoin St [Draper St]
617-282-1998 • $$
Something for everyone—grilled octopus to
chicken parmesean.
• Shanti: Taste of India •
1111 Dorchester Ave [Savin Hill Ave]
617-929-3900 • $$
Go for the goat.

Shopping

• Boston Winery • 26 Ericsson St [Walnut St]
617-265-9463
Make your own wine, own your own barrel.
• Coleen's Flower Shop •
912 Dorchester Ave [Grafton St]
617-282-0468
Cute florist on Dot Ave.
• Euromart • 808 Dorchester Ave [Locust St]
617-825-1969
Polish meats, beers, and pirogies.
• Greenhill's Irish Bakery •
780 Adams St [Henderson Rd]
617-825-8187
Soda bread, scones and sandwiches with
blood pudding.

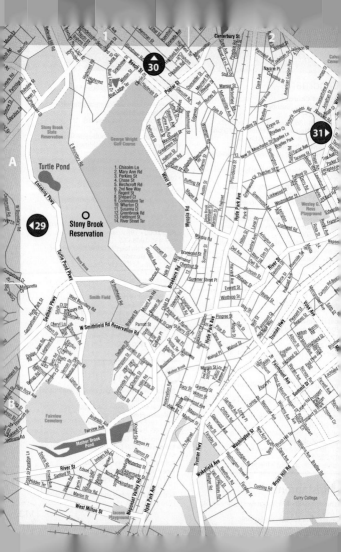

almost as large as Franklin Park, **Stony Brook Reservation** covers 475 acres and includes y hills, dense woods, rock outcroppings, and marshland. The park's largest feature is tle Pond, where you can fish for perch and sunfish. There are also several miles of ycle paths and the most extensive hiking opportunities within the city limits. Among park's many recreational facilities is the John F. Thompson Center, New England's first reational facility designed specifically to accommodate handicapped visitors.

Landmarks

Stony Brook Reservation • Turtle Pond Pkwy
17-333-7404
Great option for biking and hiking.

Nightlife

Master McGrath • 1154 River St [Winthrop Rd]
517-364-3662
Like a real life Cheers.

Restaurants

- **Rincon Caribeno** • 18 Fairmount Ave [River St]
  617-360-9775 • $
  A new addition to Fairmont that serves
  predominately Puerto Rican food.
- **Suya Joint** • 25 Poplar St [South St]
  617-327-8810 • $$
  The fish pepper soup is a taste bud explosion.

Shopping

- **Capone Foods** • 14 Bow St [Garfield Ave]
  617-629-2296
  All your specialty food shop needs.
- **Ron's Gourmet Ice Cream** •
  1231 Hyde Park Ave [Everett St]
  617-364-5274
  Candlepins too!
- **Tutto Italiano** • 1889 River St [Solaris Rd]
  617-361-4700
  Deli. A mayoral favorite.

Overview

Copley Square is named after Boston-born portrait painter John Singleton Copley (1738–1815), America's first great artist. His portraits of America's founding fathers are on display at the Massachusetts Historical Society, across the street from the square, and at the Museum of Fine Arts. The Boston Marathon, held annually on Patriots' Day (the third Monday in April), ends on Boylston Street. A BosTix outlet, the place to score discounted theater tickets, stands at the corner of Boylston Street and Dartmouth Street. The farmers market fills the square Tuesdays and Fridays from 11 am to 6 pm, late May through November. The Friends of Copley Square sponsors its annual Holiday Tree Lighting the week after Thanksgiving. Summer months bring folk and swing dancing performances to the square on Tuesday evenings, as well as a bevy of sun-seeking loungers.

Architecture & Sculpture

The Boston Public Library is America's oldest public library. The Renaissance-revival style structure holds within it over seven million books, as well as busts of famous writers and prominent Bostonians. Big bonus: It offers wireless Internet access. Across the square you'll find the neo-Romanesque Trinity Church, designed by notable architect H.H. Richardson. The stained glass windows alone are worth a trip inside.

John Hancock Tower

The John Hancock Mutual Life Insurance Company, which already inhabited buildings on Clarendon Street and Berkeley Street, needed more space to house its employees, so it opted to build a 60-story black glass tower. What better place to put it than next to the Public Library and an old church? Designed by architect Henry Cobb, and completed in 1976, the John Hancock Tower became famous for being the tallest building in New England, and simultaneously infamous for falling apart.

Locals were upset when a foundation collapse in the early stages of construction nearly sucked Trinity Church into

the ground. They became outraged when, in January 19[...] one of the building's 10,000-plus glass windows "pop[...] off" and shattered on the ground below, followed [...] dozens more 500-pound window panes. All told, 65 pa[...] fell onto the roped-off area below the building bef[...] workers changed the solder used to mount the windo[...] In the meantime, locals had dubbed the Hancock "[...] Plywood Palace," in reference to the black plywood she[...] put in place to substitute for the fallen panes. Not lo[...] after, engineers discovered the building was in dan[...] of being sheared in half by the wind, resulting in anot[...] expensive fix. Today, the Hancock Tower stands stu[...] tall, and proud, and locals have even grown to love [...] (Classic Boston photo op: Trinity Church is reflected in [...] mirrored side of the Hancock Tower, a clichéd but perf[...] example of Boston's mix of old and new.)

The observation deck on the 60th floor, originally oper[...] to the public in response to community feedback, w[...] permanently closed for security reasons after the eve[...] of September 11, 2001. Height junkies must now he[...] over to the nearby Prudential Center for a what-a-view [...]

How to Get There—Driving

From the south, take I-93 N to Exit 18 (Massachuse[...] Avenue/Roxbury). Follow signs to Massachusetts Aven[...] and turn right. Turn right on Huntington Avenue, th[...] left onto Dartmouth Street. From the north, take I-93 S[...] Exit 26 (Storrow Drive). Follow Storrow Drive west to t[...] Copley Square exit. Turn right onto Beacon Street an[...] after two blocks, turn left onto Clarendon Street. After f[...] blocks, turn right onto St. James Avenue. This is one of tw[...] examples in the city (the other being the Pru) where t[...] "look up, locate the giant building, and drive towards[...] method of navigation works well.

How to Get There—Mass Trans[...]

Take the Green Line to the Copley stop. Alternatively, ta[...] the Orange Line to the Back Bay stop, exit, and head[...] your right along Dartmouth Street. Again, if you're n[...] sure which way to go, look for the giant glass building.

General Information

NFT Map:	6
Address:	700 Boylston St, Boston, MA 02116
Phone:	617-536-5400
Website:	www.bpl.org
Hours:	Mon–Thurs: 9 am–9 pm, Fri–Sat: 9 am–5 pm, Sun: 1 pm–5 pm (Oct–May)

Overview

The Boston Public Library, founded in 1848, was the country's first publicly-supported municipal library. The BPL was also the first public library to lend a book and the first to institute a children's room. All adult Massachusetts residents are entitled to borrowing and research privileges to the 7.5 million books currently house at the BPL. Its circulating collection and the Norman B. Leventhal Map Center (home to a whopping 350,000 maps), Rare Books and Manuscripts Department (M–F 9 am–5 pm), and many other research-oriented nooks and crannies continue to attract scholars and tourists alike. Additionally, BPL's ever-changing exhibits are always good for a free, rainy day activity, as are the frequent talks by bestselling authors.

The BPL's main branch is the Central Library, composed of two august buildings adjacent to Copley Square that hold a lot more than just books. Facing Dartmouth Street, the McKim Building (the "old wing") was designed by noted 19th-century architect Charles Follen McKim and opened in 1895. The old wing, which houses the Research Library, is built around a delightful Italianate courtyard that offers perhaps a most un-library-like place to relax with a book. A set of murals painted by John Singer Sargent hangs inside. Sargent, better known for his portraits than for large installations, intended for these mammoth murals to be his masterpiece. There's also a set of allegorical murals by Pierre Puvis de Chavannes and the architecturally significant Bates Hall.

Opened to the public in 1972, the Johnson Building was designed by legendary architect Philip Johnson. The building, which houses the General Library, faces Boylston Street and is still referred to as the "new wing." (Granted, a better nickname might be the "ugly wing.") The Johnson building has less knock-out than the McKim Building, but it does have the tiled architectural frieze *The Goose Girl*, which is worth seeking out if you're wandering through the building. The BPL offers guided tours of both the old and new wings.

Internet

If you're ever stuck without Internet access, head over to the Central Library. Both the old and new wings have PCs available for use by the general public. (All computers have Internet connections and Microsoft Office software.) The first floor of the new wing also has "express" PCs that limit use to 15 minutes—handy for a quick e-mail hit. Both buildings are also equipped with Wi-Fi access.

For the Kids

Besides the weekly and seasonal programs it offers for everyone small from infants to teens, the Central Library has an outstanding collection of materials for even the youngest readers. Most of these materials can be found in the Margret and H.A. Rey Children's Room, named for the creators of that beloved, inquisitive simian, Curious George. The Children's Room also offers access to computers with Internet-filtering software, which is helpful for protecting fragile little minds. For more information, check the website or call 617-859-2328.

Restaurants

The Central Library now has two restaurants to sate you during long hours of research. Courtyard Restaurant, the fancier of the two restaurants, is set in a spacious room overlooking the courtyard in the center of the McKim Building. (Tip: Nip in for afternoon tea, served 2:30 pm to 4 pm on weekdays.) Next door to Courtyard Restaurant, Map Room Café serves breakfast, lunch, and snacks. For reservations at Courtyard Restaurant, or for additional information, call 617-385-5660. Note that food and drink are generally prohibited from the public areas of the Central Library, so chug your coffee before entering.

How to Get There—Driving

From the north or the south, take I-93 to Exit 26 (Storrow Drive). From Storrow Drive, take the Copley Square exit. The exit dead-ends at Beacon Street. Turn right on Beacon Street, drive four blocks to Exeter Street, and make a left. Drive along Exeter Street until you reach Boylston Street. The Central Library is on the corner of Boylston Street and Exeter Street.

From the west, take the Mass Pike (I-90 E) to Exit 22 (Prudential Center/Copley Square). Move to the right lane and follow the road in the tunnel toward Copley Square. The tunnel exits onto Stuart Street. Quickly move to the far left lane of Stuart Street and make a left at the next light onto Dartmouth Street. Drive through the next set of lights. The Central Library will be on the left.

Parking

The Central Library's location near Copley Square doesn't offer much in the way of street parking. If you're feeling unlucky, try the parking garage on Stuart Street between Dartmouth Street and Exeter Street.

How to Get There—Mass Transit

Take the T's Green Line to the Copley stop or the Orange Line to the Back Bay stop. From there, it should be pretty obvious: Look for the biggest, oldest, and grayest building around.

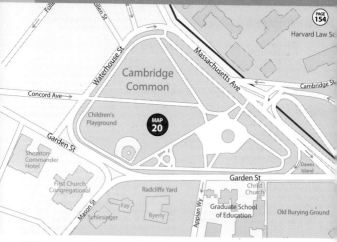

PAGE 154

Overview

Cambridge Common was the center of rebel activity in the early years of the Revolution and has been a hub of political and social activity ever since. George Washington rallied the 16,000-man Continental Army under an elm tree on the green on July 3, 1775, and the area became the primary training ground for the troops.

William Dawes, along with Paul Revere and Dr. Samuel Prescott, rode his horse across the Common on his way to warn those in Lexington and Concord that "the regulars are coming" (not that "the British are coming"). While Revere inspired a famous poem and became the namesake of many American cities, Dawes was commemorated with some lousy bronze hoof prints in the pavement of the Common.

Three cannon that the colonists seized from the Lobsterbacks still sit by the flagpole. There's also a memorial to victims of the Irish Potato Famine.

Even with the addition of a playground and a softball field, this historical urban oasis remains an important place to voice ideas and protests. Just steps away from Harvard University, the Common's corner on Mass Ave has been used by activists protesting everything from the occupation of Iraq to the existence of SUVs.

Attractions

Relaxing and people-watching are, by far, the tw best activities to undertake on the Common. With prime location next to Harvard Square, you can f like a Harvard student, without the excessive cou fees and mandatory high IQ, though tree-shad benches are available for reading if you want to pl the part.

Cambridge Common is the focal point of t Cambridge Common Historic District, whi also includes Christ Church, Old Harvard Ya Massachusetts Hall, and Gannett House (the olde surviving building on Harvard University's campus

The park has a fenced-in playground, located on t corner of Garden and Waterhouse Streets, where ki can frolic safely. The playground was last renovat in 1990 (including the addition of a wooden climbi structure, swings, bridges, slides, and benche picnic tables) and is recommended for parents wi children aged one to ten.

Sports

There's a softball field, soccer fields, and designate areas for other light recreation along with bike pat for cyclists, skaters, joggers, and walkers. Despite th close link between afternoon softball games a booze, the rules forbid alcoholic beverages on th ball field.

Parks & Places · **Charlestown Navy Yard**

eneral Information

Map: 8
ress: 1st Ave, Charlestown, MA 02129
ne: 617-242-5601 (Visitor Center);
617-242-5671 (USS Constitution)
sites: http://www.nps.gov/bost/historyculture/
cny.htm
www.cityofboston.gov/freedomtrail/
ussconstitution.asp
www.charlestownonline.net/navyyard.htm
rs: 10 am–4 pm, Thurs-Sun (Winter);
10 am–5:50 pm, Tues-Sun (Summer);
10 am–4 pm, Tues-Sun (Fall); free admission

verview

Charlestown Navy Yard is a must-see for anyone who
s big ships or US naval history. The two main attractions
the USS Cassin Young and "Old Ironsides" herself, the USS
stitution. The yard was established in 1800 as one of
naval shipyards in the country, and the Constitution is
ost as old as the country itself. When the Navy retired the
in 1974, the yard became part of the Boston National
oric Park.

ttractions

ical Fourth of July celebrations in Boston range from
kyard barbecues to beach sunbathing, but the Navy
has its own unique tradition. Independence Day is
brated with the customary turning of the Constitution—
annual practice in which the great vessel is tugged out
he dock and rotated to ensure uniform weathering. The
sin Young has battle scars from its service in both World
II and the Korean War. The nearby Commandant's House,
oldest building in the Navy Yard, is no longer a private

home, but an elegant museum, which is open to the public.
The Navy Yard Visitor Center/Bunker Hill Pavillion also serves
those visiting the nearby Bunker Hill Monument.

How to Get There—Driving

From the north, take I-93 S to Exit 28 (Sullivan Square/
Charlestown), go under I-93, and follow signs to Sullivan
Square. Bear left at the first traffic light and drive into the
Sullivan Square rotary; take the second right onto Bunker
Hill Street, turn right onto Chelsea Street, and make an
immediate left onto Fifth Street. Drive one block (Fifth Street
dead-ends) and turn left onto First Avenue.

From the south, take I-93 N to Exit 26 (Storrow Drive) and
aim for the "North Station, USS Constitution" signs. Turn left
onto Martha Road (which becomes Lomasney Way), left on
Causeway Street, then left at N Washington Street, and get
into the right lane as quickly as possible. At the end of the
bridge, turn right onto Chelsea Street.

From the west, take the Mass Pike (I-90 E) to I-93 N, and follow
the directions above.

Parking

Though public transportation is strongly recommended for
this area, discounted parking with Boston National Historical
Park validation is available from the Nautica Parking Garage
across from the park's Visitor Center on Constitution Road.

How to Get There—
Mass Transit

Visitors can take the MBTA Water Shuttle to Pier 4 at the
Navy Yard from Long Wharf for $3. (See page 258 for more
information.) Or follow the Freedom Trail from North Station.

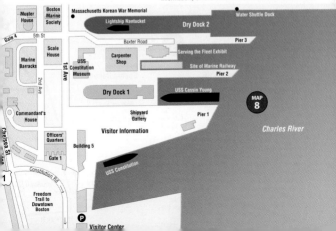

General Information

NFT Map:	3
Address:	147 Tremont St (b/w Temple Pl & West St)
Phone:	617-426-3115
Websites:	www.bostonusa.com
	www.cityofboston.gov/freedomtrail/
	bostoncommon.asp

Overview

One of the nation's oldest public parks, Boston Common was purchased by the Commonwealth of Massachusetts in 1634 to serve as livestock grazing ground. The city charged each household six shillings to pay for "the Commonage." (It was Tax-achusetts even back then!) People also used the Common to watch others being hanged at the gallows (like them cursed Quakers), for public meetings, and for military drills. The gallows were removed in 1817 and cow grazing was officially banned in 1830, around the time that urban cow ownership began falling out of fashion. In 1910, the Olmsted Brothers oversaw a massive landscape renovation, designating Boston Common as the anchor of the "Emerald Necklace," a system of connected parks that winds through many of Boston's neighborhoods. Boston Common is the beginning of the Freedom Trail and the Black Heritage Trail.

Situated across from the State House, Boston Common embodies the spirit of the city around it. Tourists, students, lunching suits, homeless Bostonians, and strolling older folks all share the park. On the lawn, squirrels and pigeons fight the latest chapter in their centuries-old gang war, while ducks enjoy free bread from park-goers. It is home to America's first and second subway stations (Park St and Boylston St), the Central Burying Ground, and the Robert Gould Shaw and Massachusetts 54th Regiment Memorial (a.k.a. the dudes from *Glory*).

Adjacent to the park is the Public Garden, former swamp that was filled in 1837. The nation's first botanical garden, Public Garden's French style of ornamental beds and pa stand in sharp contrast to the Common's informal, past English layout. This is where you can ride the famous Sv Boats and admire the *Make Way for Ducklings* sculpture.

Activities

The Freedom Trail is a 2.5-mile path through central Bos that passes by 16 of the city's historic landmarks. You'll detailed route maps and information at the Visitor Cente Boston Common. Many of the sites along the red-pain line offer free admission, others "recommend" a donation and some actually charge.

Frog Pond serves as a part-time ice-skating rink in winter a a splashing pool for children in summer. The smooth, pa paths that traverse the Common make it ideal for cyc rollerbladers, scooters, joggers, and walkers. Throughout year the park hosts concerts, plays, political rallies, and ot formal and informal gatherings.

How to Get There

Tremont, Beacon, Charles, Park, and Boylston Streets bou Boston Common. Parking is available, believe it or not, un the Common on Charles Street. By car, take the Mass P (I-90) to the Copley Square exit. Go straight at the off ra onto Stuart Street. Take a left onto Charles Street by Radisson Hotel.

By mass transit, take the Green Line or the Silver Line b to the Boylston T stop at the corner of Boylston Street a Tremont Street. This stop is heavily used by tourists a locals, so expect crowds. Another equally bustling optior to take the Red Line or Green Line to the Park Street T stop the northeastern edge of the Common.

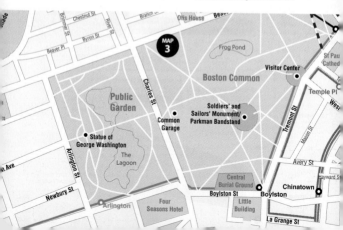

Freedom Trail & Black Heritage Trail

General Information

Maps: 1, 2, 3, 4, 8
Address: Visitor Center, 147 Tremont St,
Boston, MA 02111
Freedom Trail: www.thefreedomtrail.org
Black Heritage Trail: www.afroammuseum.org/trail.htm
Walking Tours: Available daily during spring/summer/fall,
from Boston Common to Faneuil Hall, daily:
Departs hourly, 11 am–4pm.
From Faneuil Hall to Boston Common, daily:
10:30 am, 12:30pm, and 3:30 pm.
($12 adults, $6 children, cash only)
($12 adults, $6 children, cash only)
Audio Tours: Available at the Visitor Center, or download
an MP3 version for $15 from the Freedom
Trail website.

Freedom Trail Overview

The Freedom Trail conveniently links several important colonial post-colonial historical sites. Marked by a thick red path on sidewalks, either painted or made of inlaid brick, the trail guides sightseers from the Visitor Center on Boston Common to Charlestown Navy Yard on the opposite side of the Charles River. The 2.5-mile trek passes by 16 different sites, including the location of the Boston Massacre, Paul Revere's house, a couple of cemeteries, and Bunker Hill. Walking tours led by costumed guides leave the Visitor Center or Faneuil Hall, and a complete trail walk usually lasts about 90 minutes. Audio tours are also available.

Trail Head: The Boston Common—America's oldest public park, 44-acre Boston Common is home to well-fed squirrels, pigeons, walkers, joggers, bikers, dogs, and ducks.

1. **The State House**—The Massachusetts state government sits here in this gold-domed building, the oldest on Beacon Hill, in fact. Tour Hours: Mon–Fri 10 am–3:30 pm; 617-727-3676.

2. **Park Street Church**—Constructed in 1809 and has since stood as a testament to Abolitionist faith. Lucky passersby may even be treated to a tirade being given from the outdoor pulpit. 617-523-3383. Traditional worship: 8:30 am and 11 am. Contemporary worship: 4 pm.

3. **Granary Burying Ground**—An epitaph here reads "Revere's Tomb" near the resting places of both John Hancock and Samuel Adams, along with a giant monolith paying tribute to the family of Boston-born Ben Franklin. This is the city's third-oldest burial ground, the resting place of the victims of the Boston Massacre. Open daily 9:30 am–3:30 pm, Tues-Sat; 617-635-4505.

4. **King's Chapel**—The chapel dates from 1688, and the current chapel was built in 1754 with the objective that it "would be the equal of any in England." The bell was made by Paul Revere. Summer hours: Mon, Thurs-Sat 10 am–4 pm; winter hours: 10 am–4 pm, Sat. Entry is free but there's a $2 "suggested" donation. Concerts are on Tuesdays at 12:15 pm and Sundays at 5 pm. Services are held Wednesdays 12:15 pm and Sundays 11 am; 617-227-2155.

5. **King's Chapel Burying Ground**—Older than the Granary and the final resting place of some of Boston's first settlers.

6. **Benjamin Franklin's Statue/Site of the First Public School**—Boston Latin School, founded in 1635, is still open (but it's since moved to the Fenway). The old high school is considered the top public school in Boston. A mosaic in the sidewalk marks its original site nearby to a statue of one of its famous students, Ben Franklin. Both are in the courtyard of Old City Hall, also worth a look.

6. **Old Corner Bookstore Building**—Built in 1718, this is one of Boston's oldest surviving structures. Once an apothecary, during the 19th century the building housed the publisher of classic New England titles Walden and The Scarlet Letter.

7. **Old South Meeting House**—"Voices of Protest," a permanent exhibit in the house, speaks of generations who made history under one roof, including Samuel Adams, William Dawes, Benjamin Franklin (and his parents and grandparents), Phillis Wheatley, and the instigators of the Boston Tea Party. Nov–Mar, 10 am–4 pm. Apr–Oct, 9:30 am–5 pm. Adults $5, students and seniors $4, children (6-18) $1, children under six (free); 617-482-6439.

8. **Old State House**—The oldest surviving public building in Boston, its lush exterior will draw you inside where the Bostonian Society houses a library along with its museum of Boston's past.
   Library: Open for research by appointment only; call (617) 720-1713, ext 13. Daily use fee: non-members $10; free to members.
   Museum: 9 am–5 pm, extended hours in summer, closed New Year's Day, Thanksgiving, and Christmas Day. Adults $8.50; seniors (62+) and students, $7.50; members, youth (6-18), veterans, and US military are free ; 617-720-1713.

9. **Site of the Boston Massacre**—Cobblestones now mark this historic site outside the Old State House.

10. **Faneuil Hall**—Shopping mixed with history, with some eateries to boot. If you like touristy knick-knacks, this is the place to shop. The actual hall still holds public meetings and houses an armory museum. The Marketplace is open Mon-Sat, 10 am–9 pm and 11 am–5 pm on Sundays. Historical talks every thirty minutes, 10 am–4:30 pm. See page 196.

11. **Paul Revere House**—See how Boston's favorite patriot once lived. Keep in mind that when he lived there, the area wasn't filled with Italian restaurants. Apr 15–Oct 31, 9:30 am–5:15 pm. Nov 1–Apr 14, 9:30 am–4:15 pm. Closed Mondays in Jan–Mar and on Thanksgiving, Christmas Day, and New Year's Day. Adults $3.50, seniors and college students $3, children (5-17) $1; 617-523-2338.

12. **Old North Church**—"One if by land, two if by sea," goes the poem. And so two lanterns were placed in the Old North Church, the oldest church building in Boston, warning that the British were making their way across the Charles towards Lexington and Concord. The church has held services since 1723 and is the most visited historical site in Boston. Historic site hours: 10 am–4 pm (Tues-Sun), Jan–Feb; 9 am–5 pm, Mar–May; 9 am–6 pm, June–Oct; 10 am–5 pm, Nov-Dec; 617-523-6676.

13. **Copp's Hill Burying Ground**—The site began as a cemetery in the 1660s and was later used by the British as a strategic vantage point in the Battle of Bunker Hill. Open daily 9 am–5 pm.

14. **USS Constitution**—a.k.a. "Old Ironsides," America's oldest commissioned warship, with daily flag-raising and lowering ceremonies accompanied by cannon fire. Winter hours: Thurs-Sun, 10 am–4 pm. Summer hours: Tues–Sun: 10 am–6 pm. Tours depart every half hour; 617-242-5670. See Charlestown Navy Yard, page 198.

15. **Bunker Hill Monument**—A 221-foot granite obelisk commemorates the Battle of Bunker Hill—the first major battle of the American Revolution. The monument sits atop Breed's Hill, where the misnamed battle actually took place. Exhibitions at the visitor's center explain how the battle came to be and how it was won. Hours: Open daily 9 am–5 pm and 9 am–6 pm during July and August; 617-242-5641.

Freedom Trail & Black Heritage Trail

Freedom Trail

1. State House
2. Park Street Church
3. Granary Burying Ground
4. King's Chapel
5. Ben Franklin Statue
6. Old Corner Bookstore
7. Old South Meeting House
8. Old State House
9. Boston Massacre Site
10. Faneuil Hall
11. Paul Revere House
12. Old North Church
13. Copp's Hill Burial Ground
14. Bunker Hill Monument
15. USS Constitution Museum

Black Heritage Trail

1. Shaw Memorial
2. Middleton House
3. Phillips School
4. Smith House
5. Charles Street Meeting House
6. Hayden House
7. Coburn Gaming House
8. Smith Court Residences
9. African Meeting House
10. Smith School

MAP 8

PAGE 119

PAGE 175

PAGE 188

PAGE 126

MAP 1

PAGE 120

MAP 3

MAP 4

Freedom Trail & Black Heritage Trail

Back Heritage Trail Overview

...nning north from the State House, this trail ...ognizes the historical significance of Boston's ...t-Revolution African-American community. ...ore being forced into the South End and Roxbury ...the 20th Century, the first community of free ...can-Americans actually lived in Beacon Hill after ... American Revolution, in what is now known ...the North Slope. According to the first federal ...sus in 1790, Massachusetts was the only state in ...country without slaves. The Museum of African-...erican History is housed in two of the buildings ...the Trail, the African Meeting House and the Abiel ...ith School, which are open to visitors. Most of the ...toric homes on the Trail are private residences, ...sed to the public.

Robert Gould Shaw and Massachusetts 54th Regiment Memorial—Located on Boston Common across from the State House, this monument was built in 1897 in honor of the first all-black regiment that fought for the Union Army during the Civil War.

George Middleton House—(5–7 Pinckney St) George Middleton was the commander of an all-black military company during the Revolutionary War called the Bucks of America. His house, erected in 1797, is the oldest standing wooden structure on Beacon Hill. It is a private residence.

The Phillips School—(Anderson & Pinckney Sts) One of the first Boston public schools to be integrated (in 1855) as a result of the historic court case *Roberts v. The City of Boston*, which opposed the racial segregation of the city's schools.

John J. Smith House—(86 Pinckney St) John J. Smith was born free in Virginia in 1820 and eventually moved to Boston where he opened a successful barbershop that catered to many wealthy white customers from all over the city. His shop served as a haven for anti-slavery debates, fugitive slaves, and advocates for equal education rights.

Charles Street Meeting House—(Mt Vernon & Charles Sts) Built in 1807, the Charles Street Meeting House was originally the site of the segregated Third Baptist Church. After a failed attempt to desegregate the church, Timothy Gilbert and several other abolitionist sympathizers left to form the Free Baptist Church (now the Tremont Temple), the first integrated church in America. In 1876, the Meeting House was sold to the African Methodist Episcopal Church, which eventually left Beacon Hill for Roxbury in 1939, due to changing economic conditions in the area.

6. **Lewis and Harriet Hayden House**—(66 Phillips St) Lewis and Harriet Hayden ran a boarding house out of their home, which was also a stop on the Underground Railroad. Lewis Hayden was an ardent African-American abolitionist and community leader who served as a delegate for the Republican Convention, fought for women's rights, and helped found the Museum of Fine Arts.

7. **John Coburn Gaming House**—(2 Phillips St) Home to one of Boston's wealthiest African-Americans, clothier James Coburn, the gaming house was built in 1843. Serving Boston's white elite, it became one of the most successful black-owned businesses in the city. Coburn used the profits to finance several abolitionist groups in the community, including the Massasoit Guards. Founded as an all-black military company to protect the state's troops in case of war, the Guards also patrolled Beacon Hill to protect African-Americans from slave catchers.

8. **Smith Court Residences**—(3, 5, 7, 7A, & 10 Smith Ct) Five remaining wooden houses located on Beacon Hill's north slope were all purchased by middle-class African-Americans from white landowners in the mid-1800s.

9. **The African Meeting House**—(8 Smith Ct) Founded as a response to racial discrimination in Boston's religious communities, the African Meeting House remains the oldest standing Black church building in the country. The structure was built using labor and donations from the African-American community. It was used for religious services, as a safe haven for political discussion, and as a makeshift school for black children until the Abiel Smith School came into existence. Following a six-year historic restoration, the building has been restored to its 1855 appearance. With the Abiel Smith School, it houses the Museum of African-American History.

10. **Abiel Smith School**—(46 Joy St) Built in 1834 as the first schoolhouse in America to educate black school children, the Abiel Smith School was consistently overcrowded and neglected by the city. Substandard conditions led to *Roberts v. Massachusetts* and the desegregation of schools in 1855. Hours: 10 am–4 pm, Mon-Sat. Closed Thanksgiving, Christmas, and New Year's Day. Small admission fee. 617-725-0022.

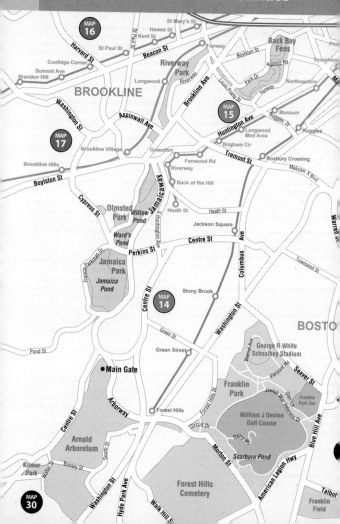

eneral Information

Maps: 14, 15, 16, 17, 30, & 31
ress: Two Brookline Pl, Brookline, MA 02445
ne: 617-232-5374
sites: www.emeraldnecklace.org
www.cityofboston.gov/parks/necklace.asp

verview

wn primarily for his work designing New York's Central
k (along with co-designer Calvert Vaux), celebrated
dscape architect Frederick Law Olmsted also created
eautiful string of Boston parks when he moved to
okline in 1883. Olmsted's Necklace was designed as
uninterrupted five-mile walkway from Back Bay to
klin Park, where Bostonians could stroll barefoot and
hout worry. The Necklace has been broken up over
years, both by the construction of the Casey Overpass
r Franklin Park and by the conversion of the Riverway,
aicaway, and Arborway from pleasant carriage paths to
or roads carrying highway-amounts of traffic. The city
conservation groups are putting together a "master
n" to connect the several sections of the Necklace and together
trying to balance path restoration with traffic concerns.
:e the completion of the Rose Kennedy Greenway, where
Central Artery once stood, all of Boston's parks are finally
ed into an actual, sorta-kinda necklace.

ranklin Park

:upying 500 acres, Franklin Park is the Necklace's largest
k and was originally designed as a country retreat in
vein of Central Park in New York. Named after Benjamin
nklin, the park encompasses the Zoo (617-541-LION),
e of the public golf courses in the country (617-265-
4), 100 acres of woodland, and the seven-acre Scarboro
d. The Franklin Park Zoo (not part of Olmsted's original
), which opened in 1911, is home to the "Butterfly
ding," a butterfly enclosure open seasonally from June
ough September. The zoo made headlines in 2003 when
lescent gorilla "Little Joe" escaped from his enclosure—
:e. The first time, he stayed on site. The second time, he
led up at a bus stop in Roxbury. Zoo entry: Adults $17,
dren (2-12) $11, seniors (62+) $14, reduced price the first
of each month, 10 am–12 pm; winter hours (Oct 1–Mar
, 10 am–4 pm; summer hours, 10 am–5 pm weekdays,
d 6 pm weekends and holidays, admission is half price the
day after Thanksgiving; www.zoonewengland.com

rnold Arboretum

: oldest arboretum in the country, Arnold Arboretum is
ned after its financier, whaling tycoon and horticulturalist
1es Arnold. Visitors come primarily to stroll amongst
exotic greenery, which includes bonsai and lilac trees.
:ause Arnold left most of his estate to Harvard and the
ool uses the arboretum as a nature museum, it seems
y fair for the city to allow the grand university to rent
land for just a dollar a year. Open every day until dusk;
Visitor Center is open Apr-Oct 11 am–6 pm, Nov-Mar 12
–4 pm, and is closed Wednesdays and holidays. Entry is
e!

amaica Park

althy Bostonians of yesteryear built their summer homes
this spot, called "the jewel in the Emerald Necklace"
:ause of the 60-acre sparkling Jamaica Pond. The largest
purest body of water in Boston, the glacier-formed

pond is fed by natural springs and is 90 feet deep in some
places. The pond is so clean that it serves as a back-up
city reservoir. Joggers and dog-walkers share the 1.5 mile
paved trail around the pond. Fishing is one of the most
popular activities, and every year the City of Boston stocks
the pond with trout, salmon, and indigenous pickerel, bass,
hornpout, and perch. The boathouse rents canoes, sailboats,
and rowboats, and, in winter, has a fireplace going. Around
Halloween, the community organization Spontaneous
Celebrations sponsors a lantern walk around the pond.

Olmsted Park

A joint project between the City of Boston and the Town
of Brookline to link the two cities together, Olmsted
Park showcases the landscape architect's unique design
philosophy with a series of ponds and wooded paths that
open onto expansive views that help you understand why
Olmsted is the Boston Brahmin equivalent of a rock star.
(The city boasts at least one Olmsted impersonator.) A
great feature of the park is the human-made Muddy River,
currently the site of a major dredging project. Leverett,
Willow, and Ward's Ponds are more secluded and less
crowded than nearby Jamaica Pond. A bike/pedestrian path
system on the Brookline side from Jamaica Pond to Boylston
Street (Route 9) was completed in 1997.

Riverway Park

Hidden below the busy street level is the narrowest park in
the system and also the only one that is completely human-
made. Riverway lies in the valley of the Muddy River (the
boundary between Boston and Brookline) and features
several small islands, wooded paths, and pretty footbridges.
Its steep tree-lined banks protect visitors from the city bustle
above. Footbridges connect the Boston and Brookline sides,
but these are poorly lit at night.

Back Bay Fens

Olmsted's first phase of the Necklace in 1878, the Back Bay
Fens was a sewage-infested saltwater marsh on the verge
of extinction when he stepped in, transforming the swampy
area into a meandering brackish creek. The creation of the
Charles River Dam in 1910 turned the Fens into a freshwater
marsh. Today, the Fens has quite a few notable attractions,
including recreational facilities, the Kelleher Rose Garden,
War Memorials, and the Victory Garden. The Victory Garden
was created in 1941, in an effort to grow extra food for troops,
and is currently tended to by local green thumbs who shell
out a small annual fee to maintain personal plots. A former
parking lot, the western end of the Fens was converted into
green space. But it's a notorious local fact that more than
mere gardening takes place on the grounds—think George
Michael.

Rose Kennedy Greenway

Opened in late 2008, the Rose Kennedy Greenway, a 15-acre
green space extending from Chinatown to the North End,
stands upon what was once the Central Artery highway. This
nuisance of a highway had torn through neighborhoods
and displaced residents for over forty years, until the Big Dig
came along and fixed everything (after it was finally fixed
itself). A joint effort of the Massachusetts Turnpike Authority,
the Commonwealth, the City of Boston, and various civic
groups, the Greenway features gardens, plazas, fountains,
and tree-lined walkways—a relaxing oasis tucked
within the busy surrounding urban environment.

General Information

NFT Map: 2
Phone: 617-523-1300
Websites: www.faneuilhallmarketplace.com
www.faneuilhall.com
www.cityofboston.gov/freedomtrail/
faneuilhall.asp
http://www.nps.gov/bost/
historyculture/fh.htm

Faneuil Hall

Faneuil Hall was built as a food and produce market/
meeting hall by Boston's wealthiest merchant, Peter
Faneuil, in 1742. It's a historically poignant section of
commercial property: At this location, Samuel Adams
rallied for independence (prior to his interest in brewing
beer), the doctrine of "no taxation without representation"
was established, and George Washington and company
celebrated our country's freedom. In later years, it was the
site of abolitionist rallies. It's still both a commercial spot
and a meeting place used by campaigning politicians,
with shops in the basement and the first floor, the Great
Hall on the second, and a museum on the third.

Since its inception, the Faneuil Hall Marketplace has been
a major shopping arena, and it's now stocked with more
than 100 stores and pushcarts and 17 sit-down restaurants
as well as a gastronomic orgy of a food hall. The
marketplace alone attracts more than 12 million visitors a
year and hosts numerous events and festivals. Local talent
includes jugglers, mimes (yes, those, too), magicians,
bands, and the occasional strolling Ben Franklin. If you're
looking to be entertained while you shop, Faneuil Hall is
your place.

Four buildings make up the marketplace: Faneuil Hall,
Quincy Market, North Market, and South Market. Touristy
and crowded at times, it's still one of the best and most
visually pleasing places to buy souvenirs, shop in a mall-
like environment, and try any number of local dishes.
Standard mall stores occupy most of North and South
Market, while local vendors and souvenir slingers can be
found in the Hall or at pushcarts in Quincy Market. The
Hall and all pushcarts are open Monday through Saturday
from 10 am to 9 pm, and from 11 am to 6 pm on Sundays.
Shopping hours in the other marketplaces vary by vendor.
The Hall and all shops are closed on Christmas.

Quincy Market

Located directly behind Faneuil Hall, Quincy Market is
where you go to chow down. The food court runs the
length of the building and far exceeds a typical mall food
court in both variety and quality of offerings. Whatever
you crave, it's hard to go away disappointed. It is usually
crowded at lunch, especially during the field trip and leaf-
peeping seasons, so avoid peak hours if you're in a rush.
Various sit-down bars and restaurants and pushcarts
encircle the food court around the perimeter. The North

Market and South Market, which stand on either side
of Quincy Market, have other places to sit for a meal,
including the still-there Durgin Park.

Like many places in Boston, Quincy Market is built on
landfill in what used to be Boston Harbor. Unlike other
sections, when you're in Quincy Market, you're standing
on bones. The butchers who used to occupy the wharf
behind Faneuil Hall would let their unusable animal parts
pile up, creating a sanitation nightmare. Then, someone
had the bright idea of throwing the bones in the water,
which eventually helped fill the wharf area and allowed for
the construction of Quincy Market.

Museum

Ancient and Honorable Artillery Company Museum; 617-
227-1638; http://www.ahac.us.com/

Located on Faneuil Hall's third floor, the museum and
library showcase the history of the Ancient and Honorable
Artillery Company. The oldest military organization in the
US (and third-oldest in the world), this august body was
established as the Military Company of Boston in 1638
and still holds military drills and participates in various
ceremonial events. The museum proudly displays the
company's artifacts. It is a unique collection that is well
worth a visit for military and history buffs. The museum is
open Monday–Friday, 9 am–3:30 pm.

How to Get There—Driving

From the south, take I-93 N to Exit 23 ("Government
Center"). Upon exiting, follow the signs to the Aquarium.
At Surface Road, turn left. Faneuil Hall will be on the right
hand side.

From the west, take the Mass Pike (I-90) to Exit 24B (I-93).
From I-93, take Exit 23 ("Government Center") and follow
the directions above.

From the north, take I-93 S to Exit 24A toward Government
Center. Stay to the right, and follow the signs for Faneuil
Hall. Immediately off the exit, turn right. Faneuil Hall will
be directly in front of you.

Parking

There are over 10,000 parking spaces within a two-mile
radius of Faneuil Hall. The 75 State Street garage near
the intersection of State Street and Broad Street offers a
discount on weekdays with validation from participating
stores, and $16 parking after 5 pm daily, all day Saturdays
and Sundays, and on select holidays.

How to Get There—Mass Transit

To get to Faneuil Hall Marketplace, take the T's Green Line
to Government Center or Haymarket, the Blue Line to State
or Aquarium, or the Orange Line to State or Haymarket.

hopping

Hat for Every Head (pushcart)
an Taylor
l Rodgers Running Center
ston Logos (pushcart)
xers To Go (pushcart)
ild A Belt (pushcart)
ltic Weavers
ach
oio
ntasy Island (pushcart)
arvest Fare (pushcart)
ad Games
Cloche (pushcart)
e is a Highway (pushcart)
chal Negrin
ghtshirts To Go (pushcart)
ne West
cs (pushcart)
a Boston USA (pushcart)
ck It To Me
ban Outfitters
ctoria's Secret

oods & Gifts

rican Collections (pushcart)
r Brush Tattoos (pushcart)
nytime (pushcart)
rman Time Company (pushcart)
rt for 'Em (pushcart)
tmosphere (pushcart)
elt Stop
est of Boston
ston Art Work (pushcart)
ston Campus Gear
ston Pewter Company
he Boston Sun Spot
ostonian Society Museum Shop
amera Center
heers Gift Shop
hristmas In New England
he Christmas Dove
onversations (pushcart)
rabtree & Evelyn
rate & Barrel
estination Boston
very Bead of My Heart (pushcart)
xotic Flowers
nusual
ateway News
eoclassics
odiva Chocolatier
appy Hangups (pushcart)
arley Davidson-Boston (pushcart)
eadlines of America (pushcart)
enri's Glassworks
usions (pushcart)
sh Eyes (pushcart)
ocal Charm

Lokta Paper (pushcart)
Lucky Decor
Magnetic Chef (pushcart)
Museum of Fine Arts Store
Musically Yours (pushcart)
Newbury Comics
On the Edge
Origins
Pillow Pets (pushcart)
Sluggers Upper Deck Kiosk
(pushcart)
Stuck on Stickpins (pushcart)
Sunglass Hut & Watch Station
Teeny Billboards (pushcart)
Yankee Candle Company
Zip It

Food

Al Mercantino
Ames Plow Tavern
Aris Barbeque
Bagelville
Bangkok Express
Berry Twist
Boston & Maine Fish Co
Boston Café
Boston Chipyard
Boston Chowda
Boston Kitchen
Boston Pretzel & Lemonade
Boston Rocks
Carol Ann's Bake Shop
Dick's Last Resort
The Dog House
Durgin Park
El Paso Enchilada
Fisherman's Net
Gourmet India
The Green Organic Bowl
Jen Lai Rice & Noodle Company
Joey's Gelateria
Kilvert & Forbes
Kingfish Hall
La Pastaria
McCormick & Schmick's
Megumi
Mija Cantina & Tequila Bar
MMMac & Cheese
The Monkey Bar
New York Deli
North End Bakery
Parris
Philadelphia Steak & Hoagie
Piccolo Panini
Pizzeria Regina
The Prime Shoppe
Quincy's Place
Salty Dog Seafood Grill & Bar
Sam's Café at Cheers
Slugger's Dugout
Sprinkles Ice Cream
Starbucks

Steve's Greek Cuisine
Ueno Sushi
Wagamama
Walrus and the Carpenter
West End Strollers
Zuma's Tex Mex Café

Bars & Entertainment

Cheers
Comedy Connection
Coogan's
Hard Rock Cafe
Jose MacIntyre's
Ned Devine's Irish Pub
Parris
The Monkey Bar
Trinity

Services

Bean Town Trolley Tours (pushcart)
BosTix Ticket Booth
City View Trolley Tours
Faneuil Hall Marketplace
Information
Old Town Trolley Tours (pushcart)
Super Duck Tours (pushcart)

Nearby Bars

The Atrium Lounge
Bell in Hand Tavern
Black Rose
Dockside Restaurant & Bar
Hennessey's
McFadden's
Kitty O'Shea's
The Rack
The Place
Purple Shamrock
Sissy K's
Union Oyster House
Vertigo

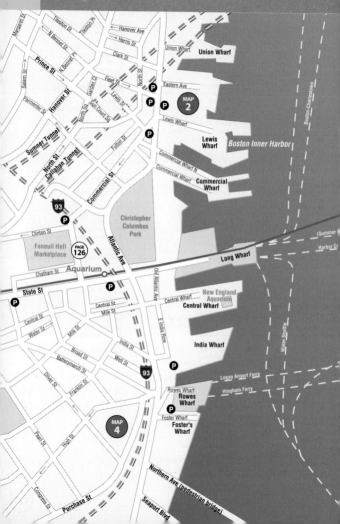

Tileston St
Hanover Ave
Harris St
Margaret St
N Bennet Pl
Clark St
Union Wharf
Union Wharf
Prince St
Salem St
N Bennet St
Fleet St
Eastern Ave
Lewis St
Parmenter St
Hanover St
Garden Ct
North St
Sun Court Sq
MAP 2
Lewis Wharf
North St
Fulton St
Lewis Wharf
Boston Inner Harbor
Sumner Tunnel
Commercial Wharf N
North St
Callahan Tunnel
Commercial Wharf
Commercial St
Commercial Wharf
93
Christopher Columbus Park
Clinton St
Faneuil Hall Marketplace
PAGE 126
Atlantic Ave
Long Wharf
(Summer
Harbor Cr
Chatham St
Aquarium
State St
Central Wharf
New England Aquarium
Central Wharf
Central St
Central St
Milk St
Water St
Milk St
India St
Broad St
Well St
India Wharf
Batterymarch St
Oliver St
93
Franklin St
Water Shuttle
Logan Airport Ferry
Rowes Wharf
Hingham Ferry
Rowes Wharf
MAP 4
Foster Wharf
Foster's Wharf
Pearl St
High St
Northern Ave (pedestrian bridge)
Congress St
Purchase St
Seaport Blvd
Boston-Charlestown
E India Row
Old Atlantic Ave

Long Wharf & Rowes Wharf

Overview

~~~inally~~~ named Boston Pier, Long Wharf juts into Boston ~~~arbor~~~ at the bottom of State Street, while Rowes Wharf is ~~~further~~~ south, near Broad Street. In the 1700s, Long Wharf ~~~extended~~~ more than one-third of a mile into Boston Harbor, ~~~but the~~~ dumping of urban landfill has resulted in a significant ~~~reduction~~~ of the pier being surrounded by land rather than ~~~water~~~. Purportedly the oldest continually operating wharf ~~~in the~~~ US, Long Wharf is also the site of the oldest existing ~~~pre-~~~Revolutionary War warehouse in Boston, the Gardiner ~~~Building~~~, which has been the home of the Chart House ~~~Restaurant~~~ since 1961.

Attractions

~~~Dur~~~ing the warmer months, stop by The Landing on Long ~~~Wh~~~arf for a drink in the sunshine. It's the perfect place to ~~~h~~~ang out and catch a Red Sox game on television after work ~~~w~~~hen you're waiting to board a ferry.

~~~The~~~ New England Aquarium is located at nearby Central ~~~Wh~~~arf and operates an IMAX Theatre next door. The ~~~aq~~~uarium allows scientists and researchers to study ~~~m~~~arine and aquatic habitats and to educate visitors about ~~~its~~~ natural habitat. One of the most exciting events to ~~~part~~~icipate in is a "release party," when an animal is returned ~~~to~~~ its natural habitat. Hours: 9 am–5 pm weekdays (6 pm ~~~sum~~~mer), 9 am–6 pm weekends (7 pm summer). Closed ~~~Tha~~~nksgiving and Christmas Day. $24.95 adults, $17.95 ~~~ch~~~ildren 3-11, $22.95 seniors (60+). www.neaq.org; 617-~~~973~~~-5200.

~~~The~~~re are several whale-watching excursions that leave from ~~~the~~~ wharves. Whale-watching season starts in April and ends ~~~in~~~ the fall.

Voyager III • Central Wharf • 617-973- 5281
Boston Harbor Cruises • 1 Long Wharf • 617-227-4321
Massachusetts Bay Lines Whale Watch •
~~~6~~~0 Rowes Wharf • 617-542-8000

~~~Lo~~~ng Wharf is also where you catch the Harbor Express boat ~~~to~~~ the Boston Harbor Islands. There are 34 islands in all, six ~~~of~~~ which are staffed and serviced by a free boat shuttle from ~~~the~~~ headquarters on Georges Island. These islands are still ~~~un~~~deutilized by locals and unfrequented by tourists. They ~~~va~~~ry in size, but most offer trails, old forts, diverse flora and ~~~fau~~~na, camping (on Grape, Lovells, and Bumpkin), and great ~~~vi~~~ews of Boston and the harbor. Spectacle Island's past as a ~~~for~~~mer quarantine island, glue factory, and garbage dump ~~~has~~~ been covered over with rubble from the Big Dig and ~~~tra~~~nsformed into an eco-friendly recreation spot. The island ~~~is~~~ now open to the public and features a visitor center and ~~~ca~~~fé. The island opens seasonally, so check the website, ~~~www~~~.bostonharborislands.org, or call 617-223-8666.

~~~If~~~ you're prone to seasickness, or if watching whales isn't ~~~yo~~~ur bag, the newly-renovated Christopher Columbus Park ~~~is~~~ a short walk from Long Wharf. The playground for the little ~~~on~~~es is top-notch, and its famous rose garden is dedicated ~~~to~~~ Rose Fitzgerald Kennedy. It's also a good viewing spot for ~~~the~~~ fireworks on First Night. Next door is Tia's, a popular after-~~~w~~~ork, meat market bar in the summer.

Architecture

~~~Ro~~~wes Wharf features a commanding arch that looks out ~~~on~~~to Boston Harbor. The Wharf is a mixed-use complex that ~~~ha~~~s won numerous design awards, including the Urban Land

Institute's "Award for Excellence." The complex is shared by the Boston Harbor Hotel, 100 luxury condominiums, and offices. There is a little-known observation area on the ninth floor named the Fosters Rotunda, offering views of both the city and harbor. Though not advertised, you can go through the hotel to gain access. In the summertime, a floating dock hosts outdoor concerts and movies under the stars.

Ferries

Both Long Wharf and Rowes Wharf serve as ferry terminals for the MBTA. F1 transports people to and from Rowes Wharf and Hingham Shipyard. F2 and F2H stop at Long Wharf, Logan Airport, and the Fore River Shipyard in Quincy. F2H also has limited service to Pemberton Point in Hull. F4, which travels to the Charlestown Navy Yard, also uses the Long Wharf terminus. The Harbor Express to Georges Island also leaves from Long Wharf. For more information on ferries, see page 254. For schedules and maps, go to www.mbta.com/schedules_and_maps/boats, or call 617-222-5000. You can also catch the high-speed catamaran ferry to Provincetown from Long Wharf. For schedules, rates, and area information visit www.bostonharborcruises.com/provincetown-ferry/default.aspx.

How to Get There—Driving

To Long Wharf from the north, take I-93 S, and get off at Exit 24A (Government Center/Aquarium). Follow signs to the Aquarium. From the south, take Exit 23 (Government Center) and follow signs to the Aquarium.

To Rowes Wharf from the north, take I-93 S and get off at Exit 23 (aim for South Station). Turn left onto Congress Street and immediately left onto Atlantic Avenue. The wharf is on the right, two blocks past the intersection of Congress Street and Atlantic Avenue.

From the south, take I-93 N to Exit 20, and follow signs to South Station. Once you proceed onto Atlantic Avenue, proceed through the Congress Street intersection and drive two blocks. The wharf will be on your right.

Parking

There is very limited street parking in the area, so if you want to forego driving around to find a free spot, you should try one of the many parking garages that are all within walking distance of the various wharves. Parking fees can cost $25 or more, depending on how long you stay, though there are usually discounted rates on weekends and after 5 pm on weekdays. If you're willing to shell out the cash, here are a few nearby garages:

- **The Rowes Wharf building** features an underground discounted parking garage with an entrance on Atlantic Avenue.
- **Harbor Garage at the Aquarium,** 70 East India Row; 617-367-3847
- **Dock Square Garage,** 200 State St; 617-367-4373
- **Laz Parking,** 290 Commercial St; 617-367-6412
- **Fitz-Inn Parking,** 269 Commercial St; 617-367-1681
- **Central Parking,** 2 Atlantic Ave; 617-854-3365

How to Get There—Mass Transit

To Long Wharf, take the T's Blue Line to the Aquarium stop. To Rowes Wharf, take either the Blue Line to Aquarium or the Red or Silver Line to South Station.

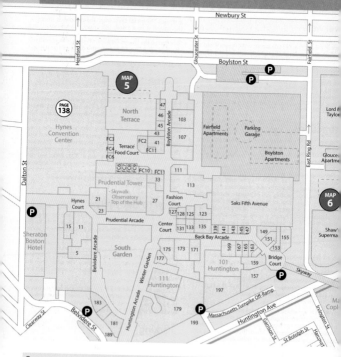

Stores

1	PF Chang's China Bistro	46	Travel 2000
5	US Post Office	47	Truffles Fine Confections
11	Ann Taylor Loft	103	Legal Sea Foods
15	Au Bon Pain	107	Sephora
17	Tossed	111	F Carriere
19	Best of Boston	113	Talbots Collection/ Talbots Kids/ Talbots Mens
21	St Francis Chapel		
23	Dunkin' Donuts	123	Olympia Sports
27	Ann Taylor	125	Chico's
33	Jasmine Sola	127	The Body Shop
39	Godiva	131	Alpha Omega
41	Free People	133	Johnston & Murphy
43	GameStop		
45	Florsheim Shoes		

135	Aldo	173	J Jill—The Store
139	Sunglass Hut		
141	Teavana	175	Club Monaco
143	Papyrus	175A	Charles David
145	Landau Collections	177	Franklin Covey
		179	Barnes & Noble
147	Optical Shop of Aspen	181	The Sharper Image
153	L'Occitane	183	Sovereign Bank
155	California Pizza Kitchen	187	Cold Stone Creamery
159	Crane & Co	189	The Cheesecake Factory
163	Lacoste		
165	Yankee Candle	193	Applebee's
167	Swarovski	197	FitCorp
169	Arden B		
171	Levenger		

Food Court

FC1	Qdoba Mexican Grill
FC2	Panda Express
FC3	Pizzeria Regina
FC4	Poulet Rotisserie Chicken
FC5	Boston Chowda
FC6	Flamers
FC7	Gourmet India
FC8	Sakkio Japan
FC9	Ben & Jerry's
FC10	Paradise Bakery & Café
FC11	Louis Barry Florist

eneral Information

Maps: 5 & 6
dress: 800 Boylston St, Boston, MA 02199
ne: 1-800-SHOP-PRU or 617-236-3100
osite: www.prudentialcenter.com

verview

Prudential Center opened in 1965 and, at 52 ries, reigned as the city's tallest building until the story John Hancock Tower was completed eleven rs later. With the exception of the top two floors, ich house an observation deck and a restaurant, Prudential Tower is used mainly as office space. Prudential Mall (not be confused with the ore highbrow Copley Place mall, attached to the idential Mall by a natty skywalk) was opened in 1990s on the lower floors and houses almost 50 ops, including Saks Fifth Avenue and numerous taurants and services. The "Pru" is also home to eral apartment buildings and is connected to the nes Convention Center and the Sheraton Boston tel. If you're not in the mood for the maddening wd, avoid the mall, which is always teeming ch tourists, hardcore browsers, and convention endees.

kywalk and Top of the Hub

e Prudential Tower gives you two options catching its spectacular views: Skywalk oservatory and Top of the Hub restaurant. Both er breathtaking sights of Boston and its suburbs, well as the harbor, Blue Hill, and—way off in the stance—Cape Cod. (By default, the Prudential enter became the best place to see Boston from high after the observatory at the John Hancock wer closed following September 11.) The Skywalk open daily from 10 am until 10 pm (8 pm in the nter). Skywalk tickets cost $15 adults, $13 seniors 2+) and students, and $10 children (6th grade and nder). As you walk around the Skywalk, focus on the uge windows, which are marked to help you locate ome of the more well-known features of the Boston yline.

Top of the Hub offers a somewhat more cost-effective viewing experience, and one that's two floors above the Skywalk, at that. Entrees are pricey, but juice and cocktails from the bar are fairly priced and served with a spectacular view. And if you're acrophobic, a little nip might be exactly what you need to be able to relax and enjoy the view as you peer down at the city or across at the top of the John Hancock Tower with beverage in hand. The restaurant and lounge get busy at night, especially when the jazz band is playing. A semi-casual but "anti-slob" dress code is in effect.

How to Get There—Driving

From the north, take I-93 S to Exit 26 (Storrow Drive) and follow it to the Copley Square exit on the left. Take a right onto Beacon Street and follow it to Exeter Street. Make a left onto Exeter Street and the Prudential Center Garage will be four blocks down on the right.

From the west, follow the Mass Pike (I-90 E) into Boston. Get off at Exit 22 (Copley Square/Prudential Center) and follow the signs for Prudential Center. This will take you directly to the Prudential Center Garage entrance on your right.

From the south, take I-93 N to Exit 26 (Storrow Drive) and follow to the Copley Square exit on the left. Take a right onto Beacon Street and follow it to Exeter Street. Take a left onto Exeter Street. The Prudential Center Garage will be four blocks down on the right.

If you get lost, try this: Look up. Find the giant building that says "Prudential" on top. Drive towards it.

How to Get There—Mass Transit

The Green Line will take you to the Prudential T stop on Huntington Avenue (E train only; FYI: Only the doors of the first car open for this stop), the Copley stop on Boylston Street at Dartmouth Street, and the Hynes/ICA stop on Newbury Street at Mass Ave. The Orange Line and the MBTA Commuter Rail both stop at Back Bay Station, just across the street from Copley Place and a short walk away.

Overview

Originally one of the least fashionable streets of Back Bay, Newbury Street has undergone quite a transformation, morphing into Boston's most popular shopping area and an excellent place to hang out and strut your stuff.

A beautiful stretch of real estate featuring late 19th- and early 20th-century architecture, Newbury Street runs eight blocks from the Public Garden west to Massachusetts Avenue. The cross streets run alphabetically from east to west, starting with Arlington, then Berkeley, Clarendon, etc. Stores pack the buildings along Newbury, which were originally designed for residential use, making for a lot of oddly shaped, quirky boutiques. The good shopping extends to either side of Newbury St with trendy stores and big name designers lining Boylston Street and many of the cross roads. Though the area features shops for all ages and tax brackets, the ambiance of Boston's most famed street may make an indulgence in $300 shoes or a $15 martini seem perfectly sensible.

In the summertime, the cafés spill out onto the sidewalk, providing a perfect spot from which to partake in unparalleled people-watching. The street is a veritable human car crash; the "hippest" elements of every age group, from 80-year-olds to eight-year-olds, interact and fight for space (and attention) on the same small sidewalk.

For an updated list of shops, see www.newbury-st.com.

History

The whole of Back Bay was swampland u about 1870, when workers completed a mas filling project. As a result, Back Bay is the c neighborhood in Boston to benefit from a mod urban planning. Streets actually cross each othe 90-degree angles, and at no point is there a rotary an eight-way intersection. Fluctuations in the wa table, however, are rotting the wooden planks which most of the area's structures sit. The res Back Bay is sinking.

The architecture on Newbury Street is fairly unifo since most of the development occurred during same half-century. Emmanuel Church, desig by Alexander Esty in 1862, was the first build completed on Newbury Street. The Church of Covenant, built in 1865, houses some spectacu stained glass windows and its steeple was described by Oliver Wendell Holmes as "absolute perfect." Its Emmaus Window shines even in t dimmest of lights.

How to Get There—Driving

Newbury Street is easy to get to. From I-93 take E 26 to Storrow Drive. Take the exit for Arlington Stre and proceed up Arlington until you hit Newbu Street (right turn only, one-way). Newbury Stree lies between Boylston Street and Commonweal Avenue, so if you get twisted around use these larg streets as landmarks.

Parks & Places • **Newbury Street**

ow to Get There—Mass Transit

n the T's Green Line you can get off at the
ngton stop, the Copley stop, or the Hynes/ICA
. Note that the Green Line's E train breaks off the
n track at Copley, so use the B, C, or D train to get
ynes/ICA.

opping

ess you have bionic feet, a shopping day on
wbury Street is going to leave your dogs barking.
kily, the layout of the veritable brownstone mall
is Newbury Street is laid out in such a way that
most expensive boutiques are found near the
ton Public Garden end of Newbury Street, with
ps gradually becoming cheaper and funkier by
time you collapse at Mass Ave.

wbury Street probably wouldn't have gotten to
ere it is today without the support of some of the
vy-hitter and high-end chain stores, so you can't
m them for being there. And, as a result, their
sence also gave the nearby little guy a steady
am of patrons. Some of the better (read: less
entatious) chains here include: **Urban Outfitters**
), **Patagonia** (346), **Puma** (333), **Johnny
cakes** (279), **1154 Lill Studio** (220), **Lush** (166),
O & Company (161). Unfortunately, between
ail space progression and the down economy,
chains appear to be taking more than their fair
re lately, so enjoy the hidden gems while they're
around. Check out **Mastu** (259), **Army Barracks**
3), **Trident Booksellers & Café** (138), **Condom
rld** (332), **Envi-Eco Fashion Boutique** (164), **Poor
le Rich Girl** (166), **Newbury Yarns** (164), **Queen
e** (85), **Paperchase** (172), **Too Timid** (297), and
ss** (221), to name a few.

Restaurants

If you don't stop to eat on Newbury Street, you're
missing half the fun. Even if you've dropped most of
your cash on shopping, you can still afford to stuff
your face with good cheap eats like **Upper Crust**
(222), **Steve's Greek** (316), **Snappy Sushi** (144),
Bottega Fiorentina (264), **Boloco** (247), **JP Licks**
(352), and **Kashmir** (279). Or pick up a little piece
of prepared food heaven at **DeLuca's Market** (239).
But if your coffers still have a little silver left in 'em,
splurge at **Stephanie's on Newbury** (190), **Tapeo
Restaurant & Tapas Bar** (268), **Capital Grille** (359),
or **Bouchee** (159). Either way, you'll never make it on
this street without some fuel in your belly.

Nightlife

Even if you only go to one store, a trip to Newbury
Street will most certainly merit a nightcap (even if
it's still day time). Unfortunately, there seems to be
a dearth of boozin' spots specifically on this street.
Fortunately, a great deal exists on adjacent streets
(see Map 5 and 6). In the meantime, the best waterin'
holes 'round these parts include the martini bar at
Sonsie (327), and **Bukowski Tavern** at the end of the
line on 50 Dalton Street.

All addresses are on Newbury Street

Clothing

A Pea in the Pod · 10 · maternity wear
AG Adriano Goldschmied · 201 ·
men's and women's clothing
Akris Boutique · 16 · shoe store
Alan Bilzerian · 34 · designer clothes
Alan Rouleau Couture · 73 · custom tailoring
Aldo · 180 · shoes and leather goods
Allen Edmonds · 36 · shoes and cedar products
American Apparel · 138 ·
men's and women's clothing
American Eagle Outfitters · 201 · youth clothes
Ana Hernandez Bridal · 165 · bridal boutique
Ann Taylor · 18 · women's clothes
Anthropologie · 203 · For the wealthy hipster.
Aria Bridesmaids · 39 · custom dresses
Army Barracks · 328 · military duds
Banana Republic · 28 ·
men's and women's clothing
Barbour by Peter Elliot · 134 ·
men's and women's clothing
BCBG Max Azaria · 71 ·
women's designer clothing
Bebe · 349 ·
women's clothing, accessories
Bella Bridesmaid · 163 ·
wedding clothing
Best of Scotland · 115 ·
sweaters at mill prices
Betsey Johnson · 201 ·
designer clothes
Betsy Jenney of Boston · 114 ·
women's unusual designer clothes
Blue Jeans Bar · 85 ·
Borelli · 73 · high-end fashion
The Boston Baked Bean · 291 ·
keychains and more
Boutique Giorgio Armani · 22 · clothes
Boutique Longchamp · 139A ·
French handbags
Brooks Brothers · 46 ·
classy clothing for men and women
Burberry Limited · 2 ·
clothes for men and women
Calypso · 114 · women's clothing
Camper Shoes · 139 · shoes

Ceri · 31 · women's clothing
Chanel · 5 · clothing and accessories
Classic Tuxedo · 223 · ummm…?
The Closet · 175 · consignment;
men's and women's clothing
Cole-Haan · 109 ·
men's and women's clothing
Cuoio · 115 ·
European shoes for women
Daniela Corte Fashion · 91 · women's fashion
Designer Shoes · 125 · designer shoes
Diesel · 339 · clothing
DKNY · 37 · clothing
Dress · 221 · women's clothing
Easter Wings · 244 · women's clothing
Ecco Newbury Street · 216 · shoes
Emporio Armani · 210-214 ·
men's and women's clothing
Envi-Eco Fashion Boutique · 164 ·
womens fashion accessories
Fiandaca · 73 · couture clothing
Flair Bridesmaid Boutique · 129 ·
wedding clothing
Footstock · 133 · shoes
French Connection · 208 ·
men's and women's clothing
G-Star Raw · 348 ·
men's and women's clothing
Guess? · 80 · clothing
H&M · 100 · men's and women's clothing
Hempest · 207 · hemp clothing
I Boutique · 251 ·
men's and women's clothing
In the Pink · 133 · women's clothing
Intermix · 186 · women's clothing
Jasmine Sola Shoes · 329 · shoes
Jessica McClintock · 201 ·
women's cocktail attire
John Fluevog Shoes · 302 · shoes
Johnny Cupcakes · 279 ·
men's and women's clothing
Juicy Couture · 12 · women's clothing
Karmaloop Boston · 160 ·
men's and women's clothing
Kate Spade Shoes · 117 ·
shoes, purses, etc.

nneth Cole Productions · 128 · shoes
ster Harry's · 115 ·
dding, children's and infant's clothing
e is Good · 285 ·
en's and women's clothing
gerie Studio · 264 · lingerie
Stores · 353 · women's clothing
ro Piana · 43 ·
en's and women's clothing, accessories,
iloring and alteration
cky Brand · 229 · denim
na Boston · 286 · accessories and handbags
aha Barson · 127 · women's clothing
arc Jacobs · 81 · fashion
atsu · 259 · handbags
ax Mara · 69 · women's clothing
udo · 205 · clothing
nette Lepore · 119 · women's clothing
ketown · 200 · everything Nike
lily · 31 ·
utch clothing for women and children
lily Women's · 32 · women's clothes
atagonia · 346 · clothing for the great outdoors
vo Real Boutique · 115 ·
omen's clothing and accessories
etit Bateau · 171 · women's clothing
ayers of Newbury · 250 ·
omen's clothing
ama · 333 · wildlife
ueen Bee · 85 · women's clothing
gg & Bone · 111 ·
alph Lauren · 95 · clothing
eiss · 132 · men's and women's clothing
elic · 116 · men's and women's clothing
ccardi Boutique · 116 · clothing
ugby Ralph Lauren · 342 ·
men's and women's clothing
ean Store · 154 · men's clothing
econd Time Around Collections · 176 & 219 ·
new and consignment clothes
erenella · 134 · European women's clothes
oudee · 293 · fashion
tel's · 334 ·
men's and women's clothing, accessories, and
ewelry
teve Madden · 324A ·
shoes and handbags

Stil · 170 · women's clothing
Technical · 230 · skate style and art
Timberland · 201 ·
Thom Brown of Boston · 337 & 331 · shoes
Ugg · 75 ·
United Colors of Benetton · 140 ·
  women's clothing
Urban Outfitters · 361 · clothing
Valentino · 47 ·
  men's and women's clothing
Vera Wang · 253 · wedding clothing
Victoria's Secret · 82 · fig leaves
Whim Boutique · 253 ·
  men's and women's clothing

Restaurants

29 Newbury · 29 · new American food
Ben & Jerry's · 174 · ice cream
Boloco Inspired Burritos · 247 · burritos
Boston Baked Bean · 291 · gourmet gifts
Bouchee · 159 · American and French food
Bostone Pizza · 225 · pizza
The Capital Grille · 359 · steak house
Charley's Eating & Drinking Saloon · 284 ·
  American food
Ciao Bella · 240 · Italian food
Daisy Buchanan's · 240 · bar
Emack & Bolio's Ice Cream · 290 · ice cream
Emporio Armani Café · 214 · Italian cuisine
Espresso Royale Café · 286 · coffee house
The Jewel of Newbury · 254 · Italian food
Kashmir · 279 · Indian food
L'Aroma Café · 85 · coffee shop
Marcello's Restaurant · 272 · Persian, Italian
Pazzo · 268 · Italian food
Piattini Wine Café · 226 · Italian food
Scoop · 177 ·
Scoozi · 237 · pizza and sandwiches
Shino Express Sushi · 144 · Japanese food
Sonsie · 327 · international cuisine
Stephanie's on Newbury · 190 · American food
Steve's · 316 · Greek-American food
Tapeo · 268 · Spanish food
Tealuxe · 108 · tea bar
Thai Basil · 132 · Thai food
The Upper Crust · 222 · pizza
Wisteria House · 264 ·
  Chinese-American cuisine

Gifts & Miscellaneous

1154 Lill Studio • 220 • handbags
A Touch of France Gallery • 173 • art gallery
Acme Fine Art • 38 •
  bought and sold modern American art
Aldo Accessories • 184 •
  accessories, handbags, jewelry
Alfred J. Walker Fine Art • 162 • art gallery
Alpha Gallery Inc • 38 • art gallery
Andrea Marquit Fine Arts • 38 • art gallery
Arden Gallery • 129 • art gallery
Atelier Janiye • 165 • jewelry
Aurum • 293 • jewelry
Axelle Fine Arts • 91 • art gallery
Back Bay Oriental Rugs • 154 • rugs
Barbara Krakow Gallery • 10 • art gallery
Bauer Wines Spirits • 330 • liquor store
Beadworks • 167 • make your own jewelry
Beth Urdang Gallery • 14 • art gallery
Bliss • 121 •
  home furnishings, cooking and dining
Brodney Antiques & Jewelry • 145 •
  antiques and jewelry
Cartier • 40 • jewelry
CD Spins • 324 • music and records
Chase Gallery • 129 • art gallery
Childs Gallery • 169 • art gallery
Cohen's Fashion Optical • 179 •
  sunglasses and glasses
Comenos Fine Arts • 9 • art gallery
Commonwealth Fine Art • 236 • art gallery
CoSo Artist's Gallery • 158 • art gallery
Crush Boutique • 264 •

Dajuli Sparkles • 304 • jewelry
Diptyque • 123 • French perfumery
Domain Home Fashions • 7 • furniture
Dona Flor • 246 • home ceramics
Dorfman Jewelers • 24 • jewelry
Down to Basics • 249 • bedding
DTR Modern Galleries • 167 • art gallery
Erwin Pearl • 4 • jewelry
European Watch Co • 232 •
  watch repair and shop
Fairy Shop • 302 • Fairies, bubbles, incense,
  jewelry, you name it
Family Treasures Bookstore •
  books and magazines
Felicia's Cosmetics • 314 • cosmetics
Firefly Jewelry and Gifts • 270 •
  jewelry and gift shop
Firestone and Parson • 8 • antique jewelry
Fresh • 121 • bath products
Galerie d'Orsay • 33 • art gallery
Gallery NAGA • 67 • art gallery
Guido Frame Studio • 118 •
  ready-to-frame prints
The Guild of Boston Artists • 162 • art gallery
Hope • 302 • unique gift shop
Howard Yezerski Gallery • 14 • art gallery
International Poster Gallery • 205 •
  poster art gallery
Inviting Company • 213 • stationery
Judi Rotenberg Gallery • 130 • art gallery
Judy Ann Goldman Fine Art • 14 • art gallery
Kiehl's • 112 • beauty products
Kitchen Arts • 161 • kitchen tools
Kitty World • 279 • Hello Kitty heaven
Knit and Needlepoint • 11 •
  crafts and sewing supplies

Boston Convention & Exhibition Center

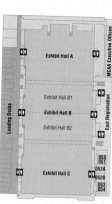

EXHIBIT LEVEL

- Exhibit Hall A
- MCAA Executive Offices
- Exhibit Hall B1
- Exhibit Hall B
- Exhibit Hall B2
- East Registration
- Loading Docks
- Exhibit Hall C

050
051
052A
052B
053
054

MAP 10

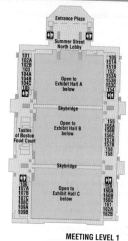

MEETING LEVEL 1

Entrance Plaza
Summer Street North Lobby

101
102A
102B
103
104A
104B
104C
105

Open to Exhibit Hall A below

Skybridge

Open to Exhibit Hall B below

Tastes of Boston Food Court

Skybridge

106
107A
107B
107C
108C
109A
109B

Open to Exhibit Hall C below

105
151A
151B
152
153A
153B
153C
154

155
156A
156B
156C
157A
157B
158
158

159
160
169A
160B
160C
161
162A
162B

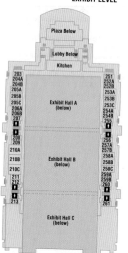

MEETING LEVEL 2

Plaza Below
Lobby Below
Kitchen

203
204A
204B
205A
205B
205C
206A
206B
207
208
209
210A
210B
210C
211
212
213

Exhibit Hall A (below)

Exhibit Hall B (below)

Exhibit Hall C (below)

251
252A
252B
253A
253B
253C
254A
254B
255
256
257A
257B
258A
258B
258C
259A
259B
260
261

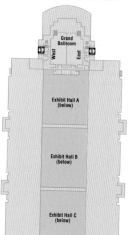

BALLROOM LEVEL

Grand Ballroom
West   East

Exhibit Hall A (below)

Exhibit Hall B (below)

Exhibit Hall C (below)

eneral Information

Map:	10
dress:	415 Summer St,
	Boston, MA 02210
one:	617-954-2000
:	617-954-2299
osites:	massconvention.com
	www.advantageboston.com

verview

:ook longer than expected to complete (what esn't in this town?) and was plagued by cost erruns and contractor squabbling, but the Boston nvention & Exhibition Center finally opened in e 2004. In our humble opinion, it was worth the it. Designed by noted architect Rafael Viñoly, e BCEC, which stands near Fort Point Channel Summer Street (about a half-mile from South ation), is a stunning addition to the South Boston terfront landscape.

t simply, the BCEC is gargantuan. With 516,000 uare feet of contiguous exhibition space, 160,000 uare feet of flexible meeting space, more than meeting rooms, and a 40,000-square-foot grand llroom, the building covers an overall area of 1.7 llion square feet. The BCEC now holds the coveted le of New England's Largest Man-Made Space and big enough to hold 16 football fields.

e new complex is the centerpiece of the city's itiative to attract more convention business to oston. As the old real estate mantra goes, it's all out "location, location, location," and a prime lling point for the BCEC is its proximity to both uth Station and Logan Airport. Only two miles om Logan, the BCEC is closer to its city airport than e convention center of any other American city.

Services

he BCEC is used for large-scale conferences, eetings, and exhibitions. To schedule an event nd be assigned a personal coordinator, contact e sales department at 617-954-2411 or sales@ assconvention.com.

atering services at the BCEC are provided by Levy estaurants. If you are planning a catered event, ontact Levy at 617-954-2382.

How to Get There—Driving

The BCEC is easy to reach from the Mass Pike (I-90). From the Pike, take Exit 25 (South Boston). Turn right onto Congress Street, then right onto D Street, then the second right onto Summer Street. The BCEC will be immediately on the left. It's hard to miss.

From the south, take I-93 N, get off at Exit 20, follow the signs to I-90 E and Exit 25. Follow the directions above.

From the north, take I-93 S, get off at Exit 23 (Purchase Street/South Station), proceed straight onto Purchase Street at the end of the exit ramp, and take a left onto Summer Street at South Station. Drive about a mile down the road to D Street and make a right.

Parking

If you must drive, you'll probably be dropping your car in a garage or fenced parking lot. The establishments listed below are the closest to the BCEC.

LAZ Parking• 10 Necco St, 617-426-1556
Fitz-Inn Auto Parks• 30-60 Necco St, 617-426-1556
Farnsworth Parking Garage• 17-31 Farnsworth St, 617-737-8161
Stanhope Garage• 338 Congress St, 617-338-5657
Stanhope Garage• 381 Congress St, 617-426-5326
Fanpier Parking Lots• 28 Northern Ave, 617-737-0910
Transpark• 390 Congress St, 617-737-3363
Transpark• 25 Northern Ave, 617-451-7732

How to Get There—Mass Transit

The Silver Line stops at the BCEC (alight at the World Trade Center stop, escalate to the top entrance, and traverse the bridge). To connect to the Silver Line from points other than Logan Airport, take the T's Red Line to South Station. The BCEC is only a few hundred yards away from South Station, so if you want to stretch your legs, take a stroll across Fort Point Channel instead of transferring to the Silver Line.

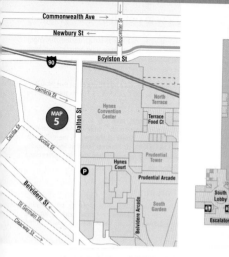

PLAZA LEVEL

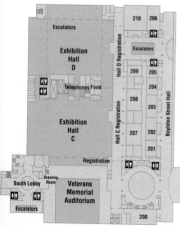

SECOND LEVEL

THIRD LEVEL

General Information

Map:	5
Address:	900 Boylston St, Boston, MA 02115
Phone:	617-954-2000
Websites:	massconvention.com
	www.advantageboston.com

Overview

The John B. Hynes Veterans Memorial Convention Center is a relatively small center, with just 176,480 square feet of exhibit space, a 25,000-square-foot ballroom, and 38 meeting rooms. The Hynes is conveniently located in Back Bay with many hotels, historical sites, and tourist attractions within close proximity. Only a short walk from the Green Line's Hynes Convention Center stop.

Once the big name in town for would-be conventioneers, the Hynes Convention Center now plays second fiddle to the Boston Convention and Exhibition Center (see page 204). Because the Hynes adjoins the Prudential complex and sits in the midst of a few thousand hotel rooms, it continues to attract convention business, focusing on mid-size meetings (like the American Association of Immunologists and the National Council of Teachers of Mathematics) while letting the biggest fish (like the International Boston Seafood Show) swim to the Southie Starship.

Services

The Hynes is used for conferences, meetings, exhibitions, and most other events where groups of people gather. (Word to the wise: Stay far, far away during CollegeFest.) To schedule an event and be assigned a personal coordinator, contact the sales department by phone at 617-954-2411, or by email sales@massconvention.com.

Catering services at the Hynes are provided by Levy Restaurants. If you are planning a catered event, contact Levy at 617-954-2382.

How to Get There—Driving

The Hynes is only four miles from Logan Airport. Two major roadways, I-93 and the Mass Pike (I-90), will deliver you close to the venue. From I-93, take Exit 26 (Storrow Drive). Follow Storrow Drive for about two miles to the Fenway/Kenmore exit and head towards Fenway. Continue to the first set of lights and merge left onto Boylston Street.

From the Mass Pike, take Exit 22 (Prudential/Copley Place), stay left as you exit, and turn onto Huntington Avenue. At the next set of lights (Belvidere Street), take a right, follow the curve, and bear right onto Dalton Street. At the lights, turn right onto Boylston Street.

The main entrance to the Hynes is at 900 Boylston Street and is easily accessible to taxis and buses via an access lane, which is set apart from Boylston Street.

Parking

There are numerous parking garages within a three-block walk of the Hynes, totaling more than 4,400 spaces. There is metered parking available around the Hynes and adjacent streets, but these spots are hard to come by.

- **Prudential Center Parking Garage**, 800 Boylston St, 2–10 hours for $36, and the daily maximum is $39. 617-236-3060.
- **Copley Place Parking Garage**, 100 Huntington Ave (corner of Huntington Ave & Dartmouth St), $9 for the first half hour with an increase of $4 for every additional half hour, $30 for 3–10 hours, but only $10 for three hours with validation. Maximum day rate is $35. 617-369-5025.
- **Boston Marriott Hotel Copley Place**, 100 Huntington Ave, self-parking $35 per day, valet parking, $41 per day. 617-236-5800.
- **Westin Copley Place Parking Garage**, 10 Huntington Ave, $16 for up to 1 hour; $24 for 1-3 hours, $32 for 3-5 hours, $36 for 5-8 hours, $46 for 8-24 hours, $48 for overnight. 617-262-9600.
- **Colonnade Hotel Parking Garage**, 120 Huntington Ave, $12 for the first hour, with a $4 increase every additional hour; $24 for 3–12 hours. $36 for overnight parking. 617-424-7000.
- **Back Bay Hilton Hotel Parking Garage**, 40 Dalton St, $5 for 1/2 hour, $12 for 1 hour, $20 for 1–2 hours. $22 for 2–3 hours, $24 for 3–12 hours, $35 for overnight parking, $39 for overnight parking with valet service. 617-236-1100.

How to Get There—Mass Transit

The subway stops just two blocks away from the Hynes. Take the Green Line (B, C, or D train) to the Hynes Convention Center stop. Once you get off the subway, exit at any entrance and follow signs to the Hynes.

The library, which overlooks Boston Harbor fr
windswept Columbia Point, was designed
architect I.M. Pei (who also designed the Christ
Science Center next to the Pru). The centerpiece
the complex is a nine-story concrete tower fron
by a glass-enclosed pavilion. The adjacent Steph
E. Smith Center, used for educational programs a
conferences, opened in 1991. Outside on the la
sits *Victura*, JFK's 26-foot sloop.

What's Inside

The JFK Library holds 8.4 million pages of president
papers, 180,000 still photographs, six million fe
of film and videotape, and 15,000 catalogu
museum objects. The library also houses the work
most comprehensive collection of the papers a
mementos of Ernest Hemingway, but they a
available to professional researchers only. If you are
scholar who seeks access to Papa's papers, check t
library's website to review the restrictive rules.

The library's Centennial Room displays rotati
exhibits showcasing the Kennedy White Hous
embrace of cultural values and the arts. Visito
can watch a 17-minute film about the Kenne
administration before entering the main exhi
space. On weekends, the 2 pm showing of t
introductory film is replaced by a 30-minute fi
about JFK's brother/attorney general, Robert
Kennedy. Visitors can also watch a 20-minute fi
about the Cuban Missile Crisis.

A museum café serves light meals and snacks fro
9 am to 5 pm, and the gift shop is open durir
visiting hours.

How to Get There—Driving

The JFK Library is off Morrissey Boulevard next
the UMass Boston campus. From the north or th
south, take I-93 to Exit 14 (Morrissey Boulevard) ar
follow the signs. From the west, take the Mass Pik
(I-90) east to the intersection with I-93. Take the ex
toward I-93 S, get off I-93 at Exit 14, and follow t
signs. The library provides free on-site parking.

How to Get There—Mass Transi

Take the T's Red Line to the JFK/UMass stop. A fre
shuttle bus runs between the T stop and the librar
Shuttle buses run every 20 minutes between 8 an
and 5 pm.

General Information

NFT Map:	32
Address:	Columbia Point
	Boston, MA 02125
Phone:	617-514-1600
Website:	www.jfklibrary.org
Hours:	9 am–5 pm daily except Thanksgiving, Christmas, and New Year's Day
	Research Library is open M–F 8:30–4:30 by appointment
Admission:	Adults $12, seniors and students $10, children $9, free for children 12 and under

Overview

The John F. Kennedy Library and Museum, dedicated
to our 35th president on October 20, 1979, houses
25 multimedia exhibits examining the life and work
of JFK, his administration, his family, and his legacy.
The library is one of thirteen presidential libraries
administered by the National Archives and Records
Administration, a federal government agency.
The library draws approximately 200,000 visitors
each year.

General Information

Cape Cod Chamber of Commerce:
508-362-3225; www.capecodchamber.org
Wellfleet Bay Wildlife Sanctuary:
508-349-2615; www.massaudbon.org/Nature_
Connection/Sanctuaries/Wellfleet/index.php
Cape Cod National Seashore Salt Pond Visitor Center:
508-349-3785; www.nps.gov/caco

Overview

Thanks to the eternal appeal of picturesque beaches, fried seafood, and miniature golf, Cape Cod is one of New England's most popular getaway destinations. Separated from mainland Massachusetts by the Cape Cod Canal, the region is located on the portion of the state that looks like a strong, flexing arm. There are only two roads that cross the canal, both via bridge; those Cape Cod Canal Tunnel stickers on locals' cars are just a sly hand played on the out-of-towners.

The Cape is composed of 15 towns, with a permanent population of roughly 230,000 that swells to over 550,000 in the summer months. The islands of Martha's Vineyard and Nantucket are not officially part of Cape Cod, but are generally considered the same destination region. Each town has its own character: Bustling and bawdy Provincetown is home to a large and proud gay community, while Falmouth is a more tranquil, wooded locale.

Highlights and Essentials:

Beaches—With a total of 559.6 miles of coastline, the Cape is perhaps most well-known for its beaches, many of which are open to the public for a modest daily parking fee. The northern ocean water resists warming though, so swimming is generally, let's say, refreshing.

Seafood—Fried clams, twin lobsters, steamers, baked stuffed quahogs...need we say more?

Christmas Tree Shops—The merchandise sold at this thriving retail chain can be best described as discount "stuff." The company has expanded beyond its Cape Cod origins, but there is no better place to go when you need picture frames, beach toys, or souvenir tchotchkes.

Miniature Golf—The Cape has elevated mini-golf landscaping to a fine art. Whether you prefer putting in a serene garden setting or braving darkened caves in a pirate-inspired golf adventure, Cape Cod has something for you.

Lighthouses—If you have time to visit a lighthouse or two, we recommend the Nobska Point Lighthouse at Woods Hole, an oft-photographed white tower at the southwestern tip of Cape Cod, the Highland (Cape Cod) Lighthouse in North Truro, or the Chatham Lighthouse on the southeastern corner of the Cape.

Whale Watches—Hop aboard a whale watch voyage out of Woods Hole, Hyannis, or Provincetown to experience the truly breathtaking phenomenon of cruising alongside some of the world's largest and most powerful creatures.

The Towns

The Cape, about 70 miles in length, is often divided into three regions:

The Upper Cape—The first area you reach after crossing the canal, the Upper Cape includes the towns of Falmouth, Mashpee, Sandwich, and Bourne. For the best views and smoothest journey, avoid the highways and take surface routes, such as 28A, that take you close to the water. Film buffs might consider a visit to Woods Hole, where part of the movie Jaws was filmed.

The Mid Cape—Continuing eastward, the next area you will reach includes Dennis, Yarmouth, and Barnstable, a town containing seven villages: Hyannis, Osterville, Centerville, Cotuit, West Barnstable, Barnstable Village, and Marstons Mills. Almost 70% of the Cape's permanent population resides in the Hyannis area, so the downtown remains busy throughout the year, and it is about the only place in the area to find such national chains as Barnes and Noble or Old Navy. If such conventional commercialism isn't on your vacation itinerary, take the Old King's Highway (Route 6A) to stay in the Cape mood.

The Outer Cape—Home of the peaceful Cape Cod National Seashore, Nickerson State Park, and the quiet towns of Brewster, Orleans, Eastham, Wellfleet, Chatham, Harwich, and Truro, it's difficult to imagine the spectacle sitting at the tip of the Outer Cape: Provincetown. At land's end sits one of the most "out" towns, where gay couples are as plentiful as seagulls, and the prevailing aesthetic can best be described as "flamboyant." After a day in the sun, cruise into P-town for a night of revelry. Gay or straight, the town knows how to party. For full effect, visit during Carnival in August. More information is available at www.provincetown.com.

The Islands—Martha's Vineyard and Nantucket each possess a distinct feel. Martha's Vineyard is known for great beaches, ocean vistas, and the annual (and controversial) Monster Shark Tournament. It's even better known for its well-heeled rich folk and the Kennedy Compound. Nantucket, only three and a half by fourteen miles, is a quaint New England destination where tourists roam the cobble-stoned streets year-round. In addition to shops and galleries, the downtown is home to the Nantucket Whaling Museum. The best way around the island is to rent a moped or a bicycle but remember to pack a lunch if you head to the beaches because there are no restaurants or snack bars.

The Outdoors

Sculpted dunes, haunting marshlands, and miles of hiking trails make the Cape an ideal area for outdoor exploration. If the water calls, you can splash about at one of the Cape's many bay or ocean beaches, take a boat out to sea, dive or snorkel in the bay, canoe or kayak, parasail, kiteboard, or enjoy one of the whale- or seal-watching excursions offered.

Flora and fauna enthusiasts come here to explore the lush plant and animal life at the Cape's many sanctuaries. The Audubon Society's Wellfleet Bay Wildlife Sanctuary is the only sanctuary with a visitor's center. It boasts 1,000 acres of woodlands, wetlands, and grasslands that attract an exciting variety of wildlife, including songbirds and shorebirds. Five miles of scenic trails wind through

143

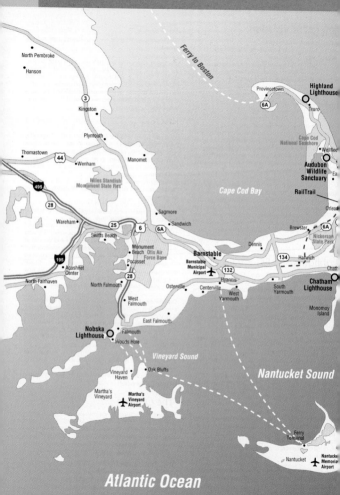

North Pembroke

Hanson

3

Kingston

Plymouth

Thomastown

44

Wenham

Manomet

Miles Standish
Monument State Res

495

28

Wareham

25

Swifts Beach

195

Acushnet
Center

North Fairhaven

6

Sagmore

6A   Sandwich

Monument
Beach   Otis Air
Force Base
Pocasset

28

North Falmouth

West
Falmouth

East Falmouth

Nobska
Lighthouse

Falmouth

Woods Hole

Vineyard Sound

Vineyard
Haven

Oak Bluffs

Martha's
Vineyard

Martha's
Vineyard
Airport

Atlantic Ocean

Ferry to Boston

Provincetown

6A

Highland
Lighthouse

Truro

Cape Cod
National Seashore

Wellfleet

Audubon
Wildlife
Sanctuary

Ea

Cape Cod Bay

RailTrail

Orleans

Brewster

6A

Nickerson
State Park

Dennis

134

Harwich

Barnstable

Barnstable
Municipal
Airport

132

Hyannis

Osterville   Centerville

West
Yarmouth

South Yarmouth

Chatham
Lighthouse

Chatt

Monomoy
Island

Nantucket Sound

Ferry
Terminal

Nantucket

Nantucke
Memorial
Airport

various habitats, while the newly renovated Nature
[cen]ter includes "green" elements such as solar heating and
[co]mposting toilets. Inside the nature center, you'll find two
[1]0-gallon aquariums that feature the underwater worlds of
[the] salt marsh and tidal flats. Other sanctuaries on the Cape
[inc]lude Long Pasture near Barnstable, Skunknett River near
[Cen]terville, Sampson's Island (accessible only by private boat
[fr]om local marinas and town landings), and Ashumet Holly
[nea]r Falmouth. The Cape Cod National Seashore Salt Pond
[Vis]itor center in Eastham offers guided tours and nature walks
[thr]ough the salt marshes.

[Mon]omoy Island, established in 1944 as a National Wildlife
[Ref]uge, is a barrier island that sits ten miles south of Chatham.
[It i]s prime habitat for migratory birds and a seal population
[th]at has grown in recent years. It is not uncommon to sit on
[a b]uset beach to the north and see seals swimming regularly
[al]ong the shoreline, which wasn't the case ten years ago.
[Mon]omoy has hiking trails and bird watching opportunities
[as] well as commercial boat tours for seal-watching. Check out
[ww]w.fws.gov/northeast/monomoy.

Sports

[Ca]pe Cod is an ideal location for sport fishing. Charters and
[to]urs are available and, for those looking to have a little fun on
[the] water, ships such as the Yankee offer party cruises, perfect
[for] those who hate lugging around a heavy cooler. Be warned:
[dr]inking and waves are not always the best combo.

[Go]lf is also popular here. There are a dozen or so courses
[in] the Cape, varying in price, size, and level of difficulty.
[De]nnis Pines and Dennis Highlands are two highly-respected
[mu]nicipal courses where a challenging game can be had for a
[rea]sonable price, and Highland Links in Truro is perched atop
[she]er bluffs that overlook the ocean.

[Hi]king is another favorite pastime in the area, with free trails
[in]cluding the epic 22-mile RailTrail at Cape Cod National Park.
[Th]e trail runs along the bed of a defunct railroad (hence the
[na]me) from Dennis (get on at Route 134 just south of Exit 9
[fr]om Route 6) to the South Wellfleet General Store.

[Die]hard baseball fans shouldn't miss the 104-year-old Cape
[Co]d League, where top college athletes are recruited to play
[in] the summer, many of whom go on to the majors. Thurman
[Mu]nson, "Nomah" Garciaparra, Jason Varitek, and other stars
[on]ce played for one of the league's ten teams. Attending one
[of] their early evening games is what summer is all about.
[Br]ing your beach chair, grab a hot dog, and watch the little
[ki]ds scramble for foul balls.

Arts and Culture

[Alt]hough best-known for its natural splendor, Cape Cod also
[bo]asts a thriving arts community. Every summer, the Cape
[Co]d Melody Tent in Hyannis hosts popular music and comedy
[ac]ts ranging from Willie Nelson to Lewis Black. In Dennis, the
[Ca]pe Playhouse mounts theatrical productions such as Guys
[an]d Dolls and Thoroughly Modern Millie.

[Ga]lleries, studios, specialty museums, and whimsical artisan
[sh]ops are to be found on almost every corner. For help
[na]vigating, download the Cape Cod, Nantucket, or Martha's
[V]ineyard ArtsApp from the Cape Cod Chamber of Commerce
[we]bsite (www.capecodchamber.org/artsapp). For something

a little more analog, to locate a copy of Arts and Artisans
Trails, a book featuring self-guided tours of the Cape and
Islands that highlight the best of the area's arts scene.

Ever since Henry David Thoreau penned Cape Cod, the region
has also been the full-time or summer home of a number
of notable authors. Literary greats Norman Mailer and Kurt
Vonnegut, and the mystery maven Mary Higgins Clark have
been among the Cape's more notable literary residents over
the years.

If you aspire to join this tradition, check out the Fine Arts
Work Center in Provincetown, where summer workshops
in painting, drawing, and writing could help you find your
hidden muse.

How to Get There

By Car: The only two driving routes onto Cape Cod are via the
overburdened Bourne and Sagamore bridges. This limited
access has traditionally resulted in multi-mile gridlock on
Friday evenings and Saturday mornings. The Sagamore Rotary
has recently been replaced with a direct ramp known as the
flyover, intended to tame the traffic. Plan to travel outside of
the peak times and slowdowns should be minimal. Once on the
Cape, most places are easily drivable, though downtown areas
such as Hyannis and Provincetown can get a bit tangled up.

By Ferry: Avoid traffic and cut down on gas expenditures by
hopping a ferry to Provincetown or on the Islands. Bringing along
a car or bike generally increases the fare, but the price may
be a bargain if you have limited patience for the traffic that
driving across the Canal can entail. Keep your eyes peeled for
Secretary of State John Kerry in the summertime. At 6'4", he's
hard to miss.

Bay State Cruise Company • 617-748-1428 •
www.boston-ptown.com
Boston-Provincetown. May–October.
Round-trip fare: $46 on weekend excursion ferry, $62-$83 on
daily fast ferry. $12 for bikes.

Boston Harbor Cruises Provincetown Fast Ferry •
617-227-4321 • www.bostonharborcruises.com
Boston-Provincetown. May–October.
Round-trip fare: $63-$83. $7 for bikes.

Hy-Line Cruises • 800-492-8082 • hylinecruises.com
Hyannis-Martha's Vineyard. High-speed ferry,
April–October. Standard ferry, May–October.
Hyannis-Nantucket, High-speed ferry year-round.
Standard ferry, May–October.
Martha's Vineyard-Nantucket. June–September
Round-trip fare: $45-$77. $7 for bikes.

Island Queen Ferry • 508-548-4800 • www.islandqueen.com
Falmouth Harbor- Martha's Vineyard. June–September.
Round-trip fare: $8-$20. $8 for bikes.

Steamship Authority • 508-693-9130 •
http://steamshipauthority.com
Woods Hole-Martha's Vineyard. Year-round.
Hyannis-Nantucket, Year-round.
Woods Hole-Martha's Vineyard round-trip fare:
$8-$16. $8 for a bike. $85-$155 for a car.
Hyannis-Nantucket round-trip fare:
$34-$67. $14 for a bike. $280-$450 for a car.

Berklee College of Music

1. 130 Massachusetts Avenue
2. Berklee Performance Center
3. 150 Massachusetts Avenue
4. 155 Massachusetts Avenue
5. 171 Massachusetts Avenue
6. The Berklee Bookstore
7. 120 Belvidere Street
8. 19 Belvidere Street
9. 1140 Boylston Street
10. 22 The Fenway

11. 198 Hemingway Street
12. Boston ArchitecturaCenter
13. 921 Boylston Street
14. 264-270 Commonwealth Avenue
15. 100 Massachusetts Avenue
16. 168 Massachusetts Avenue
17. 899 Boylan Street
18. 867 Boylan Street
19. 855 Boylan Street

Commonwealth A

Commonwealth

Gloucester St

Hynes
Convention
Center

12

13   17

15

Cambria St

Hynes
Conventi
Cente

PAGE
138

1

Boylston St

6

2

3

Scotia St

St Cecilia St

Dalton St

7

9

Haviland St

4

Belvidere St

16   8

St Germain St

The Fenway

10

Stonehalm St

Norway St

5

Clearway St

Hemenway St

Edgerly Rd

Massachusetts Ave

MAP
5

Christian
Science
Center

Burbank St

Westland Ave

11

Huntington Av

Symphony Rd

Symphony

General Information

T Map: 5
dress: 1140 Boylston St, Boston, MA 02215
one: 617-266-1400
ebsite: www.berklee.edu

Overview

rklee is the largest independent music college in
e world and calls itself the "premier institution for
e study of contemporary music." Founded in 1945
 pianist and MIT-trained engineer Lawrence Berk,
e school became accredited in 1973. Berklee offers
ur-year degrees as well as diploma programs that
ow students to forego the liberal arts and focus
clusively on music. Facilities include more than 250
vate practice rooms. In addition to performance,
udents study Music Business/Management, Music
ucation, and Music Therapy. During the summer,
e school offers specialized programs including
rklee in Los Angeles.

e college enrolls close to 4,000 students, with the
ghest percentage (about 26%) of international
udents of any college in the United States from
ore than 70 different countries. The student body
 a funky, diverse lot, with many musicians from
pan, Korea, Germany, Switzerland, and Brazil.
ey tend to congregate on Mass Ave, particularly
tside the Berklee Performance Center where
draggled musical geniuses stand around with
eir instruments. Tracy Bonham, Melissa Etheridge,
tty Larkin, Branford Marsalis, Howard Shore, and
nee Mann are among Berklee's notable alumni.
rthermore, Berklee was the first college to
cognize the guitar as a principal instrument and
velop a curriculum for it back in the '60s.

Tuition

rrently, tuition fees hover around $35,000 and
using will run you an extra $17,000 or so per year.

Sports

There are no college-level athletics at Berklee,
but student clubs do offer soccer, basketball,
softball, and yoga, among others. Nearby fitness
facilities, including the YMCA, the Tennis and
Racquet Club, and Boston Kung-Fu Tai-Chi Institute
offer discounted rates for students. Much more
popular than sports are the 350-plus student music
ensembles in an impressive range of styles.

Culture on Campus

Housed in the historic Fenway Theater, the 1,220-seat
Berklee Performance Center (BPC) stands as one of
the finest concert halls on the East Coast. Located
at 136 Massachusetts Avenue near the intersection
with Boylston Street, the BPC offers numerous
performances by major concert promoters as well
as faculty and student concerts throughout the year.
To attend a performance, check out the Event
Calendar at www.berklee.edu/BPC or call the box
office at 617-747-2261.

Departments

Admissions 617-747-2047
Financial Aid . . . . 617-747-2274 or 800-538-3844
Registrar. 617-747-2240
Housing 617-747-2292
Alumni Relations. 617-747-2236
Berklee Performance Center. 617-747-2474
Library. 617-747-2258

Colleges & Universities · **Boston College**

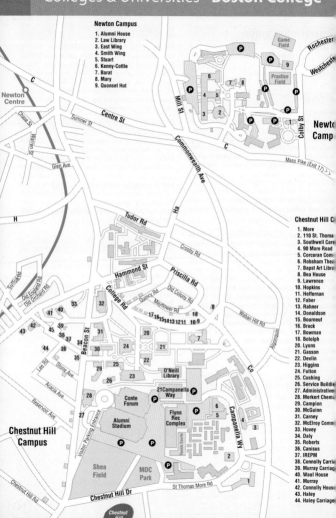

Newton Campus

1. Alumni House
2. Law Library
3. East Wing
4. Smith Wing
5. Stuart
6. Kenny-Cottle
7. Barat
8. Mary
9. Quonset Hut

Chestnut Hill C

1. More
2. 110 St. Thoma
3. Southwell Care
4. 90 More Road
5. Corcoran Comm
6. Robsham Thea
7. Bapst Art Libra
8. Bea House
9. Lawrence
10. Hopkins
11. Heffernan
12. Faber
13. Rahner
14. Donaldson
15. Bourneuf
16. Brock
17. Bowman
18. Botolph
19. Lyons
20. Gasson
21. Devlin
22. Higgins
23. Fulton
24. Cushing
25. Service Buildin
26. Administrative
27. Merkert Chema
28. Campion
29. McGuinn
30. Carney
31. McElroy Comm
32. Hovey
33. Daly
34. Roberts
35. Canisius
36. IREPM
37. Connolly Carria
38. Murray Carriag
39. Waul House
40. Murray
41. Connolly House
42. Haley
43. Haley Carriage

Colleges & Universities · **Boston College**

General Information

Main Campus:	140 Commonwealth Ave, Chestnut Hill, MA 02467
Newton Campus:	885 Centre St, Newton Center, MA 02459
Phone:	617-552-8000
Website:	www.bc.edu

Overview

It all began one day in Paris in 1534, when a group of students at the University of Paris got together and decided to combine their devotion to God with their commitment to bettering society. They called themselves the Society of Jesus, or the Jesuits. A few centuries later, in 1863, three Jesuits opened a college in the South End and cleverly named it Boston College. The college began with just 22 students, but even then the Jesuit profs envisioned a grander institution that would integrate intellectual development with religious and ethical growth.

Over the past century-and-a-half, the school has drifted a bit, both geographically and ethically. Once located in Boston proper, the school now sits six miles to the west, sprawling over 117 acres in Chestnut Hill and another 40 in Newton. And while the college is still officially Jesuit through and through, today's 14,500 undergraduates and graduate students students come from 80 countries and all 50 states and all religions and creeds.

In the past BC perhaps had a bit of a Doug Flutie-style chip on its shoulders, what with Boston's competitive and crowded academic scene. Often overlooked is BC's excellent academic reputation. Its eight colleges and schools offer degree programs in more than fifty fields of study, and the school continues to be ranked as one of the best universities in the country by *U.S. News & World Report*.

Tuition

Currently, undergraduate tuition, room and board and fees amount to around $57,000.

Sports

Supporting 31 varsity and 38 club and intramural sports, Boston College boasts a diverse and strong athletic department. The varsity teams all compete at the NCAA Division I level. The BC Eagles football program is strong and the team continues to reach bowl games. The biggest game every year is against Notre Dame. The men's hockey team has been perennially successful, winning a national championship in 2001 and losing in the semifinals of the Frozen Four in 2004. In 2008 and 2012, however, Boston College won, much to BU's chagrin. In 2010 Boston College won the Beanpot, which is a hockey tournament amongst Boston colleges.

Culture on Campus

The Robsham Theater Arts Center is Boston College's creative center. Built in 1981, the theater seats 591 people. The building also includes a black box theater that seats 150–200 people. The three main departments housed in the facility are the Department of Theater Arts, the Robsham Dance and Theater Company, and the Boston Liturgical Dance Ensemble. The university presents four faculty-directed and two student-directed productions each year, and 20 musical and dance groups perform throughout the year. BC also has its share of improv and sketch comedy troupes including one that puts on comedic, part-improv murder mysteries once per semester. Worth checking out to get a better sense of the school's culture is the (now archived) website for "The BC" (the-bc.com), a send-up of "The OC" that is set at the Heights (local-speak for BC's Chestnut Hill campus). Download one of the show's commercials such as "Jon Bon Jesuits" for an hysterical, rocking-good time.

Another source of culture at Boston College is the McMullen Museum of Art. Located on the first floor of Devlin Hall, the museum is housed in one of the many Neo-Gothic buildings on the main campus. Aside from its notable permanent collection, the museum has frequent exhibitions of international and scholarly importance from all periods and cultures. The museum is free and open to the public. Hours: Mon–Fri 11 am–4 pm and Sat–Sun 12 pm–5 pm.

Departments

Undergraduate Admissions	617-552-3100
A&S Graduate Admissions	617-552-3265
Carroll Graduate School of Management	617-552-3920
Connell School of Nursing	617-552-4928
Law School Admissions	617-552-4350
Lynch School of Education	617-552-4214
Graduate School of Social Work	617-552-4024
Student Services	617-552-3300
Athletic Departments and Tickets	617-552-GoBC
O'Neill Library	617-552-4470

General Information

NFT Map: 16
Address: One Silber Way, Boston, MA 02215
Phone: 617-353-2000
Website: www.bu.edu

Overview

If you really want to go to school in Boston, BU is the school for you. Consisting of a strip of buildings along Commonwealth Avenue, BU's campus doesn't win any points for style, beauty, or landscape architecture (since that would require having a clearly defined landscape). Aside from several thousand red banners on the lampposts that say "Boston University," and a larger than usual concentration of jaywalking young folk along Comm Ave, there's little indication that you've entered BU's domain.

The fourth-largest private university in the country, the school's "campus" is the learning center for all students and the residence of many of its 30,000 undergraduates and grad students. The upshot of the ill-defined BU campus is that its students are truly living in the city. BU students make the best of the little green space they have. "The Beach," a strip of greenery on the inbound side of Storrow Drive (which runs along the Charles), is a springtime hotspot for socializing and sunbathing.

When the university was founded in 1839, it was intended to be a theological school for ministers of the Methodist Episcopal Church. As the years went by, the university expanded its curriculum in order to accommodate the needs and interests of its growing student population. Today, there are 11 schools and colleges and over 250 different degree programs. Boston University students represent all 50 states, as well as 140 countries. BU also holds the distinction of having the most property owned by a non-government institution in the City of Boston. The university also boasts a bevy of outspoken alumni

including Howard Stern, Bill O'Reilly, and Rosie O'Donn (who didn't graduate).

Longtime president and infamous curmudgeon Jo Silber stepped down in 1996 after more than thir years of leading the school to wherever he pleased. replacement, former NASA chief Daniel Goldin, was call off the job even before he began his first day due conflicting ideas about how the university should be r Goldin said he took the job on the condition that Sil would not occupy a seat on the board of trustees. T Executive Committee balked at this stipulation and, af a little mud was slung, Goldin's termination was signe thereby embarrassing the university in national headlin Following the reign of an interim president since t resignation of Jon Westling in 2002, BU's tenth and curre president, Robert A. Brown, was inaugurated to the p in April 2006.

Tuition

Undergraduate tuition costs run at about $51,000 per ye with room board and fees. Graduate student tuition, fe and expenses vary by college.

Sports

Notwithstanding the termination of the universi football program in 1997, the Terriers have quite impressive athletics department. With 24 NCAA Divis I varsity sports, Boston University provides a r environment for sports lovers. The department prid itself on its equal emphasis on women's and men's vars sports. The men's varsity ice hockey team is, by far, the m popular sports team at BU, with the most enthusias community support. There is fierce competition ev year for the Beanpot—the "New England Invitatior tournament. BU has won the Beanpot 29 times, wi Boston College being their biggest rival for the title. T university's hockey and basketball teams play in Agganis Arena, a spiffy new facility that also hosts ot sporting and entertainment events.

Culture on Campus

The first university to have a music program, BU remains committed to the arts. The Boston University Art Gallery is located at 855 Commonwealth Avenue. Although the gallery has no permanent collection, the architecture of the building is like an exhibit unto itself. Alluding to both the Classical and the Medieval, the columns that adorn the facade are a rare beauty and have attracted many people on that basis alone. You would never guess that the building is actually a converted Buick dealership. If this piques your interest, you'll be happy to learn that the gallery is open and free to the public, but only during the academic school year: Tues–Fri 10 am–5 pm and Sat–Sun 1 pm–5 pm.

Departments

Undergraduate Admissions	617-353-2300
Graduate Admissions	617-353-2696
Graduate School of Management	617-353-9720
School of Medicine	617-638-4630
School of Law	617-353-3100
School of Education	617-353-4237
School of Public Health	617-638-4640
School of Social Work	617-353-3765
Athletic Department and Ticket Office	617-353-GoBU
Mugar Memorial Library	617-353-3732

Building Legend

1. 1019 Commonwealth Ave (major residence)
2. Case Athletic Center
3. West Campus (major residence)
4. Office of Housing
5. Fitness and Recreation Center
6. 10 Buick St (major residence)
7. Center for English Language and Orientation Programs
8. Comptroller; Financial Assistance; Registrar; Student Health Services
9. College of General Studies
10. College of Fine Arts; University Art Gallery
11. School of Hospitality Administration; Metropolitan College Academic departments and other programs
12. Boston University Academy
13. George Sherman Union; Dean of Students; Student Activities Center; Howard Thurman Center
14. Mugar Memorial Library; University Information Center
15. School of Law
16. Metropolitan College; Summer Term
17. School of Theology; University Professors Program
18. Marsh Chapel
19. Photonics Center
20. College of Arts and Sciences
21. School of Social Work
22. Graduate School of Arts and Sciences
23. The Tsai Performance Art Center
24. The Castle
25. Warren Towers (major residence)
26. Office of Information Technology
27. College of Engineering
28. Sargent College of Health and Rehabilitation Sciences
29. College of Communication
30. School of Education
31. Morse Auditorium
32. Biological and Physics Research Buildings
33. The Towers (major residence)
34. Chancellor's Office; President's Office; Provost's Office; Development and Alumni Relations
35. School of Management
36. 575 Commonwealth Ave (major residence)
37. Metcalf Science Center
38. Admissions Reception Center
39. Kenmore Classroom Building
40. Shelton Hall (major residence)
41. International Students and Scholars Office; Career Services; Disability Services; Judicial Affairs & Student Safety
42. University Computers
43. Barnes & Noble at BU; Asian Archeology & Cultural History
44. Hotel Commonwealth
45. Miles Standish Hall (major residence)
46. Danielsen Hall (major residence) (off map)
47. Agganis Arena

General Information

NFT Maps: 3 & 6
Address: 120 Boylston St, Boston, MA 02116
Phone: 617-824-8500
Website: www.emerson.edu

Overview

Emerson College is the country's only comprehensive college or university dedicated solely to communication and the arts in a liberal arts context. In close proximity to Boston's Theater District, Emerson is near all of the city's major media interests. Founded as a small oratory school in 1880, Emerson has expanded its curriculum over the years to include other forms of communication. Today, Emerson specializes in communications, marketing, communication sciences and disorders, journalism, the performing arts, the visual and media arts, and writing, literature, and publishing. Emerson also operates semester-study programs in Los Angeles and the Netherlands. There is also a thriving continuing education department, recently renamed the Department of Professional Studies and Special Programs, which offers—besides communications classes—certificate programs in media, publishing, and screenwriting.

The college enrolls about 3,000 full-time undergraduates and 1,000 graduate students, many of whom can be found sporting funky haircuts and smoking outside Emerson buildings between classes. Students take pride in their award-winning radio station, WERS (88.9 FM). Most alumni go on to pursue careers in the communications and entertainment fields. Notable alumni include talk show host Jay Leno, actor Denis Leary, comedian Steven Wright, and entrepreneur and make-up artist Bobbi Brown.

Tuition

Undergraduate tuition fees are about $35,000. Room and board adds about $14,000. Add on books, service fees, activity fees, and personal expenses. Graduate student tuition, fees, and expenses vary by the number of credits taken.

Sports

Although Emerson does have an athletic department, it has never been one of the school's top priorities. Since most of the students attending Emerson College are interested primarily in the fields of communications and performing arts, sports are considered nothing more than a lighthearted diversion. Still, Emerson College sponsors 13 men's and women's varsity teams that compete in the NCAA's Division III.

Culture on Campus

Because Emerson considers itself an arts school, it takes great pride in its theater. The aptly named Majestic Theatre was built in 1903 as an opera house. In 2001, the college closed the theater temporarily for renovation and reopened its doors in 20[ ]. Today, the historic venue seats 1,200 people and has become an integral part of the campus. Not only does it provide a venue for all types of productions by Emerson students, it also serves the greater New England community. It hosts more operas than any other theater in New England and is the top stop for many touring dance companies. To visit the theater or check out a performance, go to the theater box office located at 219 Tremont Street in Boston or visit the website: cutlermajestic.org.

Departments

Undergraduate Admissions Office 617-824-86
Graduate Admissions Office 617-824-86
Majestic Theatre 617-824-86
Athletics Department 617-824-86
Fitness Center 617-824-86
Library 617-824-86

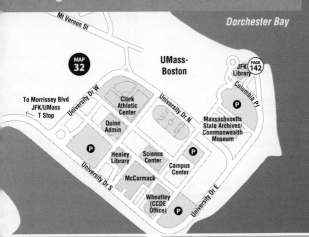

Mt Vernon St

Dorchester Bay

UMass-Boston

MAP 32

To Morrissey Blvd
JFK/UMass
T Stop

University Dr W

University Dr N

Clark Athletic Center

Quinn Admin

Healey Library

Science Center

University Dr S

McCormack

Campus Center

Wheatley (CCDE Office)

University Dr E

JFK Library PAGE 142

Columbia Pl

Massachusetts State Archives/ Commonwealth Museum

General Information

Map:	32
Address:	100 Morrissey Blvd, Boston, MA 02125
Phone:	617-287-5000
Website:	www.umb.edu

Overview

The University of Massachusetts Boston is one of five UMass campuses. The campus opened in 1982 when UMass acquired Boston State College. The university has been described as a "sensibly priced, high-quality college that provides excellent academic programs to people from all walks of life. UMass Boston aims "to bring technical, intellectual, and human resources to the community."

The school's most famous alum is Boston Mayor Thomas M. Menino. Not exactly renowned for his oratory skills, he is nevertheless a well respected champion of the low-income neighborhoods. Menino graduated from UMass Boston at the age of 45 in 1988 with a degree in community planning. UMass Boston's campus, which has been described as a "concrete jungle", is only three miles from downtown Boston and is pretty easy to reach by public transportation. (Take the Red Line to JFK/UMass Station, then jump on the shuttle buses, which run almost constantly.)

While on campus, be sure to check out the Campus Center—simply look for the most modern-looking (and attractive) building on campus. A graceful building featuring huge windows that overlook magnificent Boston Harbor, the Center makes it easy to forget that the rest of the campus is pockmarked by bomb-shelteresque architecture. Also, a trip to campus should always include a quick walk or drive over to the JFK Presidential Library, which shares Columbia Point Peninsula with UMASS Boston.

Tuition

Undergraduate tuition runs about $28,000 per year for outsiders, but around $14,000 for staties. Graduate tuition costs run at about $28,000 per year for out-of-towners and $14,000 for in-state residents.

Sports

UMass offers 14 varsity sports, including basketball, soccer, lacrosse, and ice hockey. All teams compete in the NCAA's Division III. The Beacon Fitness Center is open to all students and staff free of charge. The UMass teams are called the Beacons, carry the slogan "Follow the Light," and have been named All-Americans 64 times in seven sports. UMass Boston provides a community service program which offers, for free or at very low cost, the use of all athletic facilities and coaches to the general public.

Culture on Campus

Often considered a commuter-centric school, UMass Boston is nonetheless a mini-mecca of culture, offering everything from rampant community-service opportunities to myriad student-run publications. The current Performing Arts Department is actually a conglomerate of three previously separate theater arts, music, and dance departments. Music courses provide grounding in music theory, history, and performance. Private music lessons are also available for one credit. The college Jazz Band, Chamber Orchestra, and Chamber Singers all give public performances at the end of each semester.

Departments

Undergraduate Admissions	617-287-6100
Graduate Admissions	617-287-5700
Graduate College of Education	617-287-7600
College of Nursing & Health Sciences	617-287-7500
Performing Arts Department	617-287-5640
Athletic Department	617-287-7801
Healey Library	617-287-5900
Honors Program	617-287-5520
Campus Center	617-287-4800

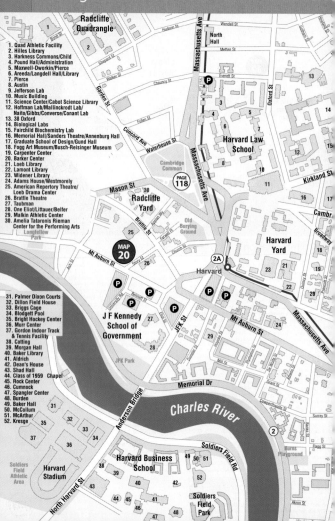

1. Quad Athletic Facility
2. Hilles Library
3. Harkness Commons/Child
4. Pound Hall/Administration
5. Maxwell-Dworkin/Pierce
6. Areeda/Langdell Hall/Library
7. Pierce
8. Austin
9. Jefferson Lab
10. Music Building
11. Science Center/Cabot Science Library
12. Hoffman Lab/Mallinckrodt Lab/
    Naito/Gibbs/Converse/Conant Lab
13. 38 Oxford
14. Biological Labs
15. Fairchild Biochemistry Lab
16. Memorial Hall/Sanders Theatre/Annenburg Hall
17. Graduate School of Design/Gund Hall
18. Fogg Art Museum/Busch-Reisinger Museum
19. Carpenter Center
20. Barker Center
21. Loeb Library
22. Lamont Library
23. Widener Library
24. Adams House/Westmorely
25. American Repertory Theatre/
    Loeb Drama Center
26. Brattle Theatre
27. Taubman
28. One Eliot/Littauer/Belfer
29. Malkin Athletic Center
30. Amelia Tataronis Rieman
    Center for the Performing Arts

31. Palmer Dixon Courts
32. Dillon Field House
33. Briggs Cage
34. Blodgett Pool
35. Bright Hockey Center
36. Murr Center
37. Gordon Indoor Track
    & Tennis Facility
38. Cotting
39. Morgan Hall
40. Baker Library
41. Aldrich
42. Dean's House
43. Shad Hall
44. Class of 1959 Chapel
45. Rock Center
46. Cumnock
47. Spangler Center
48. Burden
49. Baker Hall
50. McCollum
51. McArthur
52. Kresge

General Information

Map: 20
dress: University Hall, Cambridge, MA 02138
one: 617-495-1000
bsite: www.harvard.edu

Overview

I've probably heard quite a bit about Harvard. Chances
you associate it with academic excellence, cutting-
ge research, red brick, and students with at least two
man numerals after their names.

stereotype hits the nail at least partly on the head.
unded in 1636, Harvard remains the richest and most
ered university in the country (and perhaps even the
ld). True to myth, its pool of 19,000+ undergrads and
d students include children of royalty, famous actors,
s, heiresses, and an assortment of other fortunate sons
daughters. But the truth is that these folks are more
 exception than the rule. Harvard's deep pockets have
wed it to offer generous scholarships and increase the
ural and financial diversity of its student population
d to allow such great intellectuals like Conan O'Brien
ttend). The same loot also helps them net world-class
fessors in each of its 11 schools and colleges.

h the goal of properly housing and educating "the
t of the best" in all fields from arts and humanities to
iness and technology, Harvard is hungry for more than
 talented minds. The university continues to gobble
 land in Cambridge and across the river in Allston,
gruntling some locals.

haps Harvard needs more space for its livestock. A
ase coined to mock the local accent states that you
not "pahk the cah in Havahd Yahd," since automobile
fic is prohibited there. However, an old contract clause
ws each full professor to pasture one cow in the Yard.
stant faculty members are allowed a sheep. Luckily
Harvard, no professor in recent memory has taken
antage of this opportunity.

rly 2007, Harvard made news yet again by naming its
 female president, historian Drew G. Faust.

Tuition

dergraduate tuition, room, board, and college fees
ount to about $56,000. Graduate school tuition varies
 ending on the program.

Sports

etics at Harvard began around 1780, when a small
up of students began challenging each other to
stling matches, thereby starting an early version of
 t Club. Since then, the spirit of athletic competition
 remained integral to the Harvard experience.
vard introduced its crew team in 1844, and won its
 championship just two years later. Since then, the
's heavyweight and lightweight crew teams have

won 15 championships between them and the women's
lightweight crew team has won five championships.
Years ago, Harvard was a football powerhouse, always
ranked among the top ten in the nation. Harvard still
consistently tops the Ivy League, and games against the
likes of Yale continue to fill century-old Harvard Stadium
on fall afternoons. The men's tennis team has also been
a source of pride in the athletic department, consistently
producing top-class players, many of whom have gone
on to play professionally. In the fall of 2004, the team
captured its second consecutive Eastern College
Athletic Conference title.

Not all jocks are dumb: Since 1920, Harvard athletes have
netted 46 Rhodes Scholarships.

Not all nerds suck at sports: More than 100 Harvard
athletes have participated in the Olympics.

Culture on Campus

Harvard boasts four art museums (free every day after 4:30 pm
and from 10 am until noon on Saturdays), each showcasing
art from different parts of the world. The university also
runs an extensive music and theater program. Music department performances are held in the prestigious Sanders
Theater, renowned for its acoustics and design. Aside
from hosting most of the orchestral and choral performances by Harvard groups, Sanders Theatre is also a
popular venue for professional groups such as the Boston
Philharmonic, the Boston Chamber Music Society, and the
Boston Baroque.

Harvard's various dance troupes perform at the Amelia
Tataronis Rieman Center for the Performing Arts.

The country's only not-for-profit theater company
housing a resident acting company and an international
training conservatory, the American Repertory Theater
(A.R.T.) operates out of the Harvard University campus.

A building shaped suspiciously like "Linguo, the Grammar
Robot" of *Simpsons* fame houses the offices of the Harvard
Lampoon on Mt Auburn Street. Graduates of this famed
humor publication have gone on to work for *Saturday
Night Live*, *The Simpsons*, and *The Office*.

Departments

Undergraduate Admissions 617-495-1551
Graduate School of Arts and Sciences 617-495-1814
Graduate School of Education 617-495-0740
Kennedy School of Government 617-495-1100
Harvard Crimson 617-576-6565
Harvard Law School 617-495-3100
Harvard Medical School 617-432-1000
Harvard Business School 617-495-6000
Athletics Department Ticket Office 877-GO-HARVARD
                                             or 617-495-2211
Sanders Theatre 617-496-2222

(155)

General Information

NFT Maps: 26 & 27
Address: 77 Massachusetts Ave, Cambridge, MA 02139
Phone: 617-253-1000
Website: www.mit.edu

Overview

Just down the Chuck River from Harvard, MIT is one of the top tech schools in the world. The school's 1022 faculty and over 11,000 slide-rule-bearing graduate and undergraduate students inhabit a 168-acre "factory of learning" that features both neoclassical domes and some of the most aggressively modernist buildings in Boston (including the Stata Center, designed by world-renowned architect Frank Gehry).

MIT profs are infamous for assigning massive amounts of work, but some students can't seem to get enough of engineering, spending their downtime planning and executing "hacks,"

technically elaborate pranks. A frequent target of hackers is M Great Dome. In 1994, a replica of an MIT police cruiser appea atop the dome. In 1996, it was adorned with a gigantic bea cap complete with a fully functioning propeller. Just before release of Star Wars Episode One: The Phantom Menace, stude decorated the dome to look like the robot R2-D2. Harvar another frequent target of hackers. During a 1990 Harvard-football game, players and spectators alike were surprised w an 8.5' x 3.5' rocket-propelled banner with the letters MIT spr up from under the end zone as Yale lined up to kick a field go

Tuition

Undergraduate tuition fees, room, and board total about $54,

Sports

Whoever said science nerds can't play sports was totally r. Nevertheless, they keep trying, posting moderate success in b Division II and III. Believe it or not, MIT actually boasts the lar

1. Pierce Laboratory
2. Fluid Dynamic Laboratory/ Dept of Mathematics
3. Maclaurin Buildings
4. Maclaurin Buildings
5. Pratt School
6. Eastman Laboratories
6B. Solvent Storage
7. Rogers Building
8. 21 Ames Street
9. Center for Advanced Educational Services
10. Maclaurin Building/Alumni Center
11. Homberg Building
12. 60 Vassar Street
12A. Waste Chemical Storage
13. Bush Building
14. Hayden Memorial Library
15. Wright Brothers Wind Tunnel
16. Dorrance Building
17. Dreyfus Building
24. CANES/Center for Nanofluids Technology ESG/Dept of Nuclear Science and Engineering
26. Compton Laboratories
32. Sloan Laboratories
33. State Center
33. Guggenheim Laboratory
34. EG & G Education Center
35. Sloan Laboratory
36. Fairchild Building

37. McNair Building
38. Fairchild Building
39. Brown Building
40. Lean Aerospace Initiative/ Fuel Cell Lab
41. Power Plant
42. Power Plant Annex
43. Cyclotron
44. Brain and Cognitive Sciences
48. Parsons Laboratory
50. Walker Memorial
51. Wood Sailing Pavilion
54. Green Building
56. Whitaker Building
57. MIT Alumni Pool
62. Alumni Houses: Munroe Hayden Wood
64. Alumni Houses: Walcott Bemis Goodale

66. Landau Building
68. Koch Biology Building
E1. Gray House
E2. Senior House
E15. Wiesner Building
E17. Mudd Building
E18. Ford Building
E19. Ford Building
E23. Health Services
E25. Whitaker College
E28. Publishing Services Bureau (PSB)/Reference Publications Office (RPO)
E33. Rinaldi Tile

E34. Earth Re
E38. Suffolk
E39. MIT Pre
E40. Muckle
E48. MIT Inv Compar
E51. Tang Ce
E52. Sloan Bu
E53. Hermar

West Campus

MAP 27

Briggs Field

Harry G Steinbrenner Stadium

Indoor Tennis Facility
W53

Barry Astroturf Field

...ber of NCAA-sponsored programs in the nation, and the
...hes and students have received numerous awards for sports
...ellence. The heavyweight crew squads and the men's cross-
...ntry and track teams have garnered accolades for the university.

...ulture on Campus

...time when art and technology are often indistinguishable,
...not hard to believe that MIT has a happening arts program,
... We highly recommend a visit to the MIT Museum.
...ographic images, scientific photographs, and mechanical
...ctures with names like "Untitled Fragile Machine" show just
... beautiful math-type stuff can be.

...Wiesner Building (designed by I.M. Pei and housing the
...ia Laboratory) opened in 1985 and was used, for much of a
...decade, to explore digital video and multimedia. The Media
... allows for interdisciplinary research, and the developing
...s of study is on how electronic information affects our daily
...—how we use it to think, express, and communicate ideas.
...y of the Media Lab's research projects are made possible

through corporate sponsorship, and the lab fosters a positive
relationship between academia and industry.

According to the MIT website, the Media Lab "houses a gigabit
fiber-optic plant that connects a heterogeneous network of
computers, ranging from fine-grained, embedded processors
to supercomputers." Unfortunately, in its role as an academic
research laboratory, the Media Lab is not able to accommodate
visits from the general public.

Departments

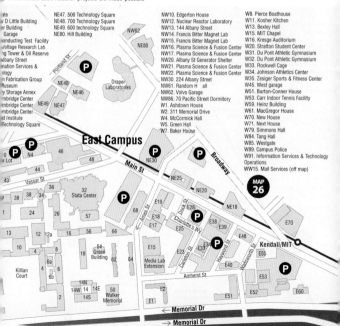

NE47. 500 Technology Square
NE48. 700 Technology Square
NE49. 600 technology Square
NE80. Hill Building

NW10. Edgerton House
NW12. Nuclear Reactor Laboratory
NW13. 144 Albany Street
NW14. Francis Bitter Magnet Lab
NW15. Francis Bitter Magnet Lab
NW16. Plasma Science & Fusion Center
NW17. Plasma Science & Fusion Center
NW20. Albany St Generator Shelter
NW21. Plasma Science & Fusion Center
NW22. Plasma Science & Fusion Center
NW30. 224 Albany Street
NW61. Random H all
NW62. Volvo Garage
NW86. 70 Pacific Street Dormitory
W1. Ashdown House
W2. 311 Memorial Drive
W4. McCormick Hall
W5. Green Hall
W7. Baker House

W8. Pierce Boathouse
W11. Kosher Kitchen
W13. Bexley Hall
W15. MIT Chapel
W16. Kresge Auditorium
W20. Stratton Student Center
W31. Du Pont Athletic Gymnasium
W32. Du Pont Athletic Gymnasium
W33. Rockwell Cage
W34. Johnson Athletics Center
W35. Zesiger Sports & Fitness Center
W45. West garage
W51. Burton-Conner House
W53. Carr Indoor Tennis Facility
W59. Heinz Building
W61. MacGregor House
W70. New House
W71. Next House
W79. Simmons Hall
W84. Tang Hall
W85. Westgate
W89. Campus Police
W91. Information Services & Technology
Operations
WW15. Mail Services (off map)

Northeastern University

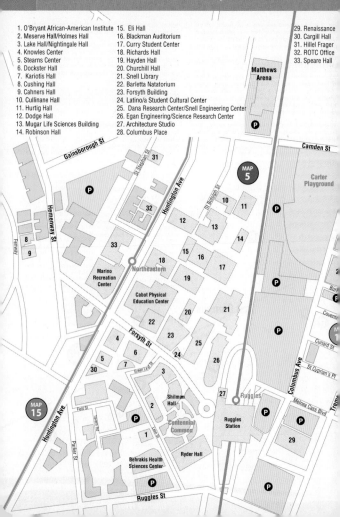

1. O'Bryant African-American Institute
2. Meserve Hall/Holmes Hall
3. Lake Hall/Nightingale Hall
4. Knowles Center
5. Stearns Center
6. Dockster Hall
7. Kariotis Hall
8. Cushing Hall
9. Cahners Hall
10. Cullinane Hall
11. Hurtig Hall
12. Dodge Hall
13. Mugar Life Sciences Building
14. Robinson Hall

15. Eli Hall
16. Blackman Auditorium
17. Curry Student Center
18. Richards Hall
19. Hayden Hall
20. Churchill Hall
21. Snell Library
22. Barletta Natatorium
23. Forsyth Building
24. Latino/a Student Cultural Center
25. Dana Research Center/Snell Engineering Center
26. Egan Engineering/Science Research Center
27. Architecture Studio
28. Columbus Place

29. Renaissance
30. Cargill Hall
31. Hillel Frager
32. ROTC Office
33. Speare Hall

Matthews Arena

Camden St

Gainsborough St

St Stephen St

MAP 5

Carter Playground

Huntington Ave

St Botolph St

Hemenway St

Fenway

Northeastern

Marino Recreation Center

Cabot Physical Education Center

Forsyth St

Green Leaf St

Columbus Ave

St Cyprian's Pl

Coventry

Cunard St

MAP 1

Melnea Cass Blvd

Huntington Ave

Field St

Team Rd

Leon St

Shillman Hall

Ruggles

Ruggles Station

MAP 15

Parker St

Behrakis Health Sciences Center

Centennial Common

Ryder Hall

Ruggles St

eneral Information

Maps: 5, 13, & 15
dress: 360 Huntington Ave, Boston, MA 02115
one: 617-373-2000
ebsite: www.northeastern.edu

verview

theastern University has come a long way from ng a commuter school with a fairly unimpressive an campus. In recent years, the university emerged as an important national research itution with sparkly new academic, athletic, residential facilities. NU originally began as a -year school with an academic model called actice-Oriented Education," a program that bines education and internships (co-op) and is rnatively dubbed "real-life learning" by school cials. The school added more four- and five-year ons, along with online study for a number of rees.

nded in 1898 as a part-time night school, theastern is located on more than 67 acres g Huntington Avenue and served by three en Line E train stops. The current enrollment at is approximately 16,300 full-time undergraduate ents and around 4,800 graduate students with ale-to-female ratio that is pretty evenly matched. vever, cultural diversity isn't something for ch the university is known. The most popular ree programs on offer are in Business, Health, Engineering/Technology. The University Honors gram is also a big draw for potential undergrads.

ition

ergraduate tuition costs run at about $40,700 per with room and board adding up to an additional 600. Books, lab fees, and personal expenses are, lways, extra. Graduate student tuition and fees by college, as do individual online courses.

ports

Northeastern Huskies compete in Division I with ity teams in nine men's and ten women's sports. school's various teams had their finest collective ormance ever in the 2002-03 season. The Huskies four teams to the NCAA playoffs and won a l of seven conference titles—Northeastern's st ever in both categories. Every February, men's key takes part in the Beanpot, the largest college rting event in Boston

Culture on Campus

While Northeastern University doesn't offer much in the way of the arts, it is located in a prime spot for cultural enrichment. Huntington Avenue, also known as "Avenue of the Arts," runs through the urban campus, making it easy to visit the neighborhood museums. Among the most notable are the Isabella Stewart Gardner Museum, a ten-minute walk from the center of campus, and the Museum of Fine Arts (page 326), a four-minute walk from the main quad. Massachusetts College of Art is also located just a few T stops away and Symphony Hall (BSO, anyone?) is next door. Thai, soul food, and pizza abound—whether you walk or T it, you can hit anywhere from five to infinite restaurants with one stone.

For on-campus entertainment, afterHOURS, the campus's late-night club, welcomes many musical acts, ranging from local unknowns to bigger names like Gavin DeGraw. Additionally, the Curry Student Center is a magnet for Huskies in search of a bite (the Food Court includes everything from a salad bar to a Taco Bell) or an e-mail fix.

Departments

Admissions	617-373-2200
	(TTY) 617-373-3768
Library	617-373-2350
Registrar	617-373-2300
Athletics Department	617-373-2672
Athletics Ticket Office	617-373-4700

Undergraduate:

Admissions	617-373-2200
College of Arts & Sciences	617-373-3980
Bouvé College of Health Sciences	617-373-3321
College of Business Administration	617-373-3270
College of Computer & Information Science	617-373-2462
College of Criminal Justice	617-373-3327
College of Engineering	617-373-2152
School of Engineering Technology	617-373-7777
School of Nursing	617-373-3649

Graduate:

Bouvé College of Health Sciences	617-373-2708
College of Arts & Sciences	617-373-3982
College of Business Administration	617-373-5992
College of Computer & Information Science	617-373-2464
College of Criminal Justice	617-373-3327
College of Engineering	617-373-2711
Law School	617-373-2395
School of Professional & Continuing Studies	617-373-2400

Colleges & Universities · **Tufts University**

1. Mugar Hall
2. Dowling Hall
3. Goddard Hall
4. Granhoff Family Hillel Center
5. Dana Lab
6. Barnum Hall
7. Ballou Hall
8. Goddard Chapel
9. Eaton Hall
10. Miner Hall
11. Paige Hall
12. Lincoln-Filene Center
13. Braker Hall
14. East Hall
15. Packard Hall
16. Bendelson Hall
17. Central Heating Plant
18. Lane Hall

20. Dewick-MacPhie Hall
21. Bookstore
22. Elizabeth Van Huyson Mayer Campus Center
23. 55 Talbot Ave
24. Pearson Chemical Laboratory
25. Michael Lab
26. Academic Computing Building
27. Costume Shop
28. Jackson Gym
29. Baltch Arena Theatre
30. Remis Sculpture/ Leir Hall
31. Cohen Auditorium
32. Aidekman Arts Center
33. Baronian Field House
34. Anderson Hall
35. Robinson Hall
36. Bromfield-Pearson

37. Hamilton Pool
38. Halligan Hall
39. 177 College Ave
40. Office Services
41. Curtis Hall
42. Psychology Building
43. Bray Laboratory
44. Central Services
45. Bacon Hall
46. Science and Technology Center
47. Eliot-Pearson Child Development Center
48. Eliot-Pearson Children's School
49. West Hall
50. Olin Center
51. Cabot Center
52. Scene Shop

General Information

Map:	22
Admin Building:	169 Holland St, Somerville, MA 02144
Medford/Somerville Campus:	Medford, MA 02155
Boston Campus:	136 Harrison Ave, Boston, MA 02111
North Grafton Campus:	200 Westboro Rd, North Grafton, MA 01536
General Phone:	617-628-5000
Website:	www.tufts.edu

Overview

There's a perception that Tufts is a school for kids who can't get into Harvard, just two Red Line stops away. This is (mostly) not true. Tufts possesses academic prowess in its own right, especially in its engineering, veterinary, international relations, and science departments. The Fletcher School is the country's oldest graduate school of international affairs, and its prestige and strong curriculum lure students from across the globe. To boot, Tufts boasts a kick-ass study-abroad program (pick a continent, any continent) and a laudable community-service focus.

The university has three campuses. The main Medford/Somerville campus is where approximately 5,500 students, mostly liberal arts undergrads, live and learn. The Medford/Somerville campus also houses the School of Engineering, the Graduate School of Arts and Sciences, and the School of Special Studies. Tufts prides itself on diversity: A whole center is devoted to lesbian, gay, bisexual, and transgender students, and on any given day the "viewpoints" section of The Tufts Daily—the school's impressive and professional-looking student newspaper—will have several pieces about the LGBT community. As touchy-feely as campus politics may be, though, academics remain pretty hardcore.

The centrally located Boston campus houses the School of Medicine, School of Dental Medicine, Sackler School of Graduate Biomedical Sciences, Jean Mayer USDA Human Nutrition Research Center on Aging, and The Gerald J. and Dorothy R. Friedman School of Nutrition Science and Policy.

Tuition

Undergraduate tuition fees total around $43,600. Room and board cost an additional $12,000. Books, service fees, activity fees, and personal expenses are extra. Graduate student tuition, fees, and expenses vary by college.

Sports

If you ever find yourself at Tufts University and, more specifically, in the office of the Athletic Director, you might notice a peanut butter jar with ashes in it. Don't be frightened; it's only Jumbo. Jumbo is the elephant mascot of Tufts University. P.T. Barnum, of the Barnum and Bailey Circus, was one of the University's original trustees. His prize act was an elephant named Jumbo, who was hit by a train and killed in 1885. His stuffed body was donated to Tufts, where it was stored in a museum on campus that eventually became a student lounge. Sadly, however, the museum burned in 1975 and Jumbo went up with it. The ashes in the jar are said to be those of Jumbo, though university officials say they have no evidence that that is the case. Luckily, they have his tail in a cardboard folder in their archives. (Extra trivia fun: Jumbo also has the honor of being the only mascot mentioned in Webster's. Take that, Ivy Leaguers.)

If that isn't enough to attract you to the sports, then maybe the recent successes of the golf and women's sailing teams will pique your interest.

There's also an old campus joke: "What's Brown and Blue and loses every weekend?" Answer: "The Tufts football team." It's not really funny, but often accurate.

Culture on Campus

If sports aren't your thing, cultural activities are plentiful at Tufts. In the Aidekman Arts Center on the Medford/Somerville campus, you'll find the Tufts University Art Gallery. Again, the mantra seems to be diversity, diversity, and more diversity. The Gallery's mission is to explore art through all of its cultural complexities.

Over 70 students make up the Tufts Symphony Orchestra, which performs regularly throughout the school year. A capella groups abound, ranging from all-male to all-Jewish. The Department of Drama and Dance is where all of the performing artists can be found. Its students—a tight-knit, talented group—perform regularly at the Balch Arena Theater. Lately, though, music has been taking center stage on the Medford Campus: In February 2007, the $27-million, 55,000-square-foot Granoff Music Center opened to campus-wide accolades.

Departments

Undergraduate Admissions	617-627-3170
Graduate and Professional Studies	617-627-3395
The Fletcher School	617-627-3040
School of Medicine	617-636-7000
School of Dental Medicine	617-636-6828
Sackler School of Graduate Biomedical Sciences	617-636-6767
School of Nutrition and Science Policy	617-636-3737
School of Veterinary Medicine	508-839-5302
School of Engineering	617-627-3237
Athletics Department and Ticket Office	617-627-3232
Balch Arena Theater	617-627-3524
Tufts Symphony Orchestra	617-627-4042
Tisch Library	617-627-3460

Continuing Education in Boston

Harvard, MIT, Boston College…the city of Boston has long been associated with academic achievement. But even if you're not ready to matriculate at one of the city's famed institutions of higher learning, Boston is a great place to learn everything and anything from basic Arabic to authentic Italian cooking.

For those looking to change careers—or simply get ahead in a current position—many of the area's renowned schools offer continuing education or professional development classes. Tuition at Harvard Extension School is very reasonable and comes with unbeatable name recognition. Even community colleges like North Shore Community College, Bunker Hill, and Quincy College (Red line accessible) offer credited and non-credited courses from everything like computers to feng shui.

Those who are feeling less cerebral can try gymnastics at Cambridge's Jam'nastics or take a golf lesson at CityGolf. Got an urge to indulge your creative side? Explore painting or sculpture with a studio art class at the MFA or learn the craft of glass-blowing at Diablo Glass and Metal.

Adrenaline junkies can hop the commuter rail and head out to Trapeze School, hidden in the Jordan's Furniture complex in suburban Reading.

Continuing Education and Professional Development

Boston College Woods College of Advancing Studies, www.bc.edu, 617-552-3900, 140 Commonwealth Ave, Chestnut Hill

Boston Language Institute, www.bostonlanguage.com, 617-262-3500, 648 Beacon St, Boston

Boston University Metropolitan College, www.bu.edu/met, 617-353-6000, 755 Commonwealth Ave, Boston

Bunker Hill Community College, www.bhcc.mass.edu/, 617-228-2000, 250 New Rutherford Ave, Boston

Harvard Extension, www.dce.harvard.edu/extension, 617-495-4024, 51 Brattle St, Cambridge

MIT, www.mit.edu/education/professional, 617-253-1000, 77 Massachusetts Ave, Cambridge

North Shore Community College, www.northshore.edu, 978-762-4000, 1 Ferncroft Rd, Danvers

Northeastern University, www.ace.neu.edu, 617-373-2000, 360 Huntington Ave, Boston

Quincy College, www.quincycollege.edu/, 617-9 1700, 150 Newport Ave, Quincy

Little Bit of Everything

Boston Center for Adult Education, www.bcae.org, 617-267-4430, 5 Commonwealth Ave, Boston

Cambridge Center for Adult Education, www.ccae.org, 617-547-6789, 42 Brattle St, Cambridge

Arts and Lifestyle

Beadworks, www.beadworksboston.com, 617-247-7227, 167 Newbury St, Boston and 617-868-9777, 23 Church St, Cambridge

Boston Wine Tasting Classes, www.invinoveritas.com, 617-784-7150, 1354 Commonwealth Ave, Allston

Cambridge School of Culinary Arts, www.cambridgeculinary.com, 617-354-2020, 2020 Massachusetts Ave, Cambridge

Diablo Glass and Metal, www.diabloglassandmetal.com, 617-442-7444, 123 Terrace St, Boston

Grub Street Writing Center, www.grubstreet.or 617-695-0075, 160 Boylston St, Boston

Massachusetts College of Art, www.massart.ed 617-879-7000, 621 Huntington Ave, Boston

Mudville Pottery Classes, www.nanhamilton.com/mudville/mudville/, 617- 623-9191, 181 Pearl St, Somerville

Museum of Fine Arts, www.mfa.org, 617-267-93 465 Huntington Ave, Boston

Spark Craft Studios, www.sparkcrafts.com, 617-718-9132, 50 Grove St, Somerville

Athletics and Dance

Boston Sailing Center, www.bostonsailingcenter.com, Lewis Wharf, Boston

CityGolf Boston, www.citygolfboston.com, 617-357-4653, 38 Bromfield St, Boston

Fred Astaire Dance Studios, www.fadsboston.c 617-247-2435, 179 South St, Boston

GottaDance Cambridge, www.gottadance.org, 617-864-8675, 11 Garden St, Cambridge and 7 Temple St, Cambridge

Green Street Studios, www.greenstreetstudios. 617-864-3191, 185 Green St, Cambridge

Jam'nastics, www.jamnastics.org, 617-354-5780, 199 Columbia St, Cambridge

Trapeze School, http://boston.trapezeschool.com, 781-942-7800, 50 Walkers Brook Dr, Reading

Overview

onians love that dirty water, but we like clean water even better.
'act is best reflected by the Boston Harbor Project. Thanks to over
llion spent cleaning it up, the Hub's harbor is no longer on that
eful list of the country's dirtiest waterways, but it's still a work
ogress. So while you may still hear that damn Standells' song
ng from every bar on Lansdowne Street, you no longer need to
y about your genetic makeup should you go for a swim in the
es. However, NFT does not recommend donning your speedos
joggles just yet. Instead, consider more appropriate activities as
ed in the slew of yacht clubs and boating centers that decorate
oastline and upriver all the way to Watertown.

'ect place to start is at one of Boston Harbor's 34 beautiful islands,
h have been collectively designated a National Recreation Area.
of the islands are either fully or partially accessible to the public
a great, affordable getaway within 10-miles of downtown
on. For the most part, amenities consist of composting toilets, but
come prepared, the islands are great for a picnic or a camping
. On George's Island (Boston
or Cruises) you will find historic Fort Warren, a former Civil War
n replete with ghost—the wife of a Civil War inmate nicknamed
' in Black." The trails across 48-acre Lovell's Island pass through
s, forests, and the ruins of Fort Standish. There's a supervised
ming beach, some picnic areas, and 11 campsites. Little Brewster
is the home of Boston Light, the oldest continually used
house site in America (1716). While not open to casual visitors,
e boaters and tours are welcomed, call for specifics 617-223-
. If your boss is scheduling a Survivor-style teamwork safari or if
kids are looking for that Kevin Bacon, White Water Summer role

model, chances are you're heading to privately owned Thompson
Island. If you want to venture a bit farther out, consider Buzzards Bay
to the south. Touching more than 280 miles of the Massachusetts
coastline, the bay stretches from Rhode Island Sound to the Cape Cod
Canal. Calmer waters inside the bay make for good sailing conditions.

Back on the Charles (don't even think about pronouncing the "r"),
crew is a popular sport, particularly among the local colleges and
universities. Many of the clubs and organizations offer instruction to
the general public. The Head of the Charles Regatta, held every fall, is
the world's largest two-day rowing event. The race schedule includes
single and team events and draws competitors from around the world.
Check out www.hocr.org for more information.

The nonprofit Community Boating Inc. (located between the Charles/
MGH Red Line stop and the Hatch Shell) offers summer kayaking,
windsurfing, and sailing lessons for kids aged 10–18. (Participants
must be able to swim 75 yards.) Visit www.community-boating.org for
more information.

If you're looking for waves but find the Harbor a bit intimidating, check
out the Jamaica Pond Boat House (617-522-5061) for mini-sailboat and
rowboat rentals. At around 68-acres, the pond is the purest and largest
body of water within city limits and the only date-friendly glacial-
kettlehole in town. It's also a great place to watch kamikaze drivers
on the Jamaicaway. As they scream expletives and give each other the
finger, you can fish in the liberally stocked pond and gloat. If that isn't
relaxing, what is? Visit www.jamaicapond.com for further information.

Boston is also home to the CRASH—B World Indoor Rowing
Championships, held annually in February at Agganis Arena at Boston
University. More information is available at www.crash-b.org.

ling/Boating Centers	Address	Phone	Website
on Harbor Cruises	1 Long Wharf, Boston	617-227-4321	www.bostonharborcruises.com
on Harbor Sailing Club	58 Batterymarch St, Boston	617-720-0049	www.bostonharborsailing.com; moorings/hire/lessons racing/clothing
on Harbor Shipyard & Marina	256 Marginal St, East Boston	617-561-1400	www.bhsmarina.com; moorings/lessons
on Sailing Center	The Riverboat at Lewis Wharf	617-227-4198	www.bostonsailingcenter.com; hire/courses/lessons/racing
munity Boating	21 David Mugar Way, Boston	617-523-1038	www.community-boating.org; sailing lessons
ageous Sailing Center	One 1st Ave, Charlestown	617-242-3821	www.courageoussailing.org; lessons/racing
aica Pond Boat House	Jamaicaway at Pond St, Jamaica Plain	617-522-5061	www.jamaicapond.com
oln Sailing Center	PO Box 492, Hingham	781-741-5225	www.lincolnsailing.org; non-profit/lessons/sailing/rowing
Sailing	134 Memorial Dr, Cambridge	617-253-4884	http://sailing.mit.edu; lessons/racing
Park Sailing	95 Marginal St, East Boston	617-561-6677	www.piersparksailing.org; hire/lessons/racing/sale
ss Boston	100 Morrissey Boulevard, Boston	617-287-5404	www.UMB.edu/marineops
erfront Recreation	Boston, Fox Point Dock.		

ht Clubs	Address	Phone	Website
Haven Yacht Club	10 McPherson Dr, Beverly	978-922-9712	www.basshavenyachtclub.com
on Yacht Club	1 Front St, Marblehead	781-631-3100	www.boston.org
atree Yacht Club	9 Gordon Rd, Braintree	781-843-9730	N/A
nthian Yacht Club	1 Nahant St, Marblehead	781-631-0005	www.corinthianyc.org
versport Yacht Club	161 Elliott St, Danvers	978-774-8620	www.danversport.com
ern Yacht Club	47 Foster St, Marblehead	781-631-1400	www.easternyc.org
y Yacht Club	5 Fitzpatrick Wy, Hull	781-925-9739	www.hullyc.org
es Yacht Club	565 Sumner St, East Boston	617-567-9656	www.jeffriesyachtclub.com
ee Yacht Club	126 Water St, Beverly	978-922-9611	www.jubileeyc.net
opolitan Yacht Club	39 Vinedale Rd, Braintree	781-843-9882	www.metyc.com
Bedford Yacht Club	208 Elm St, South Dartmouth	508-997-0762	www.nbyc.com
Colony Yacht Club	235 Victory Rd, Dorchester	617-436-0513	www.oldcolonyyc.com
nsula Yacht Club	671 Summer St, Boston	617-464-7901	www.pycboston.org
outh Yacht Club	34 Union St, Plymouth	508-746-7207	www.plymouthyachtclub.com
y Bay Yacht Club	5 T Wharf, Rockport	978-546-9433	www.sandybay.org
h Boston Yacht Club	1849 Columbia Rd, South Boston	617-268-6132	www.southbostonyc.org
antum Yacht Club	646 Quincy Shore Dr, Quincy	617-770-4811	www.squantumyc.org
ano Yacht Club	101 Bridge St, Osterville	508-428-2232	www.vsb.cape.com/~wianno/
hrop Yacht Club	649 Shirley St, Winthrop	617-846-9774	www.win-yc.org

ving Clubs	Address	Phone	Website
munity Rowing (Apr–Oct)	600 Pleasant St, Watertown	617-923-7557	www.communityrowing.org
ling City Rowing Club	3 Dover St, New Bedford	508-517-1251	www.whalingcityrowing.org

General Information

City of Boston Bicycling:	www.cityofboston.gov/bikes
City of Cambridge Bicycling:	www.cambridgema.gov/CDD/Transportation/gettingaround cambridge/bybike.aspx
MassBike:	www.massbike.org
Charles River Wheelmen:	www.crw.org
Hubway (Bike Share):	www.thehubway.com
Rubel BikeMaps:	www.bikemaps.com
Bike to Bridge Boston:	www.hubonwheels.org

Overview

The city's streets are narrow, congested, and short-tempered, bike-hating drivers abound. Make no mistake, Boston is tough for cyclists.

That said, Boston and the surrounding cities are making efforts to increase the accessibility and safety of bike transportation, and it's a great way to explore the city. Relatively flat and compact, it's generally quicker to get around on a bike, and you'll find, even in the middle of winter, hardy cyclists trekking through the city, delivering packages, and heading to class. Bike-only or mixed-use bike/pedestrian paths run through most of the area's parks, paralleling major roads such as the Riverway, Storrow Drive, and Memorial Drive. While getting "doored" is a serious threat in Central Square, a much-needed repaving of Mass Ave has smoothed the bike lane connecting Boston to Harvard. In 2011, Hubway, the Boston-area bike share program, launched and it continues to expand its fleet of bike stations both in Boston and into neighboring cities.

Brookline has recently added a lane in its streets specifically for bikes, making it a much less stressful option for riding. While it isn't perfect, and there is a chance of getting "doored," it is 1000 times better than having to contend with cars in a shared lane or pedestrians on a sidewalk

Danger lurks around every non-perpendicular corner. To avoid catastrophe, have your best cycling wits about you and be especially wary of:

- **Drivers**—Boston drivers reserve some of their most venomous roadrage for cyclists. They're also notoriously self-centered, erratic, prone to underestimate your speed, and quick to double-park to dash in for liquor or donuts.

- **Potholes**—They can sneak up on you, espec at night. The bigger ones will swallow you wh while bumping over the little ones lead to n bruises in the nether regions.

- **Trolley Tracks**—Green Line tracks will flip over and buckle your wheel, especially in par Mission Hill, Jamaica Plain, and in Cleveland Ci If you're going to cross the tracks, take them 90-degree angle.

- **Bridges**—All the bridges across the Charles narrow and heavily trafficked.

- **Pedestrians**—They jaywalk into your path, text while doing so, and they can't hear screams because their iPod is set to volume l "jet engine." Also, keep in mind that even if they hear you scream "On Your Left," 99% of them step directly to the left to ensure that you die.

If you plan on biking in Boston and you have a b that you'd like to keep, invest in a helmet an battery-powered red light to place below your or on your back. Front lights and rear reflectors the law after dark.

The city offers many options for recreational ric including the popular 11-mile Minuteman Bike through Lexington and the 17-mile Charles F Bikeway growing past Watertown. Shorter handy for commuting, the Southwest Corridor se you from Northeastern along the Orange Line Forest Hills. Recent funding should improve on the serious flaws of the Boston bike system: un of cross-trail connections, crossing lights, or r markings. This makes them less than ideal for ou with small children. Of particular danger to fam are the many bridge intersections along the so Charles River Bikeway. If light jogging traffic doe bug you, another great option is the 38-mile-Boston Harborwalk, which runs through Dorche Charlestown, and East Boston among c communities. The smooth pavement, pictures views, and prohibition of cars make it an exce choice for a long ride.

For something a little longer and farther a the Bay Circuit Trail winds its way 150 miles Newburyport on the North Shore to Duxt on the South Shore, creating a "C" shape aro Boston. Cycling enthusiasts refer to it as "Bos outer Emerald Necklace." You'll find the boy ra skipping the summer crowds on the Minutema spins around Concord and many of the cycle sponsor club teams. The Charles River Wheelm one of the nation's oldest bicycle clubs with a round calendar of rides and site full of cue sh

the distance riders, the BMB (Boston-Montreal-
ston) ride draws randonneurs from across the
untry for the grueling 90 hour, 1,200K ride.

bel BikeMaps produces maps of riding paths
d trails throughout the Greater Boston area and
well worth the six bucks. You'll likely want both
e Boston map and the Eastern Mass map. They
n be purchased at most bike shops, bookstores,
on the Rubel website. Take it to the State House
h MassBike, the primary lobbying and bicycle
vocacy group in the state. They maintain an
tensive website of all things pedal-powered
Massachusetts. Bike to Bridge Boston is a new
dition to the city and organizes free tours to
beat Boston during the summer. DIY guides to
ing Jewish Boston, the Underground Railroad,
d other routes are on their web site, and they
anize a city bike rally and ride in early October

ikes and Mass Transit

es are allowed on the Red, Orange, and Blue
es, on the MBTA Commuter Rail with some
itations, on all busses equipped with bike racks,
d on the MBTA ferries at all times. Bikes (with
exception of folding bikes) are not permitted
the Green Line and the Mattapan Trolley. Bikes
allowed on the Silver Line only if a bike rack is
ilable. On the subway and commuter rail, bikes
permitted during non-rush hours (roughly
ore 7am, between 10am–4pm, and after 7pm).
es are allowed at all subway stations except Park
eet, Downtown Crossing (except for transfer), and
vernment Center. Crosstown buses are equipped
h bike racks and can be used at any time. Other
s services do not provide racks and bikes are not
mitted on board.

ou're traveling on commuter rail, wait for the
nductor's instructions before entering or exiting
train. On subways, head for the rear of the train.
're only allowed to enter the last carriage and,
n then, there's a two-bikes-per carriage limit.
re is no additional fee for bikes on any public
nsportation. See the MBTA website for (www.
ta.com/riding_the_t/bikes) for more information.

Bike Shops and Makers

Boston's got a great variety of shops. While most
will have a low-end city cruiser or two, it's worth
getting to know your local shops for their specialties,
whether the high-end racing bikes at ATA or fixies at
Beacon Street. Oddly enough, Boston's most famous
shop and mechanic, Sheldon Brown, are way out
in West Newton at Harris Cyclery. However, if you
don't mind getting your hands dirty, we applaud the
rent-by-the-hour stands and geniuses at Broadway
Bicycle School.

· **Ace Wheelworks** ·
145 Elm St, Somerville · 617-776-2100

· **Back Bay Bicycles** ·
362 Commonwealth Ave, Boston · 617-247-2336

· **Bicycle Bill's** ·
253 North Harvard St, Allston · 617-783-5636

· **Bicycle Exchange** ·
2067 Massachusetts Ave, Cambridge · 617-864-1300

· **Bikes Not Bombs** ·
284 Amory Street, Jamaica Plain · 617-522-0222

· **Cambridge Bicycle** ·
259 Massachusetts Ave, Cambridge · 617-876-6555

· **Community Bike Supply** ·
496 Tremont St, Boston · 617-542-8623

· **Ferris Wheels Bicycle Shop** ·
66 South St, Jamaica Plain · 617-524-2453

· **International Bicycle Center** ·
89 Brighton Ave, Brighton · 617-783-5804t

· **Superb Bicycle** ·
842 Beacon St · 617-236-0752

· **Urban AdvenTours** ·
103 Atlantic Ave · 617-670-0637

When out on the road, what's better than showing
off some Yankee ingenuity? Boston's been a center
of bike fabrication since Columbia popularized the
ready-made bike in 1877. Here are some sweet handcrafted builders welding new traditions:

· **A.N.T.** ·
24 Water St, Holliston · 508-429-3350

· **Independent Fabrication** ·
86 Joy St, Somerville · 617-666-3609

· **Seven Cycles** ·
125 Walnut St, Watertown · 617-923-777

Overview

If you like the idea of lowering your center of gravity and darting around at high speeds on tiny wheels or thin blades, then Boston is the place for you. The city is jam-packed with parks and rinks that accommodate inline skaters in the summer and ice skaters in the winter.

Inline Skating

Boston drivers are no more sympathetic to skaters than they are to bikers. If you're skating for recreation, it is probably best to stick to the numerous places designated for outdoor activities. A favorite haunt of Boston skaters is Harvard's Arnold Arboretum (125 Arborway, Jamaica Plain, 617-524-1718), which offers one of the most scenic (and hilly) skates in the area. The best thing about this place is that skaters are welcome everywhere. There are two or three miles of paved paths and you don't have to worry about cars (although you might find yourself dodging strollers, cyclists, and fellow skaters, particularly on sunny weekends).

Boston Common (see page 188) is another popular skating destination, but the pedestrian traffic on the Common makes skating quite challenging. The Common is usually crowded with meandering tourists and fast-walking business folk who don't take too kindly to being mowed down by skaters. The upside, though, is that you can take in some impressive cityscapes as you zip around. The best way to get there is to take the T to Park Street. Note: Wearing skates on the T is prohibited.

For a great view of the bridges that stretch over the Charles River, try the Charles River Bike Path. The trail runs along both sides of the river between the Galen Street Bridge in Watertown and River Street Bridge in Boston, and from the Science Museum to Watertown Square. The path is about 8.5 miles each way.

Beacon Hill Skate Shop (135 Charles St S, 617-482-7400) rents top-of-the-line inline skates, roller skates, and ice skates. Rentals cost $10/hour, $15/day, and $20 overnight. Beacon Hill Skate Shop accepts cash only and requires you to leave a credit card as a deposit. All rentals come with safety equipment.

Ice Skating

Even on crisp winter days, when the cold makes it almost unbearable to be outside, Boston Common's famous Frog Pond entices many Bostonians to bundle up and head out for some good, old-fashioned ice skating—either that or some good, old-fashioned heckling from the sidelines. Skating is free for children 13 and under and $5 for everyone else. Skate rental is $5 for children and $9 for everyone else. Lockers are available for $2. Regulars might consider buying individual season passes for $150 or a family pass for $250. Lunchtime passes are valid Mon—Fri, 11 am to 2 pm (holidays excluded), and cost $100. Frog Pond is open Sun–Thurs 10 am-9 pm (except Mon when the rink closes at 5 pm) and Fri-Sat 10 am–10 pm. For more information, call 617-635-2120.

The Larz Anderson Park in Brookline is a great back-up option when Frog Pond gets too crowded (and it will be). Larz Anderson Park is located on a former 64-acre estate and is the largest park in Brookline. In addition to the outdoor skate rink, the park has picnic areas, ball fields, and an incredible view of Boston. The only downside is that the skating rink is only open a few months every ye from December to February. Skating fees cost $5 for ad residents and $7 for adult non-residents and reduced da skating rates are available for seniors, students, veteran and disabled skaters. Skate rentals are $6. The rink is op Tues and Thurs 10 am–12 pm, Fri 7:30 pm–9:30 pm, Sat–S 12 pm–5 pm. For more information, call 617-739-7518.

Ice Skating Rinks

If you have your own skates, you might opt for one of t following rinks run by the Department of Conservation a Recreation, where skating in the winter is free. Call rinks hours of operation:

Bajko Memorial Rink,
75 Turtle Pond Pkwy, Hyde Park, 617-364-9188
Jim Roche Community Ice Arena,
1275 VFW Pkwy, West Roxbury, 617-323-9532
Daly Memorial Rink,
1 Nonantum Rd, Brighton, 617-527-1741
Devine Memorial Rink,
995 Morrissey Blvd, Dorchester, 617-436-4356
Emmons Horrigan O'Neill Memorial Rink,
150 Rutherford Ave, Charlestown, 617-242-9728
Flynn Skating Rink,
2 Woodland Rd, Medford, 781-395-8492
Kelly Outdoor Skating Rink,
1 Marbury Ter, Jamaica Plain, 617-727-7000
LoConte Memorial Rink,
3449 Veterans Pkwy, Medford, 781-395-9594
Murphy Memorial Rink,
1880 William J Day Blvd, South Boston, 617-269-7060
Porazzo Memorial Rink,
20 Coleridge St, East Boston, 617-567-9571
Reilly Skating Rink,
355 Chestnut Hill Ave, Brighton, 617-277-7822
Skating Club of Boston,
1240 Soldiers Field Rd, Brighton, 617-782-5900
Simoni Memorial Rink,
155 Gore St, Cambridge, 781-982-8166
Steriti Memorial Rink,
561 Commercial St, Boston, 617-523-9327
Veterans Memorial Rink,
570 Somerville Ave, Somerville, 617- 623-3523

Skateboarding

The Charles River Skatepark, 40,000 square feet of pip ramps, and rails, will be constructed at North Po Park along the Charles River where Cambridge mee Charlestown. Ongoing issues are still causing delays w construction here, so the original goal of a 2010 opening long gone. If it ever gets finished, it will be one of the large skateparks in the country, perfect for catching air like To Hawk or busting backside lipslides like Ryan Sheckler. Un the mythical park opens, the best option in Boston is t Reservation Skatepark in Hyde Park. The park is small, b it does have a very nice pool setup and a few good sets stairs. The park is just steps away from the Hyde Park st on the Providence/Stoughton commuter rail line.

Gear

Beacon Hill Skate Shop,
135 Charles St S, Boston, 617-482-7400
Orchard Skate Shop,
156 Harvard Ave, Boston, 617-782-7777

General Information

Boston Parks and Recreation Office
Phone: 617-635-4505
Hotline: 617-635-PARK
Website: www.cityofboston.gov/parks

Cambridge Recreation Department
Phone: 617-349-6200
Website: www.cambridgema.gov

Department of Conservation and Recreation
(Division of Urban Parks)
Phone: 617-626-1250

Outdoor Courts—Open to the Public

These public courts operate on a first-come, first-served basis. Most courts are not equipped with lights, so get there early to get your game in. Although many courts are in good condition, some have pretty major divots, à la the Boston Garden's parquet floor, making the ball spin in unexpected directions. Courts are managed by the city or the town recreation department, or by the Commonwealth's Department of Conservation and Recreation's Division of Urban Parks (DCR). Until recently, the DCR was the Metropolitan District Commission (MDC), so the courts might still be labeled with the wrong acronym. Don't let it affect your game! Many locals also use the well-maintained school courts in the university-rich area. Each school has a different policy regarding outsiders depending on season, location, and the mood of the athletic director on a particular day. Contact the schools or just take your chances.

Tennis Courts	Address	Type	# of Courts	Map
Charlesbank Park (DCR)	Boylston St & Charles St	Public	4	1
North End Park (DCR)	Commercial St & Cooper St	Public	2	2
Boston Common	Boylston St & Charles St	Public	2	3
Pagoda Park	Kneeland St	Public	1	4
Cook Street Playground	Hill St & Cook St	Public	1	8
Porzio Park	Maverick Sq	Public	2	9
Boston Athletic Club	653 Summer St	Private		11
Marine Park (DCR)	Day Blvd	Public	1	11
Clifford Playground	Norfolk Ave & Proctor St	Public	1	12
Carter Playground	Columbus Ave & Camden St	Public	5	13
Rep Jones Park	King St	Public	1	13
Malcolm X Park	Dale St & Bainbridge St	Public	2	13
Trotter School Playground	Humboldt Ave & Waumbeck St	Public	1	13
Mission Hill Deck (DCR)	Southwest Corridor Park	Public	2	14
South Street Mall	South St & Carolina Ave	Public	2	14
Stony Brook Deck (DCR)	Southwest Corridor Park	Public	2	14
Amory Clay Tennis Courts	Amory St	Public		16
Ringwood Playground Park	Newall Rd off Kent St	Public	3	16
Waldstein Playground	37 Dean Rd	Public	8	17
Rogers Park	Lake St & Foster St	Public	2	18
Coolidge Playground	Kenwood St b/w Harvard St & Columbia St	Public	1	19
Devotion Playground	Steadman St off Harvard St	Public	3	19
Driscoll School	Westbourne St	Public	2	19
Ringer Playground	Allston St & Griggs Pl	Public	2	19
Anderson Courts	Pemberton St & Haskell St	Public		22
George Dilboy Field (DCR)	Alewife Brook Pkwy	Public		22
Maxton J Foss Park (DCR)	McGrath Hwy & Broadway	Public	2	24
Hoyt Field	Western Ave & Howard St	Public	2	27
Riverside Press Park	River St & Memorial Dr	Public		27
Harvard Street Park	Harvard St & Clark St	Public		28
Joan Lorentz Park at Cambridge Public Library	Broadway & Ellery St	Public		28
Hunt Playground	Blue Hill Ave & Almont St	Public		31

Public Courses

Public Courses	Address	Phone	Par	Fees (WD/WE)	Map
Fresh Pond Golf Course	691 Huron Ave	617-349-6282	35/70	$30 WD / $36 WE	
Presidents Golf Course	357 W Squantum St, Quincy	617-328-3444	70	$35 WD / $44 WE	
Putterham Meadows Golf Club	1281 W Roxbury Pkwy, Chestnut Hill	617-730-2078	71	$35 WD / $38 WE	
William J. Devine Golf Course	1 Circuit Dr, Dorchester	617-265-4084	72	$23–26 WD / $29–34 WE	

Driving Ranges

Driving Ranges	Address	Phone	Fees (WD/WE)	Map
City Golf Boston	38 Bromfield St	617-357-4653	$10/bucket	3

Bowling

First and foremost, if you prefer tenpin over candlepin bowling than you are clearly not from Boston. If you a trying to fit in with the cutters or if want your girlfriend to think you're the real life Will Hunting, then you bette learn how to hit those skinny sticks. On the other hand, if you are comfortable admitting that you were born upstate New York and that you collected Don Mattingly cards when you were a kid, then embrace the tenpi no one will think less of you for it (yeah, right).

All kidding aside, bowling has become hip and bowling has become expensive. Take **Kings (Map 16)**, f instance. Go there on a Friday night and it's filled with people who wouldn't have been caught dead bowling o a Friday night back in high school. Then there's **Lucky Strike Lanes (Map 16)** with a friggin' dress code. If tha your idea of bowling, by all means, have at it. If you're an old-school bowler, the kind that embraces leagu and finds no kitsch value in a button up short sleeve with your name in cursive on it (your real name), then yo must head straight to **Lanes & Games,** order yourself a Bud and some steak tips, and get out your lucky glov Another similar option is **Sacco's Bowl Haven (Map 22)** in Somerville (candlepin only). And here's one of thos moments that remind you why you bought this little awesome book in the first place—**Boston Bowl Fami Fun Center (Map 32)** on Morrissey Boulevard is open all night! You read correctly: In the squarest late-nigh town in America, where your options are your buddy's stained futon or the South Street Diner, Boston Bowl ha you covered 24 hours a day.

Bowling Lanes

Bowling Lanes	Address	Phone	Fees	Map
King's Boston	50 Dalton St	617-266-2695	$5.50/game, $4/shoes	5
Central Park Lanes	10 Saratoga St	617-567-7073	$2.50/game, $1/shoes	
South Boston Candlepin	543 E Broadway	617-464-4858	$3.50/game, $1.50 shoes	11
Lucky Strike Lanes	145 Ipswich St	617-437-0300	$4/game, $3/shoes	16
Sacco's Bowl Haven	45 Day St	617-776-0552	$3/game, $2/shoes	22
Boston Bowl (24 hrs)	820 Morrissey Blvd,	617-825-3800	$4.95/game, $4.25/shoes	32
Lanes & Games	195 Concord Tpke	617-876-5533	$4.75/game, $2.75/shoes	n/a

Billiards

Billiards	Address	Phone	Fees	Map
Boston Beer Works	112 Canal St	617-896-2337	$10/hr	2
King's Boston	50 Dalton St	617-266-2695	$14/hr	5
4 X 4 Billiards	1260 Boylston St	617-424-6326	$12/hr	15
Big City	138 Brighton Ave	617-782-2020	$10/hr	19
Sacco's Bowl Haven	45 Day St	617-776-0552	$7.50/hr	22
Flat Top Johnny's	One Kendall Sq, Bldg 200	617-494-9565	$12/hr	26
Boston Bowl (open 24hrs)	820 Morrissey Blvd	617-825-3800	$13/hr	32
Columbia Billiard CO	Columbia Rd	617-265-1828	$6.60/hr	32

General Information

Phone: 617-236-1652

Website: www.baa.org

Overview

One of the great perks that comes with living in Boston is Patriots' Day, a little gem of a holiday that is celebrated on the third Monday of April. Schools and most jobs get the day off, opening the door for the best athletic day of the year in Beantown. The Sox play an 11:05 a.m. home game, the Bruins and/or Celtics usually have a playoff game, and the Boston Marathon draws the best distance runners in the world to the hub. The Marathon's history goes back to the 19th century, making it the oldest annual road race in the world. Today, nearly 25,000 people ran in the Marathon, which boasts one of the most famous and peculiar courses in the world.

The race stretches from Hopkinton to Copley Square, and features plenty of unique hills and obstacles. Anyone preparing to run the race (props to you for running a qualifying time) should take into account the legendary Newton hills that rear their heads around the 19th mile, and the Cleveland Circle train tracks that must be crossed at the 23rd mile. There is usually a wind at your back when you are running, making the race a bit more tolerable. Boston's weather varies so much in April that in 2011, the winning time for the marathon was a record setting 2:03:02 and in 2012, it was nearly 10 minutes slower, at 2:12:52. Runners can expect temperatures from the 40s to mid-90s, making training very difficult.

If running is not your thing, and you want to watch one of the best races in the country, there are plenty of great options for viewing the race. Obviously, the finish line is the prime spot, but if you don't like waking up at 5:00 in the morning on a day off from work, there are better options. Kenmore Square has plenty going for it. It's only a mile away from the finish, there are plenty of great places to eat and it's shady on one side. It gets very loud at around 2 p.m. as thousands of Sox fans stream out from Fenway Park to support the runners as they make the final push towards the finish line. Coolidge Corner in Brookline is also a great spot, and Heartbreak Hill is easily the most dramatic spot on the course. If you know someone running in the race, you might want to set up there to help will them up the slope.

The weekend leading up to Patriots' Day is a blast. The Sports and Fitness Expo at the Seaport World Trade Center is a must for any runner. All of the top names in the fitness business are eager to show off their new creations and hand out tons of free swag at the convention, which runs on the Friday, Saturday and Sunday leading up to the big race. The Marathon begins on Patriots' Day Monday ("Marathon Monday") at 9 a.m., so be sure to set up by 11:00 if you're spectating in Boston.

How to Get There—Driving

This would be a pretty touristy move if there ever was one. Don't drive, for the love of all things holy, just don't. If you HAVE to, take I-93 to exit 6, and follow signs to the Braintree Red Line T station. If you're watching in Newton or Brookline, driving shouldn't be that bad, as long as you give yourself an extra half hour for traffic. Take I-95 to exit 19 or 20, depending on where you want to watch.

Parking

Good luck. A ton of roads are shut down along the race route, so spots are very scarce, try to get lucky and find a meter, but it's basically a lost cause.

How to Get There—Mass Transit

Ahh—now we're talking. Take the green line to Arlington if you're planning on watching from the finish line, or Kenmore if you're going to Kenmore Square (note that Copley is closed on Marathon Monday). Take the C train to the stop of your choice if you're planning on watching in Brookline (it runs parallel to the race). The D train will get you to Newton. If you're coming in from out of town, take the commuter rail to Back Bay and walk to the Arlington T stop, or simply walk a block and you're at the finish line. Fares run from $2 to $8.75.

Hiking in Boston

While it may not be the greatest city for driving, Boston is a great walking city. Whether you're in the mood for a casual stroll or a major trek, the city offers a surprisingly wide array of hikes and walks from which to choose. The trails closest to the city tend to be more scenic walks than hikes—appropriate for strolling students or families who want to get out and about in the city. If you're hungering for some real hiking, you'll need to be prepared for a drive. Boston's outskirts offer plenty of rigorous hiking trails with breathtaking views of the city and a taste of Massachusetts nature. If none of that is hardcore enough for you, the White Mountains of New Hampshire are just a Zipcar (see page 193) away.

Boston Harbor Islands

Seven miles from downtown Boston, this cluster of pretty much undiscovered islands is a great day trip to walk among historical forts and bucolic landscapes, birdwatch, or do some beachcombing. The inexpensive ferry from Long Wharf drops you off at Georges Island, where you can explore Fort Warren, a former Civil War prison that supposedly has its own ghost, "The Lady in Black." From there you can take free shuttles to the other islands. Peddocks Island has the longest coastline of all the islands and the most diverse set of trails. Grape Island takes you through forests, orchards, and rocky shoreline. Lovells has nice sand dunes and swimming beaches. Ferry service runs six times a day to Spectacle Island, a former dump site, which has been refurbished with excavated dirt from the Big Dig. It features a renewable energy visitor center, electric cars, a marina, beaches, and five miles of trails. There is camping on Peddocks, Grape, Lovells, and Bumpkin, but you must pack in and pack out everything yourself. Ferries to Spectacle Island and Georges Island operate from 9 am until sunset in the summer. Roundtrip tickets cost $15 for adults, $11 for seniors (65+), $9 for children (ages 4-11), and children under 4 ride for free. For more information, go to www.bostonharborislands.org or call 617-223-8666 for schedules.

HarborWalk

With the cleaning up of Boston Harbor (though we still wouldn't swim in it) and the removal of the Central Artery, the waterfront has become more beautiful and accessible to pedestrian traffic. Finally realizing that people are attracted to a picturesque waterfront, Boston decided to capitalize on its coastal setting and incorporate it into the life of the city. The HarborWalk is a multi-use attraction consisting of walkways, parks, benches, artwork, restaurants, and swimming spots extending from Chelsea to Neponset. Currently 38 miles long, it is 80% complete and meanders through diverse waterfront neighborhoods with views of the Harbor Islands and Boston skyline. A don't miss highlight is the Institute of Contemporary Art (ICA), with its glass structure perched over the waterfront. It is really quite pleasant on warm summer nights to wander among the boats and the lights of the city and revisit neighborhoods from a whole new perspective. With the Rose Kennedy Greenway complete (and catching flack for not having enough people on it), feel free to give that a stroll from where it parallels the Harbor Walk on Atlantic Ave. The signs might be the best part—especially the one that speaks directly to your pooch.

Arnold Arboretum

Harvard's Arnold Arboretum, located in Jamaica Pla[...] occupies 265 acres and boasts a dizzying array of woo[...] plants, more than 700 of which are over 100 years old. Y[...] can take a free guided tour of the grounds (call 617-52[...] 1718 for tour schedules) or amble along the three-mile t[...] at your own pace. The arboretum welcomes dogs as long [...] they're kept on a leash. The botanical haven is just two bloc[...] away from the Forest Hills T stop (Orange Line) and parking[...] available outside the main gate (although spots can be ha[...] to come by on certain days, such as Sundays and summ[...] holidays). Restrooms are located next to the entrance gate[...] the Hunnewell Visitor Center. The grounds are open every [...] of the year during daylight hours. For more information, vi[...] www.arboretum.harvard.edu.

Fresh Pond Reservation

This is a favorite of local residents and Harvard studen[...] Located just one mile from the university and six miles fro[...] downtown Boston, the Fresh Pond Reservation offers [...] rather easy 2.25-mile paved trail around comely Fresh Pon[...] the 155-acre reservoir. The trail has become a hot spot f[...] joggers, cyclists, and skaters. If you take your dog, be sure [...] check out the pooper-scooper dispensers! But it's not just th[...] athletic types that reap the benefits of the reservation—th[...] reservoir provides drinking water to many residents an[...] businesses in Cambridge. To reach the reservation by trai[...] take the Red Line to Alewife (last stop). By car, follow Rou[...] 2 east or west to Fresh Pond Parkway. The reservation lies o[...] the corner of Huron Avenue and Fresh Pond Parkway. You[...] find the best entrance to the reservation directly across fro[...] Wheeler Street. Parking in the reservation is reserved for ca[...] with a Cambridge permit. There is parking after hours at th[...] Tobin School, or take bus #72, #74, #75, or #78. For mo[...] information, visit www.friendsoffreshpond.org or call 61[...] 349-6319.

Mount Auburn Cemetery

Hailed as America's first landscaped cemetery and a Nationa[...] Historic Landmark, Mount Auburn provides two miles o[...] leisurely walking, alternating between paved walkway[...] and unpaved footpaths, and is considered one of the bes[...] birding spots in the state. Aside from the 86,000 graves, th[...] cemetery is home to over 5,000 native and foreign tree[...] Located just 1.5 miles west of Harvard Square, the cemeter[...] can be reached via Route 2 or 3 to Route 16 at the Moun[...] Auburn/Brattle Street intersection on Fresh Pond Parkway. I[...] you follow Mount Auburn Street (Rte 16) west for two block[...] you will reach the entrance. Contact the Friends of Moun[...] Auburn Cemetery (617-547-7105) for information abou[...] guided tours and lectures or visit their website at www[...] mountauburn.org. No dogs allowed.

Forest Hills Cemetery

Jamaica Plain's Forest Hills Cemetery is overshadowed i[...] popularity (perhaps unfairly) by Mount Auburn Cemeter[...] Established in 1848, it's one of the country's oldest buria[...] grounds, featuring 275 acres of beautifully sculpte[...] landscape. The cemetery offers books, brochures, an[...] maps to help visitors create their own tours of the ground[...] and its famous residents, including Eugene O'Neill and[...]

, cummings. One of its most impressive features is Lake Hibiscus, which hosts the Buddhist-inspired lantern lighting festival held annually in the summer season. Another highlight is the Sculpture Path, a revolving exhibit of work by contemporary local and national artists. The cemetery is located conveniently next to the Forest Hills T stop. If you're driving, take the Arborway east over the Casey overpass and follow signs for the cemetery exit, located on the right on Shea Circle. The grounds are open year-round during daylight hours. For more information, visit www. foresthillscemetery.com or call 617-524-0128.

Hammond Pond Reservation

Hammond Pond is located behind a suburban mall in Chestnut Hill—an unlikely place to find a reservation. You can see the department stores as you hike through the 114 acres of woodlands. It's also one of the few outdoor places in Boston where you can rock climb. The best place to start is at the entrance to the reservation, located on the left of Hammond Pond at the north side of the parking lot. Walk through the metal gate and remain on the wide main path through the woods. If you're interested in rock climbing, you'll see rocks to your left a little way along the path. If climbing rocks is not your thing, continue on for two miles of easy walking or try fishing in the pond. Hammond Pond Reservation can be reached by foot from the Chestnut Hill T stop. Hammond Pond Reservation is open year-round during daylight hours. For more information, call 617-698-1802.

Breakheart Reservation

Hidden amidst strip malls and fast-food joints along Route 1, this 640-acre hardwood forest is a treasure for hikers lucky enough to stumble across it. The reservation offers many miles of scenic views and plenty of strenuous trails to get your heart pumping. Fishing, bird watching, cross-country skiing, swimming, and biking are other attractions that lure nature lovers out to Breakheart. As there's really no way to get there by mass transit, you'll have to drive. Take Route 1 to the Lynn Fells Parkway exit towards Melrose and Stoneham. Turn right onto Forest Street, and follow the signs to Breakheart Reservation. A good place to begin your hike is on the paved Pine Tops Road, located next to the parking lot adjacent to the headquarters building. For more information, call 781-233-0834.

Skyline Trail

This seven-mile trail is located in Blue Hills Reservation (near Milton), the largest open space within 35 miles of Boston. The Skyline Trail winds through rocky hills and provides scenic views of the city. With an elevation gain of 2,500 feet, this hike is not for the faint of heart. This is a strenuous hike that will take at least half a day. But don't fret! If you're not up for a real workout, there are plenty of less challenging trails in the park and the color-coded trail map available at the headquarters building will help you find your way around. To get there, take Route I-93 to Exit 3 towards Houghton's Pond. After exiting, turn right at the stop sign onto Hillside Street and travel about a mile until you reach Houghton's Pond. The trail is open year-round from sunrise until sunset. Also in the Reservation is the Ponkapoag Pond trail, a four-mile

loop around the pond, the highlight of which is a boardwalk trail (two miles roundtrip) through a rare Atlantic white cedar swamp. It's fun and different, but be warned: Wear waterproof shoes. Seriously. The boardwalk is made up of half submerged logs.

Middlesex Fells Reservation Eastern Section

Located seven miles north of Boston, Middlesex Fells is a 2,060-acre reservation where you'll find some of the area's most challenging hikes, many of which are considered some of the Boston area's best kept secrets. (If anyone asks, you didn't hear about it from us.) Middlesex Fells is off I-93 past the Stone Zoo. Parking is available on Pond Street. The beginning of the trail is located on the south side of Pond Street and begins behind a Virginia Wood sign near Gate 42. The trail is approximately 5.5 miles long, but can be extended to 16 miles if you connect trails. All of the hikes in this area are fairly strenuous and involve climbing and descending rocky slopes.

Moose Hill Wildlife Sanctuary

This is the oldest and second-largest Massachusetts Audubon Society (MAS) sanctuary. Moose Hill covers 1,984 acres that teem with wildlife and offers more than 25 miles of well-marked trails. One trail in particular, the Warner Trail, provides an exceptional view of the surrounding area from 491 feet. (You have to earn the view by climbing up Bluff Head.) Admission is $4 for adults, $3 for seniors and children aged 3–12. Members come for free. Trails are open daily from dawn to dusk. The best way to get to Moose Hill is off of Route 128/I-95 S. Take Exit 10. At the end of the ramp, make a left; then travel a quarter-mile and turn right onto Route 27 towards Walpole. After half a mile, turn left onto Moose Hill Street. Follow the MAS signs to the parking lot on the left. Find your way to the Visitor Center. All of the trails stem from there. For more information call 781-784-5691.

Walden Woods

Henry David Thoreau's account of his two-year stay in Walden is credited with sparking the conservation movement. Though nestled between railroad tracks and busy Route 2, Walden Pond is still a peaceful and pleasant setting for an afternoon walk no matter what season. The 102-foot deep Walden Pond is just one part of the 2680-acre Walden Woods. There is an easy loop trail around the pond, which passes by the site of Thoreau's house (a replica sits in the parking lot). If you get too hot, you can always stop for a quick dip. Easy interconnecting trails link up with the neighboring Walden Woods and Lincoln Conservation Trust. The main parking area is on Route 126 off of Route 2. Parking ($5) is limited to 350 spaces and fills up quickly on hot summer days. If there is no ranger at the gate, you will need exact change for the annoying automated ticket machine, inevitably causing longer delays than dealing with a live person. On crowded days, there are designated times of the day when they let people in. Call ahead at 781-259-4700, and visit www.walden.org for more information.

General Information

City of Boston Swimming:	www.cityofboston.gov/bcyf/facilities.asp
Department of Conservation Resources:	www.mass.gov/eea/state-parks-beaches/pools-beaches-boating
MIT Zesiger Center:	mitrecsports.com/index.php/aquatics
YMCA of Greater Boston:	www.ymcaboston.org
New England Masters Swimming:	www.swimnem.org

Overview

With your swimming options including universities, the oldest Y in the country, and local gyms, it's easier to skip the ma[...] poorly maintained pools of the city with their odd hours. While the city's pools are the cheapest option (meaning free) they're only open from mid-June to mid-August. You'll find the city's website provides little help in locating pools and th[...] only way to get schedules is to call each pool directly. For serious lap swimmers, the largest indoor pool in Boston is **MIT's Zesiger Center** (Map 27), running short course all winter and changing lanes to a 50 m for the summer. Day pass[...] are available. New England Masters maintains a comprehensive listing on swimming clubs, workout locations, and stro[...] clinics. There are also YMCAs scattered around the metro area.

In the summer, the DCR operates many outdoor swimming and wading pools and public beaches along the Bay and a[...] local ponds. Their website lists the hours and locations. The most famous wading pool is the Frog Pond in Boston Commo[...] If fighting for pool space amongst hordes of screaming children is not your thing, favorite alternatives include taking [...] dip in Walden Pond in Concord (get there early, as the parking lot fills up fast) and strolling the busy beaches at Reve[...] and Wollaston, which can be accessed by the Blue and Red Lines respectively. The Standells might "love that dirty wate[...] but ongoing efforts to improve the once dangerous water quality of the Charles River continue, and the Charles Rive[...] Swimming Club held its first ever one-mile swim in 2007 to demonstrate its safety (toxic algae postponed it in 2006), bu[...] recreational swimming is not encouraged, especially after a heavy rain. For those of you with a little extra cash burnin[...] some holes in your designer swim trunks, the **Colonnade Hotel** (Map 6) has a rooftop pool that has a $50 weekday pas[...] for the public. It's like a club scene up there though, so make sure to spray tan on some abs if you're on the flabbier side.

Where to Swim

	Address	Phone	Fees	Map
Lee Memorial Wading Pool	Charles St	617-523-9746	Free	1
Boston Harbor Island National Park Beach	ferry leaves from Long Wharf outside Marriott Hotel, State St	617-223-8666	Free (but unavoidable $10–12 ferry ticket)	2
Mirabella Pool	585 Commercial St	617-635-5235	$10 adults, kids under 5 free	2
Boston Chinatown Neighborhood Center Pool	Ash St	617-635-5129	$75 per year, $30 children	4
Huntington Avenue YMCA	316 Huntington Ave	617-536-6950	Membership $55.60 per month. Plus $100 joining fee	5
Colonnade Hotel	120 Huntington Ave	617-424-7000	$30 per day pass	6
Blackstone Community Center	50 W Brookline St	617-635-5162	$25 per year, children $5	7
Charlestown Community Center	255 Medford St	617-635-5169	$25 per year adults, $5 children	8
Harborside Community Center	312 Border St	617-635-5114	$25 per year adults, $5 children	9
Paris Street Pool	113 Paris St	617-635-5125	$20 per year adults, $5 children	9
Condon Community Center	200 D St	617-635-5100	$5 adults, $3 youth	10
Curley Community Center	1663 Columbia Rd	617-635-5104	$25 per year	11
Madison Park Community Center	55 New Dudley St	617-635-5206	$10 per year adults, $4 children	13
Curtis Hall Community Center	20 South St	617-635-5193	$25 per year adults, $5 children	14
Hennigan Community Center	200 Heath St	617-635-5198	$25 per year adults, $5 children	15
Clougherty Pool	Bunker Hill St	617-635-5173	Free	16
Dealtry Memorial Pool	114 Pleasant St	617-923-0073	Free	16
Kirrane Aquatic Center	60 Tappan St	617-713-5435	$5 adults, $3 students	17
Brighton-Allston Swimming & Wading Pool	380 N Beacon St	617-254-2965	Free	18
Oak Square YMCA	615 Washington St	617-782-3535	$58/month	18
Reilly Memorial Swimming Pool	Chestnut Hill Ave	617-277-7822	Free	18
Artesani Wading Pool	Soldiers Field Rd	-	-	19
McCrehan Memorial Swimming & Wading	356 Rindge Ave	617-354-9154	Free	22
Vietnam Veterans Memorial	Carter St	617-884-9630	Free	25
Cambridge Family YMCA	820 Massachusetts Ave	617-661-9622	$48 per month & $50 joining fee	27
Veterans Memorial Swimming & Wading	719 Memorial Dr	617-354-9381	Free	27
Zesiger Sports and Fitness Center	120 Vassar St	617-452-3690	$12 per day adults, $7 children	27
Mason Pool	176 Norfolk St	617-635-5241	$10 per year (adult), $5 (under 18)	28
Cass Memorial	120 Washington St	617-445-0062	Free	
Moynihan Wading Pool	920 Truman Pkwy		Free	
Olsen Swimming & Wading	95 Turtle Pond Pkwy	617-364-9524		

General Information

Map:	16
Address:	4 Yawkey Wy
	Boston, MA 02215
Phone:	617-REDSOX9
	(617-733-7699)
Website:	boston.redsox.mlb.com

Overview

It would be only the slightest of exaggerations to say that, in Boston, the Red Sox are a religion and Fenway Park is a house of worship. Situated just outside Kenmore Square, Fenway Park is a place where the staunchly unfriendly locals find fellowship in their deep love of the Sox and an even deeper hatred of the Yankees. In fact, Red Sox Nation is still (and will forever be) gloating over the historic 2004 comeback win against arch-evil men in pinstripes before crushing the St. Louis Cardinals in the Fall Classic. Yet, our gloating increased quite a bit in 2007, as the Sox once again brought home the World Series Trophy with a four game sweep of the Colorado Rockies, while the Yankees were at home washing their uniforms. That's two World Series wins in four seasons, after an 86-year drought. Boston is truly in its baseball renaissance.

Despite this devotion, even the most die-hard fan cannot deny two basic truths: Fenway is old and Fenway is small. Fenway Park celebrated it's 100th anniversary in 2012 the first game at Fenway Park, played on April 20, 1912, it bumped off the front page of the newspapers for the breaking news of the Titanic sinking a few days earlier. With only 37,493 seats, it is the smallest park in the majors, though management has recently added a few thousand more seats in some very creative locations to expand capacity.

With age, however, comes a rich sense of history, and the dusty corners of Fenway have more personality than perhaps any other park in the game. The best-known of these character traits is the towering Green Monster, the 37-foot left field wall whose odd location can turn pop flies into homers and homers into singles. Marking the right field foul line is Pesky's Pole, named for Red Sox legend Johnny Pesky. On the manually operated scoreboard in left field, Morse Code dots and dashes spell out the initials of Red Sox owner Tom Yawkey and his wife.

Walking on Yawkey Way before a game is one of the best experiences you can have in Boston. Make sure to arrive at the game at least 45 minutes before first pitch, so you can experience the action around the park, which includes a live band, plenty of souvenir shops, and some of the best hot dogs in the world, "Fenway Franks" (Fenway Park sells more hot dogs than any other park in the country). Note, only ticketed fans are allowed on Yawkey Way before games.

Truly patriotic citizens of Red Sox Nation should take the Fenway Park tour. A tour leaves from Yawkey Way every hour Mon–Sun 9 am–5 pm. On game days, the last tour is offered 3 hours before the start of the game (so 4 pm. for a 7 pm. game). Tours are $16.00 for adults, $14.00 for seniors, and $12.00 for children and students. Tickets for tours can be purchased at the Gate D Ticket Booth on the corner of Yawkey Way and Van Ness Street. When the booth is closed, they are available at the team store on Yawkey Way. Tours last for 50 minutes.

How to Get There—Mass Transit

Take the Green Line to Kenmore and follow the crowd to the ballpark. The MBTA Commuter Rail's Worcester/Framingham line also goes to Yawkey, a short walk from Fenway Park. There's also a free game-day-only shuttle that connects Gate B at Fenway Park with the Ruggles stop, served by the T's Orange Line and the MBTA Commuter Rail's Providence/Stoughton, Needham, and Franklin lines. Subway fare is $2; commuter rail fares range from $2 to $11, and a $3 surcharge if you buy tickets aboard the train.

How to Get Tickets

Always difficult to score, the first places to try for individual game and season ticket information, are the Red Sox box office at 877-REDSOX9 and the team's website. Ticket prices range from $12 bleacher seats to $312 dugout box seats. If you are willing to wait in line, a great way to get tickets is to head to the gate E window around 2 and a half hours before game time (4:40 on weeknights). Tickets that had been held for players' families are sold at face value at the window. It's the only way to get face value seats on a whim the day of a game. Fans are allowed to start lining up five hours before game time (2 p.m. on weeknights), but you would only need to wait that long for a marquee game, such as the first Yankee game, or opening day), and tickets go on sale two hours before first pitch. Everyone that wants to go to the game must be on hand to buy a ticket, holding places in line is strictly prohibited. There is a "scalp free" zone at gate B on game days, where ticket holders can sell extra seats to fans at face value. Red Sox personnel are on hand to observe every sale.

A good tip for getting tickets is showing up to the game after an inning and a half or so, say 7:40 for a 7:10 game, when scalpers slash prices dramatically. Fans can get as low as $15 for $55 tickets. Another good tip is to look for standing room tickets either down the first base line or on the Budweiser right field roof deck. The tickets are only $20-$30 and can usually be purchased the day of the game at the Red Sox ticket office. The Bud Deck has especially great views, better than the Green Monster, so $30 is well worth it.

General Information

Address: One Patriot Pl
Foxborough, MA 02035
Phone: 508-543-1776
Websites: www.gillettestadium.com
www.patriots.com
www.revolutionsoccer.net

Overview

As far as NFL franchises go, the New England Patriots were a joke until Bill Parcells took over as head coach in 1993 and Robert Kraft bought the team in 1994. The team continued to play in a mediocre stadium until 2002. Old Schaefer/Sullivan/Foxboro Stadium was an unsightly, obsolete, charmless concrete slab, but the Pats sent it packing in style. The last game at Foxboro Stadium was the hotly debated "Snow Bowl" vs. the Oakland Raiders. Depending on your loyalties, QB Tom Brady either fumbled or "tucked" the ball during a key late-game possession. (It was a tuck.) The Pats won, propelling them to victory in Super Bowl 36.

The 2002 season was ushered in by the opening of Gillette Stadium, where the Patriots proved that their first championship season was no fluke, winning two more Super Bowls over the next three years. The stadium has been accessorized with a 12-story lighthouse and a replica of the Longfellow Bridge at one end of the field. A high definition screen, nearly 1,300 square feet in size, hangs over each end zone.

With a seating capacity of over 68,000, Gillette Stadium does triple duty, also acting as the home of Major League Soccer's New England Revolution and a major concert venue. It can be a good place to catch big names like the Rolling Stones or U2. Gillette also hosts the biggest annual country music festival in the northeast during the last weekend of August, with perennial headliner Kenny Chesney and a loaded lineup of Nashville talent. Given the size of the stadium, make sure to bring a pair of binoculars if you have anything but the best seats.

On non-game days, the Hall At Patriot's Place is a great destination for any football fan. Located steps away from the stadium, with an entrance through the team's pro shop, the hall of fame has plenty of interactive exhibits as well as relics from throughout Patriots history in a state-of-the-art facility that was opened in 2008. Some notable exhibits include the team's three Super Bowl trophies, the infamous snow plow from 1982 and a film chronicling the Pats' rise to the top of the football world. The hall opens at 10 a.m. every day and closes at 7 p.m. every day except for Saturday, when it closes at 9 p.m. Admission is $5 for adults, $7 for seniors and $5 for children aged 12 or younger. For more information, visit www.thehallatpatriotplace.com.

Patriot Place, the gigantic mall that's sprung up around the stadium, is now in full swing, with every option imaginable for you to purchase on your way in or out of a game. The movie theater there, which has an adults only section, recently kicked Justin Bieber out for being underage, proving that the Patriots always make good decisions.

How to Get There—Driving

From Boston, take I-93 S to I-95 S; take I-95 S to Exit 9 (Wrentham) onto Route 1 S. Follow Route 1 S approximately three miles to Gillette Stadium (on the left).

Upper Level, Corner/End Zone
Upper Level, Sideline
Mezzanine Level, Corner/End Zone
Lower Level, Corne
Lower Level, Sidelin
* N/A=Non-Alcoholic

Parking

The lots open four hours before Pats games, three ho before concerts and other events, and two hours befo Revolution games, leaving plenty of time for tailgating an opportunity fans use to the fullest. The lots tend to up well before game time, so make sure you give yours ample time to get there. Pre-game Route 1 traffic legendary, so give yourself at least 90 more minutes th you think you'll need when heading out to the gar even more in bad weather. General Seating ticket holde should enter lot P2, P5, or P10 from Route 1. Follow sig for "General Stadium Parking." Disabled parkers and lim should head for P2, buses for P5, and RVs for P10. Patriots games, car parking costs $40, RV and limo parki costs $125, and bus parking costs $200. Prices vary other Gillette events.

How to Get There— Mass Transit

MBTA commuter rail trains leave South Station for Foxbo Station on game days. A round-trip ticket costs around $ The train departs from the stadium 30 minutes after th game. For more information and a complete schedule, vi www.mbta.com/riding_the_t/patriots/

How to Get Tickets

With the Pat's Dynasty status firmly cemented as the tea of the Century, and the Greatest Football Team to Ev Exist (fact), you're going to have some ticket trouble especially since Tom Brady is still throwing bombs. To g on the season ticket waiting list, visit the Patriots' websi and have $100 a seat on hand for a deposit. For regul tickets (or concert tickets), call Ticketmaster at 617-93 2222 or visit www.ticketmaster.com. Game tickets rang from $59 to $125. The ubiquitous scalpers can be four roaming the parking lots and entrances to the stadium StubHub.com, eBay, and Craiglist also accommodate foll who are selling and buying tickets, but be careful—seaso ticket holders have been known to lose their seats whe being caught selling extra tickets online.

eneral Information

Map: 1
ress: 150 Causeway St
Boston, MA 02114
ne: 617-624-1000
Celtics: 617-854-8000
Bruins: 617-624-1900
sites: www.tdgarden.com
www.nba.com/celtics
bruins.nhl.com

verview

ater Boston's long regional sports nightmare
ver. Once again Celtics and Bruins fans can
urately say that their teams compete in "the
den." The original Boston Garden, which opened
928, earned the adoration of Bostonians as the
na in which Bird, McHale, and Parish propelled
Celts to dynasty status. In footage of the team's
4 NBA finals victory over the Lakers, fans crowd
sidelines and rush the court with time left on
clock. Bruins games could be even less civil and,
espondingly, even more fun.

Loge   Club   Balcony

the 1980s drew to a close, however, both the
tics and the Garden lost a bit of their luster. The team
gan a slow decline from glory and the venue grew more
I more decrepit. Finally in 1995, the FleetCenter was
nstructed next door and both the Celtics and the Bruins
d goodbye to their old stomping grounds. The new
ne took years to catch on among the area's stubborn
ditionalists. When Fleet was acquired by Bank of America,
e new parent company sold the naming rights—for $6
lion a year—to TD Banknorth, who promptly restored
e proper name. Then in 2009 TD Banknorth became TD
now we have TD Garden. Can we just replace TD with
ston" and get this over with? The 17,565-seat (18,624 for
ketball) TD Garden has all that you would expect from
modern arena—rocket-launched t-shirts, overpriced food
d beer, luxury box TVs, and airline and casino promotions
ring timeouts—but still holds on to touches of tradition,
luding the Celts' legendary parquet floor. Nonetheless,
en with the relative success of the Celts and Bs in recent
ars, the new venue just doesn't seem to inspire the same
at of loyal as did its dilapidated predecessor. Having said
at, the Celtics NBA Record 17th Banner now hangs from
ese new rafters, hopefully ushering in a new dynasty for
e boys in Green. Even more fitting was the fact that we
n it against those old purple and gold Lakers, at home,
ving once again that in NBA history it's Celtics first,
kers a solid and distant second. Just don't remind us what
appened during the rematch in 2010.

e Bruins, the only major league team in Boston (the
volution? They don't count!), that was left without a recent
ampionship, has fully cemented Boston as Titletown, USA
bringing the Stanley Cup home in 2011 with a victory
r the Vancouver Canucks. That's seven, count them again
ar god, seven major championships in 10 years. To break
t down further, that's the Pats with three, the Sox with
o, and the C's and B's with one each. We've had so many
ampionship parades that people are lining up for the next
e already, just to get a good spot. BEST. CITY. EVER.

addition to sporting events, the TD Garden hosts the circus
d concerts by artists ranging from Beyonce to U2. It is also
me to the sports museum, which houses many of the
ost important pieces from the old Garden, including Larry
d's locker, and the Bruins' penalty box. For more info, go to
ww.sportsmuseum.org.

ow to Get There—Driving

iving to the Garden is no more difficult than getting any
ere else in Boston by car—which is to say that it is quite

difficult. From the north, take I-93 S to Exit 26A (Leverett
Circle/Cambridge). Follow the signs (if construction hasn't
relocated them) towards North Station/TD Garden. Take a
right at the end of the ramp; the arena will be on your left.
From the south, take I-93 N to Exit 26 (Storrow Drive). After
the exit, keep left and follow the signs (see above warning)
for TD Garden. Watch out, it's a left-hand exit. The Garden will
be on your left.

Parking

Parking is provided directly underneath the Garden in the
North Station garage, which charges $30 for events. The
lot doesn't block cars in, so it's a pretty good option. It will
fill up, as it only has 1,200 spaces. The T is the way to go, it's
cheaper and you don't have to show up an hour early for a
game. Unlike Fenway Park, before a game, you're staring at
a hardwood floor or a clean sheet of ice, which can get old
after around 90 seconds.

How to Get There—
Mass Transit

The TD Garden sits atop the North Station commuter rail
station, which services the northern suburbs. Directly
underneath is a new "superstation" that finally puts
North Station's Green Line and Orange Line T stops in the
same location. The Charles/MGH Red Line stop and the
Bowdoin Blue Line stop are less than a ten-minute walk
away. Commuter rails fares range from $2 to $11, with a $3
surcharge if you buy the ticket on board the train.

How to Get Tickets

To get Celtics season tickets, call 866-4CELTIX or visit the
Celtics' website. They offer full-season, half-season, and
multi-game packages. Individual ticket prices range from
$25 nosebleed seats to $275 courtside seats. The mid-range
$55 end-court seats offer an excellent value.

To get Bruins season tickets, call 617-624-BEAR or visit the
Bruins' website. The Bs offer full-season, half-season, and ten-
game packages, with individual ticket prices ranging from $26
to $101, topping out with the mysteriously un-priced Premium
Club. If you have to ask, you can't afford them.) Craigslist is a
good option the night before a game. You can probably find
tickets at face value or below.

If you don't have tickets but have cash to burn, scalpers
can be found on Causeway Street on game days.

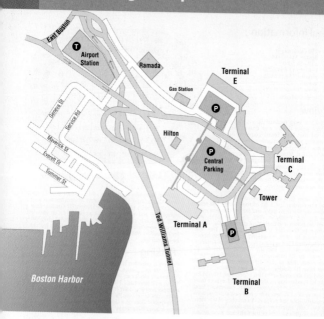

Airline	Terminal	Phone Number
Aer Lingus	E	800-474-7424
Air Canada/ Air Canada Jazz	B	888-247-2262
Air France	E	800-237-2747
AirTran	C	800-247-8726
Alaska Airlines	B	800-252-7522
Alitalia	E	800-223-5730
American (except int'l arrivals)	B	800-433-7300
American (int'l arrivals only)	E	800-433-7300
American Eagle	B	800-433-7300
British Airways	E	800-247-9297
Cape Air	C	800-352-0714
Copa Airlines	E	800-359-2672
Delta Air Lines	A	800-221-1212
Delta Connection/Com Air	A	800-354-9822
Delta Shuttle	A	800-221-1212
Finnair	E	800-950-5000
Iberia	E	800-772-4642
Icelandair	E	800-223-5500
Japan Airlines	E	800-525-3663

Airline	Terminal	Phone Number
JetBlue (except int'l arrivals)	C	800-538-258
JetBlue (int'l arrivals only)	E	800-538-258
Lufthansa	E	800-645-388
PenAir	B	800-448-422
Porter Airlines	E	800-619-862
SATA	E	800-762-999
Southwest Airlines	E	800-435-979
Spirit Airlines	B	800-772-711
Sun Country	E	800-359-678
Swiss	E	877-359-794
TACV	E	866-359-822
United	C	800-241-652
United Express	C	800-241-6522
US Airways	B	800-428-432
US Airways Express	B	800-428-432
US Airways Shuttle	B	800-428-432,
Virgin America	B	877-359-847
Virgin Atlantic	E	800-862-862

General Information

Website:	www.massport.com/logan-airport
Customer Service:	617-561-1800
Ground Transportation Info:	800-23-LOGAN
Logan Lost and Found:	617-561-1714
Parking Office:	617-561-1673

Overview

The country's 12th busiest airport (according to Bureau of Transportation Statistics), Logan International Airport features all the serpentine security lines and two-mile gate runs of most major airports and is located in an area of the country where weather can ground planes at any time of the year. But thanks to the completion of the Big Dig and the extension of the Silver Line, getting to Logan is now much easier.

Jutting into the harbor from East Boston, Logan opened in 1923 as the "temporary occupant" on landfill originally intended to be a port. By 1939, flying contraptions had proven their worth and the site was made permanent. The airport is named after Lt. General Edward Lawrence Logan, a local and a Harvard grad who served in the Spanish-American War, the Massachusetts House of Representatives, and the Senate.

The decade-long Logan Modernization Project yielded new and improved Terminals A and C, a new T station, an extended Silver Line, a new international arrivals hall serving Terminal E, standardized and improved signage, and improved access to the Central Parking Garage. In 2009, Health Magazine ranked Logan as the healthiest airport in the country. Terminal A is the world's first airport terminal certified by the U.S. Green Building Council for using the highest green construction standards, with a heat reflecting roof, low-flow faucets, waterless urinals, self-dimming lights, and recycled construction materials.

If good planning or bad weather leaves you with time to kill before your flight, you can grab a gourmet snack at Todd English's Bonfire or one of the three Legal Seafood locations, relax in one of 50 wooden rocking chairs (16 decorated by local artists), or just spend an hour letting yourself be hypnotized by the rhythmic movements of billiard balls through the kinetic sculpture in Terminal C.

How to Get There—Driving

To get to Logan from the west, take the Mass Pike (I-90) E through the Ted Williams Tunnel until the highway ends. From the south, use I-93 N and take Exit 20 to I-90 E. From the north, take I-93 S and follow the signs to the Callahan Tunnel. Check www.massport.com for traffic and construction updates.

Parking

Hourly and daily parking are available at Central Parking Garage, Terminal B Garage, and Terminal E Parking Lots 1 and 2. Rates range from $3 to $24 during the day and $36 to $48 a day for overnight parking. The Economy Parking lot charges a daily rate of $27 and a weekly rate of $108.

How to Get There—Mass Transit

Seriously, do yourself a favor by taking the T. It's a quick ride on the Blue Line from downtown to the Airport stop. A free shuttle bus that runs 4am–1am (and prevents 7 tons of emissions from polluting the atmosphere every year by running on compressed natural gas), will take you from the T stop to your terminal. Or take the Red Line to South Station and transfer for the Silver Line bus, which stops at each airport terminal. If you're coming in from the 'burbs, check out the Logan Express buses that service Braintree, Framingham, Peabody, and Woburn. A Park-and-Ride system is in place, and although the prices for parking and buses vary, they will always be cheaper than taking a cab, especially if you're downtown near the water, the MBTA's Harbor Express water taxi can get you from Long Wharf to the airport in less than ten minutes.

How to Get There—Taxi

It's hard to get to Logan from anywhere except Eastie for less than $20. Boston Cab: 617-536-5010; Checker Taxi: 617-536-7000; City Cab: 617-536-5100; Green Cab (Somerville): 617-623-6000; Cambridge Cab: 617-776-5000.

Rental Cars

Advantage	800-777-5500
Alamo	800-327-9633
Avis	800-831-2847
Budget	800-527-0700
Dollar	800-800-4000
Hertz	800-654-3131
National	800-227-7368
Enterprise	800-325-8007 (off-airport)
Thrifty	800-367-2277 (off-airport)

Hotels

Courtyard Boston Tremont · 275 Tremont St · 617-426-1400
Embassy Suites · 207 Porter St · 617-567-5000
Hampton Inn · 230 Lee Burbank Hwy · 781-286-5665
Hilton · 85 Terminal Rd · 617-568-6700
Holiday Inn · 225 McClellan Hwy · 617-569-5250
Hyatt · 101 Harborside Dr · 617-568-1234 · 800-633-7313
Marriott Long Wharf · 296 State St · 617-227-0800
Omni Parker House · 60 School St · 617-227-8600
Hilton Boston Downtown ·
89 Broad St · 617-556-0006

177

Transit • **The Big Dig**

History

The story begins just after World War II. When the good people at the Massachusetts Department of Public Works noticed the increasing popularity of automobiles and the stream of people leaving the city for the suburbs, they decided to make plans to build some major highways. The first highway to be completed was I-93, the Central Artery, hailed at the time as "a futuristic highway in the sky."

It soon became apparent that I-93 totally sucked. It was ugly, disruptive to neighborhoods, and boasted a high accident rate due to the excessive number of entry and exit ramps along the 1.5-mile stretch through the city. Recognizing that the Central Artery was a disaster, community groups fought successfully to stop other major highway projects. Two plans that never came to fruition were the Inner Belt (unbuilt I-695), which would have taken traffic around I-93 via a new, ten-lane BU bridge, and the Southwest Corridor Highway (unbuilt I-95), which would have run from the 93/128 split up through Hyde Park and JP to central Boston.

While averting construction of two new highways was a small victory for city dwellers, I-93 was still operating at triple its capacity, resulting in traffic jams at most hours of the day. The solution to the congestion was to dig a highway under the city—a solution that rather resembled performing open-heart surgery on a fully awake patient. Planning the project took the entirety of the 1980s and construction finally began in September 1991. After fifteen years and almost fifteen billion dollars, the project is officially finished. Hallelujah!

What Is the Big Dig?

As most Bostonians know, the substantially completed "Central Artery/Tunnel Project" was, as the Massachusetts Turnpike Authority puts it, "the largest, most complex and technologically challenging highway project ever." The most important element of the Big Dig is the routing of I-93 from the Central Artery to a new (and leaky) tunnel. Other major aspects of the Dig include the extension of the Mass Pike to Logan Airport through the Ted Williams Tunnel, the construction of the beautiful Leonard P. Zakim Bunker Hill Memorial Bridge (yeah, it's a ridiculously long name), the erection of the Leverett Circle Connector Bridge, and a complete overhaul of the roads and traffic patterns around Logan Airport. The 2006 opening of the Albany Street off-ramp from I-93 S marked the point when all of the Dig's tunnels and bridges and their connection and

ramps to surface roads were open to general traffic. But when exactly does a civil engineering project of this magnitude "end"? Is it when the last orange pylon is removed from the road, or when the litigation finally wraps up? The I-93 tunnel (O'Neill Tunnel) sprouted a leak in 2004 shortly after opening to traffic. In its design for the tunnel, contractor Bechtel/Parsons Brinckerhoff recommended an approach that had never been used for another highway tunnel in the US, rejecting the more conventional design of lining the huge slurry walls with a concrete "tunnel box" in favor of making the slurry walls the tunnel's *only* walls. When the tunnel construction later necessitated waterproofing, the lack of interior walls caused some major problems. While the leaky walls and the endless construction are causes of concern and ennui for the daily commuters, the faulty bolts that fasten the concrete ceiling tiles are another issue all together. In July 2006, a woman was killed by one such tile falling on her car in the I-90 connector on her way to Logan Airport, a tragic event that lead to comprehensive inspections within the tunnels and the discovery of dangerous structural flaws and evidence of negligence. After extensive closings and traffic rerouting, the tunnel ceiling tiles have all reportedly been reinforced, though, and we are told that travel is once again wet and safe, but the loss of human life has added an unfortunate and serious undertone to the Big Dig's already infamous story.

Park Development

In December 2007, the Big Dig was officially completed, with the final price tag ringing up at $14.8 billion (not including interest which could raise the "real" cost to around $24 billion—ouch!), which Bostonians may end up paying for via toll and mass transportation rate hikes. Either way, someone has to pay the piper . . . er, digger. On a more positive note, the old elevated 93 was finally demolished, leading to a great deal more walking traffic from Faneuil Hall to the North End via the lovely Rose Kennedy Greenway, a 15-acre green space extending from Chinatown to the North End. Post-Dig park construction included pedestrian-friendly spots along the Fort Point Channel, in the Wharf District, and in the North End.

General Information

ss Highway Department:	www.massdot.state.ma.us/highway/Main.aspx
ssport:	www.massport.com
Dig:	www.massdot.state.ma.us/highway/TheBigDig.aspx

Overview

e first bridge built in the American colonies (a pile bridge, cidentally) was completed in 1662, connecting Cambridge and ghton. It stood where the Larz Anderson Bridge stands today. t-forward 350 years and you'll find no fewer than ten bridges anning the Charles River from the Inner Harbor to Brighton, luding the Boston University Bridge, the Harvard Bridge ka. the Mass Ave Bridge), and the Longfellow Bridge (with its t-and-pepper-shaker towers), all of which offer great views of e skyline. (The view from the BU Bridge is our favorite.) Other dges further upstream cross the river at River Street, Western enue, JFK Street/North Harvard Street (the Larz Anderson dge), and Gerry's Landing Road/Soldiers Field Road (the Eliot dge).

e Hub's new pet landmark is the Leonard P. Zakim Bunker I Memorial Bridge. No postcard of the Boston skyline seems mplete without the Zakim, which connects downtown Boston with Charlestown. Perhaps the only Big Dig undertaking worth its salt, the Zakim is the widest cable-stayed bridge in the world, with soaring towers designed to reflect nearby Bunker Hill Monument. The bridge gives off a luminous glow at night, adding to its impressive appearance. According to the *Portsmouth Herald*, some call it the "Bill Buckner Bridge" as traffic passes through an inverted Y-shaped structure like the ball that passed through the legs of the Red Sox first baseman during the 1986 World Series. Poor Bill Buckner. Unlike the other bridges crossing the Charles, the Zakim is unfortunately not open to pedestrians. The Charlestown Bridge, now somewhat overshadowed by the Zakim, connects the North End and Charlestown and was once the scene of many Irish/Italian gang fights.

The old green lady crossing the Mystic River and connecting Charlestown with Chelsea is the Tobin Bridge. The three lanes on the lower level run northbound; the three lanes on the upper level run southbound. Drivers heading south on the Tobin must pay a toll (30 cents with a resident commuter permit and $3 for everyone else).

The Evelyn Moakley Bridge, built in the mid-1990s over the Fort Point Channel to divert traffic from the historic-but-decaying Northern Avenue Bridge, is itself decaying at an alarmingly fast pace. Be careful walking across the bridge at high tide.

And remember: The Callahan Tunnel takes you to the airport (no toll) and the Sumner Tunnel takes you from the airport (yes, toll).

ridge	Engineer (E); Architect (A)	Length	Opened
oston University Bridge	Desmond and Lord (A)		1928
	John Rablin (E)		
harlestown (N Washington St) Bridge			1901
ongress Street Bridge			1930
iot Bridge	Maurice Witner (A)		1950
	Burns & Kennerson (E)		
velyn Moakley Bridge	Ammann & Whitney (A)	800'	1996
	Modern Continental (E)		
arvard Bridge	William Jackson (E)	364.4 smoots, one ear	1891
arz Anderson Bridge	Wheelright, Haven, and Hoyt (A)		1915
	John Rablin (E)		
everett Circle Connector Bridge	HNTB Corporation (E)	830'	1999
ongfellow Bridge	Edmund M. Wheelwright (A)	1,768'	1906
	William Jackson (E)		
Malden (Alford St) Bridge		2420'	
Northern Avenue Bridge		636'	1908
iver Street Bridge	Robert Bellows (A)	330'	1926
	John Rablin (E)		
ummer Street Bridge	John Cheney (A)		1899
	William Jackson (E)		
obin Memorial Bridge	JE Grenier Co (A)	1,525'	1950
Veeks Footbridge	McKim, Mead, and White (A)		1924
	John Rablin (E)		
Western Avenue Bridge	John Rablin (E)	328'	1924
eonard P. Zakim Bunker Hill Bridge	Christian Menn (designer)	1,457'	2002
	Miguel Rosales (A)		
	HNTB Corporation (E)		

Tunnel	Engineer	Length	Opened
Callahan Tunnel			1961
O'Neill Tunnel	Bechtel/Parsons Brinckerhoff (E)		2003
Sumner Tunnel			1934
Ted Williams Tunnel	Jacobs Engineering Group (designer)	8,500'	1995
	Bechtel/Parsons Brinckerhoff (E)		

General Information

Websites:
Boston: with: www.cityofboston.gov/parking
Brookline: www.brooklinema.gov
Cambridge: www2.cambridgema.gov/traffic
Somerville: www.ci.somerville.ma.us
Mass. RMV: www.massrmv.com
Phones:
Boston: 617-635-4680
Brookline: 617-730-2177
Cambridge: 617-349-4700
Somerville: 617-666-3311

Overview

Boston drivers have somehow made order out of chaos. We offer very few signs, have roadways simultaneously labeled both North and South (causing you to believe you've found the nexus of the universe), and claim, with pride mind you, the most aggressive road-ragers in the entire Northeast. Driving in the city itself is done more by "feel" than by specific directions, as every trip becomes an adventure in side streets, wrong turns, and clusterf**ks. And don't even ask about the endless civil war between drivers, bikers, and pedestrians.

The road system (if you can call it that) in Boston grew organically as the city expanded, not, as legend has it, out of cow paths (though it's a reasonable misconception). Little, if any, urban planning took place. The result is the chaos of today: an exasperating, exhilarating tangle of streets that are a source of pride to those who master them. The only exception to this pandemonium is Back Bay, which was given the benefit of foresight in its planning when this former marshland was filled and developed in the 1850's. The result: a grid-like pattern and alphabetized street names. But where's the fun in that?

State legislation prohibits the majority of national auto insurance providers from doing business in Massachusetts, though it's easy to just assume that they'd be insane to insure Bostonian drivers in the first place. But as a rule, we are both aggressive and competent. We know precisely how far we can push the envelope on sudden lane changes and risky passing maneuvers.

The novice may find himself reduced to tears on the side of the road, but the initial challenge makes the eventual mastery that much more satisfying.

Learn the Vocabulary

The Boston Turnaround: the act of turning one's a full 180 degrees in the middle of the street with regard for oncoming traffic in either direction.

The Boston Creep: the act of executing a tu by slowly creeping one's car into the middle of intersection, which eventually leads to a comple blockage of both lanes of oncoming traffic. T allows the driver to successfully negotiate the turr or cause an accident.

Rotary: Known in other parts of the country as roundabout or traffic circle. Usually, vehicles alrea in the rotary have right-of-way. But no one in Bost follows this rule. Watch out.

Square: A location at which several feeder stree connect in odd formations and strange angles (s Harvard or Davis). Squares are rarely, if ever, square

Masshole: From the mouths of out-of-staters, derogatory term. For a true Boston driver, a lab worn with pride.

Registry of Motor Vehicles (RMV): Known in oth parts of the country as the DMV. The main RMV is Chinatown, but other, equally disgruntled branch exist in Watertown, Cambridge, and the suburb You will have to pay the RMV $100 to become officially licensed Masshole if you're changing fro out-of-state.

Survival Tips

Be aggressive: You're never gonna make it in th town without a thick skin. Seriously, we will run yo off the road.

Pay it forward: If you want people to let you in, yo have to let them in—once in a while.

Be wary of cabs and buses: They WILL cut you o if you don't gun it.

Be color blind: A yellow light (and the first te seconds of a red light) are considered the function equivalent of a green light. This goes both way though, so be careful. But the faster you gun it, th less honks you'll hear.

Trust your instincts: If you think that unlabele street is the one you want, it probably is. If you thin that guy is going to cut you off, he probably wi Tailgate the lady in front of you as a preventativ measure.

You will get lost: Resistance is futile. A GPS wor save you. Neither will Google Maps. Leave yourse some extra time. We promise, one day it will star making sense. Or you'll have a nervous breakdow and never drive again.

General Information

bsites:
on: www.cityofboston.gov/parking
okline: www.brooklinema.gov
bridge: www.cambridgema.gov/Traffic/
index.cfm
erville: www.ci.somerville.ma.us

nes:
on: 617-635-4680
okline: 617-730-2230
bridge: 617-349-4700
erville: 617-625-6600

Overview

n parking within the city, you'll need time, se, and a sixth sense for parking spots that are ut to open up. With a few notable exceptions (near way during Sox games comes to mind), careful ing of a target area will eventually yield results. If ence fails, a willingness to pay the outrageous fees parking garage is also helpful. There are, however, gains to be found; the rates at the Post Office Square ge are amazing considering its location and the bridgeside Galleria charges only $2 per hour.

ending on where you live, and whether parking oston causes you to regularly lose your temper, might want to reconsider even owning a car. To quish driving is to lower your blood pressure siderably. The North End and Allston are crowded ghborhoods with narrow streets jam-packed with ked cars. When it snows (and it will snow), Boston dents become fiercely protective of their parking ts, illegally using traffic cones, lawn chairs, and er assorted paraphernalia to claim their freshly eveled out spaces. Fisticuffs over disputed parking s are not unheard of. Somerville, Cambridge, and okline, however, aren't quite as bad for parking, in due to vast "resident-only parking" zones, plus fact that there is no overnight parking allowed rookline. Remember, if you own a car and live in city, always lock your doors, tuck in your mirrors, remove any valuables. The Club ain't a bad estment, either.

mately, if you live in Boston and own a car, you receive *at least* one ticket a month. Maybe there was street cleaning the night before. Maybe there arking ban because of snow. Or maybe you got eed because there's a construction project and you sed the half-hidden "Tow Zone" sign that workers itioned conveniently on the sidewalk under a carded pizza box. It doesn't matter what you do how careful you are—*they will get you*—so just l it to the monthly budget.

How to Get Permits

In Somerville, take a current bill or bank statement with your address and your registration to 133 Holland Street. In Boston, take your registration and a current bill with your address to City Hall, Room 224, at Government Center. All Brookline wants is $25 and, apparently, they don't care where you live. Brookline Town Hall is at 333 Washington Street. In the People's Republic of Cambridge, you need your registration saying that either you or your car (it's not clear which) weighs less than 2.5 tons and proof of residency (other than a lease). You can visit the website, download the form, and send copies of the above with a check for $25 to: Traffic, Parking & Transportation, City of Cambridge, 344 Broadway, Cambridge, MA 02139.

Towing

Cars get towed for snow emergencies, street cleaning, and other emergency violations, so keep an eye out for Nor'easters, third Thursdays, and massive construction. If your car gets towed, it'll cost you at least $100 to get it back.

The Boston BTD Tow Lot is located at 200 Frontage Road, near the Andrew T stop in Dorchester/Southie where you can hail a cab or hoof the .8 miles to the tow lot. Another option is to take the Red Line to the Broadway stop and then walk .8 miles to the lot.

Brookline, Somerville, and Cambridge use private, commercial lots to store your newly towed car. Call one of the numbers above, and they'll (hopefully) be able to tell you where your car is.

The Somerville tow lot is, for reasons unknown, Pat's Auto Body on McGrath Highway near Union Square.

Cambridge either has a top-secret tow lot, or it rotates. If your car gets towed, they ask you to call the police (617-349-3300), who will presumably then tell you where your car is.

Brookline has a similarly clandestine car imprisonment system. A call to their transportation/parking office should unearth your car.

Tickets

Because it allows them to take your money immediately, all four places offer online ticket payment. Tickets are dispensed for offenses such as double-parking, expired meters, non-resident parking on a resident-only street, street cleaning violations, and the city/town needing money. Regardless of the city, you're looking at about 50 bucks per infringement.

LEGEND

- Transit lines & stop
- Commuter rail & station
- Terminal station
- Interchange with other lines
- Accessible Station
- P Parking

*Boylston: Accessible for Silver Line only
State: Blue line wheelchair access outbound side only. Inbound riders transfer to outbound train at Government Center. Exit State outbound

Water Transportation Services

Hingham Shipyard to Rowes Wharf, Boston

Quincy & Hull to Logan Airport & Long Wharf, Boston

Customer service & travel information......(617) 222-3200
Visit our website at: www.mbta.com

General Information

Website: www.mbta.com
Phone: 617-222-5000

Overview

Maps of the T show its four subway lines (Red, Orange, Blue, and Green) and the Silver Line (the T's mash-up of a subway line and a bus). All of the T lines except the Green Line's B train move you across the city at a decent clip. But if you need to get from Da Square (Somerville) to Cleveland Circle (Brighto well…it's not easy. Despite the proximity of the t places, you have to go downtown on one line (Re and back out on another (Green)—an 11-mile t connecting destinations that are 6.5 miles apa Another T peeve is that the last trains depart fro stations between midnight and 1 am, even thou last call at Boston bars is between 1 and 2 am. (So Redcoat traditions live on.) Late-night revelers a left to shell out for cabs.

Red Line: The T's flagship line, the Red Line runs Alewife in Cambridge through Davis Square, ard Square, MIT, the Esplanade (where you can ire the sparkling new Charles/MGH station,) the mon, Southie, and Dorchester. At the JFK/UMass , the line splits in two: The Ashmont train goes to chester (with a connecting trolley to Mattapan,) the Braintree train runs through Quincy. A fun e to play on the Red Line: Bet with your friends ut which student riders and professorial-looking s will get off at which university stops.

Green Line: This is the oldest operational vay in the country, and it shows. Not a grown-ubway like the Red, Orange, and Blue Lines, the en Line features light-rail "trolleys"—130-foot-green Twinkies—that shoot you beneath the of Boston before emerging onto streets and ing stuck in traffic.

Green Line runs from Lechmere in Cambridge ar as Kenmore in Boston. Stops along the way ude the Museum of Science, TD Garden, Faneuil the Common, Back Bay, and Fenway Park. At more, the B (Boston College), C (Cleveland Circle), D (Riverside) trains diverge and emerge from the and as trolleys. The E train parts ways two stops k at Copley. The B is the slowest train because god id the Boston University kids walk anywhere. Lots ops + lots of red lights = long rides. The B takes through BU, Allston, Brighton, and as far as Boston ege. The C runs along Beacon Street through lidge Corner (in Brookline) to Cleveland Circle (in hton). When getting off the train at Cleveland e, note the trolley making a wide circular turn ugh four-way traffic, which, inexplicably, leads lot of accidents. The D runs through Fenway Brookline Village to Chestnut Hill before hitting eral Newton neighborhoods. The E (Heath Street) splits before Kenmore at Copley and services phony Hall, Mission Hill, Northeastern University, Museum of Fine Arts, and Longwood Medical Don't believe the maps that tell you E trains ninate at Forest Hills. This service was "temporarily" pended in 1986—meanwhile, the 39 bus will take from Heath Street to Forest Hills.

nerville residents have been patiently waiting the arrival of a long-promised, but controversial, ension of the Green Line. This extension, which uld take the Green Line from Lechmere through aust-clogged Union Square to West Medford, is v expected in 2016-2017—but that delayed date most likely be pushed back.

Orange Line: The Southwest Corridor Park the Orange Line follow a path originally gned for the extension of I-95 through Boston. mmunity groups defeated the proposal in 1979, vincing officials to put a subway and park on land instead. The Orange Line runs from Oak Grove in Malden to Forest Hills in Jamaica Plain. Stops along the way include Sullivan Square, Bunker Hill Community College, TD Garden, Faneuil Hall, Downtown Crossing, Chinatown, New England Medical Center, Back Bay/South End, as well as a few stops in Roxbury and Jamaica Plain.

The Blue Line: Who rides the Blue Line? MBTA ridership figures show a little over 55,000 daily boardings on the Blue Line, compared to 154,000 on the Orange, 210,500 on the Red, and about 205,000 on the Green. Running from Bowdoin Street downtown to Wonderland in Revere, this is the line you want to ride if you're going fishing, flying, or betting on horses. On your way east, you'll pass the Aquarium, Logan Airport, Suffolk Downs, and Revere Beach before winding up at Wonderland. The stations at Aquarium and Logan have been renovated and made more accessible; other stations on the Blue Line are due to get the same treatment over the next couple of years.

The Silver Line: Now the most convenient way to the airport, this is actually a high-speed bus line. Don't ask.

Parking

Your chances of finding parking increase as you move further away from downtown, but generally only end cap stations and suburban stations provide day parking. Garages and lots fill up quickly on weekdays. Prices vary. Parking in resident-only spots will result in a ticket and, in some areas, a keying.

Fares and Passes

In 2007, the MBTA replaced subway tokens with the magnetic-stripe CharlieCard and the paper CharlieTicket. (The "Charlie" moniker was taken from the Kingston Trio's 1959 hit, "Charlie on the MTA.") A subway ride costs $2 using the CharlieCard, and $2.50 with the paper CharlieTicket. The monthly subway/bus "Linkpass" costs $70, and reduced fares are available for seniors, people with disabilities, and junior-high and high school students. Children under 11 ride free when accompanied by an adult. Passes are sold at certain T stops and in some stores, however—the T has stated that it will no longer give away the rechargeable plastic CharlieCard, and will instead charge a fee for new and replacement cards. To find out where to buy a pass or to purchase one online, visit www.mbta.com.

MBTA Buses

Website: www.mbta.com
Phone: 617-222-3200

Every day, intrepid T bus drivers pilot their behemoth vehicles down too-narrow streets filled with angry drivers, errant pedestrians, unfortunate bikers, and, in the winter, ice and snow. (A simple "thank you" to the driver as you get off the bus isn't too much to ask.) MBTA buses run everywhere the subway doesn't, and some places it does. Usually at least one of any bus route's end points is a subway station. The T also runs several popular express buses from outlying neighborhoods to downtown along the Mass Pike and other highways.

The T is in the process of replacing the bulk of its aging diesel fleet with new Compressed Natural Gas (CNG) buses. Identifiable by their blue strip and the low roar of their engines, the new buses reduce emissions by up to 90 percent and, so far, are cleaner on the inside as well (just give them a few years). Some buses on busy routes feature low floors and articulated midsections, such as those used along the Silver Line and JP's 39 bus.

In 2005, the MBTA discontinued its popular but unprofitable Night Owl service (is a public service supposed to be profitable, anyway?). The Night Owl used to run buses along the subway routes until 2:30 am on Friday and Saturday nights, helping late-night partiers with a lift home. There is still no word from the MBTA on whether this service will ever reappear.

With a fare increase in June 2012, buses cost $2 if you use the paper Charlie Ticket or $1.50 if you use the plastic Charlie Card. The fares on the express buses are also different depending on if you use the ticket ($4.50 for inner express buses and $6.50 for outer express) or card ($3.50 for inner express and $5 for outer express). Monthly bus passes are $48 and subway/bus combos cost as little as $70 for a subway/local bus packages, while express bus combos are either $110 or $168. Students, seniors, and disabled persons can purchase monthly passes at reduced rates. Bus passes can be bought at several T stations or online at www.mbta.com. And you should be able to pick up a Charlie Card at customer service booths in T stations or buy a pre-loaded one at the T's website.

Silver Line

Website: www.mbta.com/schedules_and_maps/
            subway/lines/default.asp?route=SILVER
Phone: 617-222-3200

Although the Silver Line appears on the MBTA's subway map, it is actually a high-speed bus line (a "state-of-the-art Bus Rapid Transit system," no less) that, according to the MBTA, "combines the quality of rail transit with the flexibility of buses." The MBTA's public relations materials

may be as gassy as the CNG used by some of the buses, but in fact the new system provides much-ne additional public transport options for Roxbury resid and is proving handy to airport travelers, Mo Courthouse staff, and people working at constru sites along the waterfront. It's also a convenient way t to the Bank of America Pavilion for concerts or to o the many Seaport district restaurants, like the Lega Kitchen or Anthony's Pier Four, for dinner and drinks.

The Silver Line is being constructed in three ph Completed Phase I runs between Downtown Cros and Dudley Square in Roxbury. Phase II, also comple runs from South Station to Logan Airport, Boston M Industrial Park, and City Point. (The MBTA is waffling o original plan to extend the Silver Line to the Andrew T in South Boston/Dorchester.

Phase III is scheduled to be completed in 2016, because there hasn't yet been a decision taken on how buses will actually get into the tunnel, it's anyone's when Phase III will go on-line.

The Silver Line Waterfront fare follows the above structure for the subway (subway passes are valid) the Silver Line Washington Street follows that of the (bus passes are valid), with Charlie Tickets and Car effect for both.

Cambridge EZRide

Website: www.charlesrivertma.org/program_
            ezride.htm
Phone: 617-839-4636

Cantabrigians who traverse the Charles each mor on their daily commute should check out the EZ bus service, whose cheery sky-blue coaches run thro Cambridge to North Station. The EZRide route be in Cambridgeport and passes through University Kendall Square, and East Cambridge, making a doze so stops along the way.

EZRide operates Monday through Friday only, and not run on holidays. Service in the morning runs approximately 6:15 am to 10:45 am; afternoon service from approximately 3:30 pm to 7:30 pm. A limited mic service is also available, from Kendall Square to Pa Street, from about 11 am until 3 pm.

A trip on EZRide costs $2. Students, seniors, disa persons, and children aged 5–11 traveling with an a pay 50 cents. Flashing an MIT ID lets you ride for free.

eyhound

ite:	www.greyhound.com
e:	800-231-2222

hound buses leave from the South Station bus terminal
4) and they'll take you *anywhere*. It ain't the Concorde,
'll eventually get you to one of its 3,700 stations across
n America. Round-trip tickets to New York usually cost
$65 round-trip to Washington DC is $132–$142, and
on to Philadelphia is $92–$118 round-trip.

n Station is on Atlantic Avenue, one block down from
ner Street. The bus terminal is the taller building behind
ail building.

et to South Station from the Mass Pike (I-90), take Exit 24A.
exit drops you onto Atlantic Avenue—the bus terminal is
he right side. From I-93 N, take Exit 20 and follow signs for
ntown and South Station. At the lights, continue straight
Atlantic Avenue.

I-93 S, take Exit 23 onto Purchase Street, make a left on
eland Street, continue to the end of the street, and then
a left onto Atlantic Avenue. On-street parking is scarce.
u're pinched, try the bus terminal's parking garage. The
ance is on Kneeland Street.

Red T line has a stop at South Station, also the end
t for the southern routes of the commuter rail. Walk
ugh the train station and past the tracks to reach the bus
on entrance.

hinatown Buses

ou want to get to New York City for really cheap, take
bus. A round-trip ticket will cost you around
on Boston Deluxe or on Sunshine Travel. The quality of
atown buses can be hit or miss, but the price is right. In
3, two of the best known Chinatown bus companies, Fung
and Lucky Star, were forced to shut down due to safety
es. Sadly, their shutterings may be permanent.

u take a late Chinatown bus from NYC, you will get to
on after the T closes, meaning you'll have to pay for a
that will cost more than the 200-plus-mile journey from
York.

ton Deluxe

w.gotobus.com/bostondeluxe/; 617-354-2101
stian Science Plaza, 175 Huntington Ave (Map 5)

up the Boston Deluxe near the Prudential Center for trips
ew York City and Hartford. New York-bound buses depart
ay through Sunday at 8:30 am, 11 am, 1 pm, 4:30 pm, 6
and 10:30 am and drop off at Broadway and 32nd Street
well as E 86th Street and Second Avenue. Buses to Hartford
art Friday to Sunday at 8:30 am, 11 am, 1 pm, 6 pm, and
30 pm and drop off at 365 Capitol Avenue (Charter Oak
ermarket). Both routes cost $30 round-trip.

nshine Travel

w.sunshinebus.com;
-328-0862 or 617-695-1989
Harrison Ave, Boston (Map 4);
Donald's Plaza, Fields Corner, Dorchester (Map 32)

ng with buses departing hourly for NYC ($15 each way, $25
he 2 am bus), Sunshine Travel offers two-, three-, and four-
tours to places like Tennessee (four days, $178), Chicago
ur days, $269), Washington DC (three days, $118), Niagara
s (two days, $105), and destinations in eastern Canada
28–$278). Buses to the Mohegan Sun casino in Connecticut
part five times daily, picking up in Dorchester, Boston, and
ncy. Round-trip tickets cost $10, and you'll receive a $20
mbling voucher and a $15 dining voucher if you're 21 years
age or older.

Bolt Bus

Website:	www.boltbus.com/
Phone:	1-877-BOLTBUS

Bolt Bus provides service between Boston and New York City,
and connecting service to Philadelphia, Baltimore, Cherry Hill,
and Washington DC out of New York. Round-trip tickets to
New York run about $30, although the earlier you book your
trip, the more the price goes down (it can go as low as $1!).
Each bus includes free wireless internet, three extra inches of
legroom per seat, and power outlets throughout.

Megabus

Website:	www.megabus.com/us/
Phone:	877-GO2-MEGA

Megabus provides service from Boston to Hartford and
New York, and connecting service from New York to Albany,
Atlantic City, Baltimore, Buffalo, Niagra Falls, Philadelphia,
Rochester, Syracuse, Toronto, and Washington. As with Bolt
Bus, the earlier you book, the less you're likely to pay. Round
trip tickets to New York round out to about $36 (maximum).
Many locations of Megabus stops are on public streets
(usually either outside train stations or transportation hubs),
college campuses, or at park-and-ride lots. All Megabus buses
are equipped with free Wi-Fi.

Go Buses

Website:	www.gobuses.com
Phone:	855-888-7160
	Alewife Bus Station (Map 22),
	Alewife Brook Parkway, Cambridge

Go Buses (formerly World Wide Bus) is another option for
taking the bus to NYC by offering service out of Alewife
Station in Cambridge—a far less crowded, busy option than
South Station. Buses to New York (with a stop in Newtown on
the way out of town) depart six times a day Monday-Thursday,
eight times a day on Fridays and Sundays, and five times a
day on Saturdays. Round-trip tickets cost around $30-$60,
depending on the time of day. All Go Buses are equipped with
free WiFi and power outlets in every seat.

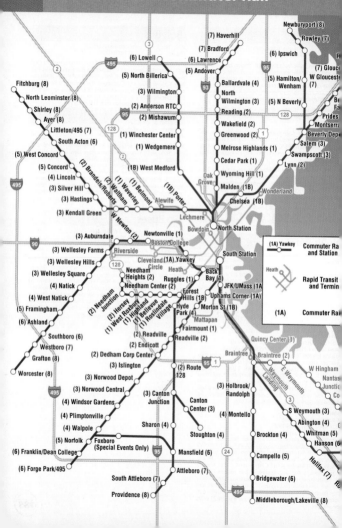

eneral Information

site: www.mbta.com
e: 617-222-3200 or 800-392-6100

verview

commuter rail is a series of train lines that service outer limits of Greater Boston, the suburbs, and nts as far out as Worcester and Providence, Rhode nd. Northbound routes leave from North Station, southbound routes depart from South Station. npared to the commuter rail systems of other Coast cities, Boston's trains make for a relatively asant experience. Massachusetts is working to ovate all of the stations, outfitting them with new forms, electronic signaling, and new ramps and vators to make them handicapped accessible. As n any major transit network, there are occasional d: daily) delays on the commuter rail. Still, a ride the rails is 1,000 percent less stressful than driving nd out of the city every day.

commuter rail is also a great option for day-pers going in either direction. Taking the train ws inbound visitors to enjoy, rather than just get in, the city. City-dwellers who want to escape the iliar urban landscape can head up to Gloucester a day at the beach, venture to Plymouth for a tory lesson, or just explore a new city down in vidence.

you're looking at the commuter rail map for first time, you might think that the lack of a nnection between North Station and South tion is a mistake. Well, it may be a mistake, but on the part of the mapmakers. To get from one tion to another, you'll have to use the T (and nsfer to a second T), take a cab, or walk. Seriously. additional information about North Station and uth Station, see the next page.

the long term, Gov. Deval Patrick has pledged to ng commuter rail service back to the cities of New dford and Fall River by 2016.

Parking

Parking is available at every commuter rail station except Back Bay, Belmont Center, Chelsea, JFK/ UMass, Morton Street, Porter Square, River Works, Ruggles, Silver Hill, Uphams Corner, Waverley, Windsor Gardens, and Yawkey. Rates vary, with some as low as $1 per day.

Fares and Passes

Commuter rail tickets range in price from $2 to $11. Each destination is assigned a zone number that determines the price of your ticket. Tickets can be purchased on the train, but depending on how busy the train is and the ticket-taker's mood, a surcharge may be added to the price. Kids 5–11, high school students, seniors, and disabled persons ride for half-price. Children under five and blind people ride free. The cost of monthly passes ranges from $70 to $345, depending on the zone. Some monthly passes offer varying perks like free subway, bus, and ferry use. Passes are sold at certain T stops and other locations (usually a local shop close to the station), as well as online at www.mbta.com. If you're buying your ticket at a T stop, be sure to look up your zone number ahead of time on the MBTA website. And make sure you're boarding a commuter rail train and not an Amtrak train. (This happens more often than you'd think.)

MAP
1

93

PAGE
175

TD
Garden

North
Station

Auerbach Wy

O'Neil
Federal
Building

Lomasney Wy

35 Stanford

Charlestown Bridge

Commercial St

Battery St

Causeway St

Canal St

Lancaster St

Friend St

Valenti Way

Portland St

N Washington St

Thacher St

N Margin St

Cooper St

Hull St

Snelling

Snowhill St

Charter St

Hanover St

Prince St

Tileston St

Parmenter St

North St

Richmond St

Fleet St

Garden Court St

Moon St

Fulton St

Commercial St

Merrimack St

Market St

New Chardon St

○ North Station

New Sudbury St

○○ Haymarket

Bowdoin ○

Cross St

Cross St

Clinton St

Cambridge St

Hancock St

Temple St

Ridgeway La

Bowdoin St

Somerset St

New Sudbury St

Government ○
Center

City
Hall

Congress St

Faneuil
Hall

PAGE
126

Quincy Market

Christopher
Columbus
Park

○ Aquarium

Ashburton Pl

State St

State St

○ State

Congress St

Kilby St

Water St

India St

India Row Wy

East

Beacon St

School St

Milk St

Oliver St

Broad St

PAGE
120

○ Park Street

Park St

Tremont St

Bromfield St

Washington St

Province St

Devonshire St

Federal St

Water St

Pearl St

High St

Temple Pl ○

○ Downtown
Crossing

Franklin St

Boston
Common

West St

Mason St

Hawley St

Arch St

Avery St

Summer St

Chauncy St

Bedford St

Lincoln St

Kingston St

Purchase St

Atlantic Ave

North

Seaport

Ave de Lafayette

Harvard St

Boylston ○

Essex St

Beach St

Chinatown ○

Lagrange St

Harrison Ave

Kneeland St

Tyler St

Oak St

Summer St

South
Station

○ South
Station

Atlantic Ave

Dorchester Ave

Congress St Bridge

Fort Point
Channel

MAP
4

General Information

Maps: 1 & 4
Websites: www.amtrak.com (Amtrak)
www.mbta.com (MBTA)
Amtrak: 800-872-7245 (800-USA-RAIL)
MBTA: 617-222-5215

Overview

North Station and South Station are the main Amtrak and MBTA Commuter Rail depots in Boston. North Station, near the North End and underneath TD Garden, sits above the T's new "superstation" that (finally) connects the Green Line and Orange Line. South Station, on Atlantic Avenue and Summer Street at the gateway to South Boston, is served by MBTA and Amtrak and also has a bus terminal, a food court in the domed arrival hall, a bar, a newsstand, and a bookstore.

Traveling between Stations

There is a one-mile gap between the two Amtrak stations. The North Station stop is on the Orange and Green Lines of the MBTA subway, and the South Station stop is on the Red Line. Yes, it is crazy that the stations aren't on the same line and don't directly connect to each other. No, they're not going to do anything to correct the problem in the near future. Yes, they could have rolled it into the Big Dig project, since they were digging under the city anyway. No, we don't know why they didn't. And yes, it does seem odd that they spent billions to improve automobile transportation while ignoring public transportation. As it stands, travelers going from New York to Maine have to get off the train at South Station and either take a cab, take two subway trains, or walk to get to North Station to continue their journey. Where's "Amtrak Joe" Biden when you need him?

How to Get There—Driving

Both stations are located off I-93 in downtown Boston. For North Station, take Exit 26 (Storrow Drive), and for South Station, take Exit 23 (Purchase Street/South Station). To get to South Station from the Mass Pike (I-90), take Exit 24B to Atlantic Avenue.

Parking

The MBTA says there's no parking at either station, but "street or private parking may exist." Helpful, huh? In fact, both North Station and South Station are served by nearby, expensive parking garages, and neither station offers much in the way of street parking. Lovely.

How to Get There—Mass Transit

North Station is on the T's Green and Orange Lines. South Station is on the Red Line.

Amtrak

Amtrak trains leave out of North Station and South Station going north to Portland, Maine and south to NYC and beyond. When you go north, they call it the Downeaster (that's Mainer for "near Canada"). When you go south, they call it a bunch of things, including "the Federal," "the Acela," and the mundanely titled "Regional." The Acela is Amtrak's flagship route, offering "high-speed" service from South Station to NYC, Philly, and DC, with stops along the way. On a good day, the Acela chugs from Boston to New York in 3.5 hours, which is still only slightly faster than a bus and, at $100 a ticket, costs much more than taking one of the Chinatown buses or Greyhound.

Baggage Check

Three items of baggage weighing up to 50 lbs each may be checked up to 30 minutes prior to train departure. For an additional fee of $10 per bag, three additional pieces can be checked. Each passenger is allowed two carry-on items on board. No dangerous, fragile, valuable items, animals, or household goods can be checked. Bikes, skis, and other odd-shaped equipment usually count as one checked bag and should not be carried aboard the train. With the exception of service animals, all pets are prohibited on Amtrak trains.

How to Get Tickets

To purchase train tickets, call Amtrak or visit their website. The website sometimes offers discounts for purchasing online, so it's worth checking the website before heading to the station.

Going to New York

One-way fares start at $62 and the journey takes about 4.5 hours from South Station. You could cut an hour off your commute by riding express on the Acela, but the comfort and convenience will cost ya ($100 or more).

Going to Philadelphia

One-way fares start at $60 and the ride takes about six hours. Fares on the speedier Acela Express start at $115 and cut about an hour off of the journey.

Going to Washington DC

A trip to Washington on the regular Amtrak train will cost you at least $65 and will take you between eight and nine hours. Acela Express tickets start at $124 and the trip takes between six and seven hours.

CHARLESTOWN

MAP 8

46

Navy Yard

43

22

Charles River

F4

Commercial Wharf
19

18

Long Wharf
16

15

Aquarium

14

Rowes Wharf

Courthouse
7

9 8

World Trade Center

5

MAP 10

4

Fleet Boston Pavilion (summer only)

2

Reserved Channel

Fort Point Channel

BOSTON

MAP 1

MAP 2

EAST BOSTON

MAP 9

East Boston Piers

Boston Marina

6B

Boston Inner Harbor

F2/F2H

1

Logan Airport

Logan International Airport

PAGE 176

F1

F1

F2/F2H

Boston Harbor

SOUTH BOSTON

MAP 11

Black Falcon Terminal

Pleasure Bay

F2H only

Dorchester Bay

F2/F2H

Pemberton Point (limited service)

F1

QUINCY

Fore River Shipyard

Hingham Shipyard

HINGHAM

Legend:
— Commuter Boats
- - - Limited Service
— Inner Harbor Ferries
○ Ferry Station
● Rowes Wharf Water Taxi
② City Water Taxi

General Information (Ferries)

TA:	www.mbta.com/schedules_and_maps/boats/; 617-222-5215
ston Harbor Cruises:	www.bostonharborcruises.com/commuter-boat-services; 877-733-9425

Overview

e MBTA Commuter and Excursion Boat Service nnects Boston to Logan Airport and is one of the best utes in and out of Charlestown and other shore side mmunities. One thing that makes the T boat better than a nice day, paying three bucks for a quick jaunt across e harbor feels like a steal. And on any day, not having to al with Boston traffic is priceless. The views of the city om the water are gorgeous, and since the routes are in e Inner Harbor, the ride remains relatively smooth even bad weather. There is also that delicious old-time feeling at comes with ferrying across the harbor. You'll want to ep in mind that boat schedules are more limited than s schedules (particularly on weekends) and are more sceptible to disruptions due to inclement weather.

ost ferries operated by the MBTA leave from Long Wharf d travel to the Charlestown Navy Yard (F4), the Fore ver Shipyard in Quincy (F2), and Pemberton Point in ull (F2H). The F1 boat travels between Rowes Wharf and ngham Shipyard.

e F2 and the F2H boats, catamarans operated by Boston arbor Cruises, stop at Logan Airport, but not at all times the day—check the MBTA website for timetables. uring rush hour (and decent weather) the Boston Harbor uises is a sensible choice for getting to the airport. It kes a mere seven minutes to get to the airport dock from ong Wharf and about 25 minutes from Quincy and Hull. om the airport dock, take the free Water Shuttle bus 66 the terminals. The 66 bus takes about 15 minutes to visit l terminals and return to the dock.

ll ferry stops are accessible to wheelchair users. Bicycles an also be taken on board for free.

Parking

arking for commuter ferry stops in the Inner Harbor available only on the street or in a garage. Parking in uincy costs $1 for a day and $6 overnight. In Hingham, arking costs $1 for a day and $1.75 overnight. Free arking is available at Hull High School.

Fares

trip on a boat between destinations in the Inner Harbor osts $3 (pay a crewmember when boarding the boat). rips from Hull, Quincy, and Hingham to the Inner Harbor Rowes Wharf or Long Wharf) cost $8 ($4 for kids, seniors, nd disabled persons). Trips from Quincy and Hull to Logan irport on the Boston Harbor Cruises are $13 ($7.50 for eniors, students, and kids 5–11). Pay a crewmember when oarding the boat.

General Information (Water Taxis)

City Water Taxi:	www.citywatertaxi.com; 617-422-0392
Rowes Wharf Water Taxi:	www.roweswharfwatertransport.com/RWWT_2010/HOME.html; 617-406-8584
Massport:	www.massport.com/logan-airport/Pages/WaterTransport.aspx; 800-23-LOGAN

Overview

On the charmed waters of the Inner Harbor, two water taxi companies ply their trade. During the warmer months, water taxis provide an enjoyable way to cross the Inner Harbor. Both water taxi companies stop at the Logan Airport dock.

City Water Taxi

City Water Taxi offers direct service to the entire Boston waterfront, year-round, with enclosed boats that are heated when the weather is bad. (Mon–Sat 7 am–10 pm; Sun 7 am–8 pm). In addition to the airport dock, City Water Taxi serves 16 other points, including Bank of America Pavilion, Fan Pier, Charlestown Navy Yard, Black Falcon Terminal, and all the major wharves in the Inner Harbor. (To get to the Boston Convention and Exhibition Center, aim for the World Trade Center.) To catch a City Water Taxi from the airport, take Massport's 66 bus to the water dock. Use the call box at the dock to call for a boat if there isn't one already there. From other destinations, call City Water Taxi to arrange a pick-up.

Tickets are sold on board the boat. Fares to downtown points and Logan Airport cost $10 one-way and $17 round-trip. There is a $20 minimum to Charlestown, North Station, and Black Falcon Terminal, but if you have a traveling companion, the fare is $15 each.

Rowes Wharf Water Taxi

Also operating year-round, Rowes Wharf Water Taxi provides on-call service to 31 points in the Inner Harbor (from Nov 2–April 1, service runs 7 am–7 pm; from April 2–Nov 1, service runs from 7 am–10 pm Mon–Sat and 7 am–8 pm on Sun). After-hours service available upon request. Rowes Wharf Water Taxi serves 17 different docks and now operates a Seaport Express providing weekday service between Rowes Wharf, Central Wharf, and the Seaport World Trade Center for $1.70. For the complete schedule, look online. To hail a boat from the airport dock, use the company's call box; from other destinations, give them a call from your own phone.

Tickets are sold on board. The fare costs $10 one way and $17 round-trip.

Car Rental

Map 1 • Beacon Hill / West End
Avis	3 Center Plz	617-534-1400

Map 2 • North End / Faneuil Hall
Enterprise	1 Congress St	617-723-8077

Map 3 • Downtown Crossing / Park Square / Bay Village
Hertz	30 Park Plz	617-338-1500

Map 4 • Financial District / Chinatown
Alamo	270 Atlantic Ave	617-557-7179
Hertz	Summer St & Atlantic Ave	617-338-1503
National	270 Atlantic Ave	617-557-7179

Map 5 • Back Bay (West) / Fenway (East)
Enterprise	800 Boylston St	617-262-8222
Hertz	39 Dalton St	617-338-1506

Map 6 • Back Bay (East) / South End (Upper)
Avis	100 Clarendon St	617-534-1404
Dollar	110 Huntington Ave	617-578-0025
Hertz	10 Huntington Ave	617-338-1506

Map 9 • East Boston
Affordable	84 Condor St	617-561-7000
Alamo	6 Tomahawk Dr	617-561-4100
Avis	202 Porter St	617-561-3500
Budget	20 Tomahawk Dr	617-497-3733
Enterprise	2 Tomahawk Dr	617-561-4488

Map 12 • Newmarket / Andrew Square
Enterprise	230 Dorchester Ave	617-268-1411

Map 13 • Roxbury
Enterprise	17 Melnea Cass Blvd	617-442-7500

Map 18 • Brighton
Hertz	1686 Commonwealth Ave	617-232-189

Map 19 • Allston (South) / Brookline (North)
Adventure Vehicle	27 Harvard Ave	617-783-300
Budget	95 Brighton Ave	617-497-360
Enterprise	292 Western Ave	617-783-224
Enterprise	996 Commonwealth Ave	617-738-600
Hertz	414 Cambridge St	617-787-289
U-Save Auto	25 Harvard Ave	617-629-309

Map 20 • Harvard Square / Allston (North)
Avis	1 Bennett St	617-534-1430
Hertz	24 Eliot St	617-338-1520
Thrifty	110 Mt Auburn St	617-876-2758

Map 23 • Central Somerville / Porter Square
Hertz	646 Somerville Av	617-625-7958

Map 24 • Winter Hill / Union Square
Americar	190 Highland Ave	617-776-4640

Map 25 • East Somerville / Sullivan Square
Enterprise	37 Mystic Ave	617-625-1766

Map 27 • Central Square / Cambridgeport
Budget	20 Sidney St	617-577-7606
Enterprise	25 River St	617-547-7400

Map 28 • Inman Square
Adventure Vehicle	72 Prospect St	617-623-6408
U-Save Auto	70 Prospect St	617-625-6704

Map 30 • Roslindale
Enterprise	4009 Washington St	617-327-6688

pcar General Information

bsite: www.zipcar.com

one: 617-933-5070

ackground

ocar rents out cars by the hour. The company, which now runs similar services DC, New Jersey, New York, and elsewhere, was founded at MIT: "People would hieve transportation nirvana by having a transit pass and a Zipcard in their ckets. The result would be reduced congestion, fewer auto emissions, more en space, and a revolution in urban planning." That's Cantabrigians for "Give us /hr, we'll give you a Jetta." This seems like the smartest idea on wheels if you live congested areas like the North End, Allston, or Harvard Square and you need get somewhere the T can't take you. For infrequent drivers, the $25 application e and minimum annual fee of $60 still make Zipcar service cheaper than owning ar.

ow It Works

ou're 21 or older, in possession of a valid driver's license, and you've completed e online application, all you need to do is call or go online to reserve one of the ndreds of cars available at zipcar.com. (You get to choose from a fleet of BMWs, nis, pick-ups, and others.) Your Zipcard unlocks the car that has been reserved you, which you pick up at the most convenient of their many locations. Cars ust be returned to the same spot where they were picked up. The car unlocks en a valid Zipcard is held to the windshield; your card will only open the car ring the time you have reserved it.

osts

e cost of Zipcar varies depending on the pick-up location, but rates start at .25 an hour. A reservation for 24 hours, the maximum amount of time that a car n be reserved, starts at about $84. The first 180 miles are free; each additional le costs about 45 cents. Membership costs are additional. Make sure to return ur car on time, as Zipcar charges exorbitant hourly late fees on unreturned cars. e best part: gas and insurance are included with every reservation.

If you've just moved to Boston and need a crash course on the "sights," you must check out the **Freedom Trail** (see page 189). Yes, it's touristy, but it's the best self-guided tour of Revolution-era Boston and gives you the skinny on aspects of Boston colonial history that every resident should know. To gain a better appreciation of just where it is you live, hit the top of the **Prudential Tower (Map 5)** for a bird's eye view, which will show you that Boston has a lot more hills and water than you might have suspected. For a more human perspective, get familiar with the Charles River with a stroll along the **Esplanade (Map 6)**, or, for a walk with an impressive view of Beacon Hill and Back Bay, cross the **Harvard Bridge (Map 26)** and take a stroll along Memorial Drive in Cambridge. For a nice rest, grab a snack in Harvard Square, and find a tree in **Harvard Yard (Map 20)** under which to chill.

If winter keeps you from str[...] outside, there's plenty to s[...] indoors. The **Museum of Fine A[...] (Map 15)** (see page 326) is wor[...] class. Across the street, the **Isabe[...] Stewart Gardner Museum (M[...] 15)** has a first-rate collection, and t[...] setting (inspired by a 15th-cent[...] Venetian palace) is stunning. T[...] ornate interior of **Trinity Chu[...] (Map 6)** and the Sargent Murals [...] the **Boston Public Library (Map [...]** (see page 185) are also impressi[...] Boston's best concert halls are in t[...] neighborhood, so why not catch[...] show at internationally acclaim[...] **Boston Symphony Hall (Map [...]** or one of the many free shows [...] the New England Conservator[...] **Jordan Hall (Map 5)**. For ro[...] music, comedy and high-qual[...] musical theater head to the Wilb[...] and Wang theaters in the Thea[...] District near the Boylston Gre[...] Line T stop. The Orpheum, near t[...] Park Street T station, is home [...] national and international acts in[...] seated, classic concert hall setti[...] You'll also not want to overlook t[...] many museums of Harvard, nota[...] the **Fogg Art Museum (Map 2[...]** (focusing on Western art) and t[...] **Natural History Museum (Map 2[...]** (with its brilliant glass flowers).

you've already checked out
ston's big hits, there are plenty
quirky spots to fill your time.
e the skull of Phineas Gage, the
th century medical oddity who
rvived a thirteen-pound rod of
el shot through his brain at the
**arren Anatomical Museum (Map
). The Boston Athenaeum (Map
** has a true crime account bound
th the skin of it's author. If that's
t to your sense of everlasting
e, you could sip coffee in the
rth End and wander over to see
Peter Baldassari is home and his
ksy **All Saints Way (Map 2)** is
en. Roxbury has the only scale
bian tomb at the **Museum of the
tional Center for Afro-American
tists (Map 13)**. The Mapparium at
e **Christian Science Center(Map
** highlights the ambitions of Mary
ker Eddy and her clean-living
ovement. Those with a more
minal bent can find mobster
unts like "Whitey" Bulger's old
uthie **liquor store (Map 10)** or
e garage of the **Brink's Job (Map
** in the North End.

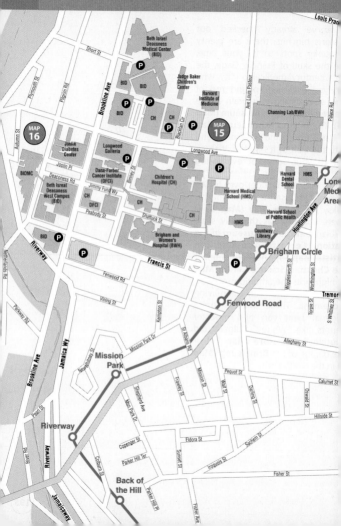

ospitals

ton's medical facilities rank among the best in the world. Many medical firsts happened in Boston, including the:

rst public demonstration of anesthesia during surgery, at Massachusetts General Hospital (1846).

rst identification and analysis of appendicitis, at Massachusetts General Hospital (1886).

rst surgical procedure to correct a congenital cardiovascular defect, performed by Dr. Robert Gross (1938).

rst successful fertilization of a human ovum in a test tube, by researchers at Peter Bent Brigham Hospital 944).

rst successful pediatric remission of acute leukemia, achieved by Dr. Sidney Farber (1947).

rst isolation of the polio virus, at Children's Hospital (1948).

rst successful kidney transplant, at Peter Bent Brigham Hospital (1954).

rst demonstration of the effectiveness of an oral contraceptive, by Dr. John C. Rock (1959).

Longwood Medical Area (see map on the facing page) compresses a dozen medical institutions into andful of blocks below Mission Hill. These institutions, including **Brigham and Women's Hospital (Map Beth Israel Deaconess Medical Center (Map 16), Children's Hospital (Map 15), Dana-Farber Cancer titute (Map 15), Joslin Diabetes Center (Map 16), the CBR Institute for Biomedical Research (Map 16),** Harvard's medical, dental, and public health schools, comprise what is probably the world's leading center health care and medicine.

ssachusetts General Hospital (Map 1), which opened in 1811, is the oldest and largest hospital in New land. Each year MGH admits over 45,000 in-patients, processes over 76,000 emergency visits, and, at its West main campus and four satellite facilities, handles more than 1.5 million outpatient visits.

unt Auburn Hospital (Map 21) is a Harvard Medical School teaching hospital and the most prominent pital in Cambridge.

ergency Rooms	Address	Phone	Map
ssachusetts Eye and Ear Infirmary	243 Charles St	617-523-7900	1
ssachusetts General Hospital	55 Fruit St	617-726-2000	1
ts Medical Center	750 Washington St	617-636-5000	3
ston Medical Center	1 Boston Medical Ctr Pl	617-638-8000	7
gham and Women's Hospital	75 Francis St	617-732-5500	15
ildren's Hospital	300 Longwood Ave	617-355-6000	15
th Israel Deaconess Medical Center	330 Brookline Ave	617-667-7000	16
Elizabeth's Medical Center	736 Cambridge St	617-789-3000	18
ount Auburn	330 Mt Auburn St	617-492-3500	21
A Somerville Hospital	230 Highland Ave	617-591-4500	23
e Cambridge Hospital	1493 Cambridge St	617-665-1000	28

her Hospitals	Address	Phone	Map
ston Shriners Hospital	51 Blossom St	617-722-3000	1
aulding Rehabilitation Hospital	125 Nashua St	617-573-7000	1
wish Memorial Hospital & Rehabilitation Center	59 Townsend St	617-989-8315	13
bour Hospital	49 Robinwood Ave	617-522-4400	14
na-Farber Cancer Institute	44 Binney St	617-632-3000	15
mune Disease Institue	220 Longwood Ave	617-734-9500	15
w England Baptist Hospital	125 Parker Hill Ave	617-754-5800	15
. Boston-Jamaica Plain Campus	150 S Huntington Ave	617-232-9500	15
slin Diabetes Center	1 Joslin Pl	617-732-2400	16
anciscan Hospital for Children	30 Warren St	617-254-3800	18
Elizabeth's Medical Center	736 Cambridge St	617-789-3000	18
e Boston Center	14 Fordham Rd	617-783-9676	19
uville Hospital & Rehabilitation Center	1575 Cambridge St	617-876-4344	28

Post Offices & Zip Codes

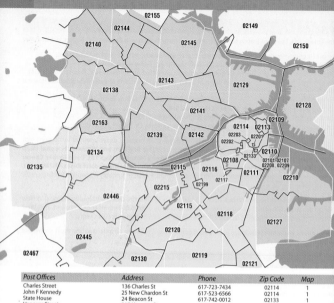

Post Offices	Address	Phone	Zip Code	Map
Charles Street	136 Charles St	617-723-7434	02114	1
John F Kennedy	25 New Chardon St	617-523-6566	02114	1
State House	24 Beacon St	617-742-0012	02133	1
Hanover Street	217 Hanover St	617-723-6397	02113	2
Lafayette	7 Ave de Lafayette	617-423-7822	02111	4
Milk Street	31 Milk St	617-482-1956	02109	4
Astor	207 Massachusetts Ave	617-247-2429	02115	5
Prudential Center	800 Boylston St	617-267-4164	02199	5
Back Bay	133 Clarendon St	617-587-5260	02117	6
Cathedral	59 W Dedham St	617-266-0989	02118	7
Charlestown	23 Austin St	617-241-5322	02129	8
East Boston	50 Meridian St	617-561-3900	02128	9
South Boston	444 E 3rd St	617-269-9948	02127	10
Roxbury	55 Roxbury St	617-427-4898	02119	13
Jamaica Plain	655 Centre St	617-524-3620	02130	14
Mission Hill	1575 Tremont St	617-566-2040	02120	15
Kenmore	11 Deerfield St	617-437-1113	02215	16
Brookline	1295 Beacon St	617-738-1649	02446	17
Brookline Village	207 Washington St	617-566-1557	02445	17
Brighton	424 Washington St	617-254-5026	02135	18
Allston	47 Harvard Ave	617-789-3769	02134	19
Soldiers Field	117 Western Ave	617-354-0131	02163	19
Harvard Square	125 Mt Auburn St	617-876-3883	02138	20
West Somerville	58 Day St	617-666-2255	02144	22
Porter Square	1953 Massachusetts Ave	617-876-5599	02140	23
Somerville	237 Washington St	617-666-2332	02143	24
Winter Hill	320 Broadway	617-666-5225	02145	24
East Cambridge	303 Cambridge St	617-876-8558	02141	26
Kendall Square	250 Main St	617-876-5155	02142	26
MIT	84 Massachusetts Ave	617-494-5511	02139	26
Cambridge	770 Massachusetts Ave	617-575-8700	02139	27
Inman Square	1311 Cambridge St	617-864-4344	02139	28
Uphams Corner	551 Columbia Rd	617-287-9626	02125	32

General Information

Emergencies: 911
Crime Stoppers: 800-494-TIPS
Boston Area Rape Crisis Center (BARCC): 617-492-RAPE
State Police: 617-727-7775
Boston: www.ci.boston.ma.us/police
Brookline: www.brooklinepolice.com
Cambridge: www.ci.cambridge.ma.us/~CPD/
Somerville: www.ci.somerville.ma.us

Police Stations

	Address	Phone	Map
District A-1	40 New Sudbury St	617-343-4240	1
District D-4	650 Harrison Ave	617-343-4250	7
District A-7	69 Paris St	617-343-4220	9
District C-6	101 W Broadway	617-343-4730	10
District B-2	135 Dudley St	617-343-4270	13
District E-13	3345 Washington St	617-343-5630	14
Brookline Police Department	350 Washington St	617-730-2222	17
District D-14	301 Washington St	617-343-4260	18
Somerville Police Department	220 Washington St	617-625-1600	24
Cambridge Police Department	125 6th St	617-349-3300	26

Though Boston is chiefly known for its college-town feel, there is plenty for the younger set to enjoy. You're bound to find something to hold the attention of your little ones among the many, MANY museums and parks.

The Best of the Best

- **Best Kid-Friendly Restaurant:** Full Moon (344 Huron Ave, Cambridge, 617-354-6699). Full Moon is the brainchild of two restaurateurs who also happen to be moms. The result is a restaurant that features a sophisticated menu with an extensive wine list for adults and a tasty assortment of kids' tried-and-true favorites. With sippy cups, toy buckets at every table, and a play area stocked with pretty much every toy imaginable, Full Moon gives you "grown-up dining with a kid-friendly twist."
- **Quaintest Activity:** Swan Boats in the Public Garden (Public Garden, Boston, 617-522-1966). Owned and operated by the same family for over 120 years, the swan boats have directly inspired two children's classics: Robert McCloskey's *Make Way for Ducklings* and E.B. White's *The Trumpet of the Swan*. The people-paddled boats can hold up to 20 passengers during the 15-minute cruise around the lagoon and under the world's smallest suspension bridge. An inexpensive and adorable treat for all. Open April–Sept.
- **Funnest Park:** Rafferty Park (799 Concord Ave, Cambridge). One of the area's best-hidden playgrounds, this wooded park provides tons of fun stuff for older children, including a new metal climbing structure with a twisty slide, wobbly bridge, boat-shaped sand box, and a mini schoolhouse with a chalkboard roof. Basketball hoops, tennis courts, and a baseball field reside next door.
- **Best Rainy Day Activity:** Children's Museum (300 Congress St, Boston, 617-426-8855). This world-renowned museum—reopened in spring 2007 after a pricey and well-received renovation and expansion—has designed early learning experiences for kids of all ages with its inventive hands-on exhibits. Permanent exhibits include the Japanese House, where children experience the culture of Kyoto, Japan through a replica of a silk merchant's house, as well as a Hall of Toys, in which children can look at toys of the past, but not touch.
- **(The World's Only)** Curious George Store: Re-opened in April 2012 at the same iconic, fork-in-the-road spot at 1 JFK Street. Only Curious George store still has plenty of children's and young adult books, exclusive apparel and, yes, toys.
- **Cutest Event:** The Annual Ducklings Day Parade (Boston Common). Held every year on Mother's Day, the parade commemorates Robert McCloskey's children's book *Make Way for Ducklings* set on Boston Common. Children come dressed as their favorite duckling character and ready to parade.
- **Neatest Store:** Irving's Toy and Card Shop (371 Harvard St, Brookline, 617-566-9327). Since 1939, Irving's has been a favorite neighborhood source for ice cream, candy, and little nostalgic toys galore. This small store is packed with everything you never knew you needed from kazoos, to jacks, to tiny plastic farm animals.

Shopping Essentials

- **Nine Months Maternity and Infant Wear** (mom & baby clothes) 272 Newbury St, Boston, 617-236-5523
- **Barefoot Books Store** (kids' books) 1771 Massachusetts Ave, Cambridge, 617-349-1610
- **Black Ink** (stamps):
  101 Charles St, Boston, 617-723-3883
  5 Brattle St, Cambridge, 617-497-1221
- **Boing!** (toys) 729 Centre St, Jamaica Plain, 617-522-7800
- **Calliope** (toys & kids' clothes) 33 Brattle St, Cambridge, 617-876-4149
- **The Children's Book Shop** (kids' books) 237 Washington St, Brookline, 617-734-7323
- **Co-op for Kids at the Harvard Co-op** (kids' books) 1400 Massachusetts Ave, Harvard Square, Cambridge, 617-499-2000
- **Discovery Channel Store** (educational gifts) 40 South Market Building, Faneuil Hall, 617-227-5005
- **Eureka! Puzzles and Games** (endless supply of brain-teasers and boardgames)1349 Beacon Street, Coolidge Corner, 617-738-7352
- **Henry Bear's Park** (kids' books & toys) 361 Huron Ave, Cambridge, 617-547-8424
- **KB Toys** (toys) 100 Cambridgeside Pl, Cambridgeside Galleria, Cambridge, 617-494-8519
- **Oilily** (up-scale kids' clothes) 32 Newbury St, Boston, 617-247-9299
- **PriKidz** (tween girls' clothes and accessories) 1378 Beacon Street Suite B, Coolidge Corner, 617-682-0998
- **The Red Wagon** (kids' toys & clothes) 69 Charles St, Boston, 617-523-9402
- **Stellabella Toys** (toys)
  1360 Cambridge St, Inman Square, Cambridge, 617-491-6290
  1967 Massachusetts Ave, Porter Square, Cambridge, 617-864-6290
- **Under Henry Bear's Park** (additional location) 19 Harvard Street, Brookline, 617-264-2422

Parks for Playing

Kids need fresh air. And singing into the rotating fan does not count. Take them out for a swing. In addition to the roomy Boston Common and Cambridge Common, Boston boasts many smaller neighborhood parks:

- **Alden Playground** (Oxford St and Sacramento St, Cambridge). A great neighborhood playground located in the shadow of Baldwin School and Lesley University, this toddler and big kid-friendly park includes a mini-track, a zooming climbing equipment, and what may be the World's Coolest Slide.
- **Charlesbank/Esplanade Playground** (Charles St at Longfellow Bridge). This large play area features several climbing structures, slides, and swings for all ages with a nearby snack bar, open during the summer months.
- **Christopher Columbus Park** (Atlantic Ave & Commercial Wharf, Boston). One large climbing structure dominates this playground that is mostly geared towards the six-and-under set.
- **Clarendon Street Playground** (Clarendon St & Commonwealth Ave, Boston). This fenced and gated area provides ample scope for the imagination of children of all ages. The park features several climbing structures, slides, swings, and a sand area, along with a larger, open area for games of tag and soccer.
- **Constitution Beach** (Orient Heights, East Boston). Lifeguarded swimming areas, a bathhouse with a snack bar, tennis courts and a playground with lots of climbing and sliding prospects make this a great destination to take the kids.
- **Emerson Park** (Davis Ave & Emerson St, Brookline). The Park boasts one of the town's oldest spray pools, with lots of trees for shade and a casual open space for tag.
- **Green Street Playground** (Green St, Jamaica Plain). On summer days, the city turns on the water, and kids in bathing suits splash around in the fountains. Families set up picnics around the periphery, and there is a sandy jungle gym and swingset area nearby.
- **Huron Avenue Playground** (Huron Ave, Cambridge). This newly renovated play area has two climbing structures for children of all ages, as well as a play train and spray fountain for the summer months. The lack of tree shade may bother some parents.

angone Park (Commercial St, Boston). The park features a brand-new playground with multi-age, multi-level climbing structures, and a swing set hovering on the edge of the harbor, great for that flying-across-water feeling. There are also three bocce courts and a baseball field.

arz Anderson Park (Newton, Avon, & Goddard Sts, Brookline). The largest park in Brookline holds an enclosed playground, picnic areas, ball fields, and an outdoor skating rink open December though February.

Millennium Park (VFW Pkwy & Gardner St, West Roxbury). This park is larger than the Boston Common and TD Banknorth Garden combined and located on the site of the former Gardner Street landfill. The park provides picnic areas, play structures, and hiking and walking trails, as well as access to the river for boating and fishing.

Myrtle Street Playground (Myrtle St & Irving St, Boston). Situated at the top of Beacon Hill, this playground features several climbing structures, a glider, a fire pole, swings, and a crazy daisy.

Public Garden (Between Arlington St & Charles St, Boston). The first public botanical garden in the US, the Public Garden has 24 acres of flowers and green in the middle of the bustling city. Among the park's winding pathways and tranquil lagoon are the prized bronze statues of a mama duck and her brood commemorating Robert McClosky's famous children's book, *Make Way for Ducklings.*

Rafferty Park (799 Concord Ave, Cambridge). One of the area's best-hidden playgrounds, this wooded park provides tons of fun activities for older children, including a new metal climbing structure with a twisty slide, wobbly bridge, boat-shaped sand box, and a mini-schoolhouse with a chalkboard roof. Basketball hoops, tennis courts, and a baseball field reside next door.

Raymond Street Park (Walden St & Raymond St, Cambridge). Located on the shady side of the field, this playground is split up into two sections: one sandy, sunken area for the younger toddlers and one area for older children, equipped with a large climbing structure. Play gear ranges from a bridge to swing sets, including one handicapped swing seat.

Stoneman Playground (Fairfield Ave & Massachusetts Ave, Cambridge). This playground is divided into a toddler area and an older children's space, with entertaining activities for both groups. Supervised model sailboat racing and fishing takes place on Sundays in the summer months.

Rainy Day Activities

t rains in Boston. A lot. It's also one of the windiest cities in the country. Foul weather can drench even the highest aspirations for outdoor fun. Here are some day alternatives:

Museums with Kid Appeal

- **Museum of Afro-American History** (46 Joy St, Boston, 617-725-0022). The first publicly-funded grammar school for African-Americans now has interactive exhibits for kids. www.afroamuseum.org
- **Children's Museum** (300 Congress St, Boston, 617-426-8855). This world-renowned museum, freshly renovated, has designed early learning experiences for children of all ages with its inventive hands-on exhibits. Permanent exhibits include the Japanese House, where children get to experience the culture of Kyoto, Japan through a replica of a silk merchant's house, as well as a Hall of Toys where children can look at toys of the past, but not touch. www.bostonkids.org
- **New England Aquarium** (Central Wharf, 617-973-5200). Among the many exhibits you'll find here are the sea lion show

and a supervised hands-on demonstration that allows children to touch sea stars, snails, and mussels. Whale-watching trips and summer classes are also offered through the aquarium. www.neaq.org

- **Larz Anderson Auto Museum** (Larz Anderson Park, 15 Newton St, Brookline, 617-522-6547). Located in the grand Carriage House, the museum features an extensive exhibit on the history of the automobile, as well as America's oldest car collection. www.mot.org
- **Museum of Science** (Science Park, 617-723-2500). This award-winning interactive science museum features permanent and changing exhibits, including a Virtual Fish Tank, where children see life through the eyes of a fish. The museum also houses the Charles Hayden Planetarium, featuring sky and laser shows, and the five-story IMAX Mugar Omni Theater. Various science classes are also available. www.mos.org
- **Harvard Museum of Natural History** (26 Oxford St, Cambridge, 617-495-3045). This museum has great educational programs and exhibits for little explorers interested in botany, zoology, and geology. The Sunday afternoon programs and lectures are highly recommended for families with middle school children. www.hmnh.harvard.edu

Other Indoor Distractions

- **The Clayroom** (1408 Beacon St, Brookline, 617-566-7575). Paint your own pottery place. Great for parties. www.clayroom.com
- **Lanes and Games** (195 Concord Tpke, Rte 2, Cambridge, 617-876-5533). Candlepin bowling and ten-pin lanes for the whole family. www.lanesgames.com
- **Puppet Showplace Theater** (32 Station St, Brookline, 617-731-6400). This 100-seat theater has been staging shows for Boston's young brood for over 30 years. The company stages classic puppet shows, as well as many original productions. Shows are recommended for children five and older. Great for parties. www.puppetshowplace.org

Outdoor and Educational

For when you've come to realize your children are a little too pale from sitting inside and playing video games all day.

- **Boston Duck Tours** (departure points: Prudential Center and Museum of Science, information: 617-267-DUCK). The Boston Duck is an original WWII amphibious landing vehicle that takes guests on an 80-minute tour (rain or shine) around the city by land and by sea. Kids are encouraged to quack at passersby. Tickets are sold inside the Prudential Center and Museum of Science beginning at 8:30 am. An additional ticketing location is at Faneuil Hall. Operating season: March 27th–Nov 26th. www.bostonducktours.com
- **Zoo New England** (1 Franklin Park Rd, Boston, 617-541-LION). The zoo holds all the standard zoo fare, plus the Butterfly Landing exhibit, a tented outdoor area where you can walk among more than 1,000 butterflies in free flight. (Smaller but still fun is the other Zoo New England site, Stone Zoo, in suburban Stoneham.) Adults: $9.50, seniors: $8, children (2–12): $5.50, under 2: free, and half-price tickets the first Sat of each month 10 am–12 pm. www.zoonewengland.com

Classes

Boston kids can participate in any number of structured activities that could help to mold and shape them like the blobs of clay that they are.

- **Boston Ballet School** (19 Clarendon St, Boston, 617-695-6950). Ballet classes for kids ages three and up. www.bostonballet.com
- **Boston Casting** (129 Braintree St, Suite 107, Allston, 617-254-1001). Acting classes for kids ages five and up. www.bostoncasting.com
- **Boston Children's Theatre** (321 Columbus Ave (Studio/Office), Boston, 617-424-6634). "Theatre for children by children," this theatre group has children involved in all phases of production. The theatre also offers acting classes and a summer creative arts program, in which kids learn stage combat, clowning, and juggling. www.bostonchildrenstheatre.org
- **Brookline Arts Center** (86 Monmouth St, Brookline, 617-566-5715). A non-degree school for the visual arts, the Brookline Arts Center offers classes for children ages two to teen in subjects ranging from jewelry-making to sculpture. www.brooklineartscenter.org
- **The Brookline Ballet School** (1431 Beacon Street, Brookline, 617-879-9988). Ballet as well as other dance and fitness classes. www.brooklineballet.com
- **Cambridge Multicultural Arts Center** (41 Second St, Cambridge, 617-577-1400). A program designed for Cambridge residents to promote cross-cultural interchange using dance, music, writing, theater, and the visual arts. www.cmacusa.org
- **Community Music Center of Boston** (34 Warren St, Boston, 617-482-7494). A music program designed to promote musical development through experimental learning for kids of all ages. The center also offers visual arts classes, summer programs, and individual instruction. www.cmcb.org
- **The Dance Complex** (536 Massachusetts Avenue, Central Square, 617-547-9363). Volunteer-based, artist-run organization located in historic Odd Fellows Hall. www.dancecomplex.org
- **French Library and Cultural Center** (53 Marlborough St, Boston, 617-912-0400). French classes for children ages three to ten. www.frenchlib.org
- **Full Moon** (344 Huron Ave, Cambridge, 617-354-6699). This kid-friendly restaurant offers cooking classes for parents and children ages three and up. www.fullmoonrestaurant.com
- **Grace Arts Project** (Grace United Methodist Church, 56 Magazine St, Cambridge, 617-864-1123). The program offers non-sectarian classes in music.
- **Grub Street Writers, Inc.** (160 Boylston St, Boston, 617-695-0075). Boston's only private writing school offers workshops and summer courses for young adults. www.grubstreet.org
- **Happily Ever After** (799 Concord Ave, Cambridge, 617-492-0090). The classes use fitness with creative stories and games for children aged three to six. Great for birthday parties. www.evergreendayschool.org
- **Hill House** (127 Mt. Vernon St, Boston, 617-227-5838). A non-profit community center that offers activities such as inline skating, karate, and youth soccer teams to downtown residents. www.hillhouseboston.org
- **John Payne Music Center** (kids' and adults' classes and ensembles with patient teachers) (9 Station Street, Brookline, 617-277-3438). Kids and adult classes and ensembles with patient teachers. www.jpmc.us
- **Isis Maternity** (Two Brookline Pl, Brookline, 781-429-1599; 397 Massachusetts Ave, Arlington, 781-429-1598; 110 2nd Ave, Needham, 617-429-1597). The brainchild of Boston-area moms and health professionals, each Isis Center offers classes to stimulate everyone from the newly born to those about to bop into kindergarten. Infant massage, anyone? www.isismaterr com

- **Jeanette Neill Children's Dance Studio** (261 Friend St, Boston, 617-523-1355). Since 1979, the progr has offered children ages three to 12 an "intelligent da alternative" with its focus on education, not preparation. ww jndance.com
- **Jose Mateo's Ballet Studio** (Old Cambridge Baptist Chur 400 Harvard St, Cambridge, 617-354-7467). A professio performance company that provides ballet instruction children ages three through 18. www.ballettheatre.org
- **Longy School of Music** (1 Follen St, Cambridge, 617-876-0956). Music instruction for children ages 1 to 18. www.longy.edu
- **Made By Me in Harvard Square** (1685 Massachusetts A Cambridge, 617-354-8111). A paint-your-own-pottery studio Great for birthday parties. www.made-by-me.com
- **Make Art Studio** (44 N Bennett St, Boston, 617-227-077 Children ages four to 13 are encouraged to "choose th own medium" with guidance and instruction in small, a appropriate classes.
- **Mudflat Studio** (149 Broadway, Somerville, 617-628-0589). F the past 30 years, the studio has offered hand-building, p throwing, and individual workshops for children ages four an up. www.mudflat.org
- **Museum of Fine Arts** (465 Huntington Ave, Boston, 617-267-9300). The museum offers weekday and Saturd instruction that combines gallery study and creative expressio for children ages five to 18. www.mfa.org/learn/index.asp?key=3117
- **New School of Music** (25 Lowell St, Cambridge, 617-492-810 Newborns and up are provided with musical instruction for a levels of interest and skill, as well as musical theater classes f the older kids. www.cambridgemusic.org
- **North Cambridge Family Opera** (23 North St, Cambridge 617-492-4095). Adults and children ages seven to 14 ca participate in theatrical and operatic production. www.familyopera.org
- **North End Music and Performing Arts Center** (Paul Revere Mall, between Hanover St and Unity St, Bostor 617-227-2270). The center offers classes in music, language and the performing arts to North End residents. www.nempac.org
- **New England Conservatory** (290 Huntington Ave, Bostor 617-585-1130). Music lessons for kids ages four and up at th oldest independent school of music in the US. www.newenglandconservatory.edu
- **Oak Square YMCA** (615 Washington St, Brighton, 617-782-3535). The center offers instruction in swimming gymnastics, basketball, and art as well as after school program for kids of all ages. www.ymcaboston.org
- **The Skating Club of Boston** (1240 Soldiers Field Rd, Brightor 617-782-5900). Classes for skaters and hockey players of al levels. www.scboston.org
- **Topf Center for Dance Education** (551 Tremont St, Boston 617-482-0351). The center provides underserved youth access to classes in jazz, tap, ballet, hip hop, and African dancing www.topfcenter.org
- **Upon a Star** (441 Stuart St, Studio 4, Boston, 617-797-5562) Music and movement classes for children ages 14 months to three. www.uponastar.net
- **Wang YMCA of Chinatown** (8 Oak St W, Boston, 617-426-2237). Activities ranging from swimming instruction to music and art classes for children of all ages. www.ymcaboston.org
- **Wheelock Family Theatre** (180 The Riverway, Boston, 617-879-2147). The theatre offers classes for kids ages four to 17. www.wheelock.edu/wft

For more information, visit www.gocitykids.com

Overview

The Boston Public Library, founded in 1848, was the first publicly supported municipal library in the United States, and is the only public library in the United States that is also a Presidential library, that of John Adams. It is also the first library to open and operate neighborhood branches. By far the coolest looking branch, the **Honan-Allston (Map 19)**, was designed by Machado & Silvetti Associates, Inc. and features tree guards and bike racks created by artist Josh Duca. The BPL now operates 24 branch libraries, each of which offers free wireless Internet access. Check out the details on the BPL's website. If you're looking for a getaway in Copley Square, the Italian courtyard is the perfect place to sit down with a book and a bagged lunch. For more information on the BPL's main branch and just how much cultural heat it's packing check out BPL Central Library **(see page 185)**.

Brookline, Cambridge, and Somerville have their own public libraries, which are part of the Minuteman system. The Brookline Public Library houses government documents, Russian and Chinese materials, Brookline high school yearbooks and newspapers, well-stocked CD collection, DVDs,

videos, new books, and local newspapers. The **Cambridge Public Library's Main Library (Map 28)** has occupied the same building since 1889. After moving to a temporary location while the building underwent renovations and an expansion, it reopened to the public 2009. The library now has seating for over 200 patrons, 100 public computers, both a Children's Room and a Teen Room, and WiFi throughout. Most noteworthy in the new addition is the Cambridge Room, which houses the CPL's Archives and Special Collections. Here you'll find historic maps, photographs, city directories and other genealogy resources, and the Historic Cambridge Newspaper Collection. Neat. The 93-year old **Somerville Public Library (Map 24)** holds its own serving its community by providing access to all kinds of information, in analog and digital form, via its three branches. Both Cambridge and Somerville libraries offer residents free passes to visit the Children's Museum, Harvard University Museum of Natural History, the JFK Library and Museum, the Museum of Fine Arts, the New England Aquarium, the Roger Williams Park Zoo, and others. To reserve FREE tickets, call 617-623-5000 (Somerville) or 617-349-4040 (Cambridge). For more information about hours, collections, and special events, check the library websites.

Library	Address	Phone	Map
Boston Public Library - West End	151 Cambridge St	617-523-3957	1
Boston Public Library - North End	25 Parmenter St	617-227-8135	2
The Mary Baker Eddy Library	200 Massachusetts Ave	617-450-7000	5
Boston Public Library - Central	700 Boylston St	617-536-5400	6
Boston Public Library - Kirstein Business	700 Boylston St	617-859-2142	6
Boston Public Library - South End	685 Tremont St	617-536-8241	7
Boston Public Library - Charlestown	179 Main St	617-242-1248	8
Boston Public Library - East Boston	276 Meridian St	617-569-0271	9
Boston Public Library - South Boston	646 E Broadway	617-268-0180	11
Boston Public Library - Dudley	65 Warren St	617-442-6186	13
Boston Public Library - Connolly	433 Centre St	617-522-1960	14
Boston Public Library - Jamaica Plain	12 Sedgwick St	617-524-2053	14
Boston Public Library - Parker Hill	1497 Tremont St	617-427-3820	15
Brookline Public Library	361 Washington St	617-730-2370	17
Boston Public Library - Brighton	40 Academy Hill Rd	617-782-6032	18
Boston Public Library - Faneuil	419 Faneuil St	617-782-6705	18
Boston Public Library - Honan-Allston	300 N Harvard St	617-787-6313	19
Brookline Public Library - Coolidge Corner	31 Pleasant St	617-730-2380	19
Cambridge Public Library - Boudreau	245 Concord Ave	617-349-4017	21
Cambridge Public Library - O'Neill	70 Rindge Ave	617-349-4023	22
Somerville Public Library - West	40 College Ave	617-623-5000	22
Somerville Public Library	79 Highland Ave	617-623-5000	24
Somerville Public Library - East	115 Broadway	617-623-5000	24
Cambridge Public Library - O'Connell	48 Sixth St	617-349-4019	26
Cambridge Public Library - Central Square	45 Pearl St	617-349-4010	27
Cambridge Public Library	449 Broadway	617-349-4040	28
Cambridge Public Library - Valente	826 Cambridge St	617-349-4015	28

General Information · LGBT

Websites

Boston Gay Men's Chorus · www.bgmc.org
Now in its 24th year, the BGMC, through its collaboration with The Boston Pops, was the first gay chorus in the world to be recorded with a major orchestra on a major label.

craigslist · http://boston.craigslist.org
General community site (for straights, gays, and everyone else) that offers heavily trafficked "men seeking men" and "women seeking women" sections, as well as other community-related listings and information.

EDGE Boston · www.edgeboston.com
Gay Boston news and entertainment.

Gay & Lesbian Advocates & Defenders (GLAD) · www.glad.org
New England's leading legal rights organization dedicated to ending discrimination based on sexual orientation.

Greater Boston Business Council · www.gbbc.org
Promotes the vitality of Boston's LGBT business and professional community.

Out In Boston · www.outinboston.com
Local news and events, personal ads, business ads, chat, and community message boards.

PinkWeb · www.pinkweb.com
The LGBT yellow pages for New England and beyond.

Provincetown Business Guild · www.ptown.org
A gay and lesbian guide to P'town.

Publications

Bay Windows—New England's largest gay and lesbian newspaper is a weekly publication that prints local, national, and international news as well as community events and guides. www.baywindows.com.

Boston Spirit Magazine—Free glossy bimonthly magazine www.bostonspiritmagazine.com.

In Newsweekly—News and entertainment weekly, including a calendar of events and a club guide. www.innewsweekly.com.

Bookstores

Calamus Bookstore · 92B South St, Boston · 617-338-1931 · www.calamusbooks.com

Sports

Beantown Softball League · www.beantownsoftball.com
LGBT softball since 1978.

Boston Bay Blades · www.bayblades.org/boston
For rowers and scullers.

Boston Boasts Squash League · www.bostonboasts.com
The country's oldest and largest gay and lesbian squash league.

Boston Gay Basketball League · www.bgbl.com
The country's largest LGBT basketball league.

Boston Strikers · www.bostonstrikers.com
Indoor and outdoor soccer league for gay and straight players of all levels.

Cambridge-Boston Volleyball Association · www.gayvolleyball.net
Indoor league with three levels of play.

Chiltern Mountain Club · www.chiltern.org
New England's largest LGBT outdoor recreation club.

East Coast Wrestling Club · www.eastcoastwrestlingclub.org
Gay men's wrestling group for athletes of all abilities.

FLAG Flag Football · http://flagflagfootball.tripod.com/flagflagfootballonline
Plays a full fall season and an abbreviated spring season.

FrontRunners Boston · www.mindspring.com/~frontrunners/index.htm
Welcomes joggers, walkers, and runners of all experience levels.

PrideSports Boston · 617-937-5858 · www.geocities.com/pridesportsboston
Gay & lesbian athletic alliance with more than 20 sports clubs.

ealth Centers & Support rganizations

ston Alliance of Gay Lesbian Bisexual and nsgender Youth · 617-227-4313 · www.bagly.org young people 22 and under.

gnity Boston · 617-421-1915 · ww.dignityboston.org inclusive community of LGBT Catholics.

nway Community Health · 7 Haviland St, Boston · 7-267-0900 · www.fenwayhealth.org vides high-quality medical and mental health re to Boston's gay and lesbian community; also a der in HIV care.

y Men's Domestic Violence Project · 0-832-1901 · www.gmdvp.org fers shelter, guidance, and resources to allow y, bisexual, and transgender men in crisis to nove themselves from violent situations and ationships; also operates a 24-hour free-of-charge sis center.

assEquality · 617-878-2300 · ww.massequality.org assroots advocacy group defending equal arriage rights for same-sex couples.

e Network · 617-423-SAFE · ww.thenetworklared.org ovides information and resources for battered sbian, bisexual, and transgendered women.

Annual Events

oston Pride Week · 617-262-9405 · ww.bostonpride.org egins on a Friday in June with a flag raising at City all; the parade and festival usually take place on e Saturday of the following weekend.

oston Gay/Lesbian Film/Video Festival · 7-267-9300 · www.mfa.org sually held in May at the MFA.

ass Red Ribbon Ride · 617-450-1100 · ww.massredribbonride.org his bike ride across the state raises money for AIDS rganizations. Takes place annually in August.

Venues – Lesbian

- **Aria** (Saturdays) · 246 Tremont St, Boston · 617-417-0186
- **Dyke Night Productions** · www.dykenight.com
- **Midway Cafe** (Sundays) · 3496 Washington St, Jamaica Plain · www.midwaycafe.com
- **Milky Way Lounge** (Sundays) · 284 Amory St, Jamaica Plain · 617-524-6060· www.milkywayjp.com
- **The Modern** (Thursdays) · 36 Lansdowne St, Boston · www.lesbiannightlife.com
- **Toast** (Fridays) · 70 Union Sq, Somerville · 617-623-9211 · www.toastlounge.com
- **Tribe** (at Felt) · 533 Washington St, Boston · 617-350-5555 · www.tribenightclub.com

Venues – Gay

- **The Alley** · 14 Pi Aly, Boston · 617-263-1449 · www.thealleybar.com
- **Club Cafe** · 209 Columbus Ave, Boston · 617-536-0966 · www.clubcafe.com
- **Eagle** · 520 Tremont St, Boston · 617-542-4494
- **Flaunt** (Saint Nightclub) · 90 Exeter St, Boston · 617-236-1134
- **Fritz** · 26 Chandler St, Boston · 617-482-4428 · www.fritzboston.com
- **Heroes** (Saturdays at **Toast**) · 70 Union Sq, Somerville · 617-623-9211 · www.toastlounge.com
- **Add House of Blues** Boston-15 Lansdowne Street, Boston · 888-693-2583 · http://www.houseofblues. com/venues/clubvenues/boston/
- **Jacques Cabaret** · 79 Broadway St, Boston · 617-426-8902 · www.jacquescabaret.com
- **Machine** (Thurs–Sat) · 1256 Boylston St, Boston · 617-226-2986 · www.ramrodmachine.com
- **Paradise** · 180 Massachusetts Ave, Cambridge · 617-868-3000 · www.paradisecambridge.com
- **Ramrod** · 1254 Boylston St, Boston · 617-226-2986 · www.ramrodmachine.com
- **Rise** (members only, after-hours) · 306 Stuart St, Boston · 617-423-7473 · www.riseclub.us
- **Shine Restaurant & Lounge** · 1 Kendall Sq, Cambridge · 617-621-9500 · www.shinecambridge.com
- **Venu** (Wednesdays) · 101 Warrenton St, Boston · 617-695-9500

After years of suffering from a shortage of hotel accommodations, Boston's hotel market has finally warmed up. Developers, encouraged by an improving economic climate and continued high demand for rooms, have moved forward with several large projects, most of which are located on or near the waterfront, where developers hope to leverage locations close to the Boston Convention & Exhibition Center. But it's not all just about harbor views and cafeteria-sized restaurants—boutique hotels are also popping up in various locations around town. Newcomers in the boutique market include **Hotel 140 (Map 6)** (a historic building in the shadow of the Hancock Tower), sleek **Nine Zero (Map 3)** (on Tremont Street), the **The Boxer (Map 1)** (near North Station), and the **Beacon Hill Hotel (Map 1)** (on Charles Street, near the Common). **Loews Boston Hotel (Map 6)** has opened in the fully renovated former headquarters of the Boston Police Department. **The Hampton Inn & Suites (Map 12)** (near Newmarket Square), may not be as luxurious as Loews Boston, but its suites are a decent option for long-term stays, and its proximity to I-93 and the Mass Pike make it easy to get to other locations. For visitors largely confined to happenings at the Boston Convention Center, the **Westin Boston Waterfront (Map 4)** and the **Seaport Hotel (Map 11)** are safe, convenient bets.

But Boston residents shouldn't let tourists have all the fun. Even if you're not staying the night, it's worth popping into one of Boston's classic hotels to soak up the atmosphere. The lobby of the **Fairmont Copley Plaza (Map 6)** exudes luxuriousness, as does its acclaimed restaurant, the OAK Long Bar and Kitchen. For those looking for a respite from retail therapy on nearby Newbury Street, the **Eliot Hotel (Map 5)** on Commonwealth Avenue can rejuvenate even the weariest shopper. Genteel rivals the **Four Seasons (Map 3)** and the **Taj Boston (Map 3)** (formerly home to the oldest Ritz Carlton in the country) both overlook the Public Garden. (The Bristol Lounge at the Four Seasons serves what many argue is the city's best-known

high tea.) Across the Common, towards t financial district, the **Omni Parker Hou (Map 3)** stands as a Boston institution a a literary landmark (and has been kno to flaunt its claim to fame as the birthpla of Parker rolls and Boston Cream Pie Chic boutique newcomer Liberty Hot at the former Charles Street Jail right ne to present-day Charles/MGH T stop, offe stunning atrium and hopping bar/loung The **Langham Hotel (Map 4)**, located sma dab in the middle of Boston's high-finan hub, offers a chocolate buffet on Saturda that is To Die For. If you're killing time Back Bay, check out the charming and co lobby of the **Lenox Hotel (Map 6)**. Playir up its proximity to techie heaven MIT is th lovely **Royal Sonesta Hotel Boston (Ma 26)**, with great views of the Charles River ar the Boston skyline. In Harvard Square, t **Charles Hotel (Map 20)** offers nightly jazz the Regattabar as well as organic fine dinir at Henrietta's Table. And if you're sufferir from wanderlust of the spirit, ask about th weekend retreats at the **Monastery of th Society of St. John the Evangelist (Ma 20)**. For another low-cost option, check in the new HI-Boston hostel in the Theat District/Chinatown with plenty of free per and programs.

Marriott's Custom House (Map 2) is locate in one of Boston's most prominent histor landmarks, the Custom House Tower. Th original Custom House building, complete in 1847, was described by Walt Whitma as "the noblest form of architecture in th world." The tower was added in 1915. Th open-air observation deck on the 26th floc is open to the public and offers prime view of the harbor and the open spaces create by the demolition of the Central Artery.

Whether you're booking for yourself or th in-laws, call the hotels to ask about speci and check websites such as hotels.com Orbitz, Hotwire, Travelocity, and All-Hote for discounts. Maybe you'll get lucky.

Hotel	Address	Phone	Price	Map
Beacon Hill Hotel	25 Charles St	617-723-7575	$$$	1
The Boxer	107 Merrimac Ave	617-624-0202	$$	1
Liberty Hotel	215 Charles St	617-224-4000	$$$$	1
Marriott's Custom House	3 McKinley Sq	617-310-6300	$$$$	2
Four Seasons Hotel	200 Boylston St	617-338-4400	$$$$$$	3
The Zero Hotel	90 Tremont St	617-772-5800	$$$	3
Omni Parker House	60 School St	617-227-8600	$$$	3
W Boston	15 Arlington St	617-536-5700	$$$$	3
The Langham Hotel	250 Franklin St	617-451-1900	$$$$	4
Westin Boston Waterfront	425 Summer St	617-532-4600	$$$	4
Eliot Hotel	370 Commonwealth Ave	617-267-1607	$$$	5
Fairmont Copley Plaza Hotel	138 St James Ave	617-267-5300	$$$$$	6
Hotel 140	140 Clarendon St	617-585-5600	$$	6
Lenox Hotel	61 Exeter St	617-536-5300	$$$	6
Newbury Boston Hotel	154 Berkeley St	617-266-7200	$$$$	6
Hampton Inn & Suites Boston Crosstown Center	811 Massachusetts Ave	617-445-6400	$$	7
Seaport Hotel	1 Seaport Ln	617-385-4000	$$$	11
Monastery of the Society of St John the Evangelist	980 Memorial Dr	617-876-3037	$	20
Charles Hotel	1 Bennett St	617-864-1200	$$$$	20
Royal Sonesta Hotel Boston	40 Land Blvd	617-806-4200	$$$	26

And this is good old Boston.
The home of the bean and the cod.
Where the Lowells talk to the Cabots,
And the Cabots talk only to God.
　　　　　—John Collins Bossidy (a toast given
　　　　　　　at a Harvard alumni dinner in 1910)

Useful Phone Numbers

General Info	411
Emergencies	911
Boston Globe	617-929-2000
Boston Herald	617-426-3000
Boston Public Library	617-536-5400
Boston City Hall	617-635-4000
Brookline Town Hall	617-730-2000
Cambridge City Hall	617-349-4000
Somerville City Hall	617-625-6600
Boston Board of Elections	617-635-4635
Brookline Town Clerk	617-730-2010
Cambridge Board of Elections	617-349-4361
Somerville Board of Elections	617-625-6600, ext. 4200
Boston Police Headquarters	617-343-4200
Keyspan Energy Delivery	617-469-2300
NStar	617-424-2000
Comcast	888-633-4266
Verizon	800-256-4646
Red Sox Ticket Line	877-733-7699

Websites

www.notfortourists.com/boston.aspx—
　The Boston site written by the people, for the people.
www.beantownbloggery.com—
　Anything and everything beantown.
www.boston.com—Website of the *Boston Globe*.
www.boston.craigslist.org—
　Classifieds in almost every area, with personals, apartments
　for rent, musicians, job listings, and more.
www.boston.citysearch.com—
　Portal channeling the Yellow Pages.
www.boston-online.com—
　Forums and fun facts; guide to Boston English.
www.bostonist.com—
　About Boston and everything that happens in it.
www.cambridgema.gov—
　Cambridge government resources.
http://cheapthrillsboston.blogspot.com—
　Perfect for those on an NFT salary.
www.cityofboston.com—Boston government resources.
www.ci.somerville.ma.us—
　Somerville government resources.
www.eatanddestroy.com—Amazing Boston food blog.
thephoenix.com/boston—Boston Phoenix, now online only.
www.universalhub.com—Info hub for the Hub.
www.universalhub.com—Info hub for the Hub.

We're the First!!!

- America's first public park (Boston Common, 1634)
- America's first college (Harvard, founded in 1636)
- America's first public school (Boston Latin, 1645)
- America's first public library (Boston Public Library, 1653)
- America's first post office (Richard Fairbanks' Tavern, 1704)
- America's first regularly issued newspaper (*Boston News-Letter*, 1704)
- America's first lighthouse (Boston Harbor, 1716)
- First flag of the American colonies raised on Prospect Hill (January 1, 1776)
- America's first published novel (*The Power of Sympathy*, William Hill Brown, 1789)
- First demonstration of surgical anesthesia (1845)
- First telephone call (Alexander Graham Bell, 1876)
- America's first subway (1897)
- First person-to-person network email (BBN Technolog 1971)
- First "First Night" New Year's celebration (1976)

Boston Timeline

A timeline of significant Boston events (by no means complete)

1620	Mayflower arrives in Plymouth.
1630	Dorchester founded by Gov. John Winthrop.
1630	City of Boston chartered.
1634	Boston Common, first public park in America, opens.
1636	Harvard College opens.
1639	America's first canal cut near Dedham.
1645	Boston Latin School, first public school in America, open
1692	Witchcraft trials begin in Salem.
1693	Society of Negroes founded.
1704	First regularly issued American newspaper, the *Boston News-Letter*.
1706	Benjamin Franklin born.
1716	First American lighthouse built (Boston Harbor).
1770	Boston Massacre.
1773	Boston Tea Party.
1775	Revolutionary War begins at Lexington and Concord.
1775	Battle of Bunker Hill.
1776	First flag of the American colonies raised on Prospect H in Somerville.
1776	British evacuate Boston.
1780	John Hancock becomes first elected Governor of Massachusetts.
1788	Massachusetts ratifies Constitution.
1795	The "new" State House built.
1796	John Adams, of Quincy, elected second president.
1806	African Meeting House, first church built by free African Americans, opens.
1820	Maine separates from Massachusetts.
1824	John Quincy Adams elected sixth president.
1826	Union Oyster House opens.
1831	William Lloyd Garrison publishes first abolitionist newspaper, the *Liberator*.
1837	Samuel Morse invents electric telegraph machine.
1845	Sewing machine invented by Elias Howe.
1846	Boston dentist William T.G. Morton publicly demonstrate the use of anesthesia in surgery.
1846	From 1846 to 1849, 37,000 Irish people flee the Potato Famine for Boston.
1860	From 1860 to 1870, the Back Bay is filled in, greatly increasing the landmass of Boston.
1863	University of Massachusetts at Amherst chartered.
1868	From 1868 to 1874, Boston annexes Charlestown, Brighton, Roxbury, West Roxbury, and Dorchester.
1872	*Boston Globe* prints its first newspaper.
1872	Great Fire.
1876	First telephone call by Alexander Graham Bell.
1877	Helen Magill becomes first woman Ph.D. in US (at BU).
1882	John L. Sullivan becomes bare-knuckle boxing champ.
1886	*Irish Echo* newspaper founded.
1888	Construction begins on new building for Boston Public Library.
1892	JFK grandfather John F. "Honey Fitz" Fitzgerald elected to state senate.
1894	Honey Fitz elected to US Congress.
1896	First US public beach opens in Revere.
1897	First American subway opens.
1900	Symphony Hall opens.
1901	Boston Red Sox play first game against New York Yankees.
1903	Red Sox (then the Americans) win first World Series.
1906	Honey Fitz becomes first Boston-born Irish-American mayor.

'12 Fenway Park opens.
'14 James Michael Curley elected mayor for the first time.
'15 Custom House Tower completed, tallest building in Boston at time.
'19 Great Molasses Flood kills 21 in the North End.
'20 Red Sox owner Harry Frazee sells Babe Ruth to Yankees for $100,000.
'20 Irish-Italian gang fights begin.
'20 Boston Bruins play first game.
'20 World's first mutual fund established.
'27 Sacco and Vanzetti wrongly executed for robbery shootings.
'28 Boston Garden opens.
'28 First computer invented at MIT.
'29 Bruins win their first Stanley Cup trophy.
'34 JFK's father, "Old Joe" Kennedy, named SEC chairman.
'41 Ted Williams hits .406, last player to hit over .400.
'42 Fire at Cocoanut Grove nightclub kills 491 people.
'46 JFK elected to Congress.
'46 Boston Celtics play first game.
'46 Red Sox lose World Series after tragic player error.
'47 Microwave oven invented at Raytheon.
'47 Polaroid camera invented.
'47 Dr. Sidney Farber introduces chemotherapy.
'50 Red Auerbach becomes Celtics coach.
'52 Boston Braves play final game in Boston, move to Milwaukee.
'56 Celtics draft Bill Russell.
'57 Massachusetts Turnpike opens.
'58 Celtics win first of 16 championships.
'58 Demolition of the West End neighborhood begins.
'59 Central Artery opens.
'60 Boston Patriots play first game.
'60 John F. Kennedy elected 35th president.
'60 Ted Williams homers in last at-bat for Red Sox.
'62 From 1962 to 1964, Boston Strangler kills 13 women. Albert DeSalvo is convicted and killed in prison.
'63 JFK assassinated in Dallas.
'64 Prudential Tower built.
'65 Havlicek steals the ball! Celtics win championship.
'66 Bobby Orr plays first game as a Bruin.
'66 Edward W. Brooke becomes first African-American elected to US Senate since Reconstruction.
'67 Red Sox's "Impossible Dream" season ends in defeat.
'71 First e-mail sent by BBN Technologies.
'73 John Hancock building, tallest in Boston, nears completion—giant windows start falling out.
'74 Federal court declares "de facto segregation" of Boston public schools; orders desegregation by busing. Demonstrations and violence ensue.
'75 Carlton Fisk hits 12th inning Game 6 homer, does baseline foul pole dance. Sox go on to lose Game 7.
'75 Gangster Whitey Bulger begins relationship with FBI agents, reign as Boston's biggest crime lord.
'76 First "First Night" New Year's celebration.
'78 Blizzard of '78 paralyzes Southern New England.
'78 Bucky Dent! Sox lose to Yanks.
'86 Celtics draft Len Bias dies of a drug overdose.
'86 Red Sox lose World Series Game 6 to Mets after excruciating 10th inning error, go on to lose Game 7.
'87 Big Dig construction begins in Charlestown.
'88 Cleanup of Boston Harbor begins.
'88 Governor Michael Dukakis runs for president, rides tank, loses to Bush the First.
'91 Celtics captain Reggie Lewis dies.
'93 Former Mayor Ray Flynn named ambassador to Vatican.
'93 Thomas M. "Mumbles" Menino elected Boston's first Italian-American mayor.
'95 Boston Garden closes; FleetCenter opens.
'95 Whitey Bulger goes on the lam after his FBI handlers are indicted.
'98 Boston Globe columnists Patricia Smith and Mike Barnicle fired over fabrications and plagiarism, respectively.

2001 Jane Swift becomes first female governor of Massachusetts.
2001 Planes that destroy NYC World Trade Center leave Logan Airport.
2002 After a 0-2 start, New England Patriots win their first Super Bowl.
2002 Ted Williams dies, cryogenically frozen in two pieces.
2002 Catholic clergy sexual abuse scandal explodes; Cardinal Bernard Law resigns amid controversy.
2003 Billy Bulger forced to resign as UMass president due to controversy about his gangster brother, Whitey.
2004 Supreme Judicial Court rules that gay couples have the right to marry.
2004 Demolition of Central Artery.
2004 Sox win World Series for first time since 1918.
2005 Patriots win their third Super Bowl.
2006 Massachusetts elects Deval Patrick, first black Governor of the state.
2007 Sox end three year drought by winning the World Series (again!).
2008 Cetics beat Lakers for record 17th NBA championship.
2009 Ted Kennedy passes; crowds gather the funeral procession.

15 Essential Boston Movies

The Boston Strangler (1968)	*Far and Away* (1992)
The Thomas Crown Affair (1968)	*Good Will Hunting* (1997)
Love Story (1970)	*A Civil Action* (1998)
The Paper Chase (1973)	*Monument Ave* (1998)
Between the Lines (1977)	*Next Stop, Wonderland* (1998)
The Verdict (1982)	*Mystic River* (2003)
The Bostonians (1984)	*The Departed* (2006)
Glory (1989)	*Gone Baby Gone* (2007)
	The Town (2010)

15 Essential Boston Songs

"Boston" — The Byrds
"Charlie on the MTA" — The Kingston Trio
"Dirty Water" — The Standells
"Down at the Cantab" — Little Joe Cook & the Thrillers
"Government Center" — Jonathan Richman
"Highlands" — Bob Dylan
"I Want My City Back" — The Mighty Mighty Bosstones
"Massachusetts" — The Bee Gees
"Roadrunner" — Jonathan Richman
"Rock and Roll Band" — Boston
"Sweet Baby James" — James Taylor
"Tessie" — Dropkick Murphys
"The Ballad of Sacco & Vanzetti" — Joan Baez
"Twilight in Boston" — Jonathan Richman
"UMass" — The Pixies

15 Essential Boston Books

All Souls, Michael Patrick McDonald
The Autobiography of Benjamin Franklin
Black Mass, David Lehrer and Gerard O'Neill
The Bostonians, Henry James
Dark Tide: The Great Boston Molasses Flood of 1919, Stephen Puleo
Faithful, Stewart O'Nan and Stephen King
The Handmaid's Tale, Margaret Attwood
The House of the Seven Gables, Nathaniel Hawthorne
Infinite Jest, David Foster Wallace
John Adams, David McCullough
Johnny Tremain, Esther Forbes
Little Women, Louisa May Alcott
Make Way for Ducklings, Robert McCloskey
The Trumpet of the Swan, E.B. White
Walden, Henry David Thoreau

Overview

There's always something going on in Boston—the list below is just a smattering of the hundreds of annual parades, festivals, and wing-dings. Note that dates change from year to year, so as always, it's a good idea to check an event's website when making plans. Now get out and enjoy!

· **First Night** · Dec 31/Jan 1 · www.firstnight.org · Family-oriented First Night got its start in Boston. Celebrate the new year with live performances, interactive events, and in most years, bitter cold. The purchase of a First Night Button gains you admission to participating performance centers.

· **Chinese New Year** · Early Feb · Fireworks, parades, and special banquets in Chinatown.

· **Boston Wine Expo** · Mid-Feb · www.wine-expos.com/boston · Largest consumer wine event in the country, with a long bill of celebrity chefs to boot.

· **Black History Month Music Celebration** · Feb · www.berkleebpc.com · A series of concerts at the Berklee Performance Center.

· **Winter Restaurant Week** · Early March · www.restaurantweekboston.com · Local eateries offer specially priced lunches and dinners. A chance to sample meals you could never otherwise afford!

· **Boston Flower and Garden Show** · Mid-March · www.masshort.org · Flower and craft exhibition at the Seaport World Trade Center.

· **Evacuation Day** · Mar 17 · British troop withdrawal from Boston was the perfect excuse for infamous Mayor Curley to make St. Paddy's Day an official holiday for all Suffolk County municipal workers. Gotta love the Irish.

· **St. Patrick's Day Parade** · March · www.saintpatricksdayparade.com/boston · Marching through Southie since 1737.

· **Red Sox Opening Day** · Early Apr · www.redsox.com · Unofficial holiday.

· **Boston Marathon/Patriots Day** · Apr 15 · www.baa.org · Pseudo local holiday with the 117th running of the marathon and an early Red Sox game.

· **Wake Up the Earth Festival** · May 4 · spontaneouscelebrations.org · Hippies and children alike enjoy stilt walking, puppets, live bands, and community bonding in Jamaica Plain.

· **MayFair** · First Sunday in May · www.harvardsquare.com/mayfair/ · Harvard Square festival featuring everything from Literary tours to indie rock to Morris dancers.

· **Lilac Sunday at the Arnold Arboretum** · Early May · www.arboretum.harvard.edu · Follow the perfume of the lilac and the hippie in a Morri dancing outfit. Fun atmosphere at the Arnold Arboretum for families and friends.

· **Walk for Hunger** · Early May · www.projectbread.org · 20-mile walk whose proceeds fund over 400 emergency food progran each year.

· **Anime Boston** · May 24–26 · www.animeboston. com · Japanese animation convention at the Hynes Convention Center.

· **Street Performers Festival** · Late May · Faneuil Hall carnival that's especially fun for kids. Magicians, sword swallowers, and lil' one activitie like the Kid's Kazoo Parade.

· **Feast of the Madonna di Anzano** · Early June · www.anzanoboston.com · Procession and gala feast in the North End Italian community.

· **WUMB Music Festival** · Early June · www.wumb.org/folkfest · Pickin' and grinnin'.

· **Scooper Bowl** · Early June · www.jimmyfund.org World's biggest all-you-can-eat ice cream festival. Proceeds go to the Jimmy Fund.

· **Boston Gay Pride Parade** · Early/Mid June · www.bostonpride.org · New England's largest, capping a week of pride events.

· **Cambridge River Festival** · Mid June · Summer-starting festival along Memorial Drive between JFK Street and Western Ave, featuring music, food, art, kid-stuff.

· **Dragon Boat Festival** · Early/Mid June · www.bostondragonboat.org · Celebration of Chinese Dragon Boat racing at the Weeks footbridge, on Memorial Drive. Races, food, activities all day long.

· **Bloomsday** · Jun 16 · www.artsandsociety.org · Celebration of James Joyce's Ulysses at BU.

· **Bunker Hill Parade** · Around June 17 · www.charlestononline.net · Celebration of Bunker Hill Day in Charlestown.

· **Boston Globe Blues and Jazz Festival** · Late Jun Jazz and blues on the waterfront.

Boston Harborfest · Early July · www.bostonharborfest.com · Over 200 events celebrating Boston's colonial and maritime history through reenactments, concerts, and historical tours.

Boston's Fourth of July · Guess · www.july4th.org Ridiculously crowded Boston Pops concert and fireworks on the Esplanade.

French Cultural Center's Bastille Day · Mid July · Block party in Back Bay with paid admission, crêpes and occasional world music superstars.

Bastille Day in Harvard Square · Mid July · Free admission to block party and concert/DJs, paid food spearheaded by Sandrine's Bistro."

Puerto Rican Festival · Late July · Franklin Park goes loco for 5 days with amusement rides, food, and general fun in the name of Puerto Rico. Lots of live music.

Feast of St. Agrippina · Early Aug · Featuring a procession, block party, and a giant tug-of-war.

August Moon Festival · Mid Aug · At the Chinatown Gateway arch on Harrison Ave, celebrating Chinese culture and marked by tasty flaky pastries with an interesting history,

Feast of the Madonna del Soccorso · Mid Aug · www.fishermansfeast.com · Boston's longest-running Italian festival.

St. Anthony's Feast · Late Aug · www.saintanthonysfeast.com · With Italian-American festivals in the North End every weekend throughout late July and August, this is the one to get off your coolie on. True combination of kitsch and classic.

Summer Restaurant Week · August · www.bostonusa.com · Discounted *prix-fixe* meals at scores of area restaurants—a terrific bargain.

Boston Carnival · Late Aug · www.bostoncarnival.com · Celebration of Caribbean culture in Dorchester.

Boston Film Festival · Mid/Late Sep · www.bostonfilmfestival.org · Plenty to please the most finicky cinephile.

Boston Freedom Rally · Mid/Late Sep · www.masscann.org · That ain't freedom they're smoking.

- **Phantom Gourmet Food Festival** · Late Sep · www.phantomgourmetfoodfestival.com · $40 for the Landsdowne St Grand Bouffe that's unlike any other in Boston, featuring booths hand picked by the Phantom himself.

- **Boston Tattoo Convention** · Labor Day Weekend · www.bostontattooconvention.com · Celebrating the newly legal (in Mass) art form.

- **Opening Night at the Symphony** · Sept 22 · www.bso.org · Kicks off another season of BSO goodness.

- **Harvard Square Oktoberfest** · Early Oct · www.harvardsquare.com · Don't expect liters of free beer.

- **Head of the Charles** · Oct 23–24 · www.hocr.org · The world's largest two-day rowing event.

- **Belgian Beer Fest** · Late Oct · www.beeradvocate.com/fests · *Sluit je aan bij de Bierrevolutie!*

- **Boston Jewish Film Festival** · Nov · www.bjff.org · Now in its 17th season.

- **Boston International Antiquarian Book Fair** · Mid Nov · www.bostonbookfair.com · The country's longest running antiquarian book fair features autographs, photographs, maps, and more.

- **Black Nativity** · Weekends in Dec · www.blacknativity.org · One part Harlem Renaissance, one part folk music, dance, and verse celebration of the birth of Jesus Christ. Held at the Tremont Temple.

- **Prudential Center Christmas Tree Lighting** · Early Dec · www.prudentialcenter.com · Each year Nova Scotia thanks Boston for helping Halifax recover from a 1917 disaster by sending down a huge tree.

- **Boston Tea Party Reenactment** · Mid Dec · www.oldsouthmeetinghouse.org · A fine excuse to don your tri-cornered hat.

- **Boston Common Menorah Lighting** · Late Dec · www.cityofboston.gov/arts · Celebrating the first night of Hanukkah.

Television

2	WGBH	(PBS)	www.wgbh.org
4	WBZ	(CBS)	www.wbz4.com
5	WCVB	(ABC)	www.thebostonchannel.com
7	WHDH	(NBC)	www1.whdh.com
25	WFXT	(FOX)	www.fox25.com
27	WUNI	(Univision)	www.wunitv.com
38	WSBK	(UPN)	www.upn38.com
44	WGBH	(PBS)	www.wgbh.org
56	WLVI	(WB)	www.wb56.trb.com
66	WUTF	(Telefutura)	www.univision.com
68	WBPX	(PAX)	www.paxboston.tv

AM Radio

590	WEZE	Christian radio	www.wezeradio.com
680	WRKO	Talk	www.wrko.com
740	WJIB	Instrumental Pop/Light Oldies	
850	WEEI	Sports	www.weei.com
950	WROL	Religious	
1030	WBZ	News/Talk/Sports	www.wbz.com
1060	WBIX	Business Talk	
1090	WILD	Urban	
1120	WBNW	Financial Talk	www.moneymattersradio.net
1150	WJTK	Religious	
1260	WMKI	Radio Disney	www.radio.disney.go.com/mystation/Boston/
1510	WWZN	Sports	www.1510thezone.com
1600	WUNR	Leased-time/ethnic	
1670	Allston-Brighton Free Radio		www.abfreeradio.org

FM Radio

88.1	WMBR	MIT	wmbr.mit.edu
88.9	WERS	Emerson College	www.wers.org
89.7	WGBH	NPR News/Classical	www.wgbh.com
90.3	WZBC	Boston College	www.wzbc.org
90.9	WBUR	NPR/BU	www.wbur.org
91.5	WMFO	Tufts University	www.wmfo.org
91.9	WUMB	Folk/Jazz	www.wumb.org
92.5	The River	Rock/Pop Modern	www.wxrv.com
92.9	WBOS	Modern AC	www.wbos.com
93.7	WEEI	Sports Talk Radio	www.weei.com
94.5	WJMN	Hip-Hop/R&B	www.jamn.com
95.3	WHRB	Harvard University	www.whrb.org
96.9	WTKK	Talk	www.wtkk.com
98.5	Sports Hub	Sports Talk Radio	http://boston.cbslocal.com/category/sports/
99.5	WCRB	Classical	www.wcrb.com
100.1	WBRS	Brandeis University	www.wbrs.org
100.7	WZLX	Classic Rock	www.wzlx.com
101.7	WFNX	Modern Rock	www.wfnx.com
102.5	WKLB	Country	www.wklb.com
102.9	WCFM	Caribbean Music	www.choice1029.com
103.3	WODS	Oldies	www.oldies1033.com
104.1	Mix FM	Pop	http://mix1041.radio.com/
104.9	WBOQ	Soft Rock	www.northshore1049.com
105.7	WROR	Classic Rock	www.wror.com
106.7	WMJX	Soft Rock	www.magic1067.com
107.3	WAAF	Active Rock	www.waaf.com
107.9	WXKS	Pop	www.kissfm.com

rint Media

y Windows	www.baywindows.com	617-266-6670	LGBT newsweekly.
acon Hill Times	www.beaconhilltimes.com	617-523-9490	Newsweekly serving Beacon Hill.
ston Business Journal	www.bizjournals.com/boston	617-330-1000	Business weekly.
ston Globe	www.boston.com	617-929-2000	Daily broadsheet.
ston Haitian Reporter	www.bostonhaitian.com	617-436-1222	Free monthly for Haitian-American mmunity.
ston Herald	www.bostonherald.com	617-426-3000	Daily tabloid.
ston Irish Reporter	www.bostonirish.com	617-436-1222	News from and about the Irish in Boston.
ston Metro	www.metropoint.com	617-338-7985	Weekday tabloid aimed at commuters.
ston Magazine	www.bostonmagazine.com	617-262-9700	Glossy monthly.
ston Review	www.bostonreview.net	617-258-0805	Leftish politics and culture magazine.
ston Russian Bulletin	www.russianmass.com	617-277-5398	Russian community news, in Russian.
ookline TAB	www.townonline.com/brookline	617-566-3585	Brookline newsweekly.
mbridge Chronicle	www.townonline.com/cambridge	617-577-7149	Cambridge newsweekly.
mbridge TAB	www.townonline.com/cambridge	617-497-1241	Cambridge newsweekly.
arlestown Patriot-Bridge	www.charlestownbridge.com	617-241-8500	Charlestown newsweekly.
rchester Reporter	www.dotnews.com	617-436-1222	Dorchester news.
proper Bostonian	www.improper.com	617-859-1400	Free entertainment and lifestyle magazine.
Newsweekly	www.innewsweekly.com	617-426-8246	LGBT news and entertainment.
maica Plain Gazette	www.jamaicaplaingazette.com	617-524-2626	JP news.
e Jewish Advocate	www.thejewishadvocate.com	617-367-9100	News about Boston's Jewish community.
ass High Tech	www.masshightech.com	617-242-1224	Technology news.
attapan Reporter	www.bostonneighborhoodnews.com	617-436-1222	Mattapan neighborhood news.
triot Ledger	www.patriotledger.com	617-786-7000	Daily south shore news.
ot	www.thebostonpilot.com	617-746-5889	Catholic newsweekly.
mpan	www.sampan.org	617-426-9492	Chinese/English bimonthly.
merville Journal	www.townonline.com/somerville	617-625-6300	Weekly Somerville news.
uth Boston Tribune	www.southbostoninfo.com	617-268-3440	Weekly South Boston news.
uff	www.stuffboston.com	617-859-3333	Entertainment listings and "what's hot."
eekly Dig	www.weeklydig.com	617-426-8942	Humor, news and nightlife.

Hungry?

Seafood

Boston is a seafood lover's paradise: steamers, oysters, lobster rolls, clam chowder, and every kind of fish imaginable are presented on plates all over the city. Historic **Union Oyster House (Map 2)** is Boston's oldest restaurant, and it has retained the antiquated décor; **Neptune Oyster (Map 2)** has a more contemporary vibe. For pomp and old school elegance, try **Anthony's Pier 4 (Map 10)** overlooking the harbor. The best lobster roll is at **Jasper White's Summer Shack (Map 5, 22)**, and JP's **Galway House (Map 14)** makes a mean clam chowder. Inman Square's **East Coast Grill & Raw Bar (Map 28)** is a lively local spot with a well-stocked raw bar and glorious barbeque for those who prefer land over sea. If you want something different than the standard New England-style preparations, **Peach Farm (Map 4)** specializes in shrimp and scallops with a Chinese flair. Make the obligatory trip to **Legal Sea Foods (Map 3, 6, 10, 20, 26)** first because it's a Boston institution, and second for the sinfully good fried platters. Just be prepared to drop some dough.

Italian

The scent of garlic permeates the air in the North End, Boston's charming Italian quarter. While almost any restaurant on Hanover Street is bound to be authentic and delicious, there are a few standouts, like **Maurizio's (Map 2)**, **Lucca (Map 2)**, and **Bricco (Map 2)**. **Mamma Maria (Map 2)** is a cozy spot ideal for romancing a significant other. Try **Prezza (Map 2)** for fancier fare. Outside of the North End, modern Italian restaurants like **Sportello (Map 10)** and **Via Matta (Map 3)** give the more traditional spots a run for their money. **Anchovies (Map 6)** is a Back Bay staple, while Brookliners frequent **Pomodoro (Map 17)** and **La Morra (Map 17)**. **L'Impasto (Map 22)** holds down the fort for Cambridge.

Pizza

There's a lot of diversity in Boston's pi[zza] offerings for something that's basically ma[de] of three ingredients. **Pizzeria Regina (M[ap] 2)** and the **Upper Crust (Map 7, 19, 25)** se[rve] traditional sloppy, cheesy pies, and are the [top] two for most locals. **Penguin Pizza (Map [6])** draws in the college scene with a long beer [list.] Kendall Square favorite **Emma's (Map 28)** p[uts] an upscale spin on pizza with gourmet toppin[gs,] and Cambridge's **Stone Hearth (Map 23)** cat[ers] to locavores with organic ingredients. Wh[ile] Bostonians tend to avoid anything hailing fro[m] NYC, **New York Pizza (Map 3)** is actually qu[ite] good. The uncommonly friendly staff at **Leon[e's] (Map 24)** and **Captain Nemo's (Map 14)** m[ake] it worth a visit for a neighborly chat along w[ith] your slice.

East Asian

Chinatown is to Chinese what the North En[d is] to Italian. If you're looking for full-on dim-s[um] craziness, try **China Pearl (Map 4)** or **Hei [Lai] Moon (Map 4)** for weekend brunch. If you w[ant] more sedate surroundings in Chinatown, [try] **King Fung Garden (Map 4)**, **Hong Kong Eat[ery] (Map 4)**, or **Peach Farm (Map 4)**. It's a tie for b[est] Thai between **Wonder Spice (Map 14)** and D[ok] **Bua (Map 17)**. Check out **BonChon (Map [4,] 20)** for Korean fried chicken. Sushi joints abou[nd] in Brookline; **Fugakyu (Map 17)** and **Genki [Ya] (Map 17)** are a cut above. Try **Elephant W[alk] (Map 16, 22)** for Cambodian, and **Pho Viet (M[ap] 19)** or **Xinh Xinh (Map 4)** for Vietnamese. Wh[en] in doubt, Asian fusion restaurants like **My[ers] + Chang (Map 7)** and **Thelonious Monk[er] (Map 27)** offer a little bit of everything.

outh Asian

ian restaurants can be found in almost
ery corner of the city, although many of the
st are clustered in Cambridge, like **Punjabi
aba (Map 28)**, **Diva Indian Bistro (Map 22)**,
marind Bay (Map 20)**, and **India Pavilion
ap 17)**. **Helmand (Map 26)** is a mainstay
Afghan. Back across the river, JP residents
their curry fix at **Bukhara (Map 14)**. **Mela
ap 7)** in the South End is one of the more
ordable options in the area, and even has a
ch buffet. The Back Bay has **Kashmir (Map 5)**,
assy lunch spot with a patio prime for people
tching, and Kenmore has **India Quality
staurant (Map 16)**, a small hole in the wall
h astoundingly solid food.

ars

metimes a bothersome urge to eat gets in the
y of downing beers, and in these situations
worthwhile to know that some bars serve
igher grade of grub than others. **Blarney
ne (Map 32)**, **Harry's (Map 19)**, and the
way House (Map 14)** dish up unpretentious
ner entrees on the cheap. Be warned that
barbecue chips at **Trina's Starlite Lounge
ap 28)** are dangerously addictive; same deal
h the crab guacamole at **Lolita (Map 6)**,
ts (Map 10)**, **Miracle of Science (Map 27)**,
d **Silvertone Bar & Grill (Map 3)** have lighter
rions, but to really fortify your stomach for
ne serious drinking (read: fried anything), try
Pour House (Map 5), **The Lower Depths
ap 16)**, or **Flash's (Map 6)**.

Grease

Bostonians are keener on upscale brunches
than down home diners, but there are still a few
places to get eggs and pancakes in the morning
in all their greasy glory. Head to **Mul's Diner
(Map 10)**, **South Street Diner (Map 4)**, or the
Allston Diner (Map 19) for a low-key no-frills
start to the day. **Sound Bites (Map 23)** is a half-
step up from the average diner without being
overly prissy—heck, they serve hash. For out and
out gluttony, try the funky '50s-esque **Friendly
Toast (Map 28)** if you don't mind waiting in line
with scores of hipsters. Allston's **Tavern in the
Square (Map 19)** has an all-you-can-eat brunch
buffet where college students congregate to
nurse hangovers.

Top-End

Looking to impress a date? Try **Ten Tables (Map
14)**, **Hungry I (Map 1)**, **Meritage (Map 4)**, or
Hamersley's Bistro (Map 7). Foodies that are
interested in innovative cuisine will delight
in the complex creations at **O Ya (Map 32)**,
Journeyman (Map 24), and **Bondir (Map 28)**.
Head to **Hungry Mother (Map 28)** or the **South
End Buttery (Map 7)** for upscale comfort food.
L'Espalier (Map 7), **No. 9 Park (Map 3)**, and
Mistral (Map 6) are seasoned establishments
that have only gotten better with age. **Craigie
on Main (Map 27)** and **Henrietta's Table (Map
20)** are both geared towards seasonal and local
fare. The classic elegance of **Eastern Standard
(Map 16)** is the restaurant equivalent of the little
black dress.

Arts & Entertainment • Nightlife

It's not quite the city that never sleeps, but Boston's nightlife is vast and varied, catering not only to teeming masses of college students but eager yuppies and disaffected hipsters alike. Since this is a city founded by people that were so uptight the British annoyed them (Pot paging kettle...), we are still stuck with the blue-law mentality that anything that might be fun has to be completely controlled at all times. Thus, all of our bars shutter for the evening at 1 or 2 a.m. This would be fine for most people if the MBTA, you know, the way the majority of people get around in a city with little parking, didn't manage to close by TWELVE F*@KING THIRTY. After-hours joints do exist, but are for members-only, so when those lights come up and you are doing your best Last Call Shuffle to get a number—keep in mind cabs are as easy to get after closing time as Red Sox-Yankee ticks are on opening day. Despite these best efforts, though, the variety of bars, dance clubs, and live music venues keep growing, so you'll be able to find just the right spot to be seen, be picked up, dance, throw some Red Sox-Yankee darts, or sit and share a pint with a friend while you catch a live band. Remember that clubs are always in flux, so it makes sense to call ahead and confirm what's up before rounding up your crew and hitting the town.

Beer

A wave of craft beer fanaticism has swept Boston, and while you can still get a Sam or a Harpoon just about anywhere, many bars now stock more unusual stuff. **Meadhall (Map 26)** is the holy grail for beer lovers, with over 100 beers on tap—none of them Coors, Miller, or Bud products. Nearby, **Lord Hobo (Map 28)** caters to the budding hipster beer snob. Allston's rowdy student hangout **Sunset Grill & Tap (Map 19)** serves parts of beers, while more refined Allstonians head to **Deep Ellum (Map 19)**. Two solid options in the Back Bay are **Bukowski Tavern (Map 5)** and the **Pour House (Map 5)**—the selection isn't the best at the latter but no one's complaining about the dirt cheap 22 oz. drafts. **Brendan Behan Pub (Map 14)** pours the smoothest Guinness in the city, but if you insist drinking your pint among Irish accents, head to the **Blackthorn Pub (Map 10)** in Southie. Gastropubs **Canary Square (Map 14)**, the **Squealing Pig (Map 15)**, and the **Publick House (Map 17)** all have extensive beer lists. Fenway's **Tasty Burger (Map 15, 20)** pays homage to the art of the canned beer. If you're curious to investigate the brewing process, take a tour at either the **Sam Adams (Map 14)** or Harpoon **(Map 11)** breweries. Hop on the trolley after the Sam tour to be shuttled to **Doyle's (Map 14)**, the first bar in America to serve Sam Adams. Want to get really adventurous? Buy a spin on the beer wheel at **Redbones (Map 22)**, and cross your fingers that you'll like your pick.

Sports

Almost every bar in Boston becomes a sports bar when the Red Sox, Celtics, Bruins, or Patriots are playing—just try to find a bar where the game isn't on. The best Sox bars are **Jerry Remy's (Map 15)**, **Cask 'n' Flagon (Map 16)**, **Game On! (Map 16)**, **Bleacher Bar (Map 16)**, and **The Baseball Tavern (Map 15)**. Head to The Four's **(Map 1)** or the **Greatest Bar (Map 1)** for hockey and basketball. Football fans should check out **Stadium (Map 10)**, McGreev[y]'s **(Map 5)**, **Tavern in the Square (Map 19)**, or **Stats (Map 10)**. **Coolidge Corner Clubhouse (Map 19)** is Brookli[ne's] resident sports bar, and **Orleans (Map 22)** is Somervi[lle's]. Brighton's **Cityside (Map 18)** is a relaxed, anything g[oes] spot with a killer patio, while **Champions (Map 6)** [is a] sports bar for the preppy set.

Elegant and Nice

If you feel like getting gussied up and playing socialite [for] a night, **Clink (Map 1)**, **Bond (Map 4)**, **Sonsie (Map 5)**, **City Bar (Map 6)** are some of the trendiest spots in the [city]. **Sonsie (Map 5)** has the sophistication of a Parisian ca[fé,] while **Eastern Standard (Map 16)** pours expertly m[ixed] drinks in a lavishly elegant room. Sip a calm glass of win[e at] **Parker's Bar (Map 3)** or **Upstairs on the Square (Map 3)**, or if a craft cocktail is more your speed, stop by **Local** **(Map 11)**. Relive the roaring twenties at **Cuchi Cuchi (M[ap] 27)**. **Franklin Southie (Map 12)** proves that Southie [isn't] all rough edges. While a bit pricey, **Top of the Hub (M[ap 9]** offers a birds-eye view of the city skyline from the top f[loor] of the Prudential Center. **Saloon (Map 22)** is a modern [day] speakeasy with an exhaustive whiskey list.

Dive

There are two types of dives in Boston: fun and qu[irky] holes in the wall where college students ironically c[hug] PBRs, and seriously run down places full of lotto scratch[ers] regulars. **Punter's Pub (Map 15)**, the **Silhouette Lou[nge] (Map 19)**, and the **Midway Café (Map 14)** all fall in [the] first camp. Those who'd like to leave the safety net of [the] college crowd can pull up a bar stool at the **Beacon [Hill] Pub (Map 1)**, **J.J. Foley's Fireside Tavern (Map 30)**, or [the] **Galway House (Map 14)**. **An Tain (Map 4)** and the **S[tadium] Pub (Map 22)** attract a good mix of the young and old[er].

Live Music

Boston has a thriving live music scene, its local commu[nity] of musicians nurturing each other and able to get lot[s of] exposure in a wide array of venues. The Cars, The Pix[ies,] Jonathan Richman, J. Geils, Passion Pit, Mission of Bur[ma,] and Aerosmith are just a few decent names to come ou[t of] this town. The homegrown bands get as much atten[tion] as the national acts mostly due to the sheer number th[ey're] kicking around artist boroughs Allston, Somerville, an[d...] Whether you're in the mood for rock, blues, roots, pu[nk,] folk, rockabilly, jazz, or yes, even bluegrass, somebo[dy in] Boston is playing it. If you're looking for country mus[ic,] Rhode Island is south of here. Go find it.

While huge national acts play at the Garden and Con[vention] Center, many also opt for smaller venues like the 2,800-s[eat] Orpheum Theater for its great acoustics. Berklee Coll[ege] has graduated the likes of Branford Marsalis, Qui[ncy] Jones, and Diana Krall, and at its Berklee Performa[nce] Center (**www.berklee.edu/BPC**, 617-747-2261) you [can] catch performances by big names and famous alumn[i at] cheap concerts by teachers and students. Who kno[ws?] You may be watching the next John Mayer. Ano[ther] place to catch national acts in a club atmosphere is [the] edibly awesome **House of Blues (Map 16)** that has the club corpses of Axis and Avalon. If it's summer, best venue in all of Beantown is the **Bank of America lion (Map 11)** right on the waterfront, and Bostonians e out in droves to see the Pops' famous Fourth of July cert at the **Hatch Shell (Map 6)**.

jazz, you can grab dinner and a show at the classy **attabar (Map 20)** or **Scullers (Map 19)**. Both in bridge, they host world-class performers. If you're budget, check out smaller venues like **Ryles (Map** in Inman Square, **Good Life (Map 4)** in Downtown sing, and **Wally's (Map 5)** in the South End, a tiny hborhood bar where you'll sometimes find Berklee ents sitting in with the evening's combo. Get some along with your eggs at **The Beehive's (Map 7)** jazz ches.

's rollers head to **Paradise Rock Club (Map 19)**. If downstairs is packed, go upstairs for a bird's-eye view ne band. If you get tired of moshing, the adjoining e features smaller bands and food in a more relaxed ing. In Central square, lines form out the door for **T.T. Bear's Place (Map 27)**. At next door's **Middle East p 27)**, one of the coolest clubs on the planet, you grab some grape leaves before heading to one of its e rooms of music. **Brighton Music Hall (Map 19)**, former Harper's Ferry, has continued its predecessor's cy of rock, blues, and New Orleans funk. Punk and ge bands frequent JP's **Midway Café (Map 14)**.

'u're pining for some old school blues and rock, head to **Cantab (Map 27)** on the weekend for the still standing e Joe Cook and the Thrillers. Smaller bars to catch a l groove include **O'Brien's (Map 19)**, **P.A.'s Lounge p 24)**, and **Church (Map 15)**. Great Scott (Map 19) has DJ dance nights in addition to underground bands. **nny D's (Map 22)** in Somerville reigns supreme for the r blues crowd.

ies and singer-songwriters worship at the altar that **lub Passim (Map 20)**, a 40-plus-year-old landmark cated to promoting independent musicians. Joan z, Bob Dylan, and Muddy Waters have all graced its e. Craft beer and wine is now available for purchase g with a wide array of vegetarian snacks. Are e dying to dust off that old banjo of yours, return to **Cantab (Map 27)** on Tuesday nights for its bluegrass in' party.

can find reggae, hip-hop, and Afrobeat at **Western t (Map 27)**. Latin music and salsa dancing heat up **en Street Grill (Map 27)**, **Mojitos Lounge (Map 3)**, **Bella Luna (Map 14)**, which has a dedicated lesbian wing.

t decide what mood you're in? The **Lizard Lounge p 20)**, a laid-back neighborhood hang in Cambridge, s an eclectic mix of music and performances seven ts a week, ranging from punk to acoustic, rock and experimental, and poetry slams. Dueling piano bar **vl at the Moon (Map 4)** is a novelty in Boston, and helorettes slinging cocktail 'buckets' abound. Pianists requests exclusively, so you'll hear "Piano Man" to kstreet Boys and everything in between.

Many pubs and bars feature local bands or musicians, often for free or a minimal cover charge. Check weekly listings for schedules. Some worth paying a visit to are **The Plough & Stars (Map 27)**, the **Green Briar (Map 18)**, **The Asgard (Map 27)**, and **Atwood's Tavern (Map 28)**. Probably the best of these is **Toad (Map 23)**. The room is small, and you usually have to sneak past the bass player to get to the bathroom, but the wide variety and high quality of bands make this a popular gathering place.

Clubs

Whether you're into breaking a serious sweat or just delicately nodding your head to the beat, there's a club in Boston where you can get your preferred level of groove on. Fist pumping bros flock to **Joshua Tree (Map 19)**. Don heels and a slinky dress to fit in at **District (Map 4)**, **Venu (Map 3)**, or **Rise (Map 6)**. Kick it old school at **Storyville (Map 6)**. **Tommy Doyle's (Map 20)** and **Good Life (Map 28)** have a jolly middle school dance vibe, and the varied DJ nights at **Phoenix Landing (Map 27)** draw in a different crowd every night. Hipsters who deign to dance do it at **Middlesex Lounge (Map 27)**. A booming LGBT scene can be found at **dbar (Map 32)**, **Club Café (Map 6)**, and **Machine (Map 15)**.

Karaoke

You get enough booze into even the shyest person, and suddenly repressed desires for superstardom bubble up. Grab a mic and quell those urges at the popular karaoke nights at **Tommy Doyle's (Map 20)**, **The Purple Shamrock (Map 2)**, **The Asgard (Map 27)**, **King's (Map 5)**, or **The Hong Kong (Map 2)**. The gay and lesbian crowd heads to JP for Queeraoke at the **Midway Café (Map 14)**. Belt your heart out at the **Jeanie Johnston Pub (Map 14)** or **Flann O'Brien's (Map 15)**, and you're sure to get some cheers no matter how off-key you are. For hardcore karaoke junkies, **Limelight Stage and Studio (Map 3)** applies pitch correction technology so you can finally nail that high note from "Don't Stop Believin'" in front of a large crowd or in a private studio. **Do Re Mi (Map 19)** rents private rooms for those who aren't up to performing in front of strangers. While they technically have a no alcohol policy, the owners tend to look the other way as long as you're not ostentatiously ripping shots.

It's difficult to typecast Boston shoppers, due in part to the diversity of its people, from the Burberry-sporting, Beacon Hill elite to Cambridge funksters in paint-splattered Chuck Taylors. The city's climate (11 months of winter and four weeks of spring, summer, and fall) compels most Bostonians to spend their weekends popping into climate-controlled shops that range from uncomfortably exclusive to quietly quaint to downright weird. In addition to the extreme consumerist lifestyle of many of its dwellers, the city also has its fair share of psychotic, year-round outdoor athletes, for whom purveyors of gear appear throughout the city. The fleet of moving trucks clogging this college town on the first of every month from March through October keeps the furniture and housewave hawkers in business. Despite the few malls that have weaseled their way onto the scene, the dependable disparity and constant movement of the city results in a throbbing, colorful, and sometimes shocking mass of consumers.

Clothing: New, Used & Vintage

For the label checking, what-do-you-drive-yuppies in our midst, the Boston shopping scene certainly delivers. Start in the Back Bay on Berkeley Street at **Louis Boston (Map 6)**, then head to **Brooks Brothers (Map 6)** around the corner on Newbury Street. More reasonably priced but still plenty preppy is **Eddie Bauer (Map 3)** downtown. On the other side of the coin, Boston has a ton to offer those seeking funkier duds—you just need to know where to look. The **Garment District (Map 28)** in Cambridge is a gargantuan thrift/vintage store with everything from '60s sweaters to contemporary second-hand treasures, as well as new offerings from local designers. Just a few blocks over, **Poor Little Rich Girl (Map 28)** also has a great selection of vintage duds. Even upscale Newbury Street has its share of vintage chic—the **Army Barracks (Map 5)** is an old fave. And Boston is really a walking city (you know, when it's not hailing), so outfit your feet with shoes from **Berk's (Map 20)** in Harvard Square, **The Tannery (Map 6)** in Back Bay and Harvard Square, or **Cambridge Clogs (Map 23)** in Porter Square.

For the Home/Apartment/Dorm

Though driving through Brookline and Beacon Hill on September 2—after most apartments have been vacated, their perfectly usable furniture left on the curb—is a fabulous way to outfit your own digs, you may wish to take a gander at the furniture 'n stuff offered throughout a city that's constantly turning over. If nothing else, you won't have to worry about that greenish blue stain on the free chair from the corner. Despite the terrific selection

and prices offered by the obvious **Crate & Ba (Map 6, 27)**, beware the slalom of newly-enga couples registering for gifts. **Sunshine Lucy's (M 22)** in Davis Square and **Circle Furniture (M 21)** in West Cambridge are locally owned ja offering a wide variety of furniture and applian **Economy Hardware (Map 5, 16, 26)** is a reli bet for furniture, gadgets, even paint (oh, hardware), but often comes with a complimen headache. Check out counter-intuitive spots **Urban Outfitters (Map 5, 19, 20)**, **Anthropolo (Map 6, 20)**, and **Boutique Fabulous (Map 28** finishing touches like pretty pillows, cool lamps, funky artwork. Antique hunters will be kept happ **Cambridge Antique Market's (Map 26)** five fl of yesteryear.

Sports

As the city most associated with a certain 26.2 race, Boston is well equipped to provide you whatever you need to get your heart rate pump **Marathon Sports (Map 6, 17, 20)** lets you drive their sneakers on the sidewalk to make you leave with exactly the right pair. Whatever season, you can find what you're looking for at **Sports (Map 3, 6, 19, 20, 23)**. Boston's also a b city (think pedals, not crotchrockets). Riders can tune-ups, gear, and honest advice at **Internatio Bicycle Center (Map 19)**. **REI (Map 16)** and East **Mountain Sports (Map 5, 19, 20)** are also good bikes along with anything you might need for a hangin' good time.

Computing Machines

Thanks to its many universities, hospitals, research facilities, Boston is awash with compu loving dweebs. **Micro Center (Map 27)** is swarm on the weekends. Three centrally located **Best B (Map 16, 26)** feature their usual merchandise crowds. The PC-user-repellant **Apple Store (** 26)** in the Cambridgeside Galleria is one stylin' g boutique only matched by the three-story **Ap Store (Map 6)** that sits like a see-through shrine Geekdom on Boylston St.

Music Maniacs

The rise of the iPod has given Bostonians yet ano excuse to avoid interaction with other human who dare cross their path. But plenty of options exist for those in search of discs, vinyl, and o types of tangible tunes. **Newbury Comics (M 2, 5, 20)** delivers on their offer of "a wicked g time" with not only music, but movies, novel and general craziness. For those in search of v vintage, and generally hard-to-find tunes, st along Mass Ave in Cambridge to find **Che** cords (Map 27) and Stereo Jack's (Map 20), as ll as Somerville Grooves (Map 24) in the always Union Square. Comm Ave near BU and Harvard uare are also places to troll for rare stuff with stores In Your Ear (Map 19), Nuggets (Map 16), and net Records (Map 20). If you're one of the real :-there cats looking for the most random of discs, Weirdo Records (Map 27) in Central Square for)% truth in advertising.

oodie Fanatics

u literally cannot go wrong in the North End. Mike's stry (Map 2), Modern Pastry (Map 2), and the 24/7 va's Bakery (Map 2) are three of about 1,000 places try for sweet goodies. For savory Italian treats try umeria Italiana (Map 2). Equally tempting treats be found at Athan's Bakery (Map 17) in Brookline Cardullo's (Map 20) in Harvard Square. For ice am, Christina's Homemade (Map 28) in Inman uare is a favorite, as well as J.P. Licks (Map 14, , 20), Toscanini's (Map 27), Lizzy's (Map 20), and ck & Bolio's (Maps 5, 9, 17), all with lines out the or in warmer months. Fans of more solid sweets will e just as well at Sweet (Map 3, 5, 6, 20) and KickAss pcakes (Map 22). Dave's Fresh Pasta (Map 22), y Feed & Supply (Map 14), and Pemberton Farms ap 22) carry a mix of local, organic specialty and ndard items, sandwiches, prepared foods, and sh bread. For the gourmet addicts, there's nothing the cheese counters at South End Formaggio ap 7) or Formaggio Kitchen (Map 21) to give you artisan deliciousness you've been craving. D'rool, ool.

Malls and 'hoods

ston has seemingly avoided the typical suburban sis of a mall more than other cities, but it does one better by providing several neighborhood ations where you can store-hop, grab a bite, ople watch simultaneously, with real food, not od court swill. Downtown Crossing is a high-energy nter of rabid consumerism, very convenient to the and boasting the gigantic department store Macy's ap 3) (which has recently gobbled up the beloved ene's), discount stores (Marshall's (Map 3, 6, 12, and TJ Maxx (Map 3, 19)), and other joints like &M (Map 3, 6, 26). Clothes aren't the only thing r sale around here—there are jewelers, shoe stores, eet vendors, and performers. It's also within walking tance of Faneuil Hall Market Place, another splendid altternative. Likewise, one could easily spend a id afternoon wandering around Harvard Square. wbury Comics (Map 2, 5, 20), Black Ink (Map 20), ie De Vivre (Map 23) and Leavitt & Peirce (Map 20) great for gift shopping (for yourself or anyone else),

and Urban Outfitters (Map 20) always has the latest in hipster apparel and home decor (check out their bargain basement with savings that will melt your face off). Stop for a snack at Cardullo's (Map 20) or recharge at Tealuxe (Map 20), and flip through a book at the Co-op (Map 20) or Harvard Bookstore (Map 20). Walk the length of Newbury Street and you'll find everything from bookstores (Trident Booksellers & Café (Map 5)) to foodie paraphernalia (O & Co. (Map 5)) to art (International Poster Gallery (Map 6)), plus clothes and clothes and clothes. Though most of what's found on Newbury is decidedly pricey, things do get more reasonable as you get closer to Mass Ave. Boylston Street runs parallel to Newbury with offerings like Anthropologie (Map 6) and City Sports (Maps 3, 6, 19, 20, 23). And yes, as much as we hate to admit it, Boston does have a few genuine malls—though they are well camouflaged and the word "mall" does not actually appear in their titles. The Shops at Prudential Center include Sephora (Map 5), Lord & Taylor (Map 6), and several others. It cuts through to the even higher-end Copley Place, where those of you that have the cash can drop quite a load of it at Barneys New York (Map 6). The Cambridge Side Galleria is a multi-level Mecca where MIT kids, biotech execs, and European tourists flock to the Apple Store (Map 26) to satisfy their Mac addictions. Peirce (Map 20) are great for gift shopping (for yourself or anyone else), and Urban Outfitters (Map 20) always has the latest in hipster apparel and home decor (check out their bargain basement with savings that will melt your face off). Stop for a snack at Cardullo's (Map 20) or recharge at Tealuxe (Map 20), and flip through a book at the Co-op (Map 20) or Harvard Bookstore (Map 20). Walk the length of Newbury Street and you'll find everything from bookstores (Trident Booksellers & Café (Map 5)) to foodie paraphernalia (O & Co. (Map 5)) to art (International Poster Gallery (Map 6)), plus clothes and clothes and clothes. Though most of what's found on Newbury is decidedly pricey, things do get more reasonable as you get closer to Mass Ave. Boylston Street runs parallel to Newbury with offerings like Anthropologie (Map 6) and City Sports (Maps 3, 6, 19, 20, 23). And yes, as much as we hate to admit it, Boston does have a few genuine malls—though they are well camouflaged and the word "mall" does not actually appear in their titles. The Shops at Prudential Center include Sephora (Map 5), Lord & Taylor (Map 6), and several others. It cuts through to the even higher-end Copley Place, where those of you that have the cash can drop quite a load of it at Barneys New York (Map 6). The Cambridge Side Galleria is a multi-level Mecca where MIT kids, biotech execs, and European tourists flock to the Apple Store (Map 26) to satisfy their Mac addictions.

Arts & Entertainment • **Movie Theaters**

With all the students and schools that Boston manages to cram into it's small borders, we suffer from a distinct lack of places to catch a film. Currently we're down to two locations—the **AMC Loews Boston Common (Map 3)** and **Regal Fenway 13 (Map 16)**. Be forewarned as these joints are the only players in the game, the ticket and food prices reflect the lack of competition. Also, for those of you that actually want to WATCH the movie, these locations draw a large number of teenagers who can't shut off their cell phones for 90 minutes. Still, if it's a new release that's a must see, they both deliver. If you can wait until the movie of your desire is a bit older, **The Somerville Theater (Map 22)** does a good chunk of second run business, and it also has hooch.

To watch a movie with 90% less teenager text message ringtone, then you'll have to venture to **Landmark Kendall Square Cinema (Map 26)**, the **Brattle Theatre (Map 20)**, the **Harvard Film Archive (Map 20)**, the **Museum of Fine Arts (Map 15)**, or the best damn joint to see a flick in greater Boston—the **Coolidge Corner Theatre (Map 17)**.

From the end of June through the end of August, check out Free Friday Flicks at the **Hatch Shell (Map 6)** on the Esplanade. Movies start at sundown, but arrive early to get your spot on the grass. And for heaven's sake, don't forget to bring some wine and cheese.

Huge-screen freaks should hit the **Mugar Omni Theater (Map 1)** at the Museum of Science and the **Simons IMAX Theatre (Map 2)** at the New England Aquarium. If you just have to shop for furniture before seeing a movie in IMAX or 3D, you owe yourself a trip to **Jordan's Furniture** (1-866-8JORDANS) in either Natick (ext. 2860) or Reading (ext. 6800). It might be worth the trip alone if the Red Sox are doing well in the standings, and you feel like taking them up on whatever World Series promo they have running.

Movie Theater	Address	Phone	M
Mugar Omni Theatre	1 Science Park	617-723-2500	Don't move your head, you'll puke.
Simons IMAX Theatre	1 Central Wharf	617-973-5206	MOMMY! DOLLLLPHINS!!!!
AMC Loews Boston Common 19	175 Tremont St	617-423-5801	Blockbusters.
Institute of Contemporary Art	100 Northern Ave	617-478-3100	It's contemporary art, so prepare for weirdness.
Museum of Fine Arts	465 Huntington Ave	617-369-3770	Ever changing array, filmmaker Q&A.
Regal Fenway Stadium 13	201 Brookline Ave	617-424-6111	On-site parking. Video games in the lobby.
Coolidge Corner Theatre	290 Harvard St	617-734-2500	Theme nights and film festivals.
Brattle Theatre	40 Brattle St	617-876-6837	Casablanca. Every year.
Harvard Film Archive	24 Quincy St	617-495-4700	Films you won't see at Boston Common.
Apple Cinema	168 Alewife Brook Pkwy	617-661-2900	A bit sticky.
Somerville Theatre	55 Davis Sq	617-625-5700	Now serving beer and wine.
Landmark Kendall Square Cinema	One Kendall Sq	617-499-1996	Movies for smart grown-ups.

wbury Street has Boston's largest and densest concentration of art galleries. You've probably passed the several dozen galleries on Newbury Street many times without taking a look at what's inside, t popping into just a few of them will give you some idea of the broad scope of what's on offer (even our budget means you're more likely to be striking deals at the MFA's gift shop). Commercial art s should check out **International Poster Gallery's (Map 6)** expansive collection of Italian, travel, d Soviet-era posters. The gallery of the **Copley Society of Boston (Map 6)**, also on Newbury Street, sts several competitions over the course of the year, including showcases of student work.

hile Newbury Street galleries may have the city's most established spots, the interesting velopments are happening in the South End, where a number of galleries have opened or relocated. e center of the action is the converted warehouse at 450 Harrison Avenue between Thayer Street d Randolph Street. (Take the Silver Line to East Berkeley Street, walk one block to Harrison Avenue, d hang a right.) Big na.m.es at the "SoWa Building" include **Carroll and Sons (Map 7)** and the ngston Gallery (Map 7).** If you're interested in what's emerging in Boston's contemporary art scene, ad to SoWa on the first Friday of the month to see the new exhibits. (At the very least, it's an excuse get dressed up and consume some free wine.) Elsewhere in Boston, consider seeing what's on play at **Boston Cyberarts Gallery (Map 14)** in Jamaica Plain's Green Street T Station, the **Fort Point ts Community Gallery (Map 10)**, Roxbury's **Hamill Gallery of African Art (Map 13)**, and Kenmore uare's **Panopticon Gallery of Photography (Map 15)**. Cheaper rents continue to attract artists to st Boston, where the newly reopened **Atlantic Works Gallery (Map 9)** holds regular exhibitions and tluck get-togethers.

addition to standard galleries, many of the city's neighborhoods put on "open studio" events where u can satisfy your nosy streak by poking around the studios of artists willing to open them up to the blic. Go to www.cityofboston.gov/arts.

r art too bad to be ignored, hit up MOBA (www.museumofbadart.org), with rotating locations in ookline, Somerville, and Dedham. No joke, this place is real!

Arts & Entertainment • **Bookstores**

Outside of a dog, a book is man's best friend. Inside of a dog it's too dark to read. —Groucho Marx

Big

As in so many cities, **Barnes & Noble (Map 5 & 16)** is the big dog on the Boston bookstore scene. If you're shopping for a book, but not also for a low-fat latte or a high-fat chocolate croissant, get familiar with the large independents **Brookline Booksmith (Map 19)** and the 75-year-old **Harvard Book Store (Map 20)** (unaffiliated with the university). Both focus on new titles but have cellars that handle used books.

Used

Davis Square's **McIntyre & Moore Books (Map 22)** sells an array of used books, with a bent toward school textbooks. When in Roslindale, stop by **Pazzo Books** (4268 Washington St, 617-323-2919, Map 30) for used and rare books and a round of skee-ball on the old machine in the basement. Some people think **Raven Used Books (Map 20)** in Harvard Square delivers the best bang for your buck. A good place to find used guidebooks and fiction is **Rodney's Bookstore (Map 17, 27)**, with locations in both Central Square and Brookline. Downtown Crossing's **Brattle Book Shop (Map 3)** is a well-known used book specialist—check out the outdoor book racks on dry days. Also in Central Boston, and worth checking out for antiquarian books, are **Lame Duck Books (Map 20)** and **Commonwealth Books (Map 3, 16)**. There's also the **Boston Book Annex (Map 16)**, sloppy but well stocked, a fun place for cat lovers and long-term browsing.

Specialty

Quantum Books (Map 26) is the best computer bookstore in the city. The **MIT Press Bookstore (Map 26)** is the best for social sciences, philosophy, economics, and sciences—pretty much everything MIT is best for. For little kids, take a look at Brookline's **Children's Book Shop (Map 17)**. Slightly older kids who dig gaming will enjoy **Pandemonium (Map 27)**.

Ars Libri (Map 7) has an exemplary collection of ra[...] and out-of-print fine art books. The only remainin[...] LGBT bookstore in Boston is **Calamus (Map [...]** near South Station. A big tip of the chapeau is d[...] to **Schoenhof's Foreign Books (Map 20)** for [...] broad selection. **James & Devon Grey Bookselle[...] (Map 20)** specializes in books printed before 17[...] **Lucy Parsons Center (Map 6)**, in the South En[...] stocks many progressive titles. **Trident Booksell[...] & Café (Map 5)** stocks books and a good vari[...] of mainstream and alternative magazine titles, [...] addition to serving a mean breakfast.

Cambridge

Several years ago there were more than [...] bookstores in Harvard Square, the greate[...] concentration of bookstores in the city (a[...] perhaps the country). No longer. Blame high ren[...] online retail, large chains dominating the mark[...] or a general waning interest in the printed arts, b[...] the sad fact is that many fine shops have pack[...] it in. That being said, there are still a lot of frigg[...] bookstores and they range from the nuance[...] the Coop. **Grolier Poetry Book Shop (Map 2[...]** a national poetry landmark, is nothing less than [...] beacon of art in its tiny space on Plympton Stre[...] Another Harvard Square stalwart is **Revolutio[...] Books (Map 20)**, a bookstore particularly conduci[...] to raging against the machine. **The Harva[...] Coop (Map 20)** is managed by Barnes & Nob[...] and unaffiliated with the school. The previou[...] mentioned Raven, Schoenhof's, James & Devo[...] Grey's, and probably three or four others round o[...] a full day of page flipping. If the clogged walkwa[...] and impossible parking makes Harvard Square mo[...] trouble than it's worth, there's always **Porter Squa[...] Books (Map 23)** and Inman Square's **Lorem Ipsu[...] (Map 28)**, the latter being one of the best resourc[...] for used fiction and literature in the area. Now g[...] going, you bookworm.

ap 1 • Beacon Hill / West End

folk University Bookstore	148 Cambridge St	617-227-4085	Schoolbooks and campus merchandise.

ap 2 • North End / Faneuil Hall

wbury Comics	Faneuil Hall	617-248-9992	Comics.

ap 3 • Downtown Crossing / Park Square / Bay Village

ttle Book Shop	9 West St	617-542-0210	Used; outdoor racks when warm.
mmonwealth Books	134 Bolyston St	617-338-6328	Scholarly, used, antiquarian.
erson College Bookstore	114 Bolyston St	617-824-8696	Schoolbooks and campus merchandise.
er L Stern & Co	15 Court Square	617-542-2376	Antiquarian, especially first editions.
ffolk Law School Book Store	110 Tremont St	617-227-8874	Schoolbooks and campus merchandise.

ap 4 • Financial District / Chinatown

bara's Bestsellers	2 S Station	617-443-0060	In South Station.
lamus Bookstore	92 South St	617-338-1931	Gay & lesbian.
ntral China Book Co	44 Kneeland St	617-426-0888	Chinese.
Bernett	144 Lincoln St	617-350-7778	Rare and scholarly art and architecture.
ts Health Sciences & ew England School of Law ookstore	116 Harrison Ave	617-636-6628	Schoolbooks and campus merchandise.
rld Journal	216 Lincoln St	617-542-1230	Chinese.

ap 5 • Back Bay (West) / Fenway (East)

rnes & Noble	800 Boylston St	617-247-6959	General.
rklee College of Music ookstore	1090 Boylston St	617-747-2402	Schoolbooks and campus merchandise.
wbury Comics	332 Newbury St	617-236-4930	Now featuring a large DVD section.
dent Booksellers & Café	338 Newbury St	617-267-8688	Independent; eclectic.

ap 6 • Back Bay (East) / South End (Upper)

omer Booksellers	607 Boylston St	617-247-2818	Fine, rare, and unusual.
ddenbrooks Rare Books & anuscripts	31 Newbury St	617-536-4433	Fine, rare.
cy Parsons Center	549 Columbus Ave	617-267-6272	Progressive.

ap 7 • South End (Lower)

s Libri	500 Harrison Ave	617-357-5212	Rare and out-of-print books on art.

ap 13 • Roxbury

xbury Community College ookstore	1234 Columbus Ave	617-442-8150	Schoolbooks and campus merchandise.

ap 14 • Jamaica Plain

ston Book Co	705 Centre St	617-522-2100	Antiquarian.
mmonwealth Books	9 Spring Park Ave	617-338-6328	Scholarly, used, antiquarian.
es Gatos	470 Centre St	617-477-4851	Record store, tapas bar and bookstore ingeniously fused.

Map 15 • Fenway (West) / Mission Hill

Emmanuel College Bookstore	400 The Fenway	617-739-2232	Schoolbooks and campus merchandise.
Mass College of Pharmacy & Art Bookstore	625 Huntington Ave	617-739-4772	Textbooks.
Medical Center Coop	333 Longwood Ave	617-499-3300	Schoolbooks and campus merchandise.
Northeastern University Bookstore	360 Huntington Ave	617-373-2286	Schoolbooks and campus merchandise.
Simmons College Book Store	300 The Fenway	617-521-2054	Schoolbooks and campus merchandise.
Wentworth Book Store	103 Ward St	617-445-8814	Textbooks.

Map 16 • Kenmore Square / Brookline (East)

Barnes & Noble at Boston University	660 Beacon St	617-267-8484	General/schoolbooks and campus merchandise.
Comicopia	464 Commonwealth Ave	617-266-4266	Comics.

Map 17 • Coolidge Corner / Brookline Hills

Book World	77 Harvard St	617-739-5768	Russian.
Children's Book Shop	237 Washington St	617-734-7323	Children's.
Horai-san	242 Washington St	617-277-4321	New age/spiritual.
New England Comics	316 Harvard St	617-566-0115	Comics.
Petropol	1428 Beacon St	617-232-8820	Russian.

Map 19 • Allston (South) / Brookline (North)

Brookline Booksmith	279 Harvard St	617-566-6660	Independent; used book cellar.
Cheetah Trading	214 Lincoln St	617-451-1309	Chinese.
Harvard Business School Co-op	117 Western Ave	617-499-3245	Business.
Israel Book Shop	410 Harvard St	617-566-7113	Judaica.
The Kabbalah Center	14 Green St	617-566-0808	Religious
Kolbo Fine Judaica	437 Harvard St	617-731-8743	Judaica.

Map 20 • Harvard Square / Allston (North)

Globe Corner Book Stores	90 Mt Auburn St	617-497-6277	Travel.
Grolier Poetry Book Shop	6 Plympton St	617-547-4648	Poetry books.
Harvard Book Store	1256 Massachusetts Ave	617-661-1515	Independent, with an academic bent.
Harvard Coop	1400 Massachusetts Ave	617-499-2000	General/schoolbooks and campus merchandise.
James & Devon Gray Booksellers	12 Arrow St	617-868-0752	Pre-18th-century.
Million Year Picnic	99 Mt Auburn St	617-492-6763	Comics.
New England Comics	14A Eliot St	617-354-5352	Comics.
Raven Used Books	52-B JFK St	617-441-6999	Scholarly used.
Revolution Books	1158 Massachusetts Ave	617-492-5443	Revolution.
Robin Bledsoe Books	1640 Massachusetts Ave	617-576-3634	Out-of-print books on horses and art.
Schoenhof's Foreign Books	76A Mt Auburn St	617-547-8855	Foreign languages.

Map 21 · West Cambridge

yn Mawr Book Store	373 Huron Ave	617-661-1770	Used and rare, stocked by donations.

Map 23 · Central Somerville / Porter Square

refoot Books	1771 Massachusetts Ave	617-349-1610	Picture books for the wee.
refoot Books	2067 Massachusetts Ave	617-576-0660	Picture books for the wee.
micazi	407 Highland Ave	617-666-2664	Comics.
cIntyre & Moore Booksellers	1971 Massachusetts Ave	617-229-5641	Scholarly used.
rter Square Books	25 White St	617-491-2220	Fiercely independent!

Map 24 · Winter Hill / Union Square

AD Bookstore	100 Washington St	617-625-1234	Brazilian.

Map 25 · East Somerville / Sullivan Square

nker Hill Community ollege Book Store	250 Rutherford Ave	617-241-5161	Textbooks.

Map 26 · East Cambridge / Kendall Square / MIT

IT Coop	3 Cambridge Ctr	617-499-3200	Schoolbooks and campus merchandise.
IT Press Bookstore	292 Main St	617-253-5249	MIT Press authors and quality trade.

Map 27 · Central Square / Cambridgeport

IT Coop at Stratton	84 Massachusetts Ave	617-499-3240	Schoolbooks and campus
andemonium	4 Pleasant St	617-547-3721	Sci-fi, fantasy, and gaming.
odney's Bookstore	698 Massachusetts Ave	617-876-6467	Used, out-of-print, remainders.
even Stars	731 Massachusetts Ave	617-547-1317	New Age.

Map 28 · Inman Square

orem Ipsum	1299 Cambridge St	617-497-7669	Used.

Map 29 · West Roxbury

azzo Books	1898 Centre St	617-323-2919	Used, General Interest.

Arts & Entertainment • **Museums**

If you're familiar with every painting at the **Gardner (Map 15)**, every print in the **MFA (Map 15)**, every fish in the **Aquarium (Map 2)**, and every cobblestone on the **Freedom Trail (pg 121)**, then it's time to take it to the next level by ferreting out some of the city's hidden treasures and discovering something new about some old favorites.

The new facility of the **Institute of Contemporary Art (Map 10)**, whose design evokes a laptop, opened in the winter of 2006. If you're looking for a reason to make your way over to Fan Pier, here it is.

Release your inner child on a Friday night at the **Boston Children's Museum (Map 4)**—from 5 pm to 9 pm, admission is just $1. Or, engage your inner adult at the **Museum of Science (Map 1)** with a cocktail (yes, a real cocktail!), a movie in the Mugar Omni Theater, or free stargazing at the Gilliland Observatory.

If you want to take in some art during a drive o of town, check out the **DeCordova Museum a Sculpture Park** in Lincoln (not far from Route 2 a Route 128). The DeCordova's 35 acres of woodlands the largest sculpture garden in New England. The co temporary American outdoor sculpture park chang its exhibitions on a regular basis. Admission to sculpture park is $14 for adults, $10 for students, $12 for seniors (65+). Children 12 and under, as well active duty military personnel, are admitted free. F more information, visit www.decordova.org.

And if all of those museums are just too good to true, check out the **Museum of Bad Art (MOB** way out in Dedham (580 High St, 781-444-675 Contemplate art so bad, it can't be ignored.

Museum	Address	Phone	Map
Ancient and Honorable Artillery Company	Faneuil Hall	617-227-1638	2
Arthur M Sackler Museum	485 Broadway	617-495-9400	20
Boston Athenaeum	10 Beacon St	617-227-0270	1
Boston Children's Museum	308 Congress St	617-426-6500	10
Boston Tea Party Ship & Museum	306 Congress St	617-338-1773	10
Brighton-Allston Heritage Museum	20 Chestnut Hill Ave	617-635-1436	18
Busch-Reisinger Museum	32 Quincy St	617-495-9400	20
Carpenter Center for Visual Arts	24 Quincy St	617-495-3251	20
Commonwealth Museum	220 Morrissey Blvd	617-727-9268	32
Fogg Art Museum	32 Quincy St	617-495-9400	20
Gibson House Museum	137 Beacon St	617-267-6338	6
Harvard Mineralogical & Geological Museum	24 Oxford St	617-495-3045	20
Harvard Museum of Comparative Zoology	26 Oxford St	617-495-2460	20
Harvard Museum of Natural History	26 Oxford St	617-495-3045	20
Institute of Contemporary Art	100 Northern Ave	617-478-3100	10
JFK National Historic Site	83 Beals St	617-566-7937	19
John F Kennedy Presidential Library and Museum	Morrissey Blvd & Columbia Pt	617-514-1600	32
Larz Anderson Auto Museum	15 Newton St	617-522-6547	n/a
The Loring-Greenough House	12 South St	617-524-3158	14
Mapparium/Mary Baker Eddy Library	200 Massachusetts Ave	617-450-7000	5
MIT List Visual Arts Center	20 Ames St	617-253-4680	26
Museum of African American History	46 Joy St	617-725-0022	1
Museum of Bad Art	580 High St	781-444-6757	n/a
Museum of Fine Arts	465 Huntington Ave	617-267-9300	15
Museum of Science	Science Park	617-723-2500	1
National Center for Afro-American Artists	300 Walnut Ave	617-442-8614	13
New England Aquarium	Central Wharf	617-973-5200	2
Nichols House Museum	55 Mt Vernon St	617-227-6993	1
Old South Meeting House	310 Washington St	617-482-6439	3
Old State House	206 Washington St	617-720-1713	3
Otis House	141 Cambridge St	617-994-5920	1
Paul Revere House	19 N Sq	617-523-2338	2
Paul S. Russell, MD Museum of Medical History and Innovation	2 North Grove St	617-724-8009	1
Peabody Museum of Archaeology and Ethnology	11 Divinity Ave	617-496-1027	20
Pierre Menard Gallery	10 Arrow St	617-868-2033	20
The Semitic Museum at Harvard University	6 Divinity Ave	617-495-4631	20
Somerville Museum	1 Westwood Rd	617-666-9810	23
The Sports Museum	150 Causeway St	617-624-1234	1
USS Constitution Museum	Charlestown Navy Yard	617-426-1812	8
Vilna Shul	18 Phillips St	617-523-2324	1
Warren Anatomical Museum	10 Shattuck St	617-432-6196	15

Institute of Contemporary Art

General Information

T Map:	10
dress:	100 Northern Ave
one:	617-478-3100
bsite:	www.icaboston.org
urs:	Tues, Wed, Sat, Sun: 10 am–5 pm; Thurs, Fri 10 am–9 pm; closed Mon, except on Martin Luther King, Jr. Day, Presidents' Day, Memorial Day, Labor Day, Columbus Day, and Veterans' Day. Closed Thanksgiving, Christmas, New Year's Day, and July 4.
mission:	$15 for Adults, $10 for students, $13 for seniors. Free for Members and children under 17. Free from 5 to 9 pm every Thursday night.

Overview

2006, the city's stodgy art scene got a royal kick the rear when the Institute of Contemporary unveiled its new digs on South Boston's terfront. The building's architecture by itself— awe-inspiring modern masterpiece that offers spectacular view of the harbor, an outdoor andstand, and open gallery spaces—is well worth museum's pricey $15 cover charge. Founded 1936 as The Boston Museum of Modern Art, the ginal space was a cramped laboratory where ists were encouraged to create works that both pired and provoked. Renamed in 1948, the ICA ntinued to push the envelope with a cavalcade media, ranging from visual arts, film, video, rformance, and literature. While many viewed deo and digital media as the art scene's bastard pchild in the '90s, the ICA embraced the marriage visual design and technology.

e ICA is still Boston's newest and most dynamic useum, bringing in huge shows like Shepard rey's Obey exhibit, and even hosting indie rock ncerts. It's a museum that's cooler than the osters it's attracting!

e MoMA-ized new space continues the site- ecific tradition with its Art Wall, located along e eastern interior of the museum's glass-enclosed bby. In 2006, exhibitor Chiho Aoshima unleashed r digitally manipulated monster mural, "The Divine as," on the wall. Illustrated on a Macintosh G4 nted on adhesive vinyl, the installation was a azen statement with a Gothic sensibility. With oshima's mixed-media piece, it was almost like the A was shooting a metaphorical middle finger at ose who doubted the impact digital media would entually have on our cultural landscape.

What to See

A quick stroll from South Station or directly on the Silver Line, the ICA sits right in the middle of the newly constructed Fan Pier at the top of South Boston. You'll want to take them up on their offer of an audio tour narrated by the exhibiting artists and ICA curators that you can download to your MP3 player, or you can borrow an iPod at front desk. They also offer a phone number for people to dial into the audio tours as well, but you might get some dirty looks from the art purists strolling with you. It's interesting to be able to listen to the inspiration behind something as vexing as Misaki Kawai's "Momentum 7," a free-floating-home of the future inhabited by puppets juxtaposed with the voices from the ICA's permanent collection, with luminaries like Nan Goldin, Cornelia Parker, Thomas Hirschhorn, and Paul Chan.

Nestled beneath the museum's larger-than-life cantilever is the Poss Family Mediatheque where you have access to one of the museum's 18 computer stations. Here's where you can download clips with the art and artists featured at the ICA and check out the museum's footage-archive collection which offers a glimpse of exhibitions from the museum's past. Also, the Mediatheque is where you can experience the dramatic, horizontal view of the Boston Harbor.

Amenities

The museum is handicapped accessible. All bags (including your laptop) will be checked and stored in the lobby. The ICA has limited space to hang coats and it does not have its own parking garage. However, there's a paid lot immediately adjacent to the museum. Both the men's and women's restrooms are located on the first floor.

As far as food, Wolfgang Puck's Water Café offers another stellar view—not to mention some great French-bistro cuisine—where you can open the restaurant's glass doors for outdoor dining. For those who want to skip the art and head straight for the yummy pastries, museum admission is not required to dine.

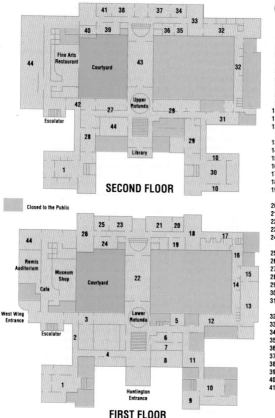

SECOND FLOOR

Closed to the Public

FIRST FLOOR

MAP 15

1. Japanese Art
2. Islamic Art
3. Brown Gallery
4. Indian Art
5. Egyptian Mummies
6. Graphics
7. Musical Instrumen
8. Nubian Art
9. Etruscan Art
10. Greek Art
11. Near-Eastern Art
12. 18th-Century Ameri
    Furniture
13. 18th-Century French
14. 18th-Century Bosto
15. English-Silver
16. 19th-Century Amer
17. American Federal
18. Copley & Contempe
19. American Neoclass
    & Romantic
20. American Folk Pain
21. 19th-Century Lands
22. American Modern
23. American Masters
24. Early 20th-Century
    & European
25. Chinese Art
26. Egyptian Art
27. Roman Art
28. Medieval Art
29. Euro Decorative Art
30. Impresses
31. 19th-Century French
    & English
32. Post-Impressionism
33. Coolidge Collection
34. 18th-Century Italian
35. Dutch & Flemish Art
36. Renaissance
37. Spanish Chapel
38. Baroque Art
39. Himalayan Art
40. Tapestries
41. Special Exhibitions

General Information

Map: 15
Address: 465 Huntington Ave
Boston, MA 02115
Phone: 617-267-9300
Website: www.mfa.org

Overview

The Museum of Fine Arts is Boston's largest and most famous art institution. The extensive permanent collection of paintings and sculpture, as well as the various lectures, films, concerts, and special traveling exhibitions, offer something for one-time sightseers and regular visitors alike. While you're there soaking up a little sophistication, enjoy a meal at one of the museum's four restaurants, and buy an artifact from the gift shop or some of their little postcards with the pretty paintings on them. Why? Because the museum needs the money. Though it's one of the largest art museums in the country, it receives little public funding. This, in part, accounts for the high admission fee. But don't worry: You get what you pay for.

In 2010, the MFA completed a ma.m.moth project that increased the size of the museum by 28%. To replace the old east wing of the museum, the MFA built a new, 0,000-square-foot four floor addition featuring the mass Art of the Americas collection. The new wing focuses heavily on the museum's peerless colonial art of New England collection, and features a gallery devoted entirely to John Singer Sargeant.

Hours

The museum is open Mon, Tues, Sat, and Sun 10 am–4:45 pm, and Wed–Fri 10 am–9:45 pm. Special exhibitions close 15 minutes before the museum closes. The gift shop is open during regular hours.

Admission Fees

Admission to the MFA costs $25 for adults, $23 for seniors (65+) and students (18+), $10 for youths 7–17 on weekdays before 3 p.m. (free at all other times), and children 6 and under are admitted for free. School group visits are discounted but must be scheduled in advanced.

Paid admission entitles visitors to one free visit within ten days of ticket purchase. On Wednesday evenings 4 pm–9:45 pm, admission is by voluntary contribution.

Tickets for entry can be purchased at the museum. Tickets for concerts, films, lectures, or special exhibitions can be purchased at the museum or online at www.mfa.org.

How to Get There—Driving

From the north, take I-93 S to Exit 26 (Storrow Drive). From Storrow Drive, take the Fenway/Kenmore exit. From the exit, take a left at the first traffic light, heading toward Boylston Street inbound. At the second traffic light, bear right onto The Fenway and proceed to the next set of lights. After passing through two stone gates, take the first right onto Hemenway Street and proceed to the end of the street. Take a left onto Forsythe Way and then a right onto Huntington Avenue. The museum is located a few lights down and on your right. Go past the museum and turn right onto Museum Road to reach the museum's parking lots.

From the south, take I-93 N to Exit 18 and follow the signs for Massachusetts Avenue. Turn right on Massachusetts Avenue, go past Columbus Avenue, and then turn left onto St. Botolph Street. Drive one block and turn right onto Gainsborough Street. Drive one block and turn left onto Huntington Avenue. The museum will be a couple of blocks down on your right. Go past the museum and turn right onto Museum Road to reach the museum's parking lots.

From the west, take the Mass Pike (I-90) E. Upon approaching the Boston city limits, look for Exit 22 (Prudential Center/Copley Square), the first exit after the Cambridge/Brighton toll plaza. You will enter a tunnel and Exit 22 will be on your right. Once on the exit ramp, get into the left lane (Prudential Center) and follow the exit to Huntington Avenue. Follow Huntington Avenue past the Christian Science Center (go through the underpass) and Northeastern University. The museum is located a few lights down on the right. Drive past the museum and turn right onto Museum Road to reach the museum's parking lots.

Parking

There is limited parking available at the museum, including two parking lots on Museum Road. Museum members pay $4 for each half-hour, $15 maximum. Non-members pay $6 for each half-hour with a $29 maximum for the day. A far cheaper option is public transportation.

How to Get There— Mass Transit

The museum is close to the Green Line's Museum stop (E train only) or the Orange Line's Ruggles stop. You can also take the 39 bus to the Museum stop or the 8 bus, 47 bus, or CT2 bus to the Ruggles stop.

Children's Museum of Boston

General Information

Address: 300 Congress Street
             Boston, MA 02210

Phone: 617-426-6500

Website: www.bostonchildrensmuseum.org

Hours: Daily 10 am–5 pm; Fridays 10 am–9 pm.
             Closed Thanksgiving and Christmas

Admission: General Admission $14, Seniors $14,
             Children (Aged 1–15) $14,
             Children (0–12 months) Free;
             Members are free.
             Friday nights 5 pm–9 pm, $1 for everybody.

Overview

A word of advice to adults visiting the Boston Children's Museum: Bring earplugs. The sound of children delighting in scientific wonder can be deafening, and this interactive hands-on museum tends to be very crowded, even on weekdays. The exhibits are fun even for adults, who most likely have forgotten everything they learned in middle school science classes, but if you've ever driven the mean streets of Boston you'll appreciate how difficult it is to fight for space at many of the activities.

Created by a group of teachers in Jamaica Plain in 1913, the Boston Children's Museum moved to its current location near Fort Point Channel on the waterfront in 1979. The goal of the original museum was to teach kids about nature, cultural diversity, and science through hands-on experiences. In the 1960s, the museum expanded and became an innovator in the concept of interactive exhibits, and today there are over 16 permanent learning areas.

Now occupying a former wool factory on the prized Boston waterfront, the small and crowded Children's Museum went through a much needed renovation and expansion in 2007. A new glass-paneled addition borders the newly expanded Harborwalk, with open spaces for additional outdoor exhibits, summer concerts, and special events. More space means more exhibits, including a 3-story climbing maze (New Balance Climb), a health and fitness area with bikes, basketballs, and interactive dance activities in Kid Power, and a brand new 160-seat theater at the Kid Stage. Popular areas include the Science Playground, where kids can engage in scientific exploration, the Japanese silk merchant's house, which is an actual house transported to the museum, the Arthur exhibit, where kids can become a part of the famous children's book and TV series, and the PlaySpace for kids under three.

The outdoor area is still being developed, but there is a Nature trail, boulders to climb on, and a waterfront park to eat lunch, escape the kids, or just sit by the water with a view of the Boston skyline. Disconcertingly, a muse promoting kids' education and healthy development o housed a McDonald's, but since the renovation, it been replaced by the somewhat healthier Au Bon P The museum is a nonprofit institution which also off workshops, seminars, and classroom kits for teacher their Teacher Leadership Center. Check its Website or about special events and concerts during the summer.

How to Get There—Driving

From the north: Take I-93 South to Exit 23 "Purch Street." At the first set of lights, take a left onto Seap Boulevard. At the next light, take a right onto Slee Street. The museum is on your right.

From the south: Take I-93 North to Exit 20 "So Station/I-90." Follow signs for I-90 East, and once in tunnel, take the first exit, labeled "South Boston." At end of the ramp, go straight onto East Service Road. At next intersection, take a right onto Seaport Boulevard. At first set of lights, turn left onto Sleeper Street. The muse is on the right.

From the east: Take I-90 West to Exit 25 "South Boston." the end of the ramp, go straight onto B Street. At the ne light, take a left onto Seaport Boulevard. At the third of lights, turn left onto Sleeper Street. The museum is your right.

From the west: Take I-90 East towards Logan Airport. O in the tunnel, take Exit 25 "South Boston." At the top of ramp, bear left towards "Seaport Boulevard." At the n set of lights, stay straight onto East Service Road all way to the end. At the next light, turn left onto Seap Boulevard. At the second set of lights, turn left o Sleeper Street. The museum is on your right.

Parking

The museum doesn't have its own lot or garage, but th are discounted prices for nearby lots. Both the Farnswo Street Garage (two blocks away) and the Stillings Str Garage (four blocks away) are $16 on weekdays and $ on weekends with museum validation. Farther away is Moakley Courthouse Parking Lot. Street parking is hard find and not recommended.

How to Get There— Mass Transit

Commuter rail and the MBTA Red Line and Silver Line dr you off at South Station, which is about a five minute w away. The MBTA Silver Line stop at Courthouse Station only a block away. Bus #4, 6, 7, and #11 all stop at Sou Station.

...ton may not have the Great White Way, but the theater ...ne—including musical venues—is alive and vibrant; ...u just might have to look a little harder for it. Where to ...t looking? Well, the most enthused patron of theatre ...he region is Larry Stark of www.theatermirror.com. If ...re's a production taking place anywhere within 100 ...es, Larry and his cast of writers are all over it. DigBoston ...n also point you to good productions.

...adway in Boston runs popular medium shows (e.g. ...ked, Swan Lake, Les Miserables) at Boston's flagship ...aters such as the **Wang Theatre (Map 3)**, neighboring ...**ubert Theater (Map 3)**, and the **Opera House (Map** ... These theaters also produce readings, dance, and ... variety of performances. Also of note in the Theater ...rict is **Emerson's Cutler Majestic Theatre (Map 3)** ...**1 the Charles Playhouse (Map 3)**, with long-running ...orites Blue Man Group and Shear Madness.

...y from the clamor of the Theater District down ...mont Street, you'll find the **Boston Center for the** ...s **(Map 7)**, containing four performance spaces that ...ommodate fare ranging from Forbidden Broadway ...one-man shows. The **Lyric Stage Company (Map 6)** ...arby on Clarendon Street showcases wide-ranging ...sons. The **Huntington Theatre (Map 5)** attracts top-...actors in local productions, while the **American**

Repertory Theater (ART) (Map 20) in Cambridge features renowned innovative stagings.

For something a little different, check out the **Puppet Showplace Theater (Map 17)** in Brookline. For laughs, try Inman Square's **ImprovBoston (Map 28)** or the North End's **ImprovAsylum (Map 2)** (both, despite the names, do more than just improv). A smaller theater worth a look is **Boston Playwrights' Theatre (Map 19)**.

If you're more of a choir and orchestra person, keep your eye on what's playing at the **Sanders Theatre (Map 20)**, which also hosts the occasional jazz, folk, or roots concert. Located in Harvard's Memorial Hall, Sanders Theatre offers terrific acoustics in a classic interior. Built to offer a 180-degree perspective for the audience, the theater was inspired by a Christopher Wren design. And of course, the Boston Symphony Orchestra at **Symphony Hall (Map 5)** has a thing or two to offer as far as classical music goes. The acoustics just can't be beat.

You can pick up half-price, same-day tickets at the BosTix booth in Copley Square or at Faneuil Hall Marketplace. You can find out performances for which tickets are available at www.bostix.org.

...eater	Address	Phone	Map
...A Plaza Black Box	539 Tremont St	617-426-5000	7
...klee Performance Center	136 Massachusetts Ave	617-747-2261	5
...ckman Auditorium/Studio Theatre	360 Huntington Ave	617-373-2247	15
...ston Center for the Arts	527 Tremont St	617-426-5000	7
...ston Children's Theater	316 Huntington Ave	617-424-6634	6
...ston Opera House	539 Washington St	617-259-3400	3
...ston Playwrights' Theatre	949 Commonwealth Ave	617-353-5443	5
...arles Playhouse	74 Warrenton St	617-426-6912	3
...onial Theatre	106 Boylston St	617-426-9366	3
...vanaughn Theatre at The Piano Factory	791 Tremont St	617-247-9777	13
...otlight Club	7A Eliot St	617-524-3200	14
...ntington Theatre Company	264 Huntington Ave	617-266-0800	5
...provAsylum	216 Hanover St	617-263-6887	2
...provBoston	40 Prospect St	617-576-1253	27
...ge Hernandez Cultural Center	85 W Newton St	866-811-4111	7
...sge Little Theatre	48 Massachusetts Ave	617-253-6294	27
...eb Drama Center	64 Brattle St	617-547-8300	20
...ic Stage Company	140 Clarendon St	617-437-7172	6
...cCormack Theatre	100 Morrissey Blvd		32
...ncy and Edward Roberts Studio Theater	539 Tremont St	617-426-5000	7
...pheum Theatre	1 Hamilton Pl	617-679-0810	3
...e Publick Theatre	1400 Soldiers Field Rd	617-782-5425	19
...ppet Showplace Theatre	32 Station St	617-731-6400	17
...mis Auditorium	465 Huntington Ave	617-369-3770	15
...aders Theatre	45 Quincy St	617-496-2222	13
...nel Theatre at Emerson College	10 Boylston Pl	617-824-8364	3
...ubert Theatre	265 Tremont St	617-482-9393	3
...art Street Playhouse	200 Stuart St	617-426-4499	3
...mphony Hall	301 Massachusetts Ave	617-266-1492	5
...eatre Cooperative	277 Broadway	n/a	24
...ver Auditorium	621 Huntington Ave	617-879-7000	15
...be Theater	67 Stuart St	617-510-4447	6
...ginia Wimberley Theatre	539 Tremont St	617-266-0800	7
...ng Center for Performing Arts	265 Tremont St	617-482-9393	3
...ng Theatre	270 Tremont St	617-482-9393	3
...eelock Family Theatre	180 The Riverway	617-879-2000	16
...bur Theatre	246 Tremont St	617-248-9700	3
...loughby and Baltic	195 Elm St	617-501-0197	23
...o Arrow Theater	0 Arrow St	617-547-8300	20

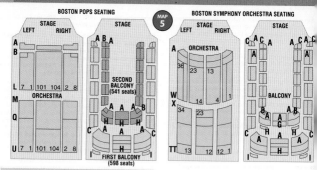

General Information

NFT Map: 5
Address: 301 Massachusetts Ave, Boston, MA 02115
Website: www.bso.org
Phone: 617-266-1492
Tickets: 617-266-1200; www.bso.org

Overview

Boston Symphony Hall, home of the Boston Symphony Orchestra and Boston Pops, is regarded as one of the finest concert halls in the world. Modeled after the German Leipzig Gewandhaus and the old Boston Music Hall, Symphony Hall was the first American hall designed to maximize acoustics, thanks to Harvard physics professor Wallace Clement Sabine (and to think you slept through your physics class!). Classical music connoisseurs recognize the hall as a space that produces a near-perfect sound experience, thanks to the sloping walls and floor of the stage and the alignment of the recessed Greek and Roman statues. The Hall, designed by New York architects McKim, Mead, & White, opened in 1900, replacing the Boston Music Hall, which was in the way of the burgeoning subway system. The hall seats 2,625 people in the Boston Symphony Orchestra (BSO) season and 2,371 in the Boston Pops Orchestra season (in the original leather seats from 1900). Don't leave without checking out the Aeolian-Skinner organ with 67 stops and 5,130 pipes. Free tours offer an insight into the history and features of Symphony Hall.

Symphony Hall contains dozens of museum-like items documenting notable events in its history. You can learn just what was so revolutionary about the acoustics and famous composers. Excitement and pride leaps from a reprinted *Boston Globe* article documenting the first performance. A 2006 renovation of the concert floor rebuilt it using the original processes, equipment manufacturers, and the exact same materials, in order to retain its premium acoustic properties.

In the past the Hall has hosted auto shows, mayoral inaugurations, meetings of the Communist Party, and a performance by Harry Houdini. You can also celebrate New Year's in style here as the orchestra performs in the background. (Bring your tux.) The tradition of hosting non-traditional events looks set to continue. In recent years, the US Open Squash Tournament has been held at Symphony Hall, using portable glass courts placed just below the stage.

If you're looking to throw your own Diddy-like party, function rooms and hall spaces can be rented for your own private shindig.

But unless you're making Manny Ramirez-style money, probably can't afford it. Renting out Symphony Hall for a ni costs between $5,400 and $6,800. Five different function spa are available for rent and cost between $1,200 and $3,900 night.

How to Get Tickets

You can purchase tickets to any of the Symphony H performances online at www.bso.org, in person at the Sympho Hall box office, or by phone on 617-266-1200 or 617-638-9 (TDD/TTY).

How to Get There—Driving

From the north, take I-93 to Storrow Drive (Exit 26). Once yo on Storrow Drive, bear left towards Copley Square/Back Bay. right onto Beacon Street. Turn left onto Clarendon Street. Tu right onto St. James Avenue. Bear left onto Huntington Aven Symphony Hall is on the corner of Huntington Avenue a Massachusetts Avenue.

From the south, take I-93 to Exit 18 and follow signs towa Massachusetts Avenue. Turn right onto Massachusetts Avenue.

From the west, take the Mass Pike (I-90) to the Prudential Cent Copley Square (Exit 27) and merge onto Huntington Avenue. Symphony Hall is on the corner of Huntington Avenue a Massachusetts Avenue.

Parking

There are two pay parking garages on Westland Avenue, anoth parking garage on Gainsborough Street next to Jordan Hall the New England Conservatory, and very limited street parking The Prudential Center Garage offers discount parking with t presentation of a performance ticket stub from the same day you enter the garage after 5 pm.

How to Get There—Mass Transi

The Green Line's E train stops at Symphony Hall. Other Green Li trains that stop at the Hynes Convention Center will get you clos Another option is to take the Orange Line to the Massachuset Avenue stop.

The #1 bus, which runs down Massachusetts Avenue from Harva Square to Dudley Square, stops mere feet from Symphony Hall.

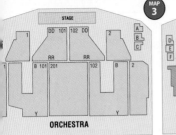

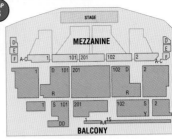

General Information

T Map:	3
ddress:	One Hamilton Pl, Boston, MA 02108
ebsite:	www.ticketmaster.com/venue/8318
none:	617-679-0810
cketmaster:	www.ticketmaster.com

Overview

e Orpheum has been around since 1852, and despite novations, it can still feel like its age, which many conder part of the charm. (Apparently, they have not heard this thing called The Internet either…) The Orpheum iginally had an eye on high-brow stuff: Tchaikovsky ong with the Boston Symphony Orchestra debuts ere. Now, it packs in close to 3,000 people to witness an lectic lineup of acts ranging from Larry the Cable Guy to orah Jones to Nine Inch Nails, and tickets often sell out uickly. Bands love the Orpheum for its premium acoustics (several live albums have been recorded here), and ew-wise there isn't a bad seat in the house, though leg om is notably sparse.

How to Get Tickets

ckets can be purchased from the Orpheum Theatre ox Office Mon–Sat, 10 am–5 pm. Tickets can also be urchased online at www.ticketmaster.com or by calling 7-679-0810.

How to Get There—Driving

From the north, take I-93 S to Exit 24A (Government Center). At the bottom of the ramp, bear right onto New Chardon Street. At the second set of lights, take a left onto Cambridge Street. Stay on the right-hand side of Cambridge Street, which will become Tremont Street as soon as you pass City Hall Plaza (on your left). Drive two blocks farther on Tremont Street. The Orpheum will be on your left on Hamilton Place.

From the south, take I-93 to Exit 23 (Government Center). At the end of the ramp, follow signs for Government Center/Faneuil Hall. At the set of lights, make a left onto North Street. Drive a quarter-mile to the end of North Street, then make a left onto Congress Street. Take your first right onto State Street, which turns into Court Street after a few feet. Follow Court Street to the end, then make a left at the fork onto Tremont Street. Drive two blocks farther on Tremont Street. The Orpheum will be on your left on Hamilton Place.

From the west, take the Mass Pike (I-90) E to Exit 24B, which will dump you onto I-93 N. From there follow the directions above for driving from the south.

Parking

Street parking will be scarce, especially during event hours. The closest parking lots are on Tremont Street, under Boston Common, and on Washington Street.

How to Get There—Mass Transit

Take the Red or Green Line to the Park Street stop or the Orange Line to Downtown Crossing. The theater is just a short walk from both stops. It's directly across from the Park Street Church.

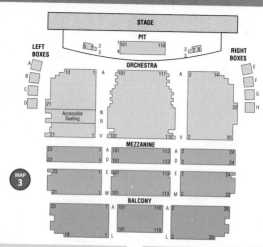

General Information

NFT Map:	3
Address:	270 Tremont St, Boston, MA 02116
Website:	www.citicenter.org/theatres/shubert
Phone:	617-482-9393
Tele-charge:	www.telecharge.com, 800-447-7400

Overview

The Shubert Theatre is the "Little Princess" to the Wang Theatre's "Grand Dame." The 1,600-seat venue opened in 1910 and has since undergone two major renovations. The theater's elaborate entranceway was destroyed during the widening of Tremont Street in 1925, and in 1996, $6 million was spent restoring and improving the theater's original ornate French Renaissance architecture. The intimacy within the Shubert remained intact, and the theater is now the home of the Boston Lyric Opera, many Boston arts organizations, as well as several touring companies. Broadway shows, including such classics as The King and I and South Pacific, debuted at the Shubert before making their way to New York. Once part of the not-for-profit Wang Center for the Performing Arts, both theaters have sadly had to sell off naming rights in an attempt to stay solvent. The Wang and Shubert are now owned by the Citigroup umbrella and carry the Citi moniker in front of their traditional names.

How to Get Tickets

You can purchase tickets for the Shubert Theatre online at www.citicenter.org/events or by calling Tele-charge at 800-447-7400. You can also buy tickets for Shubert shows (without the nasty service charges) at the Wang Theatre Box Office, which is open Tuesday through Saturday from 12 p.m. until 6 p.m.

How to Get There—Driving

From the north, take I-93 S to Exit 23 (South Station), which dumps you onto Purchase Street. Immediately after the Chinatown Gate (on your right), take a right onto Kneeland Street. Go straight for several blocks and then turn left onto Tremont Street. The Shubert Theatre is on your right.

From the south, take I-93 N to Exit 20 (South Station) and immediately get into the left-hand lane. The sign overhead will read "Detour South Station via Frontage Road." Take this left exit off the ramp and follow Frontage Road north to South Station. Turn left onto Kneeland Street. Go straight for several blocks and then turn left onto Tremont Street. The Shubert Theatre is on your right.

From the west, take the Mass Pike (I-90) E to Exit 24A. Turn left onto Kneeland Street. Go straight for several blocks and then turn left onto Tremont Street. The Shubert Theatre is on your right.

Parking

Your best bets are the parking lot on the corner of Tremont and Stuart Streets, the lot at the Radisson Hotel on Stuart Street, the Kinney Motor Mart on Stuart Street, or the Fitz-Inn lot on Kneeland Street.

How to Get There—Mass Transit

The Orange Line's New England Medical Center stop and the Green Line's Boylston Street stop are both one block away from the theater. The Red Line's Park Street stop on Tremont Street is three or so blocks from the theater.

General Information

T Map:	3
Address:	270 Tremont St, Boston, MA 02116
Website:	www.citicenter.org/theatres/wang
Phone:	617-482-9393
Tele-charge:	www.telecharge.com, 800-447-7400

Overview

Surviving several name changes and heavy renovation over the years, the Wang Theatre has retained a prominent feature of the Boston theater scene. With 3,600 seats, it is the larger of the two performance spaces once operated by the Wang Center for the Performing Arts and now owned by Citigroup (the other is the famous Shubert House across the street). Though the Wang and Shubert keep their names, the complex is now known as the Citi Performing Arts Center.

Opened in the "Roaring Twenties" (1925) as the Metropolitan Theatre, the venue was considered to be a "magnificent movie cathedral" with its ornate interior resembling something from Louis XIV's palace. Renamed the Music Hall in 1962, the theater became home to the then-fledgling Boston Ballet. As the years passed, the shiny gem began to lose some of its luster and relevance. Some minor renovations were made, but it wasn't until 1983, when Dr. An Wang stepped in to resuscitate the theater, that things took a turn for the better. Since the restoration, the theater has played host to such classics as *Les Miserables*, *The Phantom of the Opera*, and *Spamalot*, and still houses one of New England's largest movie screens. Still home to the Boston Ballet, the Wang has expanded its repertoire to include pop concerts and comedians. The *Nutcracker at the Wang* (snicker...) holiday tradition is no more (it moved to The Opera House), replaced by the very un-Boston "Radio City Christmas Spectacular" featuring high-kicking Rockettes wearing reindeer antlers.

How to Get Tickets

You can purchase tickets for the Wang Theatre online at www.citicenter.org/events or by calling Tele-charge at 800-447-7400. The Wang Theatre Box Office, open Tuesday through Saturday from 12 p.m. until 6 p.m., sells tickets without the nasty service charges levied by external vendors.

How to Get There—Driving

From the north, take I-93 S to Exit 20A (South Station), which dumps you at Purchase Street. Immediately after the Chinatown Gate (on your right) take a right onto Kneeland Street. Go straight for several blocks and then turn left onto Tremont Street. The Wang Theatre is on your left.

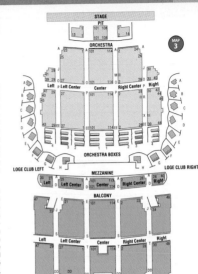

From the south, take I-93 N to Exit 20 (South Station) and immediately get into the left-hand lane. Follow signs for South Station and take the left exit for South Station/Chinatown. At the second light, turn left onto Kneeland Street. Go straight for several blocks and then turn left onto Tremont Street. The Wang Theatre is on your left.

From the west, take the Mass Pike (I-90) to Exit 24A. Turn left onto Kneeland Street. Go straight for several blocks and then turn left onto Tremont Street. The Wang Theatre is on your left.

Parking

Your best bets are the parking lot on the corner of Tremont and Stuart Streets, the lot at the Radisson Hotel on Stuart Street, the Kinney Motor Mart on Stuart Street, or the Fitz-Inn lot on Kneeland Street.

How to Get There—Mass Transit

The Orange Line's New England Medical Center stop and the Green Line's Boylston Street stop are both one block away from the theater. The Red Line's Park Street stop on Tremont Street is about three blocks from the theater.

Key to Boston neighborhoods

AL	Allston
BR	Brighton
DO	Dorchester
EB	East Boston
HP	Hyde Park
JP	Jamaica Plain
MT	Mattapan
RS	Roslindale
RX	Roxbury
SB	South Boston
WR	West Roxbury

oston

Street Index

Street Index

Street Index

Street	Page	Grid
Granfield Ave	30	B2
Granger St	32	B1
Granite Ave	32	B1
Granite St	10	A1
Grant Rd	31	A2
Grant St	32	A1
Grantley St	33	B2
Granville Ave	23	A1
Granville St	32	B1
Grassmere Rd	33	A1
Gray St	7	A1
Grayfield Ave	29	A2
Grayson St	32	B2
Greaton Rd	29	A2
Green St	14	B1/B2
Green Hill St	32	B2
Greenbaum St	12	A2
Greenbrier St		
(1-28)	31	A2
(29-199)	32	B1
Greenbrook Rd	33	A2
Greendale Rd	31	B1
Greenfield Rd	31	B1
Greenhalge St	12	B2
Greenheys St	31	A2
Greenleaf St	15	A2
Greenley St	14	B2
Greenmount St	32	A1
Greenock St	31	A1
Greenough Ave	14	B1
Greenough Ln	2	A2
Greenough Park	14	B1
Greenview Ave	14	B1
Greenville St	13	A2
Greenville Park	13	A2
Greenwich Ct	13	A2
Greenwich St [DO]	32	B1
Greenwich St [RX]	13	A2
Greenwich Park	6	B1
Greenwood Ave	33	A2
Greenwood Cir	33	A2
Greenwood Sq	33	A2
Greenwood St	31	A2
Greenwood Park	32	B1
Gretter Rd	29	A2
Grew Ave		
(1-99)	30	B2
(100-149)	33	B2
Grew Hill Rd	33	A1
Greycliff Rd	18	B1
Greylock Rd	19	B1
Greymere Rd	18	B1
Gridley St	4	
Griffin Ct	32	B1
Griggs Pl	19	B1
Griggs St	19	B1
Grimes St	10	B1
Groom St	32	A1
Groton St	7	A2
Grotto Glen Rd	14	A2
Grouse St	29	B2
Grove Pl	1	B1
Grove Rd	29	B2
Grove Sq	1	B1
Grove St	1	B1
Grove St [WR]	29	B2
Grove Ter	29	B2
Groveland St	31	B2
Grovenor Rd	14	A1
Grover Ave	30	B2
Guernsey St	29	A2
Guest St	18	A2
Guild Row	13	A1
Guild St	13	A1
Guilford St	18	A2
Gurney St	15	B2
Gustin St	10	B1
Gwinnett St	33	A2
H Ave	29	B1
H St	11	B1
H Street Pl	10	B2
Hackensack Cir	30	A1
Hackensack Ct	30	A1
Hackensack Rd		
(1-82)	30	A1
(83-199)	29	A2
Hackensack Ter	29	A2
Hadassah Way	3	B1
Hadwin Way	30	B2
Hagar St	14	B1
Hague St	19	A2
Halborn St	31	B1
Hale Ave	23	A2
Hale St	33	A1
Haley St	13	B1
Half Moon St	13	B2
Halford Rd	29	A2
Halifax St	14	A1
Hall Ave	31	A2
Hall Pl	11	B1
Hall St	14	B1/B2
Hallam St	32	A1
Halleck St	15	A1
Hallet Sq	32	B2
Hallet St	32	B2
Hallet Davis St	32	B2
Halliday St	30	B2
Hallowell St	31	B1
Hallron St	33	A1
Halsey Rd	33	B2
Halwood Rd	33	B1
Hamilton Pl	3	A2
Hamilton St [DO]	32	A1/B1
Hamilton St [HP]	32	B2
Hamlet St	32	A1
Hamlin St	10	B2
Hammond St	13	A2
Hammond Ter	13	A2
Hampden St	13	A2
Hampstead Ln	14	B1
Hampstead Rd	14	B1
Hancock St	1	B2
Hancock St [DO]	32	A1
Hannon St	31	B1
Hano St	19	A1
Hanover St	2	A2
N Hanover Ct	2	B1
Hanover Pl	2	B1
Hanover St	2	A1/A2/B1
Hansborough St	31	B1
Hansford Pl	13	B2
Hanson St	7	A1/A2
Harbell Ter	32	B1
Harbor St	11	A1
Harbor Crest Ct	32	A2
Harbor Point Blvd	32	A2
Harbor View St	32	A1
Harcourt St	6	B1
Harding Ct	10	B1
Harding Rd	30	B2
Hardwick St	18	A1
Hardwick Ter	18	A1
Hardy St	11	B1
Harem Pl	3	A2
Harlem St	31	A2
Harleston St	15	B1
Harley St	32	B1
Harlow St	13	B2
Harmon St	31	B1
Harmony St	9	
Harold Pl	11	
Harold St		
(1-219)	13	
(220-295)	31	
Harold Park	13	
Harriet St	18	A1
Harrington Ave	13	
Harris Ave	14	
Harris St	2	
Harrishof St	13	
Harrison Ave		
(1-295)	4	A1
(296-856)	7	A2/B1
(857-1199)	13	
Harrison St	30	
Harrison Archway	7	
Harrison Park	32	
Harrow St	32	
Hart Pl	11	
Hartford Ct	13	
Hartford St	13	
Hartford Ter	13	
Hartland St	32	
Hartlawn Rd	29	
Hartley Ter	13	
Hartwell St	31	A1
Harvard Ave [AL]	19	A1
Harvard Ave [DO]	31	
Harvard Ave [HP]	33	A2
Harvard Pl	3	
Harvard St	4	
Harvard St [MT]		
(1-698)	31	A1/A2
(699-1080)	30	
(1081-1099)	33	
N Harvard St		
(1-203)	20	
(204-399)	19	
Harvard Ter	19	
Harvard Way	22	
Harvard Park	31	
Harvest St	12	
Harvest Ter	12	
Harvester St	19	
Harvey Steel Rd	19	
Harwood St	31	
Haskell St	19	
Haslet St	30	
Hastings St	29	
Hatch St	11	
Hathaway St	4	
Hathaway St [JP]	14	
Hatherly Rd	18	
Hautvale St	18	
Havana St	30	
Havelock St	31	
Haven St	7	
W Haven St	7	
Haverford St	14	
Havey St	30	
Haviland St	5	B1/B…
Haviland Ter	5	
Havre St	9	A1/B…
Hawkins St	1	
Hawley Pl	4	
Hawley St	4	
Hawthorne Pl	1	
Hawthorne St [RS]	30	
Hawthorne St [RX]	13	
Hawthorne Ter	30	
Hayden St	15	
Haydn St	30	
Hayes Rd	30	
Haymarket Pl	3	

Street Index

Street	Page	Grid
Iroquois St	15	B1
Irving St	1	B2
Irwin Ave	13	B2
Isabella St	3	B1
Island St		
(1-64)	13	A2
(65-99)	12	B1
Island View Pl	32	A2
Islington St	19	A1
Islington Ter	19	A1
Itasca St	31	B1
Ivanhoe St	7	A1
Ives St	31	B1
Ivory St	29	A2
Jackson Ave	2	A1
Jackson Pl	3	A2
Jackson St	33	B2
Jacob St	31	B2
Jacqueline Rd	29	B2
Jaeger Ter	30	A1
Jalleison St	33	A2
Jamaica Pl	14	B1
Jamaica St	14	B1
Jamaicaway		
(2-98)	15	B1
(100-598)	14	A1
Jamaicaway Ct	14	A1
James St	7	B1
James St [HP]	33	A2
Jamestown Ter	31	B1
Jarvis Pl	13	B2
Jason Ter	10	B2
Jay St	11	B1
Jayjay Dr	31	B2
Jeffers St	33	A1
Jefferson St	3	A1
Jeffries St	9	B2
Jenkins St	31	B1
Jennett Ave	29	A2
Jenton Way	4	A2
Jerome St	32	A1
Jersey St	15	A2
Jeshurun St	29	B2
Jess St	14	A2
Jette Ct	18	B2
Jewett St	30	B2
Jimmy Fund Way	15	A1
Jo Anne Ter	32	B1
Joan Rd	33	B1
John A Andrew St	14	B2
John Alden Rd	29	B2
John Eliot Sq	13	A1
Johnny Ct	4	B1
Johnray Rd	31	B1
Johnson Ave	14	A2
Johnson St	29	B1/B2
Johnson Ter	31	B2
Johnston Rd	31	B1
Johnswood Rd	30	B2
Jones Ave	31	B2
Jones Way	13	B2
Joseph St	32	B1
Josephine St	32	B1
Joslin Pl	16	B1
Joy Ct	1	B2
Joy Pl	1	B2
Joy St	1	B2
Joyce Rd	33	A2
Joyce Hayes Way	10	A1/B1
Joyce Kilmer Rd	29	B1
Judge St	15	B1
Judson St	13	B2
Julian St	13	B2
Juliette St	32	A1/B1
June St	33	A1
Juniper St	13	B1
K St	11	B1
K Street Pl	11	B1
Kalada Park	13	B2
Kane St	32	A1
Kardon Rd	33	B1
Keane St	29	A2
Kearsarge Ave	13	A2
Kearsarge Ter	13	A2
Keenan Rd	18	A2
Keith St	29	A1
Kelley Ct	18	A2
Kelton St	19	B1
Kemble Pl	11	B2
Kemble St		
(1-61)	13	A2
(62-199)	12	B1
Kemp St		
(1-49)	12	B2
(50-99)	32	A1
Kempton St	15	B1
Kenberma Rd	31	A2
Kendall St	13	A2
Kenilworth St	13	A1
Kenmere Rd	32	B1
Kenmore St	16	A2
Kennebec St		
(1-209)	31	B1
(210-299)	33	A2
Kenneth St	29	A2
Kenney St	14	A2
Kenrick St	18	B1
Kensington St	13	B1
Kensington Park	13	B2
Kenton Rd		
(1-30)	14	B2
(31-99)	31	A1
Kenwood St	32	B1
Kerna Rd	29	B2
Kerr Pl	13	A1
Kerr Way	13	A1
Kershaw Rd	29	B2
Kerwin St	31	A2
Keswick St	16	A1
Kevin Rd	32	A1
Keyes Pl	30	A2
Keystone St	29	B1
Kiernan Rd	29	A1
Kilby Pl	4	A2
Kilby St		
(1-35)	2	B1
(36-98)	4	A2
Kilmarnock St	15	A2
Kilsyth Rd	23	A2
Kilsyth Ter	18	B2
Kimball St	32	B1
Kineo St	13	B2
King St		
(1-199)	32	B1/B2
Kingsboro Park	14	A2
Kingsdale St	31	A2
Kingsland Rd	29	A1
Kingsley St	19	A1
Kingston St	4	A1/B1
Kinross Rd	18	B2
Kirk St	29	A2
Kirkwood Ct	18	B1
Kittredge Ct	30	B1
Kittredge St		
(1-313)	30	B1
(314-398)	33	A1
Kittredge Ter	30	B1
Knapp St	4	B1
Kneeland St		
(1-23)	3	
(24-199)	4	
Knight St	33	
Knights Ct	14	
Knoll St	30	
Knowles St	18	
Knowlton St	10	
Knox St	3	
Kovey Ct	33	
Kovey Rd	33	
Kristin Ct	33	
L St	11	
La Grange Pl	13	
Laban Pratt Rd	32	
Laconia St	7	
Lafayette Ave	2	
Lafield St	32	
Lagrange St		B1
Lagrange St [WR]		
(1-85)	33	
(86-1408)	29	A1/A2...
Lake St	18	
Lake Shore Rd	18	
Lakeville Rd	14	
Lamartine Pl	14	
Lamartine St	14	A2/...
Lamartine Ter	14	
Lambert Ave	13	
Lambert St	13	
Lamson Ct	9	
Lamson St	9	
Lancaster St	1	
Landor Rd	31	
Landseer St	29	
Landseer Ter	29	
Lane Pl	4	
Lane Park	18	
Lanesville Ter	30	
Langdon Pl	2	
Langdon St		
(1-45)	13	
(46-99)	12	
Langdon Ter	31	
Langdon Park	31	
Langford Park	13	
Langley Rd	18	
Lansdowne St	16	
Lantern Ln	29	
Larch Pl	30	
Larch St	18	
Larchmont St	32	
Laredo St	31	
Lark St	10	
Larkhill Rd	29	
Larose Pl	18	
Lasalle Park	32	
Lasell St	29	A1/...
Lathrop Pl	2	
Latin Rd	29	
Lattimore Ct	13	
Laural St	33	
Laurel St	13	
Lauriat St	31	
Laurie Ave	29	
Lauten Pl	29	
Laval St	33	
Lawley St	32	
Lawn St	15	
Lawn Park	23	
Lawndale Ter	14	
Lawrence St		
(1-45)	13	
(46-154)	31	
Lawrence Ct	10	

Street Index

Street	Page	Grid
rence Pl	18	A2
rence St	7	A1
rence St [BR]	18	A2
son St	9	A2
rton St	33	B1
rton St	33	B1
rton Ter	33	A2
vre St	31	B2
haven Rd	31	B2
mington Rd	18	B2
anon St	32	A1
ge Hill Rd	29	B1
gebrook Rd	31	B2
gedale Rd	30	B1
gemere Rd	18	B2
gewood Rd	29	A1/A2
St	14	A2
Hill Rd	30	B1
ds St	10	B1
dsville St	32	B1
ion Pl	30	B1
cester St	18	A2/B2
ghton Rd	33	B1
and Pl	7	A2
and Rd	29	A2
and St	30	A2
nan Pl	4	A2
a Ter	31	B1/B2
niston St	30	B1
nnoco Rd	30	A2
nnon Ct	11	B2
nox St	13	A2
enox St	13	A2
oxdale Ave	32	B1
o M Birmingham Pky	18	A1/A2
on St	15	A2
onard Ct	32	B1
onard Pl	11	B1
onard St	32	B1
roy St	32	B1
seur Rd	33	B2
sher St	30	B2
slie St	32	B1
slie Park	13	B1
ster Pl	14	B1
ster St	12	B1
ston St	31	B1
tterfine Ter	13	B2
vant St	32	B1
verett Cir	1	A1
wis Pl	13	B2
wis St	2	A2/B2
wis St [EB]	9	B1
wis Wharf	2	B2
wiston St	33	A2
xington Ave	33	A2
xington Sq	9	A2
xington St	9	A1/A2
yland St	12	B1
bbey St	29	A1
berty Pl	10	B1
e St	18	A2
la Rd	30	A1
ac Ter	30	B1
lie Way	29	A2
ly St	10	B1
me St	11	B1
ncoln Pl	7	B1
ncoln Pl [BR]	18	A2
ncoln St	4	A1/B1
ncoln St [BR] (1-130)	18	A2
(131-598)	19	A1
ncoln St [DO]	32	B1
ncoln St [HP]	33	A2
ncoln Wharf	2	A2
Linda Ln	32	A2
Lindall Ct	1	B1
Lindall Pl	1	B1
Lindall St	30	B1
Linden Ave	31	B1
Linden Ct	32	A1
Linden Rd	29	B2
Linden St [AL]	19	A1
Linden St [DO]	32	A1/B1
Linden St [SB]	10	B2
Lindsey St	32	B1
Lingard St	13	B2
Linley Ter	11	B1
Linnet St	29	A2/B2
Linsky Barry Ct	10	B1
Linvale Ter	31	B1
Linwood Sq	13	A1
Linwood St [HP]	33	B1
Linwood St [RX]	13	A1
List Pl	30	B1
Liszt St	33	A1
Litchfield Ct	9	B1
Litchfield St (1-68)	18	A2
(69-199)	19	A1
Lithgow St	32	B1
Littledale St	33	A2
Livermore St (1-56)	31	B1
(57-121)	33	A2
Liverpool St	9	A1/B1
Livingstone St	31	B1
Lochdale Rd	30	B2
Lochland Rd	33	B2
Lochstead Ave	14	A1
Locke Pl	11	B1
Locksley St	14	A2
Lockwood St	33	A2
Locust St	12	B2
Lodgehill Rd	33	A1
Logan St	13	A1
Logan Way (1-45)	32	A1
(46-99)	10	B1
Logan Airport Service Dr	9	A2
Lomasney Way	1	A2
Lombard Pl	2	A1
Lombard St	32	B1
London Ct	9	A1
London St	9	A1/B1
Long Ave	19	B1
Long Ter	29	B1
Long Wharf	2	B2
Longfellow Pl	1	A2
Longfellow St	32	B1
Longmeadow St	12	B1
Longwood Ave	15	A1/A2
Lonsdale St	13	A1
Lorenzo St	32	B2
Lorette St	29	A2
Loring Pl	33	B2
Loring St [HP]	33	B2
Loring St [SB]	10	B1
Lorna Rd	31	B1/B2
Lorne St	31	A1
Lorraine St	29	A2
Lorraine Ter	19	B1
Lothian Rd	18	B2
Lothrop St	18	A2
Lotus Ave	31	A1
Lotus St (1-48)	31	A1
(49-98)	30	A2
Louders Ln	30	A1
Louis St	10	A1
Louis Ter	32	B1
Louis D Brown Way	32	B1
Louis Prang St	15	A2
Louisburg Sq	1	B1
Lourdes Ave	31	A1
Lovejoy Pl	2	A1
Lovell St	9	A2
Lovis St	10	B1
Lowell Ct	3	B2
Lower Campus Rd	18	B1
Loyola Cir	29	B2
Loyola St	13	B2
Lubec St	9	B1
Lucerne St	29	A1/A2
Lyall St	29	A1
Lyall Ter	31	B2
Lyford St	31	B2
Lynde St	1	B2
Lyndeboro Pl	3	B1
Lyndhurst St	31	A2
Lyne Rd	18	B2
Lynn St	2	A1
Lynnville Ter	31	A2
Lyon St	32	A1
M Ave	29	B1
M St	11	B1
M Street Pl	11	B1
MacNeil Way	32	A1
Macdonald St	33	A1
Machester St	29	A1
Mackin St	18	A2
Macullar Rd	29	B2
Madeline St	18	A1
Madison St	33	B1
Madison Park Ct	13	A1
Magazine St (1-62)	13	A2/B2
(63-150)	12	B1
Magdala St	32	B1
Magee St	33	A1/A2
Magnolia Pl	13	B2
Magnolia Sq	13	B2
Magnolia St (1-135)	32	A1
(136-216)	13	B2
(217-299)	31	A2
Mahler St	30	B2
Mahnis Ter	14	A2
Mahoney Pl	30	B2
Maida Ter	33	A2
W Main St	31	B1
Maitland St	16	A1
Malbert Rd	18	B1
Malcolm Rd	30	A1
Malden St	7	B2
W Malden St	7	B2
Mall St	13	A2
Mallard Ave	31	A2
Mallet St	32	B1
Mallon Rd	31	A1
Malta St	31	B1
Malvern St	19	A2
Malverna Rd	30	B1
Mamelon Cir	31	B1
Manchester St	31	B2
Manila Ave	33	B1
Manion Rd	33	A2
Manley St	32	B1
Mann St	29	B2
Manning St	30	B2
Manor St	32	B1
Mansen Ct	33	A1
Mansen Rd	33	A1
Mansfield St	19	A1
Mansur St	33	A2

Street Index

Street Index

Street Index

Street	Page	Grid
Revere Pl	2	A2
Revere St	1	B1
Revere St [JP]	14	B2
Rexford St	31	B1
Rexhame St	29	A2
Reynold Rd	33	B1
Rhoades St	31	B1
Rhoda St	29	A2
Rice St	32	B2
Rich St	31	B1
Rich Hood Ave	33	B2
Richard Ter	31	B1
Richards St	10	A1
Richardson St	18	A1
Richfield St		
(1-20)	31	A2
(21-99)	32	A1
Richfield Park	32	A1
Richmere Rd	31	B1
Richmond Pl	2	A1
Richmond St	2	B1/B2
Richmond St [DO]	31	B2
Richwood St	29	A2
Rickerhill Rd	29	A2
Ridge St	30	B2
Ridgecrest Dr	29	B2
Ridgecrest Ter	29	B2
Ridgemont St	18	A2
Ridgeview Ave	31	B1/B2
Ridgeway Ln	1	B1
Ridgewood St	32	B1
Ridlon Rd	31	B1
Riley Rd	33	B1
Rill St	32	A1
Ring Rd	5	A2
Ringgold St	7	A2
Ripley Rd	31	A2
Risley Rd	29	A2
Rita Rd	32	B2
Ritchie St	13	B1
River Rd	15	B1
River St	1	B1
River St [MT/HP]		
(1-813)	31	B1/B2
(814-1999)	33	A2/B1/B2
River Street Pl	1	B1
River Street Ter	33	A2
Riverbank St	31	B1
Riverdale Rd	31	B1
Riverdale St	19	A1
Rivermoor St	29	B1
Riverside Sq	33	A2
Riverview Rd	18	A1
Riverway		
(1-330)	16	A1/B1
(332-398)	15	B1
Riverway St	29	B1
Roach St	32	A1
Roanoke Ave	14	B2
Roanoke St	33	B2
Robbart Ln	33	B2
Robert St	30	B1
Roberts Pl	33	B1
Robeson St	31	A1
Robey St	12	B1
Robin St	29	B2
Robin Hood St	13	B2
Robinson St	32	B1
Robinwood Ave	14	A1/A2
Robken Rd	30	B1
Rock Ave	31	B2
Rock Rd	31	B1
Rock St	13	B1
Rock Ter	31	B1
Rock Hill Rd	14	A2
Rockdale St	31	B1
Rockford St	12	B1
Rockingham Ave	29	B2
Rockingham Rd	31	B1
Rockland Ave	13	B2
Rockland St [RX]	13	B1/B2
Rockland St [WR]	29	B2
Rockledge St	13	A1
Rockmere St	32	A1
Rockmount St	31	A2
Rockne Ave	32	B1
Rockvale Cir	14	B2
Rockview Pl	14	A2
Rockview St	14	A2/B2
Rockville Park	13	B2
Rockway St	31	B1
Rockwell St	31	B2
Rockwood St	30	A1
Rockwood Ter	30	A1
Rocky Nook Ter	31	A1
Rodman St	30	B2
Rodney St	18	A2
Rogers St	10	B1
Rogers Park Ave	18	B1
Rollins Ct	13	B2
Rollins Pl	1	B1
Rollins St	7	B1
Romar Ter	13	A1
Romsey Cir	32	A1
Romsey St	32	A1
Ronald St	31	A2
Ronan St	32	A1
Rosa St	33	A2
Rosaria St	32	B2
Rose Garden Cir	18	B1
Roseberry Rd	31	B1
Roseclair St	12	B2
Rosecliff St	30	B1
Rosecliff Ter	30	B1
Rosedale St	31	A2
Roseglen Rd	33	A2
Roseland St	32	B1
Rosemary St	14	B1
Rosemere St	30	B1
Rosemont St [DO]	32	B1
Rosemont St [MT]	31	B1
Roseway St	14	A2
Rosewood St	31	B1
Roslin St	32	B1
Roslindale Ave	30	B1
Roslyn Pl	14	A2
Ross Pl	11	B1
Ross Rd	32	B1
Rosselerin Rd	32	B1
Rosseter St	31	A2
Rossmore Rd		
(1-31)	14	B2
(32-34)	30	A2
(36-119)	31	A1
Roswell St	12	B1
Roucemont Pl	14	A2
Round Hill St	14	A2
Rowe Cr	30	B2
Rowe St	30	B2
Rowell St	32	A1
Rowen Ct	14	B2
Rowena St	32	B1
Rowes Wharf	4	A2
Rowley St	32	B2
Roxana St	33	B1
W Roxbury Pky	29	A2
Roxbury St	31	A1
Roxton St	31	A2
Royal St	19	A1
Royce Rd	19	B1
Roys St	14	
Rozella St	32	
Ruffing St	33	
Rugby Rd	31	
Rugdale Rd	31	
Rugg Rd	19	
Ruggles Ct	13	
Ruggles St		
(1-239)	13	A1
(240-399)	15	
Rumford Rd	29	
Rundel Park	29	
Running Brook Rd	29	
Rupert St	31	
Rusfield St	12	
Rushmore St	18	
Ruskin Rd	33	
Ruskin St	29	
Ruskindale Rd		
(1-133)	33	
(134-299)	31	
S Russell St	1	
Russett Rd	29	
Rustic Rd	29	
Rustlewood Rd	29	
Ruth St	9	
Ruthven St		
(1-25)	13	
(26-199)	31	
Ruthven Park	31	
Rutland Sq	6	
W Rutland Sq	6	
Rutland St	7	A1
Rutledge St	29	
Ruxton Rd	31	
Ryan Rd	15	
Sachem St	15	
Saco St	32	
Safford St	33	
Sagamore St	31	
Saint Alphonsus St	15	A2/B1
Saint Marys St	16	
Saint Richard St	13	
Salcombe St	32	
Salem Ct	2	
Salem St	2	A1
Salina Rd	32	
Salisbury Park	32	
Salman St	29	
Salt Ln	2	
Salutation St	2	
Sammett Ave	30	
Samoset St	32	
San Juan St	7	
San Juan Way	15	
Sanborn Ave	29	
Sanderson Pl	18	
Sanford St [HP]	33	
Sanford St [MT]	31	
Sanger St	10	
Santuit St	32	
Saranac St	32	
Saratoga Pl	9	
Saratoga St	9	A1
Sargent St	13	
Sargent Crossway	14	
Saunders St	18	
Savannah Ave	31	
Saville St	29	
Savin St	13	
Savin Hill Ave	32	A1
Savin Hill Ct	32	
Savin Hill Ln	32	
Savin Hill Ter	32	
Savoy Pl	7	

Street	Page	Grid
oolsey Sq	14	B2
oolson St	31	B1
orcester Sq	7	B1
orcester St		
(1-158)	7	A1/B1
(159-169)	6	B1
orley St	29	A2
ormwood St	10	A1
orrell St	32	B2
orthington St	15	B1
ren St	29	A2/B2
rentham St	32	B1
right St	30	B1
rights Ct	10	B1
ycliff Ave	29	B1
yman Pl	14	A2
yman St	14	A2
yola Pl	31	A2
yoming St	13	B1
yvern St	30	B2
ale Ter	31	A1
ard Way	10	A1
armouth Pl	6	B1
armouth St	6	B1
awkey Way		
(1-40)	16	A2
(41-69)	15	A2
eoman Pl	13	A2
eoman St	13	A2
ork St	31	A2
orktown St	29	A2
oungs Rd	31	B1
uill Cir	33	B1
uletide Rd	33	A2
amora Ct	14	A1
amora St	14	A1
eller St	30	B1
iegler St	13	A1/A2

Brookline

Street	Page	Grid
bbottsford Rd	19	B2
cron Rd	17	B2
dams St	19	B2
ddington Path	17	A1
ddington Rd	17	A1
llerton St	17	B2
lton Ct	17	A2
lton Pl	17	A2
mory St	16	A1
ndem Pl	16	A1
spinwall Ave	16	A1/B1
therton Rd	19	B1
uburn Ct	17	A2
uburn Pl	17	A2
uburn St	17	A2
abcock St	19	A2/B2
artlett Cres	19	B1
artlett St	19	B1
eacon St		
(1443-1793)	17	A1
(1794-2502)	18	A1
eaconsfield Path	17	A1
eaconsfield Rd	17	A1
eals St	19	B2
eech Rd	16	A1
eecher Rd	17	A1
erkeley Ct	17	A2
lake Rd	17	A1
orland St	16	A1
owker St	16	B1
oylston Pl	17	B2
oylston St	17	B1/B2
radford Ter	19	B2
rington Rd	17	B2

Street	Page	Grid
Brook St	16	A1/B1
Browne St		
(1-35)	16	A1
(36-136)	19	B2
Buckminster Rd	17	A1/B1
Cameron St	17	B2
Carlton St	16	A1
Catlin Rd	17	B1
Centre St		
(1-51)	16	A1
(52-199)	19	B1/B2
Channing Rd	16	B1
Chapel St	16	B1
Charles St	17	A2
Chatham Cir	16	A1
Chatham St	16	A1
Chesham Rd	17	A1
Chestnut Pl	17	B2
Chestnut St		
(1-221)	17	B2
(228-399)	14	A1
Chestnut Hill Ave	17	B1
Chilton St	16	A1
Churchill St	16	A1
City View Rd	19	B1
Claflin Path	17	A1
Claflin Rd	17	A1
Clarence St	19	B2
Clark Ct	17	B2
Clark Rd	17	A1
Clearwater Rd	29	A2
Clinton Path	18	B2
Clinton Rd	17	A1
Codman Rd	17	B1
Colbourne Cres	17	A1
Colbourne Path	17	A1
Colchester St	16	A1/B1
Columbia St	19	B1
Columbia Ter	19	B1
Coolidge St	19	B1/B2
Copley St	19	B2
Corey Rd		
(1-26)	17	A1
(27-89)	18	B2
Cotswold Rd	17	A1
Cottage St	17	B2
Cottage Farm Rd	16	A1
Craig Pl	19	B2
Crowninshield Rd	19	B2
Cumberland Ave	17	B2
Cushing Rd	17	B2
Cypress St	17	A2/B2
Dana St	17	A2
Davis Ave	17	A2
Davis St	17	A2
Davis Path	17	A2
Dean Rd	17	A1
Devotion St	19	B2
Downing Rd	19	B1
Druce St	17	A1
Dudley St	17	B1
Dudley Way	17	B1
Dummer St		
(1-97)	16	A1
(98-145)	19	B2
Dwight St	19	B2
Edge Hill Rd	17	B2
Edwin St	17	B2
Egmont St		
(1-46)	16	A1
(47-99)	19	B2
Elba St	19	B2
Elm St	17	A2
Emerson St	17	A2
Englewood Ave	18	A2

Street	Page	Grid
Essex St	16	A1
Euston St	16	A1
Evans Rd	19	B1
Ewe St	16	A1
Fairbanks St	17	A1
Fairmount St	17	B1
Fisher Ave	17	B1
Fisher Rd	17	B1
Foster St	17	A2
Francis St	17	A1/B1
Franklin Ct	17	B2
Franklin St	17	B2
Freeman St		
(1-173)	16	A1
(174-245)	19	B1/B2
Fuller St	17	A1
Gardner Rd	17	A1
Garrison Rd	17	A1
George Ln	17	B1
Gibbs St	19	B2
Glen Rd	17	B2
Goddard Ave	17	B1
Goodwin Pl	17	A2
Gorham Ave	17	A2
Green St	19	B2
Green Hill Rd	17	B1
Greenough Cir	17	A2
Greenough St	17	A1/A2
Greenway Ct	19	B2
Griggs Rd	17	A1/A2
Griggs Ter	17	A2
Hall Rd	17	B2
Hamilton Rd	19	B2
Hancock Rd	17	A2
Harris St	17	A2
Harrison St	16	B1
Hart St	17	B2
Harvard Ave	17	A2
Harvard Ct	17	A2
Harvard Pl	17	A2
Harvard Sq	17	A2
Harvard St	19	B1/B2
Hawes Pl	17	A2
Hawes St	16	A1/B1
Hawthorn Rd	17	B1
Hayden Rd	17	B1
Heath Hill	17	B1
Hedge Rd	17	B1
Henry St	17	B2
High St		
(1-37)	16	B1
(38-299)	17	B2
High Street Pl	17	B2
Highland Rd	17	B2
Hillside Rd	17	B2
Holden St	17	A2
Holland Rd	17	A1
Homer St	17	A1
Hurd Rd	17	B1
Hyslop Rd	17	A1
Irving St	17	B1
Ivy St	16	A1
Jamaica Rd	16	B1
James St	16	A1
Jenness Rd	19	B1
John St	19	B2
Jordan Rd	19	B1
Juniper St	16	B1
Kendall St	17	B2
Kennard Rd	17	A1
Kent Sq	16	B1
Kent St	16	A1/B1
Kenwood St	19	B1
Kerrigan Pl	17	A2
Kilsyth Rd	18	B2

Street Index

Street Index

Street	Page	Grid
ech St	23	B1/B2
l Ct	27	B1
llevue Ave	20	A1
Bellevue Ave	20	A1
llis Cir	22	B1
llis Ct	22	B1
lmont Ct	22	A1
elvidere Pl	27	A1
ennett St	20	B1
ent St	26	A1/A2/B1
rkeley Pl	20	A1
rkeley St	20	A1
rkshire Pl	28	B2
rkshire St	28	B2
gelow St	27	A1
nney St	26	A1/A2/B1
rch St	21	A1
shop Richard Allen Dr	27	A1/A2
ackstone St	27	A1
air Pl	22	B1
ake St	23	A1
akeslee St	21	A2/B2
anche St	28	A2/B2
oardman Pl	28	B2
oardman St	22	B1
olton St	20	A1
ond St	20	B2
ow St	20	A1
owdoin St	20	A1
oyle Ter	21	A2
radbury St	20	B1
rattle Sq	20	B1
rattle St (1-147)	20	A1/B1/B2
rattle St (148-227)	21	B1/B2
rewer St	20	B1
rewster St	21	B2
ristol St	28	B2
roadway (1-189)	26	B1
roadway (190-472)	28	A1/B1/B2
roadway (473-501)	20	B2
roadway Ct	28	B2
roadway Ter	28	B1
rookford St	22	A1
rookline St	27	A1/B1/B2
rown St	20	A1
ryant St	20	A2
uckingham Pl	20	A1
uckingham St	20	A1
uena Vista Park	22	B2
urns Ct	20	A1
adbury Rd	21	A2
allender St	27	A1
ambridge Ctr	26	B1
ambridge Pky	26	A2
ambridge St (1-703)	26	A1/A2/B2
ambridge St (704-1724)	28	A1/B1/B2
ambridge St (1725-1899)	20	A2/B2
ambridge Ter	22	B2
ambridge Park Dr	26	A2
ambridgeside Pl	20	B1
amden Pl	28	A1
amelia Ave	22	A2
amp St	26	A2
anal Park	26	B1
ardinal Medeiros Ave	28	B2
arleton St	26	B1
arlisle St	28	B2
arver St	20	A1
edar Sq	22	A1
edar St	22	A1/B1
entral Sq	27	A2
entre St	27	A1
Chalk St	27	A1/B1
Channing Cir	21	B2
Channing Pl	21	B2
Channing St	21	B2
Chapman Pl	20	B1
Charles St	26	A1/A2/B1
Chatham St	28	B1
Chauncy Ln	20	A1
Chauncy St	20	A1
Chauncy Ter	20	A1
Cherry Ct	27	A2
Cherry St (1-94)	27	A2
Cherry St (95-199)	26	B1
Chester St	22	B2
Chestnut St	27	B1
Chetwynd Rd	21	A2
Chilton St	21	A1/A2
Church St	20	B1/B2
Churchill Ave	22	A1
Citizens Pl	28	B2
Clary St	22	A1
Clay St	21	A2
Clement Cir	28	B1
Cleveland St	22	A1
Clifton St	27	A1
Clinton St	22	B2
Cogswell Ave	22	B2
Cogswell Pl	22	B2
Columbia St (1-124)	27	A2
Columbia St (125-152)	26	B1
Columbia St (153-599)	28	A2/B2
Columbia Ter	27	A2
Columbus Ave	22	A1
Concord Ave (1-103)	20	A1
Concord Ave (139-578)	21	A1/A2
Concord Ln	21	A1
Coolidge Hill	21	B2
Coolidge Hill Rd	21	B1
Copley St	21	A2
Corliss Pl	28	B1
Cornelius Way	26	B1
Corporal Burns Rd	27	A1
Cottage Ct	27	A1
Cottage Row	27	A1
Cottage St	27	A1
Cottage Park Ave	22	A1
Cowperthwaite St	20	B2
Craigie Cir	20	A1
Craigie St	20	A1
Crawford St	28	B1
Creighton St	22	B2
Crescent St	20	A2
Cresto Ter	26	A2
Cross St	27	B2
Crossland St	20	A1
Cutler Ave	22	B2
Cypress St	27	A1
Dana Pl		
Dana St (1-21)	27	A1
Dana St (22-99)	28	A1/B1
Davenport St	23	B1
Davis St	28	B2
Day St	22	A2/B2
Deacon St	26	B1
Decatur St	27	B1
Dewolfe St	20	B2
Dinsmore Ct	27	B1
Divinity Ave	20	A1
Doane St	20	A1
Dock St	26	B1
Dodge St	27	A1
Donnell St	21	A2
Douglas St	27	A2
Dover St	21	A2
Drummond Pl	22	B2
Dudley Ct	22	A1
Dudley St	22	A1
Dunstable Rd	21	B2
Dunster St	20	B2
East St	26	A2
Eaton St	27	A2
Edmunds St	22	A1
Education St	26	A2
Eliot St	20	B1
Ellery Pl	28	B1
Ellery Sq	28	B1
Ellery St (1-27)	27	A1
Ellery St (28-199)	28	A1/B1
Ellsworth Ave	28	B1
Ellsworth Park	28	B1
Elm St	28	B2
Elmer St	27	A1
Elmwood Ave	21	B1
Emily St	27	B1
Emmet St	26	A1
Emmons Pl	28	A1
Endicott St	27	B2
Erie St	27	B1/B2
Essex St	27	A2
Eustis St	23	B1
Evereteze Way	28	B2
Everett St	20	A2/B1
Exeter Park	23	B1
Fainwood Cir	28	B1
Fair Oaks St	22	A2
Fairfield St	22	B2
Fairmont Ave	27	A1
Fairmont St	27	A1/B1
Fallon Pl	27	A1
Farrar St	28	A1
Farwell Pl	20	B1
Fayerweather St	21	A1/A2/B1
Fayette St	28	A1/B1
Fayette Park	28	B1
Felton St	28	A1
Fenno St	21	A2
Fern St	21	A1
Fernald Dr	20	A1
Field St	21	A1/A2
Fisk Pl	27	A2
Flagg St		
Flagg St (1-77)	27	A1
Flagg St (78-99)	20	B2
Florence St		
Foch St	22	A1
Follen St	20	A1
Forest St	23	B1
Fort Washington Pl	27	B1
Foster Pl	20	A1
Foster St (1-121)	20	A1/B1
Foster St (122-199)	21	B2
Frances Pl	22	B2
Francis Ave	20	A2
Franklin Pl	27	A1
Franklin St	27	A1/A2/B2
Fresh Pond Ln	21	A1
Fresh Pond Pky	21	A1/B1
Frisbie Pl	20	A2
Front St	27	A2
Frost St (1-65)	23	B1
Frost St (66-99)	20	A2
Frost Ter	23	B1
Fulkerson St	26	A1

Street Index

Street Index

Street Index

Street Index